The Stewardship of Wealth

The Stewardship of Wealth

Successful Private Wealth Management for Investors and Their Advisors

GREGORY CURTIS

WILEY

John Wiley & Sons, Inc.

Library of Congress Cataloging-in-Publication Data:

Curtis, Gregory, 1947-
  [Creative capital]
  The stewardship of wealth : successful private wealth management for investors and their advisors / Gregory Curtis.
      pages cm. – (Wiley finance series)
  "This book is an updated and expanded edition of Creative Capital: Managing Private Wealth in a Complex World, by Gregory Curtis, copyright ? 2004 by Gregory Curtis, New York: iUniverse, Inc."–Title page verso.
  Includes index.
  ISBN 978-1-118-32186-7 (hardback); ISBN 978-1-118-42015-7 (ebk);
  ISBN 978-1-118-43410-9 (ebk); ISBN 978-1-118-42163-5 (ebk)
  1. Investments–United States. 2. Wealth–United States. 3. Finance–United States. I. Title.
  HG4910.C87 2012
  332.024'01–dc23
                                                                        2012020170

Printed in the United States of America.
10 9 8 7 6 5 4 3 2 1

"Lege feliciter!"

---

*"Read happily!" From the epigraph to *An Ecclesiastical History of the English People*, by The Venerable Bede, completed in 732. The book recorded events in Britain from the raids by Julius Caesar (55 B.C.) to the arrival in Kent of St. Augustine (597). Bede's practice of dating events from the time of Christ's birth (i.e., anno Domini or A.D.) caused that convention to come into general use. Unfortunately, the concept of zero was unknown at the time (Christ would have been age zero at birth, not age one), so Bede's dating system initially caused a great deal of mischief.

Contents

PART TWO

The Stewardship of Wealth

CHAPTER 3
Are We Living in a Permanent Financial Crisis?   53

CHAPTER 4
Risk   73

CHAPTER 8
Trusts   163

Preface

Nothing corrupts a man so deeply as writing a book.
—Nero Wolfe[1]

Over the years, thousands of investment books have been written. A precious few have become classics in the field, but the rest are long, and probably best, forgotten. Given this ponderous history, even the author himself must wonder whether he may be trying the patience of the reading public with yet another book on investing.

I plead this: I'm approaching the investment challenge from a different perspective than most—indeed, than virtually all—of my predecessors. In the first place, I'm addressing a very special audience—wealthy investors and their advisors. In the second place, the purpose of most investment books is to make us better investors. But this book has a slightly but importantly different objective: to help significant investors to become better stewards of their assets, whether or not they ever become good investors in the professional sense of the word.

Finally, this book, and especially Part One, constitutes a *cri de coeur* for the importance of private capital in the American free market economy—something too many people, including too many wealthy people, fail to understand. The so-called 1 percent—that group of people whose wealth or earnings place them above 99 percent of the rest of the population—has become a whipping boy for everything that is wrong with America.

There is certainly a lot wrong with America, and some of it involves the 1 percent. But in fact the top quartile of American society is as competitive as it has ever been—perhaps even more so. The bottom continues to struggle, as it always has, and needs help. What is new is that the middle—the great American middle class—is now struggling as it has never done before.

Much of what ails the middle class has to do with the globalization of competition—Americans who used to compete only with other Americans now must compete with Chinese, Indians, Brazilians, and so on, many of whom are far more cost competitive. But some of it is self-inflicted: The American middle class isn't prepared, educationally or by temperament, for the cutthroat world it now occupies. American public policy needs to focus on this issue, but speaking very broadly, if the middle class wants to regain its competitiveness globally, it could do a lot worse than to emulate the path taken by the 1 percent.[2]

INVESTORS VERSUS STEWARDS

As noted later in this preface, good stewardship involves much more than investing capital soundly. It involves the ongoing growth and nourishment of a family's human capital in the broadest sense. And it involves the recognition that the responsible management and creative use of private wealth is crucial to the continued vitality of the American free market democracy. Families and their advisors need to view the challenge of stewardship in this broader sense.

What is the difference between being a good investor and being a good steward of wealth? In the first place, stewardship is a much broader issue. It has to do with all the things that will bear on the long-term success of the family.[3] Investing has to do with one particular issue—the management of private capital. Although that issue is central to the question of stewardship, and is the main subject of this book, investing is only a part of the broader challenge. Indeed, it isn't necessary for every member of a wealthy family—or any members, for that matter—to become professional investors.

What *is* necessary is that members of the family—preferably all of them—gain enough of an understanding of the investment process and the capital markets to enable the family to be an astute consumer of investment services. There are many talented financial advisors out there, but there are also many—indeed, many more—who don't have a clue. At the very least, a wealthy family needs to know enough to select a good advisor and to monitor that advisor's performance.

This requires a certain amount of hard work, but it stops short of requiring that family members become investment professionals themselves. Most important, it requires that the family develop ways of working together, ways of sharing information, ways to make cohesive and intelligent and timely decisions about assets that may be widely scattered in many different family "pockets."

It's possible that the wealthiest senior generations of families can live a perfectly happy life without paying the slightest attention to the issue of stewardship. It's even possible, though far less likely, that their children won't have their lives and their happiness disrupted when they suddenly inherit large sums of money they are ill-prepared to deal with. The great probability, however, is that instead of contributing to the happiness of such families and to the betterment of the world they live in, families that ignore their stewardship obligations are probably headed for a train wreck. Money can be a great force for good, but it can also corrupt and destroy a family.

The whole point of stewardship is to avoid this train wreck. Having wealth brings with it serious responsibilities, for two reasons. The first, as noted, is that money has the power to destroy lives. We don't behave irresponsibly around dynamite or loaded pistols, and we should never behave irresponsibly around millions of dollars.

The second reason is that private capital plays a crucial role in the way America has chosen to organize its society and its economy. Failure of stewardship by a wealthy family is a very large failure, an act of irresponsibility by the very people who have been most favored by the American economic system.

Most of this book is an attempt to help wealthy families discharge their stewardship obligations more effectively. But it is also important for the wealthy—and for the nonwealthy—to understand just how crucial a matter it is that private capital be properly managed. That important point is the subject of Part One of this book.

BEST INVESTMENT PRACTICES

Anna Karenina famously begins with Tolstoy's remark that, "All happy families are alike; every unhappy family is unhappy in its own way." Whether or not Tolstoy was right about families and happiness in general, his idea certainly applies to families as investors.

All "happy" families—that is, those who are able to preserve and grow their wealth across the generations—are very much alike in the sense that they follow what I refer to in this book as best investment practices. These are practices that have demonstrated their worth in the portfolios of the world's largest and most sophisticated investors over many decades. It is a principal purpose of this book to identify best practices for taxable investors, to explain why they are important, and to show family investors how best to employ them in their own investment portfolios.

It's also the case that "unhappy" families—those whose wealth disappears—tend to be unhappy in their own ways. While there is only one certain way to preserve wealth—namely, to take stewardship very seriously—there are many, many ways to destroy wealth. Some of these tend to occur slowly over time: Poor strategies and managers and unnecessary investment costs and taxes act like portfolio cancers, slowly destroying wealth over the years. Other bad practices destroy wealth quickly, as the result of one spectacularly bad decision.

COMPLEX MARKETS

Most of us will never be forced to deal with a system more complex than the capital markets. No one completely understands how markets work or why they behave the way they do. No one can anticipate when markets will go up or down or how much they will move. Markets encompass all the complexity of the human beings who deal in and with them, as well as all the complexity of any system that is made up of millions of moving parts, some of which are related to each other and some of which aren't. And ultimately, of course, all this complexity is at the mercy of technically unrelated matters, such as the stability and vigor of the societies that provide the structures and mores through which capital markets must operate.

Thus, attempts to understand how markets work must inquire into modern portfolio theory (which builds models that, at least over long periods of time, tend to describe the operation of markets); behavioral finance (which attempts to describe how human beings respond in the face of investment decisions and market events); law (which governs the legal properties and enforceability of financial instruments); economics (which attempts to explain how economies function); chaos theory (which attempts to describe the behavior of incredibly complex systems); and so on.

On top of this complexity is the issue of the costs associated with managing private capital. No one in the financial industry works for free, and most charge not what is fair in relation to the value they bring, but rather what the market will bear. Consider that as investors we face high money management fees, the round-trip costs of brokerage commissions, the spread between bid and ask prices, the cost of market impact, variance drain,[4] and opportunity costs (price movement that occurs between the time we decide to act and the time our transaction is executed). Our wealth will be further diminished by inflation, taxes, and spending. Finally, given the complexity of the capital markets, our wealth will also be diminished by the impact of the inevitable investment mistakes we make.

A COMPLEX INDUSTRY

No one who takes an honest look at the modern financial services industry can reach any conclusion other than that it is operated in ways that are mainly hostile to the interests of investors. Most firms, for example, are organized in a manner that presents serious and ongoing conflicts of interest with their own clients. And many firms cheerfully hire large numbers of inexperienced professionals who are superb at selling investment products but who understand virtually nothing about the successful management of capital—a good working definition of hostility to the clients' interests. Finally, like any industry, the financial services business has its fair share of crooks, swindlers, con men (and women), and others for whom the term "venal" fits quite nicely.

I am as critical of the industry as anyone—indeed, I have devoted a great deal of text in this book to criticisms of the industry (see Chapter 5). But let's be realistic. All firms—not just financial firms—are in business to make money. The main reason the industry gets away with its deplorable practices is that *we are lousy clients*. Alongside the rotten firms and callous individuals there are also many superb advisory firms and many, many honest, hard-working financial professionals. Good clients easily gravitate to these people. Moreover, even imperfect advisors can be managed by well-informed clients to minimize damage to their portfolios and maximize the value the advisor is bringing to the relationship.

Yes, the financial industry badly needs to be reformed, and the fact that most of the regulators have long been asleep at the switch—or flat-out owned by the industry—is discouraging, indeed. But investors needn't wait for the regulators to wake up. By educating ourselves about the industry and the investment process, we can go a long way toward avoiding the worst the financial services industry has to offer and to create, instead, fertile partnerships with the many honest, competent advisors available to us.

COMPLEX SOCIETIES

Wealthy investors everywhere live in societies that are often hostile, and that are always indifferent, to their attempts to preserve and grow their wealth. In a way, this seems an odd circumstance.

Consider that few would deny the importance not just to the investors themselves, but to society generally, of the sound management of the portfolios of middle-income investors, pension plans, charitable endowments, and foundations. If middle-income investors mismanage their money (especially, but not exclusively, their 401(k) plans), they face an impoverished old age, an outcome that has profound social, political, and economic consequences. If corporate and public pension plans mismanage their portfolios, either taxpayers will have to bail them out (via the Pension Benefit Guaranty Corporation), or higher contributions to the plans will reduce available spending for new jobs and capital equipment, with the consequent impact on economic growth. If endowments and foundations mismanage their portfolios, a society that relies heavily on private philanthropy, rather than government funding, will find funding for services, amenities, and creative new ideas slashed.

In the special case where family wealth takes the form of control of an important corporate enterprise, no one would argue that mismanagement of the enterprise is a matter of no consequence. Most businesses in America are privately held, and some of them are spectacularly large. Privately held Cargill, Inc., headquartered outside Minneapolis, was founded in 1865, boasts annual revenues of $120 billion, and employs 142,000 people in 66 countries. Mismanagement of this form of private capital would have momentous consequences, indeed.

Yet, when it comes to the management of the passive investment portfolios of the wealthy, hostility and indifference set in. Some of this is, to be sure, nothing more than envy, or, when private capital blows up, schadenfreude. But it is more than that—it signifies a profound ignorance of the importance of private capital to American society.

PRIVATE CAPITAL AND FREE MARKET DEMOCRACIES

The serious opportunity to get seriously rich is what distinguishes America from most other free market democracies, and it has made America the most dominant civilization in the history of the world. If simply having an essentially free market were all that was required for economic domination, France and Sweden would be powerhouses. But France and Sweden are a pale version of the American free market for the simple reason that getting rich is discouraged in those countries, and being rich is despised. In America, entrepreneurs are heroes, but in much of Europe entrepreneurs are viewed more like dangerous cranks who are simply trying to make everyone else look bad.

Indeed, even cases that appear at first glance to represent the very worst aspects of American-style capitalism often prove to be quite different under more thoughtful analysis. During the Republican Party primary season in 2012, for example, even conservative Republicans savaged Mitt Romney for his private equity activities. The complaint was that private equity buyers sometimes closed firms and laid off people. Certainly if the net result of private equity activity was a reduction in the strength of the economy, that would have been a legitimate criticism.

But capitalism isn't about preserving jobs—it's about preserving *good* jobs and creating *more* good jobs. When enterprises are uncompetitive, it's very important—and a critical aspect of capitalism—that those enterprises be pruned before they drag down the entire economy. The evidence in countries like Greece, Italy, and France, where industry after uncompetitive industry is protected, should be decisive.

No one likes it when companies are shuttered and jobs eliminated. But matters would be much worse if we stuck our heads in the sand and kept weak companies on life support. Private equity is at the very heart of capitalism, because private equity firms are looking hard at enterprises that are currently operating at far less than their potential. By buying these units out from under their corporate parents and instituting real incentives (and disincentives), companies that were on their way down and out are rejuvenated.

It's true, certainly, that this process sometimes results in bloated enterprises becoming less bloated—that is, some jobs go away—but the net result of private equity activity is that many more jobs are created than are lost. In the case of Mitt Romney, the number was something like 140,000 net new jobs, and that didn't include jobs that were saved as uncompetitive companies were made more competitive.

I'm not carrying any water for Romney, but am simply making the point that capitalism necessarily involves creative destruction—not destruction, *creative* destruction. Certainly we need a safety net for folks whose jobs are eliminated, but once we begin to worry more about bad jobs lost than good jobs gained, we are in deep trouble as a society.

A NOTE TO FINANCIAL ADVISORS

Let's assume that it is true, as I maintain, that private capital is the most important capital in the world. Let's also assume that it is true, as seems self-evident, that the owners of private capital are heavily dependent on their financial advisors for success. It therefore follows that the role of financial advisor to wealthy families is one of the most crucial jobs in America. That's why this book is directed to both wealthy families *and their advisors*.

Advising wealthy families is crucial, but it is also extraordinarily difficult. I've been doing the job for more than 30 years, and if I did it for another 30 years I would still have a lot to learn. What I do know I've put in this book. It's a long book, but it only scrapes the surface of its labyrinthine subject. If you work in this field you will encounter—almost daily—challenges that you have never run up against before. I hope you have partners to confer with about these challenges, but at the end of the day you will have to rely on the knowledge and skills you have accumulated over time, and on sound judgment.

Making matters worse, there is rarely one correct answer to any issue. When it comes to families and their human and financial capital, it's very difficult to know what the right course is.

Financial advisors will note that in Part Three—the hard-core investment portion of this book—I have sprinkled throughout the text a series of Practice Tips, set off in little boxes. In these Tips I've tried to interject ideas for providing successful wealth advice that have little to do with the details of investing capital and more to do with the hands-on experience of advising families. I hope my colleagues in the industry will find these useful.

A NOTE TO SMALLER INVESTORS: THE MONEYBAGS© APP

This book is addressed to families with very substantial capital to invest. But the truth of the matter is that, just as "a rose is a rose is a rose," a best investment practice is a best investment practice, whether we are investing $10,000 or $100 million. For middle-income investors who are serious about the stewardship of their capital, this book may be worth looking into. Many best investment practices favored by large investors, after all, have been repackaged and made available to smaller investors.[5] To assist smaller investors in translating the sophisticated strategies of the rich into actionable portfolios for middle income folks, I've developed the Moneybags© app, a financial application that interprets the "best investment practices" in this book for portfolios as small as a few thousand dollars (or as large as a few million). More information about Moneybags is available at the very end of the book.

A NOTE TO INSTITUTIONAL INVESTORS

This is a book about the challenges of taxable investing, and hence many of the techniques I discuss are appropriate for family investors but may not be appropriate for nontaxable, institutional portfolios such as foundations, endowments, and pension plans. On the other hand, it will always be obvious when I am discussing a strategy that should be followed only by taxable investors. Hence the managers of institutional portfolios, and the members of endowment investment committees, may find much of interest in this book. That said, it is only fair to point out that the best book ever written on the management of nontaxable portfolios was published just a few years ago: David Swensen's *Pioneering Portfolio Management*,[6] which should be required reading for all investors, institutional or otherwise.

ORGANIZATION OF THE BOOK

Part One

Part One (Creative Capital) discusses the importance of private capital to the peculiar American version of free market democracy. Investment capital isn't something that exists in isolation from the broader society, nor is it a marginal factor in that society. If it were, the sound stewardship of capital would still be important to the families who have it, but it would be a matter of little consequence to the society at large.

In fact, however, private capital—both the lure of accumulating it and its disposition thereafter—is utterly essential to the way economic America works. It is the widespread and widely encouraged ability to become rich, and to be free to employ those riches in creative ways, that distinguishes American capitalism from its many cousins. After all, all free market democracies have strong middle classes, relatively free markets, and democratic forms of government. One might imagine that, as a result, all free market democracies would have roughly equivalent outcomes. We might assume that these economies would grow at about the same rates, with smaller economies naturally growing faster than larger economies (just as small companies grow faster than large companies), that innovation rates would be about the same across societies, that citizens of every country would work equally hard, that military strength would be roughly evenly distributed, and that each nation would export its pro rata share of the world's culture.

But, as we know, that has not been the case at all. Though it is true that most free market democracies operate on a roughly competitive plane, one of them—the United States—has so vastly outperformed the others that it has become the most dominant nation that ever existed. And even though the United States represents a huge portion of the global economy, far more than any other country, it continues to grow at rates more appropriate to emerging economies.

This has been, if we reflect on it, an astonishing outcome. In a postindustrial world of free societies, ideas migrate at the speed of light and innovation is no sooner made in one place than it is copied (or even improved) someplace else. In such a world, of all possible worlds, we would never have expected extraordinary dominance to arise.

I argue in Part One that American distinctiveness, American vitality, arises quite simply from the ongoing encouragement of American citizens to be productive by offering them the lure of great wealth, and by the resulting profusion of independently managed private capital—the most creative and least constrained source of capital in the world. I also speculate about why it

is that America, far more than any of the older free market democracies, has
managed to preserve its vigor. In other words, there are crucially important
reasons why private capital needs to be managed properly, and those reasons
go far beyond the narrow interests of the possessors of that capital. That
is the message of Part One, and it provides the context for the rest of
the book.

Part Two

Part Two (The Stewardship of Wealth) consists of six chapters (Chapters 3
through 8), each discussing a broad issue that investors of private capital
face. Chapter 3, for example, is titled "Are We Living in a Permanent
Financial Crisis?" The chapter argues that understanding what kind of world
we will be investing our capital in matters a great deal. This chapter suggests
that we are in for a great deal of difficulty in the intermediate-to-long-term
future.

Chapter 4 discusses, from a variety of angles, the crucial concept of
risk. Entire books have been written about investment risk, and even they
can only scratch the surface of this complex topic. What I've tried to do is
to give investors and their advisors a taste of the many kinds of risks capital
faces.

Chapter 5 discusses the complex and disappointing world of finance as a
business. I come down hard on my colleagues for the conflicts of interest that
pervade the financial world, for the self-interest and utter lack of concern
for clients, and for the corruption that has had global consequences.

Chapter 6 discusses the challenge of finding the right financial advisor
for your family, and Chapter 7 discusses the even greater challenge of
organizing your family to make sound and timely investment decisions.

Finally, in Chapter 8 I discuss the world of private trusts. Trusts are a
prominent feature of every wealthy family, but organizing and managing
trusts in sensible ways has become an increasing challenge as consolidation
in the banking industry has eliminated most of the local trust banks.

Part Three

Part Three, The Rich Get Richer: The Nuts and Bolts of Successful Investing,
is just that: a description of best investment practices in every important
aspect of the investment process for private investors. Part Three consists
of 14 chapters and is organized roughly in the order most families will
take up investment issues. It is thus designed to be read straight through,
from Chapter 9, which discusses the design of taxable investment portfolios,
through Chapter 22, which discusses a variety of miscellaneous issues private
investors face.

Part Three is by far the longest section of the book, and it will likely appeal more to financial advisors than to family members. However, I urge families at least to skim lightly over this material. It's very difficult to be a good client if you understand nothing about the details of the investment process.

Afterword

The afterword to this book attempts to make the important point that, after all, what matters in life is not wealth, but happiness. I argue that there is little about the struggle for happiness that is any different for wealthy families than for other families—in other words, that "All happy families are alike." It is only the specific challenges that differ from those every family faces. I also point out that the one sure way for a wealthy family to become unhappy is for the family to fail in its stewardship obligations.

■　■　■

Writing this book has been a great pleasure for me, and I hope that reading it will bring at least a modest pleasure to my readers. For a small handful of them, perhaps, it will make a difference in the quality of their stewardship—and, therefore, in their personal happiness, the happiness of their children and grandchildren, and the continued success of the society that has nurtured them. It would be a rare writer who could ask for more.

NOTES

1. Rex Stout, *The Mother Hunt* (1963).
2. See, generally, Charles Murray, *Coming Apart: The State of White America, 1960–2010* (New York: Crown Forum, 2012).
3. There are many useful books that bear on the issue of stewardship, but Jay Hughes's classic book remains the best guide. See James E. Hughes Jr., *Family Wealth—Keeping It in the Family: How Family Members and Their Advisers Preserve Human, Intellectual, and Financial Assets for Generations* (New York: Bloomberg Press, 2004). This, incidentally, is the revised and expanded edition of Hughes's original book, published in 1997.
4. See Chapter 5.
5. I am thinking of such developments as money market funds, mutual funds, exchange-traded funds (ETFs), registered hedge funds, and so on.

6. New York: Free Press, 2000.
7. Preface, *Living by the Word: Selected Writings 1973–1987* (New York: Harvest Books, 1989).
8. "Acknowledgements," *Schott's Original Miscellany* (New York: Bloomsbury, 2003).
9. The reports are available on the Berkshire Hathaway website, www.berkshirehathaway.com.
10. New York: McGraw-Hill Trade, 4th ed., 2002.
11. New York: HarperBusiness, rev. ed., 2003.
12. New York: McGraw-Hill Trade, 2nd ed., 2002.
13. Available on the TIFF website at www.tiff.org.
14. www.Windhorsegroup.com
15. New York: Free Press, 2000.

Acknowledgments

Acknowledgements often leave me with the impression that I've been lied to.

—Ben Cheever

For anyone interested in a close observation of the more basic human emotions on amusing display, it is hard to beat the acknowledgments section of most books. Here we find inadvertently laid out for inspection such passions as jealousy, ambition, insecurity, unctuousness, feckless gratitude, insincerity, lack of judgment, and, as Mr. Cheever points out in the epigraph, good old-fashioned deceit.

In bygone days, the acknowledgments section of a book was really nothing more than a dedication, typically addressed to a nonentity who happened to have deep pockets and whose favor the author was trying to curry. Insincere, to be sure, but at least with a healthy pecuniary motive.

Today, however, a really good acknowledgment, firing on all cylinders, will list several times as many contributors to the book as there are ideas in it. An even modestly energetic author will not omit to thank his neighbors, pets, sisters-in-law, fourth grade homeroom teacher, and even (in the case of Alice Walker) assorted flowers, trees, and "most especially, the animals."[7] We are left to wonder if it might not be a useful improvement to the copyright laws to deny authorship (and royalties!) to anyone who claims that more than, say, two dozen people contributed importantly to the book.

Well, far be it from me to spit into this self-absorbed headwind. I therefore cheerfully admit that everyone I have ever known or read or read about or heard about, to say nothing of the millions of people I have never heard of, have all contributed importantly to this book, and I thank them all. To paraphrase Ben Schott, if there are errors in this book, it's probably their fault.[8]

On the other hand, there actually are a small handful of people whose contributions were more direct and critical, essential in the sense that parts of the book would have been quite different, and quite worse, had these people not existed. These persons fall into the following categories:

- My clients. Though it is true that few clients are deeply knowledgeable about investment matters—they made their money being brilliant at other things altogether—every conversation we have with our clients tells us whether we are meeting their needs or not, whether we are explaining the investment world in words that can be understood.
- My partners at Greycourt. Many of the chapters in this book were originally published as Greycourt white papers, something the firm is rather famous for. Before being distributed to Greycourt's clients and to friends of the firm, those papers had to pass through an internal peer review process in which they were circulated to each Greycourt partner for comment. I did not keep detailed track of which comments were useful or nonuseful, which were incorporated intact and which simply informed a revision, or even of the many that corrected glaring errors. But much of what you will find in this book was thoroughly improved by my partners' comments. And far beyond that peer review process, my ongoing conversations with the senior professionals at Greycourt have vastly enriched my own understanding of the investment process and how its essential attributes can and cannot be communicated.
- Other writers in the field. I have read dozens and dozens of investment books over the years, and even the worst of them has probably taught me something—if only about what not to do. But it has been the best of these writings that have educated and inspired me. By "the best" I refer, in alphabetical order, to Warren Buffett's Annual Reports on Berkshire Hathaway,[9] Charles Ellis's *Winning the Loser's Game*,[10] Benjamin Graham's *The Intelligent Investor*[11] (and its in-depth original, *Security Analysis,* written with David L. Dodd),[12] David Salem's multitudinous-but-trenchant essays published by The Investment Fund for Foundations[13] and, more recently, by his new firm, Windhorse Capital Management,[14] and David Swensen's *Pioneering Portfolio Management*.[15] Anyone who reads those writings carefully will no doubt wonder why I bothered to write this book.

Finally, it is customary to thank one's spouse. A writer worth his salt should be wary of what is customary, but in this case the shoe fits. My wife, Simin, the founder and CEO of the American Middle East Institute, leads a busy professional and public service life of her own. Yet she put up with my many absences from our large and complicated family, as I stole every possible opportunity to work on this book. Her own career was put on hold while she helped me launch Greycourt into the world. If this book were to become a classic in its field, worthy of being mentioned in the same breath with the writings listed above, it could not possibly compensate her for her contributions, her kindnesses, her patience, or her love.

Credits

Most of the material in this book was written for it, but some of that material was published elsewhere before the book appeared. In particular, many of the chapters, or parts of chapters, first saw the light of day as white papers published by Greycourt & Co., Inc., the financial advisory firm I founded and where I now serve as chairman. Although I appear as sole author on most of those papers, my partners at Greycourt often supplied many helpful comments. All material has been reprinted with the permission of the original publisher. Throughout the book I have credited Greycourt and the appropriate partners who were my coauthors and have referred readers to the Greycourt website at www.Greycourt.com.

Pittsburgh
August 2012

The Stewardship of Wealth

One

The Importance of Private Capital

The role of private capital is poorly understood, both by Americans in general and also by the wealthy Americans who own that capital. Most wealthy families take the stewardship of their capital seriously, to be sure, seeing stewardship as the discharge of an important duty to their families. But beyond the importance of wealth to its owners, substantial families can legitimately wonder if private wealth is a positive or negative feature of American life. Families who work hard to maintain and grow their wealth often see their work as an intensely private activity existing outside of, unrelated to, and largely irrelevant to the major thrusts of U.S. society—a kind of fringe element in the American democracy. Nothing, however, could be further from the truth.

The building of wealth, the management of wealth, and the deployment of wealth are activities that lie at the very heart of what has made America great. Abundant private wealth is what distinguishes America from other free market democracies. It is the lure of wealth that encourages Americans (and would-be Americans) to develop and implement the ideas that drive contemporary civilization, whether those ideas are in business, science, the arts, education, entertainment, or almost any other activity that we value as human beings.

And it is the creative deployment of wealth that enriches American society far beyond the dreams of other civilizations—including other modern, postindustrial democracies. These two characteristics of wealth—its ability to bring out the competitive best in citizens and its enriching qualities that permeate society—are at the center of the special American version of free market democracy, and they are largely responsible for America's preeminence. Lying between these two aspects of wealth, and the linchpin that holds them together, is the management of private wealth. If wealth were simply created and then dissipated, it would be of little use to its owners. Far more important, it would be of little use to society.

Parts Two and Three of this book are focused particularly on the management of wealth—on the linchpin. But in Part One, I focus on the first two characteristics of wealth. Thus, Chapter 1 emphasizes how America differs from its free market cousins in the continuing encouragement of its citizens to pursue wealth. As a result, American competitiveness is the wonder of the world. In Chapter 2, I turn to the deployment of wealth—the creative use of private capital that gives this book its title.

The ultimate point of Part One is to demonstrate that wealthy families lie at the very center of the American experiment—something that is very poorly understood. Private capital is an essential, even a definitive aspect of the American version of democratic capitalism. Without private capital on a grand scale—the lure of accumulating it and the creative use of it—it would be impossible to imagine America.

Wealthy families need to be both proud of what their families have accomplished and proud of what their capital can and will continue to accomplish for America and for the world. Private capital has made America the most vigorous, the most creative, the most diverse—in short, the most powerful society ever organized. And given the increasingly feeble state of other liberal societies around the world, it is the vigor of America, and only the vigor of America, that offers hope for freedom and democracy anywhere on the globe. If America declines, freedom and democracy will have no champion worthy of the name. And the best way to ensure the decline of America is to reduce the role that private capital plays in our remarkable success.

CHAPTER 1

Wealth in America

The Indispensable Rich

Every man thinks God is on his side.
The rich and powerful know He is.

—Jean Anouilh

Few Americans—including few wealthy Americans—have given much thought to the role that wealth plays in the American polity. We tend to take it for granted that America always has and always will consist of wealthy families, middle-income families, and poor families. And when we do think about it, most Americans—including most wealthy Americans—tend to imagine that wealth constitutes, at best, a necessary flaw in the way the American democracy should work. Perhaps, we concede, the lure of wealth is necessary to encourage people to work hard, to come up with and commercialize new ideas, to build the companies that provide employment. But still and all, in a society where we are all created equal, there is something incongruous about the fact that some people have so much more money than others.

If the wealthy constitute a flaw in the way American society should work, why should we tolerate it? If we really put our minds to the problem, couldn't we come up with a system that offered similar incentives but that didn't produce wealthy families in such profusion?

What is it, then, that accounts for the persistence of wealthy families in the American democratic republic? Why do we tolerate the rich, with their godlike influence over people and affairs, when it is abundantly clear that the wealthy, like everyone else, are not endowed with godlike wisdom in deciding how to wield that influence? Certainly it is apparent that the rich, whether they are dealing with their own companies, with politics and the affairs of state, with social and cultural issues, with charitable organizations, or even with their own families, have far more impact than other citizens, for good or ill. The rich are a bit like the gods of the Greeks or Romans: not omnipotent or all-seeing sages, but powerful, fascinating, mischievous creatures we don't completely understand but which we find riveting, annoying, alarming and, like it or not, essential.

Indeed, the wealthy, *virtually alone in a democratic society*, constitute a natural, unelected aristocracy. I say "natural" not because there is anything fundamentally natural about wealthy aristocracies, but because the development of wealthy families is an organic by-product of the way we have chosen to organize our economic affairs in the United States. The American market economy is designed to pit individuals against each other in a free economic competition, the incentive to compete being the possibility of becoming rich. We believe that this sort of competition is most likely to lead to improved conditions for the broader society, including those who "lose" in the competition to create wealth (the poor), and including those who refuse to compete at all: individuals who select professions that rarely lead to wealth, such as academics, social workers, nurses, artists, and so on. (Even these people compete for power and recognition in their chosen fields.) We can easily imagine societies in which wealth-creation activities would not be valued so highly—communist, socialist and many primitive societies, for example—and in those societies different individuals would perhaps[1] constitute the "natural" aristocracy.

I say "unelected" because the wealthy are not selected by any representative body. They simply happen as the result of economic competition and opportunity, much the way great athletes simply happen when athletic competition and opportunities are made available. That's not to say that people who create wealth don't work enormously hard at it, just as great athletes work enormously hard at it. But no group of people sits down and conducts a vote to determine who the best athletes are going to be, and no one sits down to vote on who the wealthy are going to be. The same is true of great artists, musicians, writers, and so on. Rules that define excellence are established through complex cultural mechanisms, but thereafter individuals compete with each other and there will be winners, losers, and a great body of people in the middle who develop competence but not greatness—as well, of course, as people who chose not to compete at all.

Most individuals in American society who possess influence on a scale equivalent to that of the rich actually *have* been elected in one way or the other. Politicians are the most obvious example, but union chiefs, university presidents, heads of large nonprofit organizations, corporate bigwigs, and even capos of crime families have all been "elected" by some body that is considered reasonably representative in those worlds. The governor of

California, an elected official, is undoubtedly the most powerful individual in that state. But I could name eight or ten wealthy men (and two or three women) who would share top twenty billing for power-wielding in that biggest of American states, alongside a few elected officials and a few corporate CEOs. No one elected those men and women, but they made their fortunes and have used those fortunes in part to influence California affairs. Appalling as this might be to some, it is and always has been a fact of life in America.

I say "aristocracy" because, as noted in the California example, the wealthy have power and influence far beyond that of other unelected centers of excellence: They represent an aristocracy in the precise meaning of the term.[2] The difference between the wealthy and great athletes (or great artists, musicians, writers, etc.) is that the former end up, through the power of their wealth, with the ability to influence much of what we hold dear in our world, whereas the latter, except in rare instances, exercise little influence beyond their area of specialization. It is so natural to expect the rich to wield influence over important matters that we hardly stop to think about how unusual it is that one social subgroup should have been vouchsafed this influence. Why should wealth-creating skills be entitled to far greater influence than, say, the skills required to score consistently from the three-point line or the skills required to compose a piano concerto?

America didn't decide to organize a society that would produce wealthy families—far from it. America organized a society that produces wealthy families as a by-product of an economic competition that is considered desirable. That by-product may have been anticipated, but it is not universally welcomed. Indeed, in a land where "all men are created equal" it may easily be considered an unhappy by-product. Because the wealthy have *unelected* power and influence, must it not be the case that the wealthy have *illegitimate* power and influence? Do not the rich constitute a serious flaw in the way a democratic society should operate? Is it not, indeed, an important task of the democratic process to eliminate or minimize the disproportionate influence of any one group? And because there are ways to operate democratic republics without producing so many wealthy families—the Scandinavian and most Western European societies are organized in this way—might not Americans be tempted to adopt those models as well? Certainly the persistence of the rich in a democratic society is at the very least incongruous.[3]

In this introductory chapter, I will argue that private wealth persists—indeed, grows luxuriantly—in the United States for reasons that are not only sound, but that go to the very heart of America's success in its competition with other civilizations. Wealthy families are not simply a minor pothole on the grand highway leading to uniform middle-classness in America. On the contrary, the production of private wealth is a crucial aspect of the singular success of the American experiment. Private wealth, as distinct from and as a counterweight to government wealth, is both central to and the principal symbol of America. Moreover, given America's special role among nations, America's wealthy families also play a central role in the evolution of other nations and of the prospects for billions of people worldwide.

DEMOCRACY AND CAPITALISM

The apparent contradiction of private wealth in a democratic republic is best examined by viewing democracy in the only economic context in which it can flourish: a free market system. Largely capitalist economies can exist outside the context of democratic political systems (Singapore and, increasingly, China, are examples), but democratic political systems cannot exist outside the context of free market economies. We cannot be free politically but enslaved economically. The institutions of civil society that liberal democracies establish and protect—especially private property and the rule of law—enable extremely diverse populations to coexist and work together productively; they enable, in short, free civilizations to exist.[4] Because this is the case, there will be consequences flowing from the economic system that would not necessarily be welcomed if the political system could somehow exist independent of its economic context: the production of wealth that is not evenly distributed is a principal consequence.

American democracy is, far more than elsewhere, intertwined with a capitalist attitude. The opportunity to pursue one's economic aspirations—the opportunity to become rich—is inextricably a part of the American dream, a dream that captures the imaginations of the poor worldwide, as well as immigrants to America, our working poor, the lower middle classes, and aspiring middle-class families. Reinventing America to establish a society that prevented people from getting rich wouldn't hurt those who are already wealthy, but it would seriously damage the aspirations of the poor. An America that was no longer perceived as the land of opportunity would be an America essentially unrecognizable to most Americans, as well as to most non-Americans and most would-be Americans.

We are so used to the vigorous spirit animating America that it is difficult to keep firmly in mind how rare this spirit is, especially among our peer group—the largely Western[5] postindustrial liberal democracies. It is worth our time to examine in some detail the nature of these societies, if only as an example of what America would look like without private capital to fuel its competitive spirit and to irrigate its exotic garden of ideas.

CAPITALISM AND ITS CONTRADICTIONS

Karl Marx famously maintained that capitalism contained the seeds of its own destruction, that the exploitation of labor would ultimately cause the emerging, alienated working classes to rise up and crush bourgeois society, replacing capitalist systems with socialist "dictatorships of the proletariat." Although many of Marx's criticisms of capitalism were alarmingly accurate, he was notoriously wrong in his prediction of its demise. Indeed, free market democracies have proven to be the most resilient of all forms of sociopolitical organization.

In terms of social peace and economic productivity, the determinative question turns out to be not so much whether labor is or is not "exploited"[6] or how big the gap may be between rich and poor.[7] Instead, what seems to matter is whether or not citizens—including the poor especially—have a real opportunity to improve their condition on an absolute basis. If so, the relative size and stability of the resulting middle classes (the hated bourgeoisie of Marxist theory) will increase rapidly. This is, of course, exactly what has happened in all advanced industrial and postindustrial free market democracies.

In America, as elsewhere among free market democracies, the native[8] poor have come to represent an ever-smaller percentage of the population, as poor families have tended to move into the middle classes—or even to become rich—in one or two generations. This phenomenon has occurred because the vigor of free market economic activity has been so great that massive opportunities were made available to virtually anyone who wished to seize them. As a result, poor families have cared less about whether they were being exploited and more about seizing opportunities to improve their circumstances. Certainly, of course, the poor (along with African Americans, women, the handicapped, gays, etc.) have historically faced more obstacles than others along the road to economic success, and it is an important part of the job of America, and of America's rich, to demolish those obstacles. But the effort to pull down obstacles to economic success is powerfully assisted by the need of free market societies for the talents of the disenfranchised.

Marx may have been wrong in his prognosis for capitalism, but history suggests that internal contradictions, albeit of a very different sort, do seem to threaten capitalist societies. If those societies fail they will likely do so not because of the exploitation of labor, but because absolute living standards rather quickly reach such an elevated point that the very character of the societies begins to change, causing them to become almost unrecognizably different from the societies that created the wealth in the first place. That is to say, citizens in wealthy capitalist societies gradually become so affluent, so comfortable, that they become more concerned about preserving their living standards than about improving them. When this happens, the vigor of the society quickly diminishes: Its citizens demand shorter work weeks, higher wages without corresponding productivity increases, longer vacations, easier jobs, more personal autonomy ("Who the hell is my boss to tell *me* what to do?"), and so on.

Much of this is, to be sure, simple human nature. Decades ago, psychologist Abraham Maslow postulated the existence of a "hierarchy of needs."[9] According to Maslow, human beings are motivated mainly by unsatisfied needs. Moreover, certain lower needs (or, as Maslow called them, deficiency needs) must to be satisfied before the higher needs can be fulfilled, or even aspired to. Subsidiary needs are, in Maslow's terms, prepotent:, powerful and requiring that they be fulfilled before the next need in the hierarchy can be addressed.

Physiological needs are basic human needs such as air, water, food, sleep, sex, and so on. If these needs remain long unsatisfied, we experience pain. Once they are satisfied, however, we can begin to think about safety needs, which Maslow associates with maintaining stability and consistency in a world that otherwise appears to us as chaotic and uncontrollable. Only then can we aspire toward love, esteem, and, ultimately, self-actualization, the highest level in Maslow's hierarchy of needs. Self-actualization has to do with the desire to become all that we are capable of becoming, to maximize our potential, whatever it may be. We may seek oneness with our God, personal peace, knowledge of various kinds, and so on.

Whether or not Maslow's hierarchy holds water in every detail, it seems intuitively correct, and in any event accurately describes the behavior of people in societies that offer them the opportunity to satisfy increasingly complex needs. Many forms of social organization can satisfy most of the deficiency needs. Indeed, some societies that seem in many ways appalling to us came to exist precisely because they at least supplied these basic deficiency needs of their citizens better than whatever (often chaos) preceded them.

But love needs require a sense of belonging, the opportunity to associate with and communicate openly with other human beings. And they require a society open enough to permit such associations—in other words, a largely democratic society. Esteem needs require that we master increasingly complex tasks for which we are naturally suited (self-esteem) and that we be viewed positively by our peers for our accomplishments (esteem by others). These are needs best addressed by a society with an open, competitive economic system that provides an enormous range of employment, volunteer, and other options, ensuring that virtually everyone can find something to be competent at—in other words, a free market economic system.

But here is a critical point: Self-actualization—"the desire ... to become everything that one is capable of becoming," in Maslow's words—is fundamentally different from the other needs. Self-actualization does not occur naturally among individuals whose previous needs have been satisfied. Satisfaction of those needs may be a necessary condition for the achievement of self-actualization, but they are not a *sufficient* condition. Assuming that the society in which we live offers the possibility to do so, we progress naturally up the hierarchy from the deficiency needs through love and esteem; these seem to be true needs to which human beings naturally aspire. But to make the leap to full self-actualization requires intense individual effort and, therefore, intense desire. Free market democracies are forms of social organization that can provide the platform that makes the leap possible, but it will not occur automatically. Indeed, once the incentive to become rich is eliminated, the tendency to become complacent dominates.

Thus, to a very considerable extent, the comfort that advanced postindustrial civilizations offer us seems positively to interfere with the further development of our potential. With all our other needs satisfied we tend not to gather our courage for yet one more struggle—the extraordinary leap to self-actualization. Instead, the lure of becoming everything we are capable of being is lost amid the creature comforts of our lives. Worse, our desire for continued progress is overwhelmed by the fear of losing what we have already attained. Hence the odd result that societies that appear to be ideal platforms for the full expression of humanness tend at some point in their development to impede further achievement—by producing citizens who are no longer willing to strive for it, to take the risks upon which all significant achievement depends. Instead, these societies produce citizens who spend most of their time building walls around what they have. The fear of losing ground dominates all else.

Capitalist societies, then, begin as robust, competitive communities, rapidly moving their citizens up the socioeconomic ladder (and, if you will, the Maslovian hierarchy). But all too often they decay into what appears to be middle-class comfort that is actually a surface calm underlain by apprehension. As we decline to risk our current, admittedly high, level of comfort, we forfeit any possibility of achieving more. We build walls around our prosperity, and those walls ultimately stifle us.

Because they are so wealthy, it is not immediately apparent how weak many formerly robust capitalist societies have become. But as productivity declines, fewer and fewer of those societies' products can compete internationally. Formerly free market governments must now impose high trade barriers or other forms of subsidy in order to continue to produce goods and services that were formerly competitive. Inefficient industries are thereby walled off from more efficient competitors elsewhere, excused from the competition that would make them more efficient.

And if we decline to place our jobs or our social status at risk, how must we feel about placing our very lives at risk, as, for example, in the defense of our country? Societies that become risk intolerant in the economic sphere tend to become risk intolerant in many ways. The emphasis on keeping what we have, rather than incurring risk to achieve more, softens the society, allowing it to become cautious, effete. To paraphrase Louise Bogan, these formerly vigorous capitalist societies now "have no wilderness in them, they are provident instead."[10]

PROVIDENTIAL SOCIETIES

Providential societies, as we might call them (with apologies to Ms. Bogan)—societies that no longer have the stomach for economic, social, cultural, or military risk—are analogous to investors who have lost their tolerance for market risk. It is an iron law of modern portfolio theory that rewards are, at least within reason, positively associated with the risks incurred. Investors can avoid risk quite easily: by, for example, putting all their money in Treasury bills. But this is the investment equivalent of sticking one's head in the sand and hoping to become invisible. Progress marches on, carrying along with it its handmaiden, inflation. Investors who own only Treasury bills become a little poorer every day in real terms. If those investors are unfortunate enough to have to pay taxes on their meager interest, their backward progress accelerates profoundly. Investors who cannot tolerate risk therefore die a little bit each day investment-wise, becoming slightly poorer than they were before, a process that leads inevitably to economic death; that is, to poverty.

Like risk-averse investors, societies that become unwilling to take risk also die a little bit each day, becoming a little poorer relative to societies that are more vigorous. It is essential, for example, that individuals be willing to take entrepreneurial risk—otherwise, new businesses will not be formed. But taking entrepreneurial risk means accepting the risk of personal failure and the risk that cushy jobs provided by existing firms will be eliminated. It is essential that businesses be exposed to competition, including competition from foreign firms and from hostile takeovers of poorly managed businesses. Otherwise, businesses become complacent and inefficient. Societies that find themselves so risk averse that they can no longer start new businesses or permit open competition for existing businesses are societies whose growth begins, imperceptibly at first, to slow and ultimately to stop. Opportunities for further advancement begin to disappear for already-affluent citizens, but also for citizens and immigrants who have the bad luck not to be already affluent. The slowing growth of these societies also imposes severe burdens on the development of emerging economies that depend on exports for their own economic growth.

And, like it or not, it is essential that societies be vigilant in their own defense, notwithstanding the economic costs and, of course, the risk that citizens may die in battle. Indeed, this is probably the ultimate touchstone for societies that have entered a terminal stage of decline—remarkable as it may seem, societies caught in the throes of providentiality simply cannot bring themselves even to take on the costs and risks of their own defense.

This is precisely the condition in which most of the advanced postindustrial societies of Europe and Scandinavia have found themselves. Our first glimpse of European ineffectuality came in Kosovo and Bosnia in the 1990s, when, among other atrocities, a tin-pot dictator named Slobodan Milošević slaughtered thousands while (European) United Nations troops stood by and watched the carnage. Only when American troops entered the fray—very much against the wishes of the Europeans and the U.N.—was the murderous rule of Milošević brought to an end, peace imposed, and the dictator brought to trial for war crimes.

The Balkan conflict was, to some extent, a (messy) tempest in a teapot. But if the Europeans were incapable of mounting a credible military operation in their own backyard, where they faced an obvious threat to European peace and stability, what possible chance was there that they could mount credible military operations against more distant threats, such as those posed by Iraq or North Korea? The answer, of course, is none at all. In the 1991 invasion of Iraq, despite United Nations approval of the attack, the contribution from most of Europe was almost risible.[11]

In the run-up to the 2003 Iraq invasion, so-called "old Europe" was solidly opposed to the attack. Although there were certainly important reasons to examine the American case for an invasion, the Europeans were transparently opposed to the war for other reasons altogether. Some of those reasons had to do with a natural fear of massive American military and economic power and the desire to band together to limit it. Other, more selfish, reasons had to do with (legal and illegal) trade relations with Iraq. But the fundamental fact of the matter was that no European country (except Britain, which joined in the attack) had any military capacity to wage a war in Iraq, hence the notion of a "United Nations" coalition was a hollow joke from the beginning.[12]

A society that possesses an imposing military force can make the decision to use it or not, and, like America, it might make those decisions wisely or unwisely. But at least the choice is there. Europe had no choice. Despite their incredible wealth, despite being vastly more advanced socially, economically, and technologically than Iraq, the European nations were no match, individually or collectively, for Iraqi power. Hence, the European rationale for opposing the war proceeded not from substance but from a kind of disease—the disease of providentiality.

RISK AND STRENGTH

Ironically—just as in the investment world—the willingness to tolerate a reasonable amount of risk actually reduces overall systemic risk in a society, because the assets of the society become diversified, more robust. The existence of a powerful military force—and the will to employ it—means that the society is less likely to be attacked, not more likely. Exposing a society's business enterprises to foreign competition means that, overall, those enterprises will be stronger, not weaker. The knowledge that we can be fired for incompetence or indolence makes for better, not worse, employees. Thus it is that risk-averse societies are more risky overall than non-risk-averse societies, in precisely the same sense that risk-averse investors end up holding portfolios that are more risky than those of non-risk-averse investors.

Of course, there is no gainsaying that costs are paid by societies that expose themselves to risk. In my own city of Pittsburgh, years of inefficient management, obsolete plants, and a legacy of powerful, militant, and unaccountable unions destroyed the Pittsburgh steel industry in one generation. A city that, during World War II, produced more steel than all of Germany and Japan combined produces, today, not one ton of steel. In barely more than a decade, nearly 100,000 steelworkers lost their jobs. These were men (almost all were, in fact, men) wholly unsuited by training or culture for any other remotely equal employment. Thousands of businesses that relied on the steel industry also collapsed. The pain caused by this dislocation can hardly be overestimated. But the consequences for American competitiveness of propping up the Pittsburgh steel industry—by, for example, imposing high tariffs on imported steel[13]—would have been far worse.

In a very important sense, risk-averse societies—providential societies—are opposed to the idea of progress itself. In effect, these societies are saying, "I am now rich and comfortable enough that further progress is unnecessary, because it brings risks, and to hell with the consequences for others of this attitude." As noted above, we needn't look far to observe this phenomenon in full flower in much of Western Europe and Scandinavia.

It is important to keep firmly in mind that it is not that Europe lacks the inherent capability to build a strong military force or to create a more vigorous economy. The European Union encompasses 27 nations and is the single richest and largest organized bloc of nations in the world. The

Union's population is, in the aggregate, nearly 200 million people larger than that of the United States.[14] What so many in Europe (and elsewhere) lack is the *will* to do those things.

One hundred and forty years ago, Abraham Lincoln understood this point quite precisely. Speaking at the great cemetery at Gettysburg, a place as haunting today as it was in 1864, Lincoln articulated the reason why the United States would not allow democracy to die. It was not because the United States had the military power to enforce its wishes against the Confederacy—in 1864 that was still very much unclear. Nor was it that the United States possessed the industrial might to dominate the Confederacy. Nor was it, even, that God was on the side of the North. The United States would not allow democracy to die simply because we *willed* it to remain alive. Democracy would prevail as the result of a collective act of American resolve: "We here *highly resolve* ... that government of the people, by the people, and for the people shall not perish from the Earth."[15] Nearly a century and a half later, Lincoln would still recognize, in an America otherwise formidably changed, the collective American resolve to preserve democracy, a resolute will that is determined to prevail despite almost unanimous opposition from our friends and our foes alike.[16]

AMERICA AND DECLINE

Why is it, we might ask ourselves, that America seems to have been largely (albeit certainly not completely) immune to providentiality? Virtually since the United States appeared on the world stage there have been confident predictions that the country would soon enter a period of inexorable decline. Some of these predictions were based on the view that all successful civilizations pass through various stages, with a robust, dominating stage certain to be succeeded by a self-indulgent, dissipated stage, followed by collapse in the face of challenges presented by more vigorous civilizations. Other predictions have been based on underestimations of American society, estimations based on the assumption that American society is just like European society, or on peculiar conditions in America that seemed to threaten its preeminence.

After World War I, for example, most Europeans—and, for that matter, most Americans—assumed that the old order would quickly reassert itself, with London as the capital of the Anglo-Saxon world and Paris and Berlin vying for control of the Continent. America was seen as too insular to succeed to world dominance. Indeed, the German high command in World War I had made the crucial, and fatal, assumptions that America would not enter the war until it was too late and that the admittedly imposing

American economy could not switch to war production quickly enough to affect the outcome.[17] But in fact America had become the dominant world economy long before the war began, and its preeminence afterward was due only in part to the devastation the war caused to Britain and the Continental powers.[18] By 1918, the dollar had replaced sterling as the world currency, a role the dollar continues to play today, more than eight decades later. World War I certainly accelerated the rise of American dominance, but it was already preordained.

If affluence alone were sufficient to convert America into a provident society, one would have expected to see signs of it long, long ago. It was, after all, way back in the mid-eighteenth century that America surpassed all other regions of the world in living standards. Surely 250 years as the world's richest country ought to be enough to corrupt us. And, as everyone knows, the United States is not merely the world's oldest democracy—it is the world's oldest continuing government of any kind, operating under the same Constitution since 1788. That, my friends, is a long time for any kind of government to persist, notwithstanding the confident prognostications of cyclical decline theorists.

And, though it is difficult to prove, it seems likely that, by the middle of the nineteenth century, America was already the world's foremost military power. During the American Civil War, for example, the two most powerful armies on earth were both American. One hundred and fifty years of such power ought, surely, to have been long enough for America's military to fall into overconfidence, complacency, corruption, lassitude. But in the early twenty-first century America is more dominant militarily than any civilization has ever been. Granted, America did not begin to project its economic, political, and military power globally until World War I, but even that is now nine long and action-packed decades ago.

But the pundits never give up. Every time America stumbles—and we certainly stumble at least our fair share of the time—we hear that this time the final decline has begun. From the late 1940s through the 1970s, the virulence of anticommunism in America was accounted for in part by the fear that the Soviet Union had invented a more powerful military–industrial engine; that America was too free and disorganized to compete against such a disciplined juggernaut. Yet it was primarily the imposing economic and military strength of America that ultimately caused the USSR to collapse.[19]

As recently as the 1980s it was fashionable to argue that a bloated America could not possibly compete with such vigorous economies as Japan and Germany. These powerhouse societies, it was said, possessed more efficient decision-making cultures, more homogeneous populations all pulling in the same direction, more civilized labor–management relations, and were unhampered by legacy industrial plants, having been completely rebuilt after

World War II primarily with American aid. But what a difference a decade or so can make! Today, Japan is mired in a 20-year economic malaise, while the German economy has fallen to fourth place in the world (behind the United States, China, and Japan), and given its dismal demographics, is likely to be passed soon by Brazil and India. The American economy, far from succumbing to the competition, is more dominant than ever: Total U.S. GDP today is nearly twice that of Germany and Japan combined.[20]

Today, we hear that the United States will soon be crushed by the remarkable economies of China and India, and perhaps even by those of Brazil and Russia. But there are lots of things wrong with these prognostications. The first is that we've heard it all before and it never seems to happen. But let's set that aside. The second problem is that those economies aren't exactly nipping at our heels, as the doomsayers seem to suggest. China's economy, the second-largest in the world, is barely one-third the size of the United States'. Brazil's economy is 14 percent of that of the United States, India's is 13 percent, and Russia's barely 10 percent. These societies have a long way to go and a lot of potholes to navigate before they can be spoken of in the same breath with the United States.

ON CHINA

But let's focus on China for a moment, because that is the economy Americans seem to fear the most. And certainly it is true that China has been the wonder of the world for three decades, growing at an astonishing rate and lifting hundreds of millions of people out of grinding poverty into something approaching a middle-class existence. It's probably no exaggeration to say that this has been one of the most positive events in recent human history.

Indeed, we can say about China precisely what I say abut the former Soviet Union in Chapter 2: "In barely a generation, [Chinese]-style communism transformed a backward, peasant, agrarian society into the second-largest economy in the world." But it's one thing to convert an agrarian society into an industrial society. A strong and determined (communist) central government can basically decree that it will happen and it will. (Note, on the other hand, that a determined but weak—democratic—central government, as in India, will have a much tougher road.)

But for the Chinese economy to continue to grow at anything like its former glory, that economy can't remain a simple industrial society in which capital[21] is allocated mainly to create jobs and keep the populace docile. China has to transform itself into a vastly more complex postindustrial economy, where capital is allocated moment by moment to where it is needed most. And that is something that no society has ever achieved using a top-down, command economy approach. The Soviet Union collapsed when it tried to compete with the complex U.S. economy, and there is little reason to suppose that the Chinese will fare any better.

Following the catastrophic Leaps Forward orchestrated by Mao (who died in 1976), Deng Xiaoping reorganized the Chinese economy into a combination of socialism and free market principles (often called state capitalism). Since that time, domestic peace has been achieved in China via a kind of deal with the Devil, in which the citizenry gave up any hope of enjoying Western-style rights, democracy, or the rule of law in exchange for the promise of rapid economic progress that would be dispersed throughout the society.

For three decades that bargain held, with the Chinese economy growing at nearly 10 percent per year. But the bargain contains the seeds of its own destruction. As noted above, a complex postindustrial economy simply can't be managed by a small cadre of senior Party members in Beijing. Already the Chinese economy has slowed and, net of inflation, is now growing well below levels once thought to be incompatible with domestic peace. More slowing can be expected as the Chinese economy necessarily becomes ever more complicated.

In addition, corruption and nepotism are rampant, and though nearly a quarter of the population has benefited from economic growth, three-quarters (mainly the interior of the country) has not. Note, in addition, that the main beneficiaries of economic progress have been Han Chinese, while the main losers have been concentrated in other ethnic groups.

Finally, as discussed at some length in Chapter 2, the Chinese government lacks moral legitimacy. Although China is surely a freer society than was the Soviet Union, it remains the case that a government that withholds human rights but provides rapid economic growth had better keep providing rapid economic growth and it had better ensure that that growth is widely dispersed. Ultimately, the moral basis of a society matters. True, it matters less when people are starving and the central government is feeding them, but it matters more and more as citizens become more affluent and move up the Maslovian ladder. And it matters even more as the central government fails to uphold its part of the bargain.

And if the center begins to lose its hold in China, chaos can't be far away. Throughout history China has rarely been the unified country we observe today—and even in the modern era it has been unified (excluding Taiwan) only since the late 1940s. If "the center cannot hold," China is likely to fragment into a variety of autonomous countries along the lines of the former USSR. At the very least, we can expect to see Tibet, Xinjiang, Inner Mongolia, and Manchuria reorganize themselves into separate states.

The same people who believe that China will soon dominate the world, and that its totalitarian form of government is either irrelevant or a positive virtue, are the same people who were blindsided by the collapse of the Soviet Union and, more recently, by the Arab Spring.

Speaking in shorthand, the internal contradiction of Chinese society can be expressed this way: If the Chinese Communist Party (CCP) maintains its iron grip on the country, the Chinese economy will continue to slow and the CCP will have to spend more and more of its time putting down insurrections and less and less of its time trying to grow the economy. If the CCP loosens its grip and democratizes, the country will come unglued.[22]

ADDRESSING THE DECLINISTS

An example of the America-in-terminal-decline point of view is Kevin Phillips's *Wealth and Democracy*,[23] in which Phillips argues that, like Spain, Holland, and Britain before it, America exhibits all the classic symptoms of cyclical decline: a preoccupation with finance, technology, and services rather than basic manufacturing; capital markets prone to bubbles and speculation; the export of jobs and capital; the import of cheap foreign labor to do jobs Americans don't want; a growing inequality of income and wealth; and frequent and incipient wars.[24]

But Phillips has it exactly backwards: Whether or not these were symptoms of decline in societies hundreds of years ago, they are, today, symptoms of vigor, of continued dominance. Because Phillips's view of the world is widely held, let's examine each of his symptoms of decline. In brief:

- Contrary to Phillips's view, in the early twenty-first century it is important that simple (basic) manufacturing take place in societies where less expensive labor can produce goods more cheaply and efficiently. This not only contributes to economic progress in those countries, but the resulting less-expensive goods are then more affordable not merely to rich postindustrial populations, but also to people in developing societies.
- Bubbles will always be a part of capital markets and economies because they reflect not markets or economies or anything specifically American, but human nature. Nor is there anything especially modern about bubbles. Yes, America recently had its Tech Bubble and its Housing Bubble, but Holland had its Tulip Bubble (1634), England had its South Sea Bubble (1720), Japan had an entire Bubble Economy (beginning in 1984), Europe has its Debt Bubble, China has its Real Estate (and Inflation) Bubble, and so on.

- Yes, America exports capital, but that capital is used by less developed economies to build economic capacity, reducing global poverty and, ultimately, enlarging the markets for American goods and services—in addition to making the world a safer, more just, and more stable place.
- The "cheap foreign labor" that America imports (legally and quasi-illegally[25]) doesn't stay cheap very long. Within a few generations, immigrants, like those who came before them, tend to become productive citizens even by Phillips's narrow standards.
- I have already addressed the inequality of income and wealth in America—it is not the size of the disparity that matters, but the absolute level of affluence of the nonwealthy, as well as the ability of the nonwealthy to become rich.
- I have also briefly addressed the delicate issue of war. It is undoubtedly true that a warmongering America bent on world domination by military might would present a serious and undoubtedly effective means of engineering our ultimate decline. But that is a far different America from the one that stands vigilant over the free world, its vigor as the world's wealthiest and most powerful country undiminished, very much as though it were still a youthful, struggling country, rather than the world's oldest government.

Similarly, we hear virtually every day about other evidence of our decline.[26] Not long ago, for example, a friend pointed out to me that the average Japanese high school math student would rank in the top 1 percent of American high school math students. This is certainly an alarming statistic (if true), but there is a problem with such statistics—namely, that we have been hearing them year after year since at least Sputnik,[27] and, so far, at least, America has only become ever more dominant. (Indeed, the society whose educational prowess was so superior to ours in 1957 no longer exists.)

A superbly well-educated population is certainly a useful thing to have, but as in so much of life it isn't what you've got, but what you do with what you've got that matters. A truly uneducated America would undoubtedly be a recipe for disaster. But a reasonably well-educated America motivated to deploy every ounce of its competitiveness is an unstoppable juggernaut.

There are, in other words, conditions that could cause America to begin an inexorable decline into mediocrity, and it would be interesting and instructive to consider what those conditions might be. But Phillips's (and others') focus on the specific conditions of the distant past, rather than on the effect of those conditions, has led the pundits far astray. Indeed, many of the conditions that were symptoms of decline in past civilizations are now, given the dramatic change in economic and political conditions, symptoms of continued vigor.

CONCLUSION: AMERICAN DISTINCTIVENESS AND PRIVATE WEALTH

This raises again the crucial point: How is it that America has avoided becoming a providential society? Surely we are affluent enough that, long ago, we ought to have begun building postindustrial walls around our prosperity, ought to have begun to fear progress, competition, to worry more about losing what we have than about producing ever more; we ought to have reduced our military spending and avoided confrontations that might endanger the lives of our citizens. America ought, in short, to have led the headlong rush into providentiality, but we haven't. Well past two centuries old, America acts more like a young economic stallion, posting economic productivity numbers that look suspiciously like those of emerging economies, demanding ever more, not less, competitiveness from our corporations, expecting ever smarter work, ever longer hours, from our workforce. And no one on earth has the slightest doubt that, when freedom is attacked, America will respond swiftly and massively, and that the cost in dollars—and, unfortunately, in lives—will be paid as necessary.

Far from succumbing to providentiality, America, even in the minds of its detractors, seems if anything to have evolved too much in the opposite direction: We are too aggressive, too independent-minded, too bold, "interventionist bullies with no regard for the sovereignty of [other] countries."[28] America, it is argued, ought to grow up, to settle into a kind of sociopolitical middle age, to become softer, more malleable, more predictable. This is, after all, what has happened in every other advanced postindustrial free market democracy. Why hasn't it happened in the United States?

Continuing American vigor is accounted for principally by the ongoing competitive spirit that animates a society in which virtually anyone can become rich by doing something spectacularly useful for the broader society. If that spirit were to become constrained by political or cultural mechanisms, America would rather quickly come to resemble its European cousins. In order for the lure of wealth to be meaningful, America must be willing to tolerate the consequences of competition, including the possibility that some people will lose in that competition and *including the possibility that some people will become very wealthy.*

Most free market economies long ago placed serious constraints on the ability of citizens to prosper. In effect, these societies have said, "Up to this point we want you to work hard and work smart, to ensure that our society remains competitive. But beyond this point we want you to stop working hard and working smart, and if you don't we will confiscate the fruits of your labors." However well motivated this approach might be, it simply can't work. One reason it can't work is because the truly spectacular ideas that drive civilization and that lead to dominance are invariably snuffed out by economies that confiscate wealth above a certain point.

More fundamentally, no society can know at what point the trade-off between the desire to "eliminate the rich elite" begins to conflict with the desire to remain competitive. Sure, we could go ahead and place Bill Gates and the Wall Street titans into the category of "Evil Rich to be Liquidated." But what about Dan and Eve Eckels, who used their (paltry) life savings to organize the Eckels Steel Fabricating Company in 1950 and sold it for $45 million in 1998? Eckels Steel Fabricating Company didn't have anything like the impact on national productivity and competitiveness that Microsoft had. But the Eckels Company did have an important impact on competitive conditions in its own industry (which is why it flourished), and, whereas there is only one Microsoft, there are thousands of Eckels.

The fact is that constraining the fruits of hard and smart work have the same effect on a society as trying to blow up a balloon that has a hole in the other end. Competitive societies recognize the contributions of the Bill Gateses of the world by showering them with billions of dollars, and competitive societies recognize the contributions of the Dan and Eve Eckleses of the world by showering them with millions of dollars. And so on in a seamless parade of extraordinary contributions to remarkable contributions to useful contributions to no contributions to negative contributions.

It is only a kind of shorthand, therefore, to say that America dominates other free market economies because of the contributions of wealthy families to its competitive spirit. The profuse creation of private capital through the intense pursuit of the best business ideas is what distinguishes America from other capitalist systems. The possibility of becoming wealthy motivates millions of Americans to take risks and to work harder than they would otherwise be inclined to do—and than they would do if they lived in other countries.

Moreover, the competitive spirit that animates the most successful Americans creates a culture that is internalized by almost all Americans, even those who have virtually no chance of becoming wealthy. In an open society, citizens will eventually internalize the values that they observe to be legitimate and valuable. If a society claims that it wishes its citizens to be competitive, but then discourages the pursuit of wealth (via taxation or cultural disapproval, for example), citizens in that society will internalize not the message to be competitive, but the message not to be too competitive. As the most successful people in America become rich, other citizens observe the legitimacy of that activity and its value to themselves, and they internalize the competitive spirit that led to those riches. At length, all of American society is permeated with the spirit of hard work, smart work, competition, and progress. Other societies can only watch in astonishment.

If the sheer economic vigor of a society were the sole measure of its success, that would be the end of the story. We could all see clearly that America's economic success is driven by the wealth creation process, and that the possessors of that wealth are the key to understanding American competitiveness. But the lure of wealth and its impact on economic vigor is only half the story. The other half is the creative use of private capital after it has been earned. Let's turn to that subject in Chapter 2.

NOTES

1. I say "perhaps" because, whether the incentive is to create wealth, as in a market economy, or power, as in a nonmarket economy, the same kinds of people are likely to win the competition: the most competent, the hardest working and, perhaps, the most ruthless.
2. "Government by a privileged minority," *Webster's New World Dictionary* (New York: Simon & Schuster, 1996). The term "aristocracy" originally referred to a government by the best citizens in the state.
3. Many observers consider the persistence of the rich in America to be both unacceptable and a symptom of incipient decline. See, for example, Kevin Phillips, *Wealth and Democracy: A Political History of the American Rich* (New York: Broadway Books, 2002).
4. In John Gray's words, "[C]ivil society is the matrix of the market economy." John Gray, *Post-Liberalism: Studies in Political Thought* (Oxford: Routledge, 1993), 246.
5. Japan straddles this world, as an advanced postindustrial society with the trappings of liberal democracy but the soul of a civil society that is quite different from, and that developed largely independently of, Western-style democracy. Japan's distinctiveness would be far more apparent if it were not for the Western-style constitution and government imposed on Japan by the United States after World War II.
6. All labor is, in a literal sense, exploited if we accept John Roemer's Marxist definition: "[A] person is exploited if the labor that he expends in production is greater than the labor embodied in the goods he can purchase with the revenues from production." John E. Roemer, *Free to Lose: An Introduction to Marxist Economic Philosophy* (London: Century Hutchinson, 1989), 161. But such a society would be a static one, indeed. Given that labor is also exploited under any other conceivable economic system (especially socialism and communism), we ought to prefer the system that maximizes the economic well-being of the worker.

7. The wealth gap between Bill Gates and America's poorest families is very nearly as large as was the wealth gap between the Sun Kings of Egypt and their slaves. The difference is not in the size of the gap but in the fact that Egyptian slaves would always be slaves, as would their children, whereas poor citizens in America can, and do, aspire to be the next Bill Gates.

8. Poverty in America is more closely associated with immigration—no sooner does one immigrant group move up the socioeconomic ladder than they are replaced by other aspiring, but very poor, "Americans." In addition, poverty is also associated with America's semipermanent underclass associated mainly, but hardly exclusively, with our legacy of black slavery.

9. Abraham Maslow, *Motivation and Personality* (New York: Harper-Collins, 1987), originally published in 1854.

10. Louise Bogan, "Women," *Blue Estuaries: Poems 1923–1968* (New York: Farrar, Straus and Giroux, 1968). Bogan was actually speaking (ironically) of women.

11. As a random example, the French sent a few jet aircraft to Iraq, but these Mirages were so out of date that their antiquated radar left them dangerously vulnerable to Iraqi antiaircraft fire. No doubt the French pilots of these planes were as brave as their American counterparts. But their service on behalf of such an enfeebled society meant that they had to be escorted through the battle zone like noncombatants. The French were simply no match for a third world power like Iraq.

12. See, generally, the hilarious and sad article by Philip Shishkin, "How the Armies of Europe Let Their Guard Down: Guaranteed Jobs for Soldiers Leave Little Room to Train," *Wall Street Journal* (February 13, 2003): 1, 7. The main point of Shishkin's article is that "Europe's military muscle has grown soft" mainly because "so much money is spent on pay and benefits that there is less left for the technology, weapons and other gear that modern forces need." This, of course, is my point exactly: A providential society doesn't maintain a military force as a serious deterrent against possible aggression or to maintain their own security and integrity, but rather as an instrument of social policy to reduce unemployment, provide a social safety net, and respond to citizen demands for less work and more pay.

13. Tariffs have, in fact, been imposed on imported steel from time to time, most recently in 2002 (they were removed in 2003). However, these tariffs have been more about warning other countries against subsidizing their own inefficient steel industries than about subsidizing our own. Even so, tariffs are generally counterproductive because, among other things, although they may temporarily maintain employment in the

targeted industry (e.g., steelmaking), they reduce employment in all the industries that must now pay more for steel.

14. Eurostat, 2.2.7-r1821-2012-03-13, available at http://epp.eurostat.ec .europa.eu/tgm/table.do?tab=table&language=en&pcode=tps00001 &tableSelection=1&footnotes=yes&labeling=labels&plugin=1.

15. See Paul Berman's discussion of the role of resolve in the preservation of democracy: "What Lincoln Knew About War," *The New Republic* (March 3, 2003).

16. Our friends would prefer America to be as irresolute as they; our enemies would prefer us to be as irresolute as our friends.

17. In fact, however, "By the war's end, the United States had an arms-making capacity that eclipsed that of England and France combined." Ron Chernow, *The House of Morgan* (New York: Simon & Schuster, 1990), 189.

18. In 1914, Britain accounted for 8.3 percent of the world's GDP. It is interesting to compare Britain's pre-World War I "dominance" with America's dominance today: In 2011, America accounted for fully 23 percent of the world's GDP. International Monetary Fund, World Economic Outlook Database, January 24, 2012, http://www.imf.org/ external/pubs/ft/weo/2011/02/weodata/index.aspx.

19. Even Ilya Zaslavsky, the main Gorbachev advisor during Perestroika, admitted that it was Reagan's policy of "negotiating through strength that brought the Kremlin to its knees." David Remnick, *Lenin's Tomb: The Last Days of the Soviet Empire* (New York: Vintage Books, 1994), 323.

20. International Monetary Fund, World Economic Outlook Database.

21. China also faces a third challenge. Many economists have pointed out that when a rapidly industrializing society achieves a certain level of development—let's call it roughly $5,000 in capital per capita—growth inevitably slows down. While the exact mechanisms of this deceleration are a matter of dispute, the phenomenon has been observed in societies as different as the United States, the Soviet Union, post-war Germany and Japan, Taiwan, Singapore, Hong Kong, etc.

22. Somewhat similar arguments have recently been made, from very different political perspectives, by Zbigniew Brzezinski in *Strategic Vision: America and the Crisis of Global Power* (New York: Basic Books, 2012), and by Robert Kagan in *The World America Made* (New York: Alfred A. Knopf, 2012).

23. Phillips, *Wealth and Democracy*.

24. Phillips, *Wealth and Democracy*, 389 ff.

25. Illegal immigrants have so often been granted legalized status that the phrase "illegal immigrant" has little meaning.

26. A characteristic example, this time from the political left, is Edward Luce's *Time to Start Thinking: America in the Age of Descent* (New York: Atlantic Monthly Press, 2012).

27. For those of my readers who are too young to remember, Sputnik 1 was a Soviet satellite that successfully achieved an Earth orbit in October of 1957. Sputnik launched the Space Age, beating America into space and inaugurating the first of the long succession of lamentations about the poor quality of American scientific and technical education.

28. William Safire, "Myth America 2002" *New York Times* (July 8, 2002): A21.

CHAPTER 2

Creative Capital

It is as impossible for a society to be formed and lasting without self-interest as it would be to produce children without carnal desire or to think of eating without appetite.
—Voltaire, On the *Pensées* of Pascal (1734)

It is not enough that an economic system be successful economically. American-style capitalism has astonished the world, to be sure. But if we really want to observe a powerful economy in action, we need only look at the Soviet Union between 1917 and 1935. In barely a generation, Soviet-style communism transformed a backward, peasant, agrarian society into the second-largest economy in the world, an economic triumph that seems unlikely to have been surpassed by any nation in history.

The trouble with the Soviet system was that it was not a morally legitimate form of social organization. It could be sustained only by the extravagant use of state power to maintain an entrenched elite. Tens of millions of Soviet citizens would die to accomplish the remarkable economic outcomes produced by the USSR, the Soviet natural environment would be destroyed, human freedoms would be eliminated, and the moral nature of Soviet citizens would rot. Held in check by American military might for seven decades, the Soviet Union would eventually implode.

The lesson of the USSR, and of the decline of many other once-powerful civilizations, is that, ultimately, it is the moral basis of a society that matters. Remarkable as the accomplishments of the American free market might be, those accomplishments would not have persisted unless Americans in particular, and other citizens of the world in general, perceived the American system to be operating on a legitimate ethical basis. Human beings are both economic and moral creatures—that is, we are both selfish and selfless—and the organization of successful societies must recognize and nourish both aspects of our being. Thus, to fully understand the role of private capital in America's success, it is necessary to take a small detour and (briefly!) examine the moral dimension of capitalism.

A (BRIEF) MORAL HISTORY OF CAPITALISM

Even those few of my readers who have studied economic theory or the history of economics probably studied them long ago and not entirely voluntarily. As a result, names like Adam Smith have a musty scent to them, suggesting something that happened long ago and far away and that couldn't have much relevance to twenty-first century America. Whatever capitalism might have meant in the early days before the Industrial Revolution, we are thinking, surely it means something quite different today. But in fact the fundamental tenets of market theory are as profoundly important to modern economies as they were profoundly important to economies two or three centuries ago.

And what is of central importance today, as it was 300 years ago, is the *moral* character of capitalism. Serious critiques of the effectiveness of market economies versus other forms of economic organization have almost completely disappeared, buried by the stunning success of capitalism. To argue, early in the twenty-first century, that some other system might produce superior economic results would be to mark ourselves as serious ideologues. But moral critiques of capitalism have always been with us, and probably always will be. It simply can't be denied that market economies are designed in part to appeal to aspects of human nature that don't exactly represent our proudest moments. If human beings weren't selfish, weren't inclined to be lazy, didn't instinctively mistrust anyone outside our own families, didn't love power and luxury—well, in that case other, gentler, more charming economic systems would certainly be preferable.

Nor can it be denied that capitalism forces wrenching changes in traditional ways of life. If the craft guilds of Germany couldn't compete with the vast new industrial enterprises in England, the craft guilds would disappear, and along with them would disappear an entire, traditional way of life. If family farms in the American Midwest can't compete with "factory" farms, family farms will disappear, and along with them will disappear hundreds of small towns that once represented the backbone of America. To argue that nothing is lost in such transitions would be harsh, indeed.

Finally, capitalism always and everywhere results in unequal economic outcomes, with some citizens becoming remarkably wealthy while others remain poor and most end up in middle income categories.

But it is possible to mount a thoughtful defense of the moral properties of capitalism, and it is useful to remind ourselves of this fact. Indeed, virtually all the early proponents of market economies were drawn to them *precisely because they were perceived to be morally superior to other systems*. Let's briefly focus on this moral dimension of free market systems.

THE ANCIENTS

The more men value moneymaking, the less they value virtue.
—Plato, *Republic* (quoting Socrates)

Do not lay up for yourselves treasures on earth, for where your treasure is, there will your heart be also.
—Jesus, Sermon on the Mount

We could go on and on with anticapitalist quotes from the ancients ("It is easier for a camel to pass through the eye of a needle than for a rich man to enter into the Kingdom of Heaven," etc.) From Greek and Roman times through the late Middle Ages, the world was burdened by the notion that whatever wealth existed was fixed and immutable. Only in heaven could riches be created anew, and then only by God Himself. Therefore, if one man enriched himself, another man must inescapably become poorer. In such a world any sort of market activity would naturally be considered immoral:[1] " *Si unus non perdit, alter non acquirit.*"[2]

By the twelfth century, however, modern-style cities had begun to appear, commerce began to thrive, and even a hidebound Church hierarchy could not fail to notice the dramatic improvement in the condition of men. The Church was thus faced with a serious dilemma. On the one hand, commercial activity was clearly a profound social good. On the other hand, all the Church's founding documents and theories—written when the world was a more static place—had heaped scorn on this very activity. Thus began a slow and careful "reinterpretation" of Church gospel, led by such thinkers as Thomas Aquinas. Aquinas and other Scholastics marshaled religious arguments for the social necessity of private property, concluding that market systems themselves were morally neutral and their consequences socially beneficial, and focusing their scorn only on characteristic abuses of commercial activity, such as dishonesty, sharp dealing, fraud and, of course, usury.

Indeed, nowhere was the struggle to accommodate religion to capitalism more complex and strained than on the question of usury. The lending of money at interest had always been a mortal sin—had not Jesus Himself cleared the temple of moneylenders? Yet commerce could not flourish without the willingness of people with capital to lend it to people with productive ideas. The Lateran Council had banned usury in 1139—right in the teeth of the early growth of commerce and hence the need for loans. In effect, the Church had agreed that wealth in general was not a fixed commodity, but rather something that could be created by the efforts of men. The earlier, static notions now clung only to the object of money itself, which was considered sterile and incapable of growth—money does not beget money. This final dilemma was resolved not theologically, but by the expedient of creating a monopoly for Jews, who dominated moneylending for centuries.[3]

MORAL ARGUMENTS FOR CAPITALISM

Notwithstanding the early opposition of the Church, there were powerful arguments—powerful *moral* arguments—to be made for capitalism, and those arguments were advanced by the most profound thinkers of the era.[4] In the brief paragraphs below I summarize the views of this new method of organizing economies as they were expressed by Voltaire, Adam Smith, and Hegel.

Voltaire

By the time *The Wealth of Nations* appeared in 1776, capitalist economies had already flourished for more than a century. Hence Smith and his fellow "economists"[5] were not speculating about a type of political economy that might prove fruitful—they were describing and praising a system that had existed for many decades and that had proved itself remarkably adept at improving the condition of men and women.

Well before *The Wealth of Nations* appeared, the earliest and most prominent proponent of capitalism was Voltaire, who had moved to England in the 1720s to escape persecution by the French Catholic Church and government. The first public intellectual in the modern sense of the word, Voltaire was immeasurably impressed by the accomplishments of the market economy that had transformed the lives of ordinary people in Britain. Compared to the traditional French, the population of England was better dressed, better fed, and better housed. Material objects that the English considered no more than absolute necessities were still almost unknown among the mass populations on the Continent.

But what really captured Voltaire's attention was the moral impact of capitalism. He had been appalled by the almost continuous warfare on the Continent, the dreadful political machinations of the Church and the royal parties, the religious zealotry that dominated every aspect of society.

Such strife had seemed to be inherent in the human condition. Say what you will, Voltaire pointed out, men will act, and the only question is whether their energy will be directed toward discord and chaos or toward more constructive ends. For Voltaire, the great thing about the market economy of Britain was that the extraordinary energy of men was put to work constructively. Not only was human energy absorbed by the pursuit of wealth through commerce, but the outcome of that pursuit was the improvement of the condition of all men, not just those who proved most successful in the competition. Referring to the London Stock Exchange, Voltaire observed, "Here the Jew, the Mohametan and the Christian deal with one another as if they were of the same religion, and reserve the name 'infidel' for those who go bankrupt."[6]

Voltaire met head-on the charge that capitalism relied on selfishness, whereas a stable social order must be based on altruism. Blaise Pascal had powerfully argued this point, writing, "Each of us tends toward himself. That is against all order. We must tend toward the whole; and the tendency toward self-interest is the beginning of all disorder in war, in government, in economy, etc."[7] Absent a market economy to channel the self-interest of men, Pascal was probably correct. But in the context of capitalism, self-interest was transformed from a source of unrest to a source of concord and progress.

One key problem with the pursuit of self-interest in a free market economy was that it clashed with medieval and religious notions of luxury. One person's luxury is, of course, another person's necessity—better yet, an earlier generation's luxury is almost always, in market societies, a later generation's necessity. But in the later seventeenth and early eighteenth centuries, luxury was a charged word. Static notions of social order reserved luxury goods for the upper echelons of society—royalty and the aristocracy. For the masses to aspire to material well-being wasn't viewed as a natural, human inclination, but as a dangerous threat to social and religious order. Instead, Church and State encouraged monkish "virtues" such as self-denial and asceticism.

Voltaire attacked these static ideas, and glorified the struggle for material well-being, in his controversial poem "The Worldling," and its successor, "The Defense of the Worldling." The first poem—published in Paris without Voltaire's permission—caused him to flee France again, this time to Russia (where he wrote "The Defense of the Worldling"). Centuries before Abraham Maslow developed his hierarchy of needs, Voltaire asserted in these poems that prosperity was an absolute prerequisite to the progress of civilization. Voltaire even defended the "conspicuous consumption" (as we would call it) of the affluent, pointing out that demand for luxury goods increased the need for labor, which ultimately improved the lives of the nonaffluent.

In short, Voltaire correctly saw capitalism as the only serious antidote to antirational forces such as religious zealotry and absolutist governments, forces that had led to constant strife and warfare. Capitalism worked its magic, undermining extremist, antihuman forces by refocusing the attentions and energies of people into constructive, rather than destructive, activities. As the pursuit of those constructive activities raised the material welfare of the population, people began to see themselves not as helpless victims of larger forces, but as serious, independent actors, responsible for their own fate. They became far less susceptible to extreme forms of thought, religious or otherwise, and far less tolerant of being dictated to by arbitrary governments.

Adam Smith

We tend to think of *The Wealth of Nations*—then and now the finest book ever written about market economies—as a dry economic text. But it was not so perceived by Smith's contemporaries, who made the book an instant sensation and Smith an instant celebrity. Much of Smith's book is devoted to a brilliant analysis not just of what free markets can accomplish, but precisely how and why such accomplishments occur. Smith spoke not just at the level of economic theory, but at the level of the factory floor. He described in detail how the individual self-interest of workers led to greater productivity, how the division of labor allowed production to increase geometrically without longer hours or harder work. He demonstrated over and over again how capitalism rewarded efficiency, and how efficiency drove living standards.

Smith was a Scot, and he lived at a time when he could not fail to be impressed by the differences in conditions between the north and south of Scotland. In the Lowland industrializing cities of Glasgow and Edinburgh, market forces had so rapidly improved living standards that ordinary workers could, for the first time in human history, support their families on one job. In the backward Northern Highlands, however, the primitive clan culture still dominated, local chiefs wielded absolute power, market forces had not yet penetrated, and the population lived in medieval conditions. (These are, of course, precisely the conditions that continue to dominate societies that have not adopted free market systems.)

But mere material progress was not what really impressed Smith. A professor of moral philosophy at the University of Glasgow, he was far more impressed with the ethical progress that capitalism promoted among the population. Precapitalist societies were marked by superstition, a conviction of powerlessness, suspicion of anyone outside the family, and an indolence that had to be overcome by force. But populations subject to market forces quickly developed a far different character. Citizens developed behaviors characterized by fundamental decency: nonviolence, prudence, openness to the opinions of others, the ability to postpone gratification and to work for long-term objectives. These were, perhaps, modest enough virtues. But compared to the condition of men in precapitalist societies, they were cause for celebration.

Capitalism, Smith argued, encouraged good behavior because, in a market society characterized by trade and exchange, each person was dependent on others. This dependency was utterly unlike the dependence of a serf on the protection of his lord. It was a dependency of equals on equals, intermediated by the use of cash as the medium of exchange. Thus, if I treat people fairly and deliver value, people will treat me fairly in return and my living standards will rise. If I don't treat people fairly, they won't treat me fairly in return—indeed, they will refuse to deal with me at all—and I will therefore fail in my endeavor to improve conditions for myself and my family. For Adam Smith then, what Muller calls the "moral balance sheet" of capitalism[8]—its dependence on innate selfishness on one side of the ledger versus its ability to improve living conditions and the quality of human interaction—fell solidly into the black. What organized religion had failed to do for thousands of years, capitalism had succeeded in doing in a few decades, namely, enabling masses of people to live "a morally decent existence."[9]

Hegel

Adam Smith published *The Wealth of Nations* roughly half a century after Voltaire moved to England and began his observations of the British market economy. Half a century after Smith's book appeared, the moral character of capitalism was taken up in turn by Georg Wilhelm Friedrich Hegel, the German philosopher who was perhaps the most influential thinker of the nineteenth century (at least, now that Marxism is largely dead). The moral attraction of capitalism, for Hegel, lay in its ability to reify the dignity of men without resort to some higher power. In the *Philosophy of Right* (1820), and especially in the student lectures that preceded and followed publication of the book, Hegel contrasted the failure of the French Revolution with the success of capitalism.

Hegel pointed out that the leaders of the Revolution had failed because they had profoundly misunderstood the nature of liberty, considering all institutions to be impediments to human freedom. In fact, freedom cannot exist, cannot have any meaning, outside the context of institutions that are broadly accepted by members of society. If someone asserts, "I am a separate and independent person, fully entitled to all the dignity of a free man," what can that mean? What are the characteristics of such a freedom? Where does it begin and end? Absent an acknowledgement from the rest of society, such a person is not really free but only, at best, a deluded slave and, at worst, a madman.

The great thing about capitalism for Hegel was that its institutions—especially private property, the sanctity of contracts, and the need for citizens of market societies to engage in mutually beneficial trade and exchange—reified men's assertions of their separate existence, their dignity, their freedom. When a person asserts, "This is my property, no one can take it from me except with my consent and for value delivered," it may not have the same noble ring as the assertion of freedom, but in fact it is a far more profound and meaningful affirmation. Because other members of society acknowledge the institutions of private property and fair exchange—not out of some abstract benevolence, but because it is in their own interests to do so—the assertion has meaning and permanence. And because the institutions that grow up in market economies—courts, for example—define the meaning and limits of concepts such as private property, contracts, and what constitutes fair trade, there is broad understanding of and agreement about what those concepts signify.

In the Hegelian market economy, then, citizens achieve their dignity not via supplication to some higher power (a lord, the State, the Church) but by what amounts to common consent. The morality of property arises out of this common consent: men in market economies are equal, despite the fact that wealth outcomes will differ, because they are mutually acknowledged to be equal in dignity.

Contemporary Discussions

Modern discussions of the ethical nature of capitalism have strayed far from the realities of the lives of human beings, tending to turn on complex philosophical concepts such as "freedom" versus "unfreedom."[10] Perhaps this was a natural response to the horrific reality of communism under Stalin and Mao—real-world free market societies proved to be so clearly morally superior to real-world Marxist societies that the discussion could continue at all only at a theoretical level far removed from our actual experience.

Nonetheless, what all the critiques of the moral basis of capitalism have in common is their scorn for the market's focus on mankind's selfish instincts; their concern about capitalism's tendency to pull down traditional societies; and, of course, the unequal economic outcomes that occur in market economies. The defenses of capitalism respond by noting that the market's focus on selfish instincts is simply a realistic view of the dual nature of humankind; that traditional societies restrict the ability of people to achieve their full potential; and that unequal outcomes are acceptable in capitalist societies because the *average* outcome is far higher than in other economic communities.

The Moral Basis of Private Capital

What keeps the moral balance of capitalism in the positive zone is this emphasis not on what capitalism does for successful capitalists, but what capitalism does for the rest of society—the greatest good for the greatest number. Thus, let's ask ourselves the following question. We know (see Chapter 1) that private capital is at the very center of the remarkable success of the spectacularly vigorous American version of capitalism. But what is the moral argument for private capital once it has been earned and is no longer contributing directly to economic progress, no longer building new companies?

That capital is now likely to be invested passively, in portfolios consisting mainly of stocks and bonds. It might be invested wisely (see Chapters 9 through 22) or unwisely. What role does this capital play? This is, after all, the wealth that supports the lifestyles of generations of members of wealthy families, most of whom had nothing to do with the hard work of earning the wealth in the first place. Is it simply a deadweight on the American polity, an unfortunate legacy of an otherwise useful capitalist economy? Or is it perhaps a neutral element, supporting the economy's need for capital,[11] but not contributing anything of a positive nature?

My conclusion is that it is neither. This wealth—what I will call "creative capital"—is deployed in ways that enrich human lives far more than any other civil institution anywhere in the world. Creative capital—capital that has already been earned and that is being stewarded either by the founders or by subsequent generations[12]—is so critical because it is used overwhelmingly to support ideas. Ideas drive the destiny of mankind and capital is the essential nourishment that allows ideas to flourish.

Having money available to people and institutions with interesting ideas is important in two ways. First, an idea that can't be deployed, that can't be implemented or tested, is an idea that is useless to society. But it costs money to test a new idea, whether that idea is for a new business, a new arts organization, or a new intellectual journal. Creative capital supplies that money. Second, the knowledge that money is available to support new ideas encourages ideas to be generated. Creative capital acts like rainwater in the desert, encouraging that proliferation of ideas in all fields of human endeavor that is so characteristic of American society.

Let's take a look at how creative capital works and why it is so central to American preeminence in so many fields wholly unconnected to business competitiveness.

CREATIVE CAPITAL IN AMERICA

Invention is the mother of necessity.[13]

The worst way to organize an economy is for the central government to amass all the capital—by taxing its citizens heavily or by owning all enterprises itself—and then for that government to decide how the capital will be deployed. The Soviet Union paid with its life for its stubborn commitment to a centrally planned economy, and (as I noted in Chapter 1) China is headed down this same path. On a smaller scale, the economies (and, to a considerable extent, the societies) of Cuba, much of Central and South America, and most of Africa were destroyed by top-down economic systems.

The best way to manage an economy is to allow it to manage itself as freely as is possible without tolerating monopoly profits or other forms of illegal or predatory activity. In such a society, decisions about the use of capital—before and after it has been earned—will be pushed down as far as they can go. In terms of the deployment of wealth after it has been earned, those decisions are made in the United States at the individual wealthy family level. Wealthy families are, by definition, the only ones who possess excess capital, that is, wealth far beyond what will be needed to provide comfortable lives for themselves. (Middle income families, by contrast, have savings: capital that is not needed today, but that is expected to be needed by those families in the future.)

The effectiveness with which a society deploys its privately accumulated capital will in important part determine its competitive success against other societies. This is nothing more than a special case (though a very important one!) of the rule that the most successful societies will be those that most effectively maximize the talents and capabilities of their citizens. Private capital, in other words, is one of the important competitive strengths of a nation, like extensive natural resources, a democratic political system, or the vigor of its population.

Creative capital in America is a force for vitality, change, and competition in virtually every aspect of American society, from the arts to the academy to intellectual leadership to the formation of new businesses—in short, for every worthwhile endeavor that cannot support itself financially *ab initio*, if ever. We tend to recognize the role of private capital in philanthropy, but it is worth repeating: No arts or cultural organization, no institution of higher education, no journal of ideas, no small press, nor most other worthwhile social and cultural activities are able to support themselves financially without the assistance of charitable contributions.

All these activities depend on the existence of private capital and the willingness of the owners of that capital to put it at risk by supporting those activities. I say "at risk" both because there is rarely any assurance that philanthropic dollars will be used effectively, but also because it is often the case that support for cultural, intellectual, and educational activities winds up being support for individuals and ideas that are hostile to everything that allows private capital to be generated and deployed. This willingness to have the system constantly subjected to criticism and evaluation by its own dependents is one of the most astonishing things about vigorous free market democracies, and it is an aspect of the system that keeps it fresh and dynamic.

Most Americans are at least vaguely aware that our system of private philanthropy is dominated by wealthy families, but few realize just how dominant the role of those families is. There are over 300 million people in America. But I estimate that nearly 10 percent of all charitable giving—including middle class giving, which goes overwhelmingly to churches—comes from a mere 500 families. To save you from doing the math, this means that roughly 0.000002 of the people give 10 percent of the money. And if we eliminate from the notion of private philanthropy any giving that goes to religious organizations—which accounts for the overwhelming proportion of middle class giving—the dominance of the wealthy would be vastly greater.

This phenomenon can also be demonstrated by looking at how American nonprofit organizations raise the capital necessary to fund their operations. Let's look specifically at a college that has decided to mount a $100 million capital campaign. Any fundraising professional could sit down and in five minutes sketch out a capital campaign giving pyramid showing how many and what size contributions the college will have to raise to be successful in such a campaign. Specifically, the college would have to receive:

- 3 contributions of $10 million each
- 4 contributions of $5 million each
- 5 contributions of $2.5 million each
- 8 contributions of $1 million each
- 15 contributions of $500,000 each
- Many, many smaller contributions

We can easily do the math to see that contributions from wealthy donors will represent $78 million of the $100 million campaign. In other words, out of the thousands of contributions the college hopes to receive, only 35 really matter.[14] Indeed, unless and until the college receives about 60 percent of the total needed—probably from no more than a dozen people—it won't even announce the campaign publicly.

The point here is not that the wealthy are necessarily more or less generous than other citizens, but simply that the American system of private philanthropy could not persist without the creative capital of the wealthy. Our vaunted philanthropic system would not just shrink—it would collapse altogether if creative capital ceased to exist.

Certainly we could raise taxes substantially and leave it to the central government to decide which cultural activities are deserving of support, which ideas should be backed and which extinguished, who should be educated and how, which religions are legitimate and which aren't. We could, but we don't, and as a result of the richness of the millions of individual decisions made by individual families, America dominates the world of arts and ideas, and its higher education system is not merely the envy of the world, it is the only higher education system globally that is worthy of the name.

If for no other reason than this extraordinarily successful system of private charity, we ought all to care a very great deal about the quality of the stewardship of private capital in America. If we cease to allow private capital to be produced, or if we place serious constraints on how that capital can be spent, or if we allow the stewardship of private capital to be so poor that it withers or disappears, much of what makes America successful, and most of what makes the American version of capitalism so singular, will wither along with it.

Consider that at the very moment that Marxist doctrine was fueling the anger that led to the Russian Revolution, the wealthiest man in the world—Andrew Carnegie[15]—was giving away all his money. Carnegie was an extraordinary person in many ways, but he was hardly the exception that proves the rule. In other words, Carnegie was not a gentle, soft-hearted fellow who somehow managed, in competition with the most ruthless industrial captains in the world, to become the wealthiest living human. Carnegie was, in fact, a barracuda. Among other things, he was capable of ordering an end to the Homestead Steel Strike in 1892 no matter what the cost in lives,[16] then slipping out of the country so that the blame would fall on his friend and colleague, Henry Clay Frick.

Carnegie would turn out to be not an isolated example of extraordinary benevolence, but a role model for the millions of wealthy Americans who made their money in ways that benefited the society and then gave it away in ways that benefited the society yet again. Carnegie in effect invented the idea of creative capital, an idea that continues to be the definitive role of wealthy families in America to this day.

Carnegie, Rockefeller, Mellon, E. I. du Pont, Ford, Bill Gates, and Warren Buffett are examples of creative capital on a very grand scale, but, as we will see, there are innumerable examples of creative capital being deployed on a smaller, but still important, scale. Let's take a look at the role of creative capital in several spheres of American life by examining specific examples of important ideas that would not have survived but for the support of private capital.

HIGHER EDUCATION: THE CASE OF ST. JOHN'S COLLEGE

In the 1930s, tiny St. John's College was an institution on the ropes. Founded way back in 1696—only Harvard and William and Mary are older—by the middle of the Great Depression the College saw its enrollment declining, its small endowment rapidly disappearing, and its ancient physical plant crumbling. The College certainly would have disappeared altogether had not a group of radical educators, led by Scott Buchanan and Stringfellow Barr, arrived at St. John's and instituted an entirely new educational program. This program eliminated faculty departments, instituted an all-required curriculum heavy on math and science, built its courses around the classic works of Western civilization, and taught its students in seminars, not lecture halls.

The intellectual seriousness of the St. John's approach landed like a mortar round in the increasingly feeble American university world. The new program, launched in 1937, very quickly challenged other colleges and universities to examine what they were about. Though few institutions were likely to institute as rigorous a program of liberal education as St. John's, the College nonetheless established itself as the conscience of American higher education. Other institutions measured themselves against St. John's, almost always to their acute embarrassment.

But powerful and important as the idea of St. John's was, the College had a serious problem. Alumni of the "old" St. John's had little interest in the new program—as far as they were concerned, St. John's was now a completely different place. And alumni of the "new" St. John's were few, young, and generally impecunious. In fact, when a new college is started, it takes roughly half a century for its alumni base to mature to the point where the college can count on support from that quarter. How was St. John's to bridge that 50-year gap?

The answer, of course, was creative capital; in this case largely in the person of Paul Mellon. Mellon had matriculated at St. John's after having already graduated from college, starting over as a freshman "to get the education I should have gotten at Yale." His new education was interrupted by World War II, but Mellon never lost interest in St. John's—or, more precisely, in the College's vision of what a liberal education could be. For three decades Mellon's financial support allowed the College to survive, and in several cases saved it from almost certain ruin.[17] And when Mellon finally handed the reins to younger patrons of the College—led by people like Stewart H. Greenfield[18]—the job of these younger supporters was not to save the College but to help it to flourish.

The ideas behind St. John's were not created by Mellon, Greenfield, and the other patrons of the College, nor did they do the hard work of teaching and running the College. And yet, the idea that is St. John's—the idea that a serious liberal education can and should be offered to American young people—survived and flourished only because creative capital was available to support it.

POLITICS: THE CONSERVATIVE RESURGENCE

In the 1970s, the American Republican Party seemed destined for the garbage dump of history. Both houses of Congress were controlled by large Democratic majorities, virtually all state legislative houses were dominated by Democrats, moderate Republicanism—"Rockefeller Republicanism"—bored everyone stiff, and the one-note anticommunism of the Goldwaterites had been soundly rejected by the broad voting public. Yet, within a few decades Republicans would control the House and Senate, most state legislatures, and most governorships. On top of that, virtually the entire American South, which had been Democratic (or Dixiecratic) for generations, would turn solidly Republican. What happened?

Many things happened, of course, but what mainly happened was that creative capital entered the political sphere on the side of the Republicans. Two individuals in particular—Joseph Coors and Richard M. Scaife— decided that the Republican party needed a whole bevy of new ideas, and they began quietly supporting young conservative thinkers wherever they could find them. At first, to be sure, they were decidedly hard to find—young Americans had been radicalized in the 1960s and most of them had nothing but scorn for Republicans in general and conservatives in particular. But Coors and Scaife, working largely independently, relied on a core group of "talent scouts" (mainly older conservative thinkers) operating at colleges from Dartmouth to Stanford. When a young man or woman showed promise, financial support was made available. Conservative (and neoconservative) journals were launched with support from Coors, Scaife, and others. New conservative think tanks were formed (the Heritage Foundation and the Manhattan Institute, for example) and older think tanks (like the American Enterprise Institute and the Hoover Institution) were reinvigorated.

No single thing that Coors and Scaife did shook the world, but the mere existence of the creative capital they supplied encouraged more and more conservative thinkers to rise to the surface and to continue to think and publish and teach other thinkers. Ultimately, their disciplined deployment of creative capital over a long period of time would revolutionize American politics and American political ideas, for better or worse.[19]

NEW BUSINESS IDEAS: VENTURE CAPITAL IN AMERICA

In most circumstances, free market economies allocate capital through the mechanism of supply and demand. But how does capital get attracted to *new* ideas, that is, to the development and distribution of products and services that don't yet exist and for which there is, consequently, no demand, no supply, and hence no price? This is a critical question for an economy that wishes to be more than static, and it is the central question for an economy that wishes to lead the world in innovation, efficiency, growth, and power.

When Bill Gates and his team began to mess around with something called Windows, for example, few of us owned computers or could imagine why we might want to. And those few of us who did own them were using DOS and were perfectly happy with it.[20] Gates figured that computers were the future, and that if massive numbers of people were going to use computers, something far simpler than DOS had to be developed. He turned out to be right, but he could easily have been wrong. Where did he get his early capital for this odd idea?

The answer is the venture capital industry—in its broadest sense— which has a much longer history in America than is generally supposed. When we think back to the period between about 1870 and 1930, we tend to think of the great Captains of Industry (or, depending on our point of view, the Robber Barons): Carnegie, Morgan, Ford, Rockefeller, and so on. These men accumulated vast fortunes putting together the industrial enterprises that were required to meet the huge appetites of a rapidly industrializing United States. But, in retrospect, we can see that such figures could exist only during a brief period of time, a mere speck in the great sweep of history. Very quickly, the requirements for capital to build railroads, highways, steel mills, oil refineries, iron ore and coal mines, and other industries far outstripped the financial capacity of any one family. Only firms that could gain access to the *public* equity and debt markets could hope to continue to compete effectively. The Captains of Industry were, in effect, spectacular dinosaurs.

But something else was going on at about the same time that would persist far longer, namely, the support for new ideas and enterprises provided by wealthy individuals in the form of what we now think of as venture capital. The best known of these early venture capitalists was Andrew W. Mellon, then and now perhaps the greatest venture capitalist who ever lived. Mellon was one of the great industrial titans of the day (he controlled the Pennsylvania Railroad, for example), but he made his lasting impact on history through his support for a wide variety of new, start-up enterprises. Operating from the platform of the family bank (then known as T. Mellon & Sons, now Bank of New York Mellon), Mellon listened to many entrepreneurs pitch their ideas, and when he found one he liked, he backed the venture. Because these new enterprises were far too risky to justify a simple loan, Mellon took stock in the ventures as additional compensation.

Many of the new businesses failed, of course, but others grew into industrial behemoths that changed the landscape of American industry. Mellon's major venture capital successes included Gulf Oil Corporation, which rivaled Rockefeller's Standard Oil Company for control of the world oil markets; Alcoa, founded by Charles M. Hall, the inventor of the process to convert alumina to aluminum, and for many decades the world's largest producer of aluminum;[21] Carborundum Company, founded by Edward Goodrich Acheson, the first manufacturer of synthetic abrasives, which were and are critical in the mining and extraction industries; and H. Koppers Company, founded by coke oven inventor Heinrich Kopper, which created an entire industry by transforming industrial waste into usable products such as gas, tar, and sulfur.

Beyond these spectacular and enduring venture capital successes, Mellon was also instrumental in the organization or growth of many other young enterprises, such as Standard Steel Car Company, McClintic-Marshall Company, Pittsburgh Coal Company, Pittsburgh Plate Glass (now PPG Industries), Crucible Steel Corporation, and so on. Mellon also founded the Union Trust Company and, of course, dominated Mellon Bank. Other companies controlled by Mellon, or in which he exercised substantial influence, included Eastern Gas and Fuel Associates, Brooklyn Union and Brooklyn Borough Gas, Duke-Price Company, Pullman, Incorporated (into which Mellon merged Standard Steel Car), Bethlehem Steel, United States Electric Power Corporation, United Light & Power, United Light & Railways, American Light and Traction, Westinghouse Electric Corporation, Niagara Hudson Corporation, the Pennsylvania Railroad, the American Rolling Mill Company, and the Philadelphia Company, which controlled Pittsburgh's public utilities.

Andrew Mellon's eye-popping success in his venture capital activities, and the lasting impact of his investments on the American economy, did not go unnoticed, and the venture capital industry as we know it today gradually evolved as other wealthy investors attempted to emulate Mellon's triumphs. As the industry matured, the players in the industry began to specialize, with some being responsible for identifying and nurturing new ventures (the general partners of venture capital, or VC, partnerships), while others were responsible for providing the capital (the limited partners). For decades, these limited partners were virtually all wealthy families. As the industry continued to mature, however, institutional investors got into the action.

Today, however, the well-known VC partnerships are not really in the business of backing true start-ups, which are far too risky for most of the institutional limited partners. In addition, start-ups don't require enough capital to attract the attention of major VC partnerships, which these days command hundreds of millions or even billions of dollars of capital. Instead, business start-ups in America[22] continue to be underwritten almost exclusively by creative private capital. Entrepreneurs seek the earliest, smallest amounts of capital from the proverbial "friends and family" equity round: Money is raised by maxing out the entrepreneurs' credit cards and by tapping the capital of wealthier friends, neighbors, and family members. If all goes well, the fledgling business will seek out "angel" investors, wealthy individuals who enjoy backing and working with new businesses and with young (and not so young!) entrepreneurs. The next step may be to send a business plan to one of the many regional venture capital funds that almost every sizeable city boasts. Only when the business has passed all these hurdles is it likely to find favor with one of the larger VC partnerships.

Thus it is that from the founding of the venture capital business to the support for new business ideas being developed today, the only source of capital is the creative private capital that is made available only by wealthy investors. But notice one very odd aspect of the use of creative capital: It almost never provides a satisfactory return on investment in the usual sense of the word. This is obvious in the case of private philanthropy—however happy we might be with our "investment" in a nonprofit organization, we will never receive a return on our investment in the traditional sense. Our "returns" will come to us in other, nonfinancial ways.

And the same is generally true of the use of creative capital in the sense of backing for new business enterprises. At the most mature level of the VC industry, it turns out that only a tiny fraction of the hundreds of VC partnerships—the so-called top-tier funds—will ever produce an investment return that truly compensates investors for the risks they are assuming. And few investors will ever have the opportunity to invest with these top-tier firms. As we go down the VC ladder toward the regional venture capital partnerships, to the activities of angel investors, to the hapless "friends and family" who are the reluctant backers of most true start-ups, we find that almost no one receives even a positive return, much less a return that could begin to compensate for the risks. Indeed, many VC angels can spend a lifetime backing start-ups and never hit a double, much less a home run. For every local angel who backs a Google or a Cisco,[23] there are tens of thousands whose returns come, if at all, only in nonfinancial terms.

But, in both the case of private philanthropy and private venture capital, there is all the difference in the world between the return to the providers of the capital and the returns to society at large. The great good that accrues to society as the result of private charity and as the result of successful venture capital investments is obvious. But the same outcome results from the use of creative capital to back new business ventures that don't necessarily succeed in financial terms: The collective losses experienced by the providers of the capital are vastly, vastly outweighed by the enormous good that redounds to society from these activities.

CREATIVE CAPITAL AND VIBRANT SOCIETIES

Private capital is critically important because it is the progenitor of all other forms of capital. Governments possess capital, but only because they tax it away from private individuals. Corporations possess capital, but only because individuals have voluntarily invested their capital in corporate stocks and bonds. Colleges and universities and charitable foundations and nonprofit groups of all kinds possess capital (in the form of endowments and operating funds), but only because private individuals have donated that capital.

Because private capital is, at least initially, in the hands of hundreds of thousands of free individuals, individuals who can, within the limits of the law, do with their capital as they please, that capital is deployed with a diversity and richness impossible to imagine were the capital in any other hands. Private capital is the most flexible capital available to a human society, and the more of it the society possesses, the more competitive that society will be.

Ideas drive civilization, and capital is the rocket propellant behind ideas. Therefore, societies that encourage the production of wealth and its creative deployment will be far better off, far more vibrant and resilient, than societies that discourage these activities.

In America, entrepreneurs are heroes, daring individuals who incur great personal risks to pursue ideas that will make America a better place. Most of them fail, suffering the consequences of their boldness without experiencing any of the rewards. But others quickly take their place, lured by hopes of wealth and by the availability of the creative capital that makes possible even the most quixotic of dreams. Yet, how different matters are in most other free market democracies! (As George W. Bush once memorably remarked, "The French don't even have a word for 'entrepreneur.'"[24]) Throughout most of Western and Northern Europe,[25] entrepreneurs are viewed as troublemakers; arrogant iconoclasts who care more about their own potential wealth than about the welfare of their fellow citizens. These are the individuals, after all, who are advocating ideas that may render existing businesses—and the cushy jobs they provide—obsolete.

Providential societies attempt to discourage entrepreneurship by taxing away most of the gains, by imposing crushing death duties that attempt to eliminate industrious families after one generation, and—most devastating of all—by developing cultures that discourage entrepreneurship, enterprise, and innovation. Thanks to policies and cultural attitudes, little private capital is produced, and little of that can be used creatively. The ultimate result is the creation of calcified economies and, ultimately, calcified societies.

WHY DO CREATIVE CAPITALISTS PERSIST?

As I have noted, there is no financial return in the usual sense from the deployment of creative capital in philanthropic ventures, and very little in the deployment of creative capital in venture capital activities. Why, then, do creative capitalists persist in putting their money out in this way? The answer is undoubtedly complex, but I suggest that it has much to do with the peculiar conditions created by societies that are both capitalistic and democratic. Free market economies allow wealth to be created. Wealthy families in democratic republics internalize the ideals of democracy, of the dignity of every citizen, and behave accordingly. This creative use of capital after it has been earned validates the soundness of the American idea. American families who have become wealthy have richly deserved that wealth, enriching all our lives. But it is the ongoing deployment of private capital in creative ways that validates the moral acceptability of capitalism in America and that ensures the continued importance—indeed, the decisive importance—of wealthy families to America's sustained preeminence.

THE INDISPENSABLE NATION

The distinct American version of free market democracy, with wealthy families at its indispensable center, is crucial not just for Americans, but for the world at large. And not just in ways that might immediately come to mind. Yes, American economic vigor, and the resulting gigantic market we represent to other economies around the world, is certainly the main engine of global economic growth and therefore the main hope for people everywhere for material improvement in their lives. Yes, American democracy is the most widely admired form of political organization in the world and therefore represents the main hope for freedom among people everywhere. And, yes, American military might is the main guarantor of peace globally and the main fear of despots everywhere; as well as—let's face it—the main source of fear even among our allies.

But my argument goes beyond these issues, important as they are. When former Secretary of State Madeleine Albright insisted that the United States was the world's one "indispensable nation," European statesmen engaged in paroxysms of sputtering outrage. But Albright was transparently correct. Let's examine why.

In the famous "Kantian paradox," Emmanuel Kant pointed out that the only solution to constant warfare among the aggressive and all-too-adjacent European powers was the creation of a world government. But because such a government would have to be all-powerful to enforce a "state of universal peace," the world government would represent a threat to human freedom far greater than even the Hobbesian world of brutal competition and international disorder that it was intended to replace.[26] Yet, today, most European leaders seem to feel that Europe has resolved this paradox, that the European Union and its associated institutions (the United Nations, the World Court, the Court of International Justice, etc.) have created, in Kagan's words, "a post-historical paradise of peace."[27] This "paradise" is contrasted starkly with the supposed mindset of the United States, which, it is argued, remains mired in a Hobbesian world where might makes right.

But like all paradises that are supposed to exist in a world of imperfect human beings, the European "paradise of peace" is a chimera, a frail orchid of a paradise that could not, and cannot, exist outside the protective American military hothouse. Europe is, indeed, at peace, and has been for more than half a century—a happy miracle, certainly, if not a paradise. But, as Kagan points out, peace in Europe was launched not by posthistorical moral progress on the part of enlightened Europeans, but by the applied and brutal and sometimes morally ambivalent[28] use of historical military power by America in twice crushing an aggressive Germany. And European peace was further enabled by America's willingness to fund the rebuilding of Europe and to fund its military defense, especially against the USSR, leaving Europeans in the privileged, but hopelessly unrealistic, position of having little to worry about but getting along with each other.

If, at any moment during the Cold War, the United States had withdrawn its military protection from Europe, the Red Army would have overrun the Continent in a few weeks, converting our enlightened European friends into inmates in a vast Stalinist gulag. Even today, if every other free market democracy on earth disappeared, the continuing existence of the United States would ensure that the candle of freedom would continue to burn, and to burn fiercely. But if the United States disappeared, leaving all the other democracies intact, civilization could mount a deathwatch for human freedom.

European nations find themselves, in short, in the paradoxical position of having to be militarily weak in order to cooperate with each other. It's a paradox because, being weak, they are easy prey to aggressive nations who have very different (and, to European minds and our own, very much worse) visions of how societies should operate. In order to avoid being destroyed by such unpalatable societies, Europe must seek the protection of a country it identifies not with its own posthistorical ethical vision, but with the very Hobbesian vision that led to all of Europe's problems, that is, the United States.[29]

But what both Europeans and Americans seem to miss in this picture is that Europe and America, and free countries and countries struggling toward freedom everywhere, *already* exist in a world that bears at least a distant resemblance to Kagan's (and Kant's) "paradise of peace." In this ersatz version of paradise, one party—America—preserves the peace. The other party—mainly, but not exclusively, Europe—drives the search for mechanisms that might ultimately eliminate the need for a militarily enforced peace.

This circumstance doesn't *seem* like a paradise to either party, because neither party can fully participate in the activities of the other. As the guarantor and enforcer of the peace that allows our friends to work toward happy coexistence, the United States cannot fully participate because the reduction in sovereignty these experiments require would eviscerate our role as the global "hyperpuissance."[30] And as I have noted at great length in Chapter 1, our European friends cannot much participate in their own defense without first becoming as competitive and vigorous as the United States—in other words, without risking another European arms race. This odd circumstance requires each party to trust the other to do the right thing, a trust that is extraordinarily difficult to manage.

Fortunately for Europe, America is largely a *benign* hyperpuissance, a democracy with long-term interests closely aligned to those of Europe. And fortunately for America, European traditions and views on crucial issues of culture and human dignity are largely aligned with our own. Europe will never be content with America's vast military power and will always feel that we are abusing it. And America will never concede that our European friends are doing essential work that we cannot do ourselves. But, like it our not, Europe needs the United States and the United States needs Europe. One can imagine far worse outcomes than to have the most successful, the most civilized, and the most advanced societies guiding the fate of the world.

CONCLUSION: UNDERDOGS AND BULLIES

We instinctively favor the underdog in every circumstance. We boo Bluto and cheer when Popeye, having downed his trusty can of spinach, knocks the brute into orbit. If Goliath had defeated David the story would have ended there, but Goliath's defeat by the puny David created a legend that has persisted for thousands of years. In its early history, Israel was widely perceived as a small, embattled nation surrounded on all sides by large and aggressive enemies. But Israel's very success in war after war—to say nothing of having the United States in its corner—has caused this perception to change. Israel is now widely perceived around the world as the neighborhood bully—a serious political problem for the Israelis. And then there is the United States itself. Worldwide we are feared and loathed not for what we stand for or the policies we advocate. We are hated simply because we are bigger and stronger than anyone else—indeed, stronger than everyone else combined.

And this is as it should be. We can imagine a world in which we instinctively cheered for the powerful as they smashed the powerless into dust, but it is not a world most of us would like to live in. Nazi Germany was such a world—Germans still embittered by the terms imposed on them at the end of World War I cheered Hitler when he overran Poland and Czechoslovakia, and all too many Germans applauded when the Nazis hunted down and murdered Jews, even then a small, persecuted minority in Germany.

Like America itself, wealthy families will never be perceived as underdogs whose interests need to be protected. Whenever politicians can't think of principled reasons to oppose a policy or program, they can always denounce it as a sop to the rich. This is simply a fact of life and it will never change—indeed, we ought to hope it never changes, because the world that such a change would presuppose would be a world that would be anathema to most of us.

Still, the trouble with our instinctive reaction in favor of the underdog is that it sometimes interferes with cogent thought. Because we sympathize with the struggles of the American poor, because we extol the middle class as the backbone of America, we can easily forget that it is not these groups that distinguish America from other nations, or that account for its success. The poor, after all, are everywhere, and every developed society has at its center a solid middle class whose interests must be protected.

What distinguishes America is the presence, in very large and ever-growing numbers, of the rich. It is the prevalence of the rich—as a demonstration to the poor[31] and middle class that wealth is achievable—that distinguishes us from other free market democracies and that has enabled us to grow to a position of such astonishing dominance. And it is the creative use of the private capital of wealthy families that encourages the creation and supports the implementation of American ideas—the ideas that mainly fuel the drive toward a better world.

It is possible, of course, that America will prove to have been an experiment gone wrong, "the only nation that has gone from barbarism to degeneration without the usual interval of civilization," as Clemenceau put it. It is possible, indeed, that civilized behavior will one day prove to be associated entirely with gentleness, with an insistence that every problem can and must be peacefully decided. Until that day arrives, however, civilization will persist only because America's veneer of gentleness and its commitment to peace remains underlain by a hard core of steel, an adamantine resolve.

The role of private wealth in a democratic republic is and always will be a fragile one. But so long as the holders of that wealth accumulate it fairly and use it creatively, America will continue to be the wonder of the world, and, alone among all the countries of that world, the one indispensable nation.

NOTES

1. In a sense, these societies can be viewed as profoundly hypocritical. The Greek ideal could not abide trade or commerce, yet the Greeks could not even feed themselves without importing vast amounts of grain. See Paul Rahe, *Republics Ancient and Modern: Classical Republicanism and the American Revolution* (Chapel Hill: University of North Carolina Press, 1992), especially Chapter 3, "The Political Economy of Hellas." In the quote from the *Republic*, Socrates was speaking to and thinking of that tiny fraction of the Greek population who were free citizens, ignoring the fact that those citizens could avoid participating in commerce only because all their material needs were provided by slaves.
2. St. Augustine (354–430): essentially, "If no one loses, then no one gains."
3. It was not only the Jews who practiced moneylending, however. Famous figures like Voltaire himself found ways to lend large sums of money, especially to the royal houses, through the ruse of "donations" made in return for a lifetime stream of payments.
4. Much of my argument in this section of the book follows the fascinating account of Jerry Z. Muller in *The Mind and the Markets* (New York: Alfred A. Knopf, 2002).
5. The notion of economists as a separate profession did not exist in the eighteenth century. Adam Smith was a professor of moral philosophy.
6. Voltaire, *Philosophical Letters* (1734), quoted in Muller, *The Mind and the Markets*, 35.
7. From Pascal's *Pensées*, quoted in Muller, *The Mind and the Markets*, 35.
8. Muller, *The Mind and the Markets*, 72.
9. Muller, *The Mind and the Markets*, 76.
10. This happens to be the formulation of the Marxist philosopher G. A. Cohen. In other words, although it may be true that everyone in

a capitalist society has the opportunity to become wealthy, because we know that only a small percentage actually will become wealthy, the opportunity is illusory: It's not a freedom but an "unfreedom." See G. A. Cohen, *Self-Ownership, Freedom, and Equality* (Cambridge: Cambridge University Press, 1995). The trouble with such discussions, aside from their eerie other-worldliness, is that they don't particularly distinguish capitalist societies from other kinds of societies. Because no one in a Marxist society is allowed to become wealthy, it is difficult not to view that also as an "unfreedom."

11. Capital invested in Treasury securities supports the government's borrowing needs. Capital invested in corporate bonds supports the borrowing needs of corporate enterprises. Capital invested in equity securities supports the equity base of corporations, providing long-term growth capital and allowing them to borrow money as necessary (from banks or via the bond markets). Most important, capital provides the liquidity without which no one would buy stock or bonds.

12. As I note elsewhere, this capital might still be in private hands or it might be held in the form of a charitable foundation or a nonprofit endowment. But all these holding structures trace back to the original wealthy families who deployed their capital so creatively.

13. David Owen, *Copies in Seconds* (New York: Simon & Schuster, 2004), referring to the invention of the plain paper copier.

14. This isn't intended to be as elitist as it sounds. The support of thousands of small donors who are enthusiastic about the mission of the college is a good part of what justifies the campaign in the first place. In addition, of course, some smaller donations represent sacrificial gifts by donors with modest resources.

15. In 1901, Carnegie sold Carnegie Steel Company to a group led by J. P. Morgan for $250 million, forming the United States Steel Corporation.

16. The violence was supplied by an army of Pinkerton detectives hired by Carnegie Steel Company, as well as members of the Pennsylvania National Guard. The workers' strike failed and the union was virtually destroyed. On Carnegie generally, see the compelling biography by Peter Krass, *Carnegie* (New York: John Wiley & Sons, 2002).

17. On the subject of the early decades of St. John's College under the new program, see the superb account of Charles A. Nelson, *Radical Visions: Stringfellow Barr, Scott Buchanan, and Their Efforts on Behalf of Education and Politics in the Twentieth Century* (Santa Barbara: Bergin & Garvey, 2001).

18. Ironically, Greenfield is a venture capitalist himself, having cofounded Oak Investment Partners in 1978.

19. I want to emphasize that I am not endorsing the ideas of the conservative wing of the Republican Party—or of any wing of any party. I am simply pointing out what a relatively small amount of creative capital, intelligently deployed, can accomplish.

20. For those of my readers who are too young to remember the halcyon days of DOS (disk operating system), DOS commands were the language we used to communicate with our computers. DOS was, in effect, a piece of computer software that allowed us to control our computer hardware. Today, for example, if we want to backup a few files, it is the work of an instant. But in the good old days we would go to our DOS screen and type something like, "BACKUP a:[path][filename] a:[/S][/M][/A][/F:(size)] [/P][/D:date] [/T:time] [/L:[path]filename]." I'm being perfectly serious about this.

21. Alcoa is now third in the world, behind Rio Tinto Alcan and Rusal.

22. I exclude the launch of thousands of traditional small businesses that are not intended to become big businesses. Most of these local enterprises are launched by sweat equity rather than true financial capital.

23. Google and Cisco Systems got their start thanks to angel backing.

24. The remark may be apocryphal.

25. Britain, again, is something of an exception, but only since the Thatcher era (1979–1990).

26. In this discussion, I am following the argument elegantly set forth in Robert Kagan's celebrated essay, "Power and Weakness," which appeared in June 2002 in *Policy Review* 113. Kagan expanded the article into his brief but powerful book, *Of Paradise and Power: America and Europe in the New World Order* (New York: Alfred A. Knopf, 2003). My argument differs on several points from Kagan's.

27. Kagan, "Power and Weakness."

28. The carpet bombing of German cities like Cologne and Dresden occurred because bombing technology was too imprecise for Allied air forces to take out critical urban war plants without taking out entire cities. But it is certainly true that very little ethical hand-wringing took place over a strategy that was certain to, and did, lead to tens of thousands of civilian deaths and to painfully few military gains.

29. Paul Berman has pointed out that peaceful republics quite similar to those of modern-day Europe have existed before—Florence and the other economically powerful city-states that arose in the late Middle Ages, for example. These republics "blossomed splendidly for a few decades and then, in their defenseless condition, were invariably crushed under the heel of some marauding army." Paul Berman, "What Lincoln Knew About War," *The New Republic* (March 3, 2003).

30. Former French Foreign Minister Hubert Védrine's term for the United States. He did not intend it as a compliment.

31. Several years ago a young busboy in a Chicago hotel pointed to my copy of *Built from Scratch*, Bernie Marcus and Arthur Blank's story of the building of Home Depot, Inc. "Good book," he said in an English so accented I could hardly understand him. "You've read it?" I asked incredulously. "Three times," he replied matter-of-factly. "Some day I build such a company."

Two

The Stewardship of Wealth

America became wealthy and powerful, far beyond that of any other country in history, because of an economic system that produces private wealth on a massive scale and then deploys that wealth in creative ways. The holders of that wealth are the natural end result of that system and its most powerful symbol. Wealthy families are therefore central to the American experiment and therefore they are central to what we might call the near-paradise of peace that holds the promise of freedom and progress for all people globally.

As the principal beneficiaries and prime symbols of this remarkable system, wealthy families bear a serious responsibility to manage their wealth prudently, to engage in a level of stewardship appropriate to the important role our capital plays in America and in the world. We now turn our attention to the details of that demanding, and rewarding, task.

In Part Two, I will discuss the broad issues that most directly affect the ability of families to maintain their capital over long periods of time:

- Are we living in a permanent financial crisis or is this just a passing phase?
- Understanding and managing risk in all its many dimensions.
- The frankly scummy world of financial firms and what investors should do about it.
- The difficulty of finding appropriate financial advisors.

- The complexity of structuring families to make sound and disciplined investment decisions.
- Managing trusts.

Families who come to grips with these broad issues, who internalize the proper mindset of stewardship, will have gone a very long way toward ensuring the preservation of their capital across many generations.

CHAPTER 3

Are We Living in a Permanent Financial Crisis?

Before investors can even begin to think about how to structure their investment portfolios, they need to think hard about the kind of world those portfolios will be invested in:[1]

- Is it 1930, at the beginning of the Great Depression, when even the best-designed portfolios would produce dismal results for more than a decade and where investors in certain countries (Germany) would lose everything?
- Is it 1950, when the postwar economic boom was about to take off and almost any U.S.-centric portfolio would do well?
- Is it 1975, just after the worst bear market since the Depression, when stocks were screaming bargains?
- Is it 1982, when Ronald Reagan and Paul Volker had just broken the back of stagflation, setting the stage for the greatest bull market since the nineteenth century?
- Is it 1999, when stocks were at their priciest point in American history and were about to collapse?
- Is it 2006, when housing prices had peaked and leverage, preposterous exuberance, and the collapse of ethical behavior in the financial world[2] were the gathering storm ahead of the worst financial crisis since the 1930s?
- Is it 2009, when the bear market had depressed prices to their most attractive levels since the mid-1970s?
- Or is it today (early 2012 as this is being written), when a gradual economic recovery is bedeviled by unprecedented levels of public and private debt in the developed world?

Because it's today, let's consider the kind of world we might be investing our capital in.

THE END OF HISTORY (AGAIN)

In his 1989 essay,[3] and more fully in his later book,[4] Francis Fukuyama famously proclaimed "the end of history." What Fukuyama meant was that with the demise of the Soviet Union and the end of the Cold War, Western liberal democracies represented the end point of mankind's sociocultural evolution, "the universalization of Western liberal democracy as the final form of human government."[5]

I'd like to suggest, instead, that the West has reached the end of its own socioeconomic evolution and is now faced with the gargantuan task of reinventing itself. Thus, the West must create new cultures, new governing mechanisms, and new theories for how governments can support themselves. Needless to say, the investment implications of this are large and complex.

I'll begin with the proposition that the West is in a permanent financial crisis. By "permanent," I mean a period of years that is meaningful even for long-term investors. Specifically, I will consider the possibility that recent events – the credit crunch, stock market collapse, and banking crisis in the United States, and the sovereign debt problem, banking crisis, and stock market collapse in Europe—are merely symptoms of a deeper and far more complex problem that will require decades to sort out. I will also consider how investors might position themselves to avoid the destruction of their capital over an extended period of crisis.

A PERMANENT FINANCIAL CRISIS?

The current financial crisis began in the summer of 2007 with the credit crunch and continues with the European sovereign debt and banking crisis. More than four years after the crisis began, U.S. equity markets are nowhere near their 2007 high of 14,141 on the Dow. Bill Gross of PIMCO has declared the New Normal, an environment characterized by lower-than-normal economic growth, higher-than-normal unemployment, and unattractive market returns.

Yet most long-term investors have taken the position that "this, too, shall pass." That is to say, most investor portfolios are positioned near their long-term targets, targets that were developed using long-term risk and return assumptions that haven't played out for a decade. Indeed, over the past 30 years, bond returns have outpaced stock returns, an outcome that turns market theory on its head.

Investors are aware of all this, of course, but are now reduced to hoping that the markets will mean-revert, as they usually do, meaning that in the coming years returns should be much better than they have been in the past and that the traditional relationship between risk and return will reassert itself.

No doubt all that will happen, but the question is, when? In their seminal work, *This Time Is Different: Eight Centuries of Financial Folly*, Carmen M. Reinhart and Kenneth S. Rogoff make the point that recovery from the deepest financial crises takes, on average, 10 to 12 years.[6] If I measure from 2007, it's possible that we still have more than five years to go before we will have fully recovered. And if the Western countries should slip into a Japanese-style "lost two decades,"[7] well, all bets are off. Looking back from, say, 2030, our children could find to their sorrow that equity returns have been far below par for half a century.

THE CAUSE OF THE CRISIS MATTERS

I begin by asking a naive question: Why are all the Western liberal democracies so indebted?[8] Aren't these countries, I ask, the wealthiest societies in the history of civilization? If ever there were economies that could support themselves without recourse to massive borrowing, aren't these the ones? What gives?

A financial crisis can arise from a variety of causes, but the principal cause is a sovereign debt burden beyond what can be borne by the wealth of the society without causing social instability. Sovereign indebtedness can arise directly from government overborrowing, or it can arise indirectly, via (for example) guarantees of bank deposits or mortgage debt, or via government bailouts of private financial institutions.

But the important question is not simply *how* the indebtedness arises, but *why*. Imagine, as a hypothetical situation, that a country has incurred a huge external debt in order to fund significant infrastructure expansion. Presumably, this is really an investment in future growth, which should enable the country to repay the debt easily.

Suppose instead that a country has incurred its debt as a result of ongoing societal demands for current spending beyond what can be supported by the country's budget. Or imagine that private borrowers in the country have incurred massive debts to buy, for example, bigger houses. To bail out the foolish lenders to these foolish borrowers—after all, no one wants another global banking crisis—the country has to bail out the lenders, effectively transferring private borrowing into sovereign debt.

This hapless country is now faced with the problem of discharging a vast debt that is still growing, because the societal demands are still there. The situation, in other words, seems to be completely hopeless. Even if the country can somehow find the means of discharging its huge existing debt, that debt will simply rebuild itself unless something can be done about the spending demands that are responsible for the debt, or unless additional sources of revenue can be found to support the spending demands.

As a thought experiment, let's adopt the postulate that, in the advanced Western democracies, social norms have evolved to require minimum standards of living that exceed the ability of even those wealthy countries to pay. In other words, social goods that even a few decades ago would have been deemed unattainable by the great mass of the populace are now considered to be inalienable rights of all: access to universal health care (and damn the cost!), a dignified retirement and old age (whether I have saved my money or not), education through the baccalaureate degree, freedom from hunger, home ownership, and so on. These are "rights" about which there has grown up a broad consensus—indeed, anyone who espouses a reduction in these rights is usually perceived as a barbarian.

Thus there is, I am positing as part of this thought experiment, a very serious disconnect between what the citizens in Western societies believe they are owed by their governments and what those governments can actually afford to deliver. Let's step back a few hundred years and see how we've managed to get ourselves into this position.

THE INDUSTRIAL REVOLUTION AND ITS AFTERMATH

Before about 1800, the wealth of human societies had been largely stagnant for thousands of years. But once the Industrial Revolution began—surely it was the most important event in the history of human civilization—societal wealth began to grow at unprecedented rates. Between the end of the eighteenth century and the end of the twentieth century, average incomes would grow tenfold at the same time that the population was growing sixfold. This astonishing increase in human wealth came about for a variety of reasons that are still not fully understood, but clearly implicated were scientific and technological progress, the protection of property rights, the rise of representative democracies, intense competition among the industrializing countries, vastly improved health, and so on.[9]

Whatever the cause of the increased wealth of societies, it would have extraordinary consequences, not the least of which was how the wealth should be distributed. Western societies differed in how wealth should be spread around, but they all agreed that it should be vastly more widely distributed than it actually was by the late nineteenth century.

Over the course of the twentieth century, the industrializing world[10] would experiment with three strategies that were designed to capture and redistribute the wealth created by the Industrial Revolution (and, later, the

Post-Industrial Revolution). These strategies were, in rough order of their appearance:

- Seizing control of the means of production.
- Taxing wealth and income.
- Borrowing.

In each case, demands by the public for services fairly quickly overwhelmed the capacities of each strategy, causing the state to move on to the next. As noted above, our thesis is that it is simply inherent in Western liberal democracies that demands will—eventually, but always—outstrip the supply of money available to pay for them. As a result, having exhausted all three known strategies for wealth capture and redistribution, the West has reached the end of its history and must reinvent itself.

Note that I am not concerned here with the question of whether any particular wealth redistribution scheme is fair or equitable. I would note that the wealthy as a group don't seem to have been particularly harmed by the various wealth redistribution schemes (although of course individual wealthy families were decidedly harmed). And in any event whatever harm was done to the rich was far outweighed by the harm the rich have done to themselves.[11] I am only interested in the effectiveness and consequences of the wealth redistribution strategies.

Far and away the most interesting way to follow the launch, triumph, and ultimate failure of each of the three wealth distribution strategies is to look at the remarkable experiment that Western Europe has been conducting since the end of World War II.

THE GREAT (AND STRANGE) EXPERIMENT

From the fall of Rome until 1945—roughly 1,500 years—the European states were more or less constantly at war with each other. Because the Europeans quickly became the most powerful peoples on earth, there wasn't much anyone could do about this. The devastation gradually increased in savagery, reaching its cataclysm in the twentieth century when Europe launched two world wars in the span of 25 years.

But at the end of World War II, two countries—the upstart USSR and the upstart United States—emerged as vastly more powerful than the traditional European states. Determined that no more wars would come out of Europe, the USSR and the United States essentially colonized the Continent. In the east, the Soviet Union created fairly traditional colonies across Eastern Europe, establishing puppet regimes that reported to Moscow, stationing troops on Eastern European soil, demilitarizing the area, and, when the colonies got out of line, invading them (Hungary in 1956 and Czechoslovakia in 1968).

In the west, the United States took a softer line, but still imposed (democratic) regimes on countries that didn't have them, stationed troops on Western European soil (where they remain to this day[12]), and demilitarized the area. America didn't invade Europe, but that's because it didn't have to, as the Europeans remained loyal allies of the Unites States. But suppose some Western European country—let's say, Italy—had elected a Communist government and that government had seized total power, begun to build up its military might, and announced that it was leaving NATO and joining the Warsaw Pact. American troops would have been in Rome faster than you can say "lasagna."

Still, the "colonization" worked. After suffering two world wars in a quarter century, Europe has been at peace for almost 70 years. And during this long and remarkable concordance, the softer American approach allowed Western Europe to experiment with various methods of organizing itself politically and economically. (This sort of experimentation was severely restricted in Eastern Europe until the fall of the Soviet Union.)

Note, however, that this experimentation occurred in a strange petri dish of a world in which some of the wealthiest countries on the planet had no need to see to their own defense. In the history of the race, nothing like this had ever happened. Throughout history any country, wealthy or not, which failed to defend itself was soon enslaved, and this went doubly for a wealthy country. The best example, of course, was Rome, which allowed its security apparatus to decay and was promptly conquered by a bunch of naked tribes from Northern Europe.

But in Western Europe more than a dozen hyperwealthy countries have existed for seven decades without giving a thought (or a euro) to their own security, which was instead guaranteed by the U.S. nuclear umbrella. It didn't have to be this way, of course, as shortly after World War II a common European army was proposed.[13] The idea was to enable Europe to see to its own defense and, not incidentally, to keep Germany from rearming on its own. However, the proposal was defeated in France in 1954 and was never seriously reexamined.

As a result of this extraordinarily extended adolescence, none of the European countries (with the slight exception of Britain) had to develop any serious military capability. Instead of spending huge sums on defense, as the United States has done for many decades, they could spend virtually their entire annual budgets on civilian needs. And these needs grew and grew and grew.

I mention this issue because it is often overlooked. The rest of the world can take many lessons from Western Europe's 70 years of socioeconomic and political experimentation, but few countries anywhere can ever expect to be so fortunate as to emulate the European experience.

But let's set aside the fortunate circumstances of Western Europe and focus on one aspect of the Great Experiment: how to capture and redistribute the extraordinary wealth of that part of the world.[14]

SEIZE THE MEANS OF PRODUCTION!

Marx famously believed that conflicts between the middle-class owners of productive enterprises (the "bourgeoisie") and the workers in those enterprises (the "proletariat") would result in the collapse of capitalism. When this happened, the workers would seize control of the government, ban private ownership, and all profits would thereafter accrue to the state, which would redistribute the wealth far more broadly.

Such a revolution actually did occur in Russia, and the state did in fact ban private property. And for a while, this worked magnificently, as Russia evolved from a backward, peasant society into the second most powerful country in the world in less than 30 years (1917–1945). Unfortunately, once the USSR's simple industrial society found it necessary to evolve into a vastly more complex postindustrial society (to compete with the United States), top-down command strategies proved to be no match for bottom-up free market strategies, and the USSR went the way of the dodo bird.

In Western Europe, pure communism in the Marxist sense was never adopted. Instead, Europe found a "middle way." Socialist governments dominated the landscape for many years after World War II and those governments tended to nationalize not the entire economy but only the most important industry sectors—especially banks, infrastructure (transportation, communications, and energy) and large employers. Smaller enterprises were generally permitted to remain in private hands. The idea was to control the destiny of the economy and capture the profitability of the large enterprises so that wealth could be redistributed.

But Europe found, as the Soviet Union found, that state ownership of a corporation soon converted it from a golden goose into a ward of the state. Instead of enjoying large profits that could be redistributed, the Europeans found that state-owned enterprises misallocated capital so badly that they had to be subsidized to keep them from collapsing. And because they were far and away the largest employers in the countries, subsidized they were, nearly bankrupting their owners.

Eventually, even the most *dirigiste* Europeans saw the light—partly because Margaret Thatcher shined it vividly into their eyes—and began rapidly privatizing the state-owned enterprises. The first wealth-redistribution strategy, seizing the means of production, had hit the wall.

THE POWER TO TAX IS THE POWER TO DESTROY — SOCIETIES

If the Europeans couldn't succeed by seizing the ownership of productive enterprises, the next logical step in funding entitlements was to tax the profits produced by those enterprises. Profits were taxed at the corporate level, of course, but the serious money was raised by taxing individuals.[15]

When income taxes were first introduced, rates were very low (7% in the United States, for example) and compliance was laughable. But after World War II, and especially in the 1970s, when state-owned enterprises began to implode, tax rates skyrocketed. In Britain, top marginal rates stood at 98 percent as late as 1979.[16] Such rates so suppressed initiative, and so crushed private enterprise, that it seemed as if everyone in the UK was on the dole.

And in fact, everyone was on the dole, not just in Britain but across Europe. Because it wouldn't make sense for middle-class taxpayers to pay out in taxes more than they were getting back in entitlements, the only people who were net taxpayers were the wealthy. And once the wealthy had been squeezed dry, the party was over. As Margaret Thatcher was fond of pointing out, if your strategy is to pay for ever-increasing entitlements with ever-fewer people's money, you will soon run out of other people's money.

There are two fundamental problems with very high, very progressive tax regimes. The first, already mentioned, is that they destroy initiative. Even to this day, Europe (outside of post-Thatcher Britain) has virtually no venture capital industry and hardly any entrepreneurialism of any sort. In the Unites States, we tend to view entrepreneurs as economic heroes, creating jobs and developing products and services that increase human well-being. But in Europe, entrepreneurs are frequently viewed as troublemakers.

The second problem has to do with progressivity itself. Whereas certainly most people agree that higher-income taxpayers should pay more than lower-income taxpayers, the argument for highly progressive marginal rates rests on a very thin reed. Originally, progressivity was viewed in the same spirit as the communist slogan, "From each according to his ability, to each according to his need." It sounded good, but reality acted like a glass of ice water tossed in its face, and today the spirit of the slogan exists nowhere except in the tax code.[17]

When the sloganeering justification for progressivity evaporated, the arguments for highly progressive tax rates became increasingly disingenuous:

mainly, "I need the money," and "it's very popular." Obviously enough, the fact that one group of (middle-class) citizens desires more entitlements is hardly a reason to confiscate other citizens' capital: One man's "fair share" is another woman's confiscation of her hard-earned income.

The popularity issue has also evolved amusingly over time. As long as high marginal rates apply to only a few wealthy taxpayers, progressivity is naturally popular. But that doesn't make it fair. Indeed, once one's own ox begins to be gored, one's enthusiasm for progressivity evaporates very quickly. The best—and, really, the decisive—example is right here in the United States: the Alternative Minimum Tax. Originally enacted in 1969 as the Minimum Tax, it applied to a tiny handful of taxpayers—154 of them!—who reported more than $1 million of income but paid no tax (perfectly legally). The AMT was for many years the most popular provision in the tax code.

But by the late 1990s more than 600,000 taxpayers were ensnared by the AMT, and today more than four million taxpayers pay it. Guess what? It's the single most hated part of the tax code—which is saying something.

Once Margaret Thatcher was elected Prime Minister in the UK, she placed herself firmly astride the tracks down which the train wreck of Britain was hurtling. She quickly focused on reversing the disastrous policies that had led to precipitous national decline: She sold state-owned enterprises, broke the unions' stranglehold on the economy, and promoted more broadly flexible labor markets. Most important for our purposes here, she ratcheted down tax rates.

Counterparts to Mrs. Thatcher were in short supply elsewhere in Europe, but even the left-wing socialist parties gradually recognized that sky-high and ever-rising tax rates weren't improving the quality of citizens' lives. Instead, economic growth had come to a halt and Europe was falling dangerously behind the United States and the emerging economies (especially, the "BICs," ignoring Russia). Without changing their names or, nominally, their ideological positioning, Europe's socialist parties began moving rightward, and tax rates across Europe began to come down.

As had happened with seizing private property, using the power to tax to redistribute wealth had worked for a while. But the power to tax really is the power to destroy—to destroy not wealthy taxpayers, but entire economies. Europe had, in fact, run out of other people's money.

"BORROWING ... THE DISEASE IS INCURABLE"

By the end of the 1980s, you could almost see the desperation in Europe's eyes. Economic growth was flat, other economies around the world were surging ahead, and the two obvious means of raising revenues to support entitlements had died of natural causes.

But the Great Experiment isn't called the Great Experiment for nothing. In 1992 the Maastricht Treaty established the European Union under its current name and required that all countries in the EU adopt the euro.[18] From the very beginning it was recognized that one great advantage of the euro was that it would allow everyone in the currency union to borrow at rates formerly offered only to its most creditworthy states. The idea was that low borrowing rates would spur economic growth across the Continent.

This might actually have worked out as hoped—indeed, like the first two revenue-raising strategies, borrowing initially worked. In the aggregate, European growth rose, although in real terms most of that growth was isolated in the northern countries. There are, after all, good reasons for countries to borrow money. Short-term borrowing can smooth otherwise seasonal cash flows, for example. Long-term borrowing can be used to build out infrastructure—roads, railroads, pipelines, airports, the Internet backbone—which is really a form of investing in the long-term growth of the society.

When borrowing rates are low, and even more especially when low-credit countries are able to borrow at rates more appropriate to high-credit countries, and most especially of all when countries are desperate to meet entitlement demands and all their other strategies have run out of steam, the temptation to overborrow is overwhelming.

And overborrow is what the Europeans did, as we all know. The borrowing wasn't designed to smooth out seasonal cash flows and it wasn't designed to fund infrastructure spending. No, it was designed to fund current spending, with virtually all that spending being used to fund middle-class entitlements. When a country's borrowing is mainly to support current spending, it isn't long before a large part of the borrowing is used up paying interest on past borrowing: Soon enough, "current spending" mainly means paying interest on past spending, at least in terms of discretionary versus nondiscretionary spending.

At that point, the jig is pretty well up. And if interest rates demanded by bond investors should move up sharply, matters end quickly and badly.

Reinhart and Rogoff have shown that once sovereign indebtedness reaches about 90 percent of GDP, the competitiveness of a country begins to decline, as the burden of interest repayment eats into more pro-ductive spending. At ratios above 90 percent, average growth declines, according to Reinhart and Rogoff, by about 1 percent.[19] Of course, this paints with a broad brush. Economies that are especially robust can carry higher debt loads. Countries whose debt is mostly internal, rather than external, can carry higher debt loads. As noted, countries spending heavily on infrastructure can carry higher debt loads. Unfor-tunately, none of this applied to Europe, where economies were feeble, debts were externally held, and borrowing was in support of current spending.

Because the overborrowing in Europe was, at least in the intermediate term, in everybody's interest,[20] overborrowing continued endlessly while everyone winked at the Maastricht Treaty's supposed debt limits (60% debt-to-GDP) and budget deficit limits (3% of GDP) and partied on (truly, the borrowing "disease" is incurable, as Shakespeare put it so well in *Henry IV*.) As we know, this ended catastrophically for the countries that had borrowed the most, and all of Europe will be paying a steep price for decades. The last and final revenue-raising strategy has blown up in the Great Experiment's face.

NOW WHAT?

After the end of World War II, when the European Great Experiment really began, countries were faced with powerful demands for ever-increasing entitlements from the middle classes whose votes elected every government. The result was an ongoing and increasingly desperate search for ways to raise the revenue required to meet the demands. Fail, and another party would be elected that would certainly find a way to do it.

As we have seen, the main strategies employed by governments to meet rising entitlement demands were (a) seizing control of the means of production, (b) taxing wealth and income, and (c) borrowing. All worked for a time, but all eventually failed.

As this is being written, all eyes are on Europe, as the Continent struggles to avoid a domino-like collapse of sovereign countries and an associated collapse of the European banking system. But note that Europe's current troubles, calamitous as they are, are merely symptoms of the larger and vastly more formidable problem: The middle classes who elect governments are hooked on their entitlements, and those entitlements can no longer be afforded.

Yes, Europe needs to find ways to stave off its current crisis, but even assuming it is successful in avoiding the collapse of the euro and the banks and the EU, only then can it begin to deal with the larger, vastly more complex challenge of learning to live within its means. And note that almost anything Europe does to stave off collapse will likely constrain economic growth for a very long time, making the problem of living within its means even more daunting.

The question therefore arises: How are the Western democracies—very much including the United States—going to get themselves out of this mess?

Well, actually, that's not my department.[21] The reason it's not my department is that, theoretically, it's perfectly clear what has to happen:

Entitlements need to stop growing and start shrinking, and government revenue needs to grow so we can start paying down our gigantic debt burdens. And all that needs to happen without plunging the Western economies into recession or worse.

"In theory," as Yogi Berra is fond of saying, "reality and theory are the same. In reality, they're different." Everybody on the planet knows what has to happen, but getting there seems to be politically impossible, not least because none of the old ideas have worked and nobody has any new ones.

Consider Greece. If ever there was a country that had its back to the wall and was facing gathering ruin, it would be the Greeks. Yet the country has undertaken virtually no serious reforms beyond those forced on it by the bond markets. Or consider Italy. Though its economy is barely one-seventh the size of that of the United States, it is the third-largest issuer of sovereign debt in the world. We know why, and we know what Italy has been spending its spectacular borrowing on. Yet the country seems to be in serious denial. In the fall of 2011 Italy attempted to placate bond vigilantes by announcing that it was considering raising its legal retirement age from 65 to 67—over 18 years![22]

Or consider, I am sorry to say, the United States of America, where debt to GDP has gone over 100%,[23] where the economy is stalled, where Congress can't act at all, where the Super Committee collapsed in a shambles, and where any third grader can see that middle-class entitlements will sink the country very soon.

It's fun to bash Congress, and we're all in favor of it. But the fact is that Congressional deadlock merely reflects voter deadlock. Unelected commissions (e.g., Simpson-Bowles) are always coming up with perfectly sound ideas, but nobody who needs to stand for election will go anywhere near them. It's true that opinion polls show a plurality of Americans agree that the best solution to our problems involves a combination of curtailing entitlements and raising taxes. But ask the question slightly differently and watch what happens to you:

Pollster (interviewing Medicare recipient): Do you agree that Medicare should be curtailed and your taxes increased?

Medicare recipient: #@*&!

In any event, broad public opinion has little impact on what happens in Congress, because our representatives (especially) and senators are elected from specific districts and states. Imagine, for a moment, that Nancy Pelosi were to announce that she was going to vote to cut Medicare and Social Security. The poor woman would be tossed out on her ear and replaced with somebody who knew where her bread was buttered. The same goes for, say, Eric Cantor.

But the problem is actually worse than that. Congressional representatives on the political left believe very deeply that the role of government is to make people's lives better, to make the population more equal, and cutting "entitlements" is morally anathema to them. Same for folks in Congress on the political right, who believe to the core of their souls that entitlements are bankrupting America. To ask such people to vote against their most deeply held principles is a nonstarter.

The Western democracies aren't precisely out of ideas, they are out of ideas that will work and can be implemented.[24] Many commentators have observed that the Occupy Wall Street protestors haven't offered any solutions to their concerns. True enough, but who exactly *is* offering any solutions?

In addition to the paucity of realistic ideas, the West is also faced with a very disconcerting fact: We now know that all known ideas for redistributing wealth to the middle classes don't just fail (ultimately) to work, they have consequences that are cataclysmic. When state ownership of productive enterprises failed in the Soviet Union, it didn't just set the Russian people back a few years—it set them back roughly a century. Relative to other societies in Europe and elsewhere, Putin's Russia occupies about the same place in the world as Czarist Russia did in the early 1900s. Europe's "middle way" allowed it to avoid this calamity, but its long flirtation with socialism built up a culture that was, and remains, anathema to the sort of individual initiative that propels growth.

By the time high and highly progressive tax policies failed, Europe was suffering—the rich had been bled dry and there was nowhere else to turn. Britain in particular was sinking slowly into the English Channel, at whose bottom it would be lying today if Margaret Thatcher hadn't come to power.

And, of course, we all know how ruinous Europe's flirtation with borrowing turned out to be. Just to take the worst example, Greece today is the laughingstock of the world. But it wasn't always thus, and I'm not just referring to the Greece of 2,500 years ago. Not so long ago, the Greeks were a proud and virile society. As World War II was breaking out, tiny Greece (whose total population made it roughly the size of the city of Berlin) met the Axis army at its border and, astonishingly, pushed it back into Albania. Greece was doomed, of course, as it couldn't stand forever against the combined might of Germany and Italy. But when the Greeks lost the border, they fought in the villages, and when they lost the villages they fought in the mountains.[25] The pathetic sight of today's Greeks rioting in the streets, throwing Molotov cocktails into bank buildings and burning innocent women alive, all in a futile attempt to continue to retire at age 50, tells us everything we need to know about the destructive power of failed wealth redistributionist policies.[26]

Wealthy families everywhere worry incessantly and with good reason about the challenge of raising productive, disciplined children who are outwardly focused on the needs of others. Though it's a bit of an exaggeration, it's useful in assessing the scope of the challenge Europe faces to view the Europeans as the entitled, self-absorbed, feckless children of their wealthy societies. They lack a plan for moving forward, but even if they had a plan they seem to lack the character required to get it off the dime. And it's not just Greece, Spain, and Portugal: In Italy, for example, the relatively productive north has subsidized the slothlike south for many decades and has now been milked dry.

It's possible to imagine a world—possibly cheerfully inhabited by our grandchildren—in which wealth redistribution means moving money from the rich and middle classes to the poor, where the twin sorrows of human misery and lost human potential loom like neon indictments of the wealthy West. But it isn't possible to know how we're going to get there or when it's going to happen. Political incoherence is everywhere, and the implications of this for the United States (Europe isn't the canary in the coal mine, it's the gorilla in the kitchen) are many and profound.

Which—to circle back to the beginning of this chapter—raises the interesting question of how I should be investing our capital in such a world.

BUT, FIRST, A NOTE ABOUT GERMANY

My readers have no doubt noticed that many of our comments about Europe don't seem to apply to Germany. It's certainly true that Germans appear to be harder working, thriftier, and more fiscally disciplined than the rest of Europe. But there are some serious issues here.

The first is simply Germany's history. Try as they might, neither Europe nor the rest of the world is likely to allow the Germans to dominate Europe again. Thus, whatever the merits of the German prescription for the rest of Europe (austerity, fiscal discipline, firm central oversight), it isn't likely to be adopted by countries with long and dreadful memories.

More practically, the German export-led economic model[27] is simply not adoptable by Europe, for the simple reason that someone has to buy the exported goods. If, somehow, all the countries of Europe decided to become export-driven economies, they would all collapse at once—including Germany.

INVESTING CAPITAL IN A (VERY) UNCERTAIN WORLD

As I see it, there are only two possible outcomes to the mess the Western democracies have gotten themselves into:

1. This is the end of the Western democracies, at least in terms of dominating the world economically, militarily, and culturally. More vigorous nations, such as China, India, Brazil, and Russia, will soon rule the world.
2. The Western nations will, slowly but surely, get their acts together, and we'll be back on solid ground again.[28]

If you believe in (1), you should invest all your money in emerging market stocks (and bonds) and relax on your back porch while your portfolio rises and the West sinks.

If you believe in (2), as I do, one of three things will happen:

1. The Western governments will eventually take concrete steps to rein in spending and bring down debt. (I can think of this as analogous to Reagan and Volker taming inflation in the early 1980s.) When they do, you should move to a position well above your targets in risk assets.
2. The West will muddle through, never really taking conclusive action, but managing to stave off collapse. In this case, equity multiples will gradually decline into the single digits, at which point you should move to a position above your targets in risk assets.
3. The eurozone will collapse, precipitating a global crisis that will cause equity prices to plunge to levels not seen since the mid-1970s—or maybe the early 1930s. This will be a catastrophe for the world, but will offer investors a once-in-two-lifetimes opportunity to buy stocks at subterranean pricing.

In the meantime, most investors should remain positioned close to their targets in risk assets, because (a) as noted below, equity multiples are not outrageously high, and (b) I could be wrong.

The beauty of the preceding strategies in outcomes (1), (2) and (3) is not that those strategies will maximize your gains, but that they will help preserve your capital until it's possible for significant gains from risky assets to become likely again. And at that point you will have the dry powder required to back the truck up. Optionality matters.

CONCLUSION: A WORLD AT RISK

As this is being written, everyone's attention is riveted on Europe—and rightly so, because what happens there is very likely to affect the already shaky global economy in a powerful way. Will a major European bank go down, precipitating a global banking crisis? Will a major European economy default on its debt, sending Europe and probably the rest of the world into a double-dip recession or worse? Will Europe throw in the towel and reatomize into something that looks like the Europe of the 1980s?

These are urgent questions, of course, but as I've tried to show at great length in this chapter, Europe's immediate problems are only the symptoms of far deeper maladies. If Europe somehow navigates its current shoals, it can then turn its attention to the entitlement tsunami that is about to inundate the Continent.

But the problem is even worse: Whatever steps Europe takes to deal with the immediate crises of bank and sovereign insolvency are very likely to make the already Gordian long-term challenges even more intractable. For example, what the European states need more than anything else is vigorous economic growth, but what they are getting is more austerity. What the European banking system needs is to get out from under its crushing debt load, but what it is getting is more debt.[29]

Still, judged according to its original goals the Great Experiment in Europe has been an extraordinary success. Never in human history have so many wealthy countries coexisted in so small a geographical space for so long without warring with each other. The Europeans have carved out lives that are in many ways enviable, less hyperkinetic than our own, more humanistic and less market-driven. There are thousands of places in Europe that cannot be encountered without an immediate attack of *coup de coeur*.

But all this lies endangered. The danger is Europe's and the world's, and the danger puts our capital at risk. Understanding the scope and depth of the problem and investing accordingly is the best we can hope to do.

NOTES

1. This chapter is adapted from Greycourt White Paper No. 52: The End of History (Again): Why We May Be Living in a Permanent Financial Crisis (2012), available at www.Greycourt.com.
2. See Chapter 5.
3. Published in the current affairs journal, *The National Interest*.
4. *The End of History and the Last Man* (New York: Harper Perennial, 1992).

5. This probably came as news to the fundamentalist Islamic states that have cropped up since Fukuyama wrote—to say nothing of China.
6. 1st ed. (Princeton, NJ: Princeton University Press, 2009), 234–237. A separate study by David H. Papell and Ruxandra Prodan puts the average time for recovery after a financial crisis at nine years: "[T]he Great Slump is not yet half over." See *The Statistical Behavior of GDP after Financial Crises and Severe Recessions*, prepared for the Federal Reserve Bank of Boston conference on "Long-Term Effects of the Great Recession," October 18–19, 2011. Note that the Japanese crisis began in 1992 and is ongoing—20 years and counting.
7. The Nikkei Index, which measures the performance of the Japanese stock market, peaked at over 24,000 in 1992 and is now hovering around 8,000.
8. By "indebted," I include both the sovereign debt that has destroyed places like Greece and the private debt that destroyed places like Ireland and Spain.
9. See, for example, Niall Ferguson, *Civilization: The West and the Rest* (New York: Penguin Press HC, 2011).
10. We're going to focus on Europe, where the Industrial Revolution began, although of course the United States was facing the same issues at roughly the same time.
11. Shirtsleeves-to-shirtsleeves in three generations. This phenomenon is so universal that similar aphorisms exist in other cultures: rice paddies to rice paddies in three generations (Chinese); potato fields to potato fields in three generations (Irish). I am indebted to Jay Hughes for the non-U.S. versions. See James E. Hughes Jr., *Family Wealth—Keeping It in the Family: How Family Members and Their Advisers Preserve Human, Intellectual, and Financial Assets for Generations* (New York: Bloomberg Press, 2004).
12. The official occupation of Germany ended in 1955, but U.S. troops remain on German soil as part of NATO.
13. The European Defense Community (EDC) was proposed by France in 1950 and was to include West Germany, France, Italy, and the Benelux countries.
14. To simplify the discussion, I am describing the wealth-redistribution strategies as though they occurred in strict chronological order. In fact, of course, the strategies overlapped in time.
15. "The power to tax is the power to destroy" was spoken by Daniel Webster, arguing before the U.S. Supreme Court in the case of *McCulloch v. Maryland* in 1819. The question before the Court was whether a state could impose a tax on the Bank of the United States, a doomed predecessor of the Federal Reserve Bank. Chief Justice Marshall adopted

the same words in holding that it could not. I am suggesting that the power to tax is capable of destroying not just entities and individuals, but entire societies.

16. The top regular bracket was 83 percent, but there was also a 15 percent soak-the-rich surcharge on interest and dividends, bringing the total rate to 98 percent.

17. If you are skeptical, try paying your workers according to that principle and see what happens to you.

18. Actually, thus far only 17 of the 27 states of the EU use the euro. Many of the others don't meet the budgetary and monetary requirements (and others claim to but don't). Denmark and the UK opted out and Sweden, though a member of the EU, refuses to use the euro by intentionally not meeting the requirements.

19. Carmen M. Reinhart and Kenneth S. Rogoff, "Growth in a Time of Debt," paper prepared for the *American Economic Review Papers and Proceedings* (draft of January 7, 2010), 7–8.

20. That is to say, most of Europe wanted to borrow to offer ever-more-generous entitlements to their citizens, and Germany wanted everyone else to borrow so it could keep the German export economy booming.

21. I am channeling Tom Lehrer, who in his famous lyric put these words into the mouth of Wernher von Braun, the controversial German-American rocket scientist: "'Once the rockets are up, who cares where they come down?/That's not my department,' says Wernher von Braun."

22. More recently, a new-and-improved Italian government proposed that henceforth women in the private workforce would have to wait and retire at the same age as men(!).

23. See U.S. Department of Commerce, Bureau of Economic Analysis, "National Economic Accounts: Gross Domestic Product: Current-dollar and 'Real' GDP," BEA.gov, July 29, 2011.

24. It's fine for Simpson-Bowles, the Gang of Six, and others to show that entitlements need to be cut and taxes increased. The trouble is that these ideas aren't *implementable*. Until someone shows us how to get from here to there, I can safely consider that no solutions are on the table.

25. Many historians believe that the plucky Greek resistance to the Axis armies changed the course of the war. When the Italians were pushed back by the Greeks, Hitler was forced to divert German troops to help get the job done. Ultimately, this delayed the German invasion of Russia by about a month. A month may not seem like a long time, but when the Russian winter is coming on, it's an eternity. If the Greeks had simply rolled over, and if Hitler had captured Moscow, and if the Axis powers hadn't had to fight a two-front war—well, better not to go there.

26. In his recent book, *Boomerang*, Michael Lewis refers to Greece as a country in "total moral collapse" (New York: W. W. Norton & Company, 2011).
27. Exports account for almost 50 percent of German GDP, versus less than 30 percent for the United States and most other developed countries. In absolute terms, only China exports more than Germany. For a scathing look at German hypocrisy toward the rest of Europe, see our blog at www.Summitas.com/blogger/gregory-curtis.
28. A third possibility would be for the Western nations to repudiate their debt and start over. I think this is likely to happen at the fringe, but not at the core.
29. In late December 2011, the European Central Bank lent the European banks $638 billion on three-year terms.

CHAPTER 4

Risk

We helped Einstein invest his money.
What makes you think you should do it alone?
—Billboard advertising the services of TIAA-CREF

Once we possess capital of any size, our first duty as the steward of that capital is to preserve it against diminution through inattention, negligence, the ravages of inflation, incompetence or, God forbid, fraud. What we will actually do with our capital is a crucial question, of course, but if we don't husband our wealth carefully this issue will never arise—there won't be enough wealth to worry about.

In this chapter I discuss the very large and very important topic of risk. Following a general introduction to the topic, I focus on two aspects of risk that investors tend to overlook: first, the impact of variance drain on the growth of wealth, and second, the behavioral bias that all too often cause us to do exactly the wrong thing at the wrong time. I end the chapter with a description of a hypothetical investor named Edith and the many headwinds she faces as she tries to grow a nice inheritance into a large fortune.

FAMILIES AND INVESTMENT RISK

Investing is the process of putting out money today in the hope or expectation that we will receive more money in the future. If the expectation that we will receive our capital back is very high, the return we can demand on it will be very low. This is because many, many other investors are happy to take very little risk and still receive a return.[1]

Likewise, if the hope of having our capital returned intact is more speculative, we can demand a much higher return, because few other investors will have the appetite or ability to put their capital at significant risk. It's a simple matter of supply and demand, but mainly supply: There is always a great deal of demand for serious risk capital, but rarely much supply of it; there is a fairly static demand for low-risk capital (to finance the routine operations of governments and corporations), but there will always be a large supply of it.

Virtually every American family that is wealthy today got that way because someone in the family at some point took very serious risks. Yes, they also worked very hard and had a good idea. But one can work very hard and not become rich—coal miners, for example. And one can have brilliant ideas and not become rich—tinkerers and dreamers of all kinds. ("In the end, a vision without the ability to execute is probably a hallucination," as Steve Case once put it.) It is the combination of hard work, a good idea, and risk that generates wealth on any significant scale.[2] The risk typically involves doing something new and different, or doing something old in a new and different way. The grander the idea, the larger the potential wealth—but also the greater the chance of a spectacular failure.

"Low"-Risk Investments

Risk in the context of liquid portfolios—post-sale of whatever made the family wealthy—is no different, but it operates on a more modest and more controllable scale. After all, once an investor has already become wealthy, the justification for continuing to take huge risks diminishes rapidly.

But large or small, risk is a tricky subject. Consider the safest investment in the world for a U.S. investor—a United States Treasury bill. (I say "a U.S. investor" because foreign investors must take currency risk when they buy U.S. Treasuries.) The likelihood that the U.S. government will default on its promise to pay us back in 90 days is so remote that it is fair to say, for most practical purposes, that U.S. Treasuries are risk-free investments.

Huge numbers of investors like this low-risk alternative, and consequently the U.S. government typically needs to offer a return no higher than the underlying inflation rate to attract capital. Because most buyers of U.S. government paper are tax-exempt institutions, the return on U.S. Treasuries tends to equal the inflation rate *before* tax. Taxable investors who buy Treasuries can therefore expect to receive negative real returns over time.

Hence the odd result that the "safest" investment in the world will destroy vast amounts of wealth if used exclusively in family portfolios over a very long period of time. For example, if a family had invested $100 million in U.S. Treasuries beginning 50 years ago and simply rolled the

Treasuries over every 90 days for half a century, that family's wealth would have declined to the equivalent of about $60 million today (net of taxes and inflation, *but assuming no spending*). If the same family had put all its money in stocks compounding at 10 percent 50 years ago, that family would have today—net of taxes and inflation—something like $2.8 billion. *The $2.6 billion difference between these two numbers is the long-term consequence of investing exclusively in the safest investment in the world.*

"High"-Risk Investments

Let's compare the other end of the risk spectrum: early-stage venture capital investing. Venture capital is capital available to very new, untested companies. Early-stage venture capital investing involves the funding of new companies shortly after they have started up. Perhaps they have received initial capital from a "friends and family" investment round, or perhaps from a small group of angel investors. But the company is still new and untried, almost certainly unprofitable and possibly it even has no revenue stream. To say that such companies are risky investments is simply to state a truism: Many will fail altogether; others will sputter along, never completely returning their investor capital; a very few will succeed brilliantly.

Three or four decades ago, when the institutional venture capital world was in its infancy, a few intrepid investors—mainly families, not institutions—began to seek out and invest in early-stage venture companies. In those days the supply of capital for this sort of investing was almost nonexistent, given the huge risks involved and the lack of infrastructure in the industry. Consequently, annual returns could easily reach 40 percent or even 50 percent.[3] Huge fortunes were made in this way.[4]

But those kinds of returns began to attract additional capital and talent to the business. As "deal flow" increased—that is, more entrepreneurs with ideas began to come along—investors began to form partnerships to source and nurture these fledgling enterprises, with the objective of eventually taking them public or selling them to larger firms. Today, the venture capital industry is fully developed in the United States, with hundreds of venture capital partnerships offering funding and advice to tens of thousands of entrepreneurs. Billions of dollars are raised every year by these partnerships.

But of course, the law of supply and demand holds: Returns have declined. Investors making diversified investments in early-stage venture capital partnerships today can expect to receive returns in the 15 percent to 35 percent range, depending on whether they are invested with top-tier or average partnerships. Although 20 percent annual compound returns are nothing to sniff at, given the capital risks and, especially, the illiquidity of these investments, few sensible investors would participate in early-stage venture investing in the hope of receiving 15 percent per year. On the other hand, savvy investors investing directly in deals, or participating in the best partnerships and diversifying by partnership, industry, stage, and time, can have a reasonable expectation of achieving 25 percent to 35 percent annual compound returns—probably the highest returns available outside the realm of pure speculation.

But whether the returns turn out to be closer to 15 percent or 35 percent, these are stunning returns from passive investing, and, given their favorable tax treatment, can easily produce huge increases in wealth for families who take the venture capital investing process seriously. *Hence the odd result that, while the safest, low-risk investments will destroy wealth over time, the riskiest investments, properly structured, will almost certainly create significant real wealth.*

"Reasonable"-Risk Investments: Marketable Securities

The core of most wealthy family portfolios will be marketable securities—stocks and bonds—and so I want to spend some time on the nature of risk in this sector of the market.

Stocks are issued by corporations through public or private offerings, but most of us buy stocks not directly from corporations (or, technically, the underwriters of the corporate stock offering) but from other investors, typically through the mechanism of a stock exchange. Indeed, the history of America is virtually coterminous with the history of the New York Stock Exchange, the largest exchange in the world, founded under a buttonwood tree near Wall Street in 1792. (The United States Constitution, you will recall, was ratified in 1788.)

Note that when we buy from other investors on a stock exchange our buying and selling is providing the liquidity without which no one would have bought the stock in the first place.

THE LAW OF SUPPLY AND DEMAND (AGAIN)

As with other investment sectors, stocks follow the laws of supply and demand. When more investors are interested in buying than in selling a stock, the price of that stock will rise, and when more investors want to sell than buy, the price will decline. This is true not only of individual stocks, but of stocks as a whole. When investors are optimistic and in a buying mood, the level of the market itself (the S&P 500, say, or the Dow or Nasdaq) will rise. When investors are pessimistic markets will decline. Note—as we'll discuss in a moment—that individual stocks and entire markets can rise or decline based on fundamental business or economic conditions, but they can also rise and fall simply as a result of investor sentiment, whether that sentiment is factually based or not.

Supply and demand can be confusing in the capital markets context. For example, it might seem sensible to suppose that an investor—a money manager, for example—who wishes to buy a very large supply of a particular stock should get a bargain, a "quantity discount." In fact, most large purchases drive *up* the price of the stock, resulting in the odd phenomenon that money managers attempting to purchase a large block of stock will pay more than investors attempting to purchase more modest positions.[5]

Similarly, sales of large blocks of stock will push the price of the stock down, so that a large-money manager will receive less for his stock than will a small investor selling only a few shares. As a result, the main cost involved in buying or selling shares for most money managers or other large investors is not commissions or spreads between the bid and ask price—the main cost is "market impact," the increase or decrease in the stock's price caused by the investor's attempt to buy or sell it.

IDIOSYNCRATIC IDEAS ABOUT RISK

In thinking about the risks associated with investing in stocks, investors tend to think in idiosyncratic terms. What I think of as risk, for example, may be quite different from what you think of as risk. This has partly to do with our individual circumstances and partly to do with our differing temperaments. It's important, of course, to understand ourselves as investors and to know what we mean by risk. But it's far more important to understand that *the capital markets don't care about what we think of as risk*.

If risk to me means never experiencing a negative return in any calendar year, I can design a portfolio that will be highly likely to avoid that particular risk. But to do so I will have to sacrifice far more return than I probably want to give up. In other words, I'm being penny-wise and pound-foolish.

If risk to you, on the other hand, means failing to achieve at least a 15 percent annual return from a traditional stock and bond portfolio, you can probably accomplish that, too. But you will be exposing yourself to breathtaking price volatility, volatility so great that you will almost certainly abandon the portfolio long before it has generated your desired rate of return.

And the same is true of other idiosyncratic definitions of risk. Hence, it's crucially important that we understand the real risks that are embedded in the capital markets. We can still indulge our "eccentric" ideas about risk, but at least we will understand something about the costs associated with doing so.

REAL RISKS: THOSE EMBEDDED IN THE PROCESS OF INVESTING

If we are going to invest our capital, we are going to subject it to risk. Without risk, there is no return—we simply get a little poorer each day as inflation, spending, and taxes eat away at our capital. In the following paragraphs I outline the major kinds of risk we will experience as we invest.

Individual Stock Risk versus Broad Market Risk

Some risks associated with investing in stocks are unavoidable, whereas others are relatively easily avoided. The risks that can be avoided do not, except in the hands of geniuses and the very lucky, reward us for taking them. On the other hand, over time we will be rewarded for taking risks that cannot be avoided, that are inherent in the activity of owning stocks, and we should be eager to accept those risks.

The main avoidable risk is *individual stock risk*. If our stock portfolio consists of only one stock, we might make a great deal of money on that investment and we might lose everything. But unless we are Warren Buffett, or unless we know a very great deal about the company (because, perhaps, we own or run it), our investment results are likely to be both random and completely beyond our control. We aren't rewarded for taking the risk of owning one stock any more than we are rewarded for playing roulette in Las Vegas.

The reason we aren't rewarded for this behavior is that it can easily be avoided—by buying more than one stock. Owning even a small handful of carefully selected stocks dramatically reduces the risk of a one-stock portfolio, and owning 20 or 30 carefully selected stocks virtually eliminates individual stock risk. Note the words "carefully selected." This means buying stocks of companies that operate in different industries, industries that are affected differently by the same business and economic conditions. Buying five biotechnology stocks rather than one doesn't significantly reduce individual stock risk because many of the conditions that affect one of those companies will also, and similarly, affect the others.

The main risk we cannot avoid when we buy stocks is broad market risk, the risk inherent in owning equity securities. Even if we owned every stock listed on the New York Stock Exchange, we would still be exposed to market risk. On the other hand, we are compensated for accepting broad market risk, compensated by receiving a "risk premium" over the risk-free rate (typically the interest rate on Treasury bills). Over a very long period of time the risk premium for U.S. large-company stocks has been about 7 percent. Hence, if Treasuries have yielded roughly 3 percent over time, U.S. large company stocks have returned roughly 10 percent compounded over time. The size of the risk premium changes over time, but only glacially, because the risk premium seems to be imbedded in the very concept of broad ownership of productive assets on a large scale—that is, on a scale sufficiently large to be importantly affected by the growth of the broad economy. It wouldn't surprise me to learn that Ancient Egyptians were earning a risk premium of something like 7 percent when they put their capital at risk in various and sundry Egyptian enterprises.

Price Volatility

The trouble, of course, is that the risk premium we earn through broad stock ownership isn't a fixed rate of return like the return on a Treasury bill. Instead, our return fluctuates, sometimes wildly. This fluctuation is known as *price volatility,* and it is a key concept for anyone even thinking about investing in equities.

Let's look at numbers roughly close to the actual numbers to illustrate how price volatility works in the marketplace, how it affects our returns, and why it is so important. As noted above, over time U.S. large-company stocks have compounded at an annual rate of about 10 percent. But if we looked at the actual year-by-year returns over, say, 75 years, we would see that stocks almost never return 10 percent in any particular year. Instead, stock returns have occurred across a wide spectrum, from a high of +53 percent in 1954 to a low of −35 percent in 1937. In other words, stock returns fall into the familiar bell-shaped curve we all know and love.

If we assume that the annual standard deviation of stock returns—the group of outcomes that encompasses two-thirds of all annual returns—is about 20, then we would expect, two-thirds of the time, to experience returns between −10 percent and +30 percent.

This exercise illustrates several crucial points about the experience we are likely to encounter if we invest in stocks—regardless of our idiosyncratic notions about risk. The first important point is that, as discussed above, our average rate of return is likely to be about 10 percent over a very long period of time. Investors who expect better returns than this, perhaps because recent market returns have been higher, will be sorely disappointed.

The second important point is that we will rarely receive exactly 10 percent in any one year; instead, our actual annual return from equity investing will fluctuate very widely. Two-thirds of the time, as noted above, we can expect our results to be somewhere between +30 percent and −10 percent. An investor who focuses on the 10 percent average return of stocks without taking into account the standard deviation of their returns is likely to abandon stocks well before the long-term average return has been achieved.

Third, note that the range of +30 percent to −10 percent explains only two-thirds of the annual expected price volatility of the stock markets. One-sixth of the time our results will be better than +30 percent and one-sixth of the time our results will be worse than −10 percent. If we are invested over a period of 10 years—and no one should think about investing in stocks with much less of a time horizon—the odds are that in three or four of those years our results will fall outside this range, either on the upside or downside. And over an investment lifetime it is virtually certain that we will experience many years in which our investment returns will be better or worse than the standard range. Hence, as investors we simply have to understand that we will in fact experience extreme markets and that that experience is as much a part of stock investing as getting our long-term 10 percent return.[6]

Assuming that we own properly diversified stock portfolios, it is this phenomenon of price volatility that is the key risk we are exposing our assets to. Except under very specific conditions, price volatility can't be avoided without significantly reducing the return we can expect to receive. For example, we can reduce the price volatility of a 100 percent equity portfolio by converting it into a portfolio consisting of 60 percent stocks and 40 percent bonds. But we will have dramatically reduced the long-term return that portfolio will generate.

Price volatility is also symmetrical; that is, if U.S. large-cap stocks have a characteristic price volatility of 16 percent, that is 16 percent on both the upside and downside, around the 10 percent average return. It simply makes no sense to say, as many investors do, that "upside volatility" isn't risk, only "downside volatility" is risk. If you own an equity portfolio that has 20 percent upside volatility, you also own an equity portfolio that has 20 percent downside volatility, as investors in technology, growth, and momentum stocks learned after the first quarter of 2000.[7]

As we will see when we discuss asset allocation, the price volatility of investment portfolios can be reduced by thoughtfully combining asset classes in a fully diversified portfolio. For example, simply adding small amounts of diversified international stocks to a U.S. stock portfolio will simultaneously reduce the price volatility of the resulting portfolio and modestly increase its expected return—a rare "free lunch" in the investment world. Of course, it's not really a free lunch. Both the domestic and international portfolios will be as volatile as they ever were, and as investors we will experience (and heartily dislike) that volatility. It's just that the price volatility of the blended domestic-international portfolio will be lower than a simple average of the two would suggest, due to the fact that the returns of the two asset classes aren't perfectly correlated.

The phenomenon of price volatility has momentous implications for investors. The first of these implications I will call "behavioral," and the second I'll call "fundamental." That is, the first is avoidable (albeit not easily), but the second is embedded in the nature of capital in a market economy.

The "behavioral" problem presented by price volatility affects investors who simply cannot emotionally abide the ups and downs of the market. In other words, although there is no need for these investors to remove their capital from the equity market during negative periods, they nonetheless do so out of fear, and to their serious detriment. Unfortunately, this category includes the vast majority of investors, because it requires a strong stomach, an iron will, or a professional discipline to deal with the sometimes breathtaking ups and downs that are an ordinary feature of equity markets.

But there is also a "fundamental" problem with price volatility, namely, that capital—which is what the market is made up of—hates illiquidity. Capital needs to be deployed and redeployed in a vigorous economy, and the timing of the redeployment is usually unknown in advance. Unfortunately, however, capital deployed in an equity portfolio can't simply be redeployed willy-nilly. If our redeployment opportunities require us to put capital into a market near the top and take it out for redeployment elsewhere near the bottom, then we are being forced to adopt the worst possible equity investment strategy. The phenomenon of price volatility requires that capital held in equity portfolios be withdrawn only at certain optimal points in time, and those optimal times will often be inconsistent with capital redeployment opportunities elsewhere.

Finally, there is a third feature of price volatility that directly affects the rate at which our capital can grow. I discuss this aspect of volatility in a brief parable at the end of the chapter.

Wildness in the Tails

As discussed in Chapter 9, bell curves seriously underestimate the frequency and extreme nature of events that occur in the tails of the bell curve, at least when the curve is meant to describe investment returns. What, for example, must be the odds that the stock market will decline by 20 percent in two days? As noted in Chapter 9, if capital markets events were randomly distributed, such an event would be unthinkable—if we had begun investing in stocks at the time the universe was born, it would still be extremely unlikely that we would ever experience such a dramatic decline. Yet, as we all know, such a decline occurred in October 1987. Thus, we can't specify exactly what will occur or when it will occur, but we know for certain that if we invest long enough, bizarre events will decidedly occur and we had better be ready for them. There is, as someone has appropriately put it, "wildness" in those tails.

Other examples of wildness in the tails would include the 1929 Stock Market Crash (when the markets declined by 89% from the 1929 peak to the 1932 trough); the abysmal markets of 1973 and 1974 (when the markets declined in real—net of inflation—terms by 50%); the sudden evaporation of liquidity in the third quarter of 1998 (associated with Russia's default on its sovereign debt and the collapse of the Long Term Capital Management hedge fund); the collapse of the Tech Bubble in 2000; the stock market gyrations that followed the September 11, 2001 terrorist attacks; and the Financial Crisis of 2007–2009. These extreme events can be truly threatening, not only to individual investors but also to markets as a whole. For a time during the 1998 liquidity crisis, for example, the Federal Reserve feared that Long Term Capital's collapse might lead to a collapse of the entire market system.

Investor Behavior

One of the most natural, but nonetheless frightening, aspects of investing has to do with the fact that, capital markets theorists notwithstanding, investors do not behave rationally, at least not in the short term. I've just cited the example of October of 1987. Can it actually have been possible that American corporations were worth 20 percent less on October 19 than they were on October 18? It's ludicrous on its face. Either investors were irrational on October 18 or they were irrational on October 19 (or, more likely, both), but they can't have been rational on both dates.

We observe the same phenomenon over longer periods of time in bear and bull markets. Stocks rarely go from overpriced to fairly priced, or from underpriced to fairly priced. Instead, they almost always go from overpriced to underpriced, and from underpriced to overpriced. When bear markets occur, investors quickly become overly pessimistic, concluding that the world is going to hell in a handbasket (for example, 1973–1974, 2000–2003). When bull markets are roaring, investors become overly enthusiastic, convinced that stock prices will rise forever (for example, 1998–1999).

For truly rational investors, these periods of emotionalism represent tremendous opportunities, either to sell to the enthusiastic crowds at inflated prices or to buy from the terrified rabble at artificially deflated prices. Unfortunately, few of us have the moxie to take advantage of the opportunities, for the simple reason that we are *part* of the emotional crowd, not *apart* from it.

No one knows how much price volatility results from factors inherent in the capital markets and how much results from the fact that investors are human and therefore imperfect, though the work of behavioral finance experts is beginning to shed light on these issues.[8] At the margin, however, near market peaks and bottoms, it seems apparent that it is almost entirely human emotion that is driving prices. We need to realize that investors—including ourselves—aren't rational, at least over relatively short periods of time or during extreme markets, and to take that fact into account as we consider the risks of investing.

The Fear of Losing Everything Inexperienced investors often fear that if they put their money into the markets, they could lose everything. Well, yes and no. If you put all your money in one stock, it could in fact go to zero. Same for putting all your money with one hedge fund manager or one venture capital investment. But if you spread your money around in a diversified portfolio of stocks, bonds, hedge funds, and private equity, the chances of losing everything decline to the vanishing point.

I noted earlier that investors in the Weimar Republic in Germany lost everything when hyperinflation destroyed the German economy and then World War II destroyed the German state. But these are extraordinarily rare events, and can be avoided in any event by diversifying across different countries (see Chapters 9, 11, and 12).

Making a Truly Terrible Decision

Probably the biggest risk most investors face is one of their own making: that under serious stress they will make a dreadfully wrong-headed decision, permanently impairing the family's capital. In the mid-1970s, for example, thousands of family investors threw in the towel at the bottom of the market (in mid-1974, let's say), put all their money in bonds and then sat out the greatest bull market in American history. A similar phenomenon occurred in late 2008/early 2009, when investors rode the stock market all the way to the bottom, then bailed out, missing the recovery.

Note that the seeds of these catastrophic errors were often planted not during the bear market, but during the preceding bull market. In the late 1990s, people who knew nothing about the investment process quit their jobs so they could engage in "day trading." These people made quick profits and soon had virtually all their capital invested in the stock market. When that market collapsed in 2000, they were wiped out, literally bankrupted in many cases.

Overenthusiasm during bull markets combined with overpessimism during bear markets is a sure way to convert an upper-class family into a middle-class family, or a middle-class family into a working-class family.

VARIANCE DRAIN

Let's take a focused look at the concept of variance drain and the impact it can have on even a well-managed investment portfolio. The following parable, based very loosely on an actual event, is designed to drive home the important point that controlling portfolio volatility not only makes investors more comfortable, but actually grows wealth faster than more volatile portfolios with the same—or even higher—returns.

Dick and Jane and Variance Drain

Dick and Jane are twins. In case you're wondering, the answer is yes, they have a sister, Sally, and a dog named Spot. For many years they lived a cheery middle-class life. Dick would throw a stick and Spot would chase after it.

"Look, Dick, look!" Jane would say. "See Spot run!"

"Run, Spot, run!" said Dick.

All this came to an abrupt end on their twenty-first birthday, however, for on that day they received an inheritance from Weird Uncle Fred. Uncle Fred had immigrated to Switzerland many years ago, and his legacy was, like Fred, weird.

According to the Swiss trust officer, Uncle Fred had left each of them $1 million. However, the money was in trust and neither principal nor interest would be paid out until their thirty-first birthday. (This meant that the money could compound tax-free.)

But there was a further provision. Uncle Fred considered himself to be a great investor, and he wanted Dick and Jane to become great investors, too. Therefore, said the trust officer, a gnome-like gentleman, at the end of 10 years the trustee was to determine who had invested most wisely—that is, who had the most money in his or her account. That person would receive his or her entire inheritance, together with accumulated income and appreciation. The loser would have his or her inheritance tied up for another 10 years.

This provision concentrated Dick's and Jane's minds wonderfully. Dick had gone to Wharton and was a devotee of John Bogle, founder of Vanguard. "You can't control the markets," Dick was fond of saying, "But you can control your costs."

Jane had a degree in art history from Vassar and had never heard of John Bogle. She called her lawyer and her accountant, interviewed several firms, and hired an advisor whose name would be very familiar to readers of this book. That advisor designed a complicated portfolio including eight asset classes, anchored by a 15 percent position in core bonds.

Dick rather liked the 15 percent bond allocation, but as for the rest of Jane's portfolio, he laughed softly up his sleeve. Unlike Jane, Dick made only one phone call: to Vanguard. He put 15 percent of his trust in core bonds and 85 percent in an MSCI All Country World Index Fund.

Over the next 10 years, Jane spent many hours meeting with her advisor, poring over her account statements and constantly tweaking her portfolio. She made many tactical moves, as recommended by her advisor. Sometimes her managers disappointed and had to be replaced.

Dick, by contrast, looked at his portfolio precisely once each year. If the portfolio was badly out of balance, he rebalanced back to his 85/15 allocation. Otherwise, he played a lot of golf.

Later, at Le Cirque

Ten years later, Dick and Jane and the gnome-like trust officer met for dinner at Le Cirque restaurant in New York. It was a wonderful, if expensive, meal, and as Dick and Jane were polishing off their gingerbread profiteroles, the trust officer got down to business. Opening his account book, the trust officer reported that, astonishingly, both Dick's portfolio and Jane's portfolio had returned, net of fees, precisely 9 percent per year over the 10-year period.

"A dead heat!" Jane exclaimed.

"Then I win!" Dick interjected. "Poor Jane sweated blood over her portfolio for 10 years, making changes at least every quarter. I, meanwhile, invested in an elegantly simple manner. Weird Uncle Fred would certainly declare me the winner."

"You may recall," the trust officer said, "That your Uncle Fred's rules stated that the beneficiary with the largest balance in his or her trust account at the end of 10 years would win." Pausing for effect, he flipped over to the last page of his account book.

"Dick," he said, "You've done well. Your final account balance is $1,936,412."

Dick smiled modestly. "I'll pick up the check," he said.

"Jane," the trust officer said, "You've also done well. Your balance is $2,387,938."

A mouthful of Chateau Mouton Rothschild exploded out of Dick's mouth. "W-*what?*" he stammered.

"You did well, Dick," said the trust officer, "But you forgot one thing: variance drain."

After the waiter had finished applying cold compresses to Dick's fevered brow, the trust officer continued.

"Dick," he said, "I see that you have your iPhone with you."

Dick had in fact been texting his girlfriend for the past few moments. "WON WON WON," he'd texted. But now, even as the trust officer was speaking, Dick texted, "forgt abov."

"Indulge me, Dick," said the trust officer. "Tap on your calculator app and run these numbers. Suppose that a $1 million portfolio appreciated

0 percent in year 1 and declined 0 percent in Year 2. What would the value of the portfolio be?"

Tap, tap, tap went Dick's fingers. "$1 million," he said.

"Excellent. Now suppose that the portfolio appreciated 20 percent in Year 1 and declined 20 percent in Year 2."

Tap, tap, tap. "$960,000," said Dick. "Hmm."

"Now, just for fun, let's suppose the portfolio appreciated 50 percent in Year 1 and declined 50 percent in Year 2."

Tap, tap tap. "$750,000," said Dick. "I'm beginning to get the point."

"Right," said the trust officer. "Everything else being equal, the higher the volatility, the lower the final dollars. A simplified formula for calculating variance drain, as your Uncle Fred well knew, is $C = R - \sigma 2/2$, where R is the mean return and σ is the variance in the return."

Dick's eyes glazed over, but Jane was riveted. She well remembered her advisor harping on this business of variance drain, constantly reminding her that she needed to keep her portfolio volatility at the absolute minimum consistent with her return objectives.

"While you have your calculator app open," the trust officer continued, "do this quick calculation for me. Assume a $1 million portfolio that compounds at 9 percent per year at a variance of 19 percent. That happens to be the volatility of your portfolio over that period."

Tap, tap, tap, went Dick's fingers. Tap, tap, tap, tap, tap.

"$1,936,412," said Dick. "What a coincidence."

"And now, assume a $1 million portfolio that compounds at 9 percent per year at a variance of 10 percent. That happens to be the volatility of Jane's portfolio over that period."

"I don't need to do it," Dick said. "It's going to come out to $2,387,938."

"So it is," said the trust officer. "You can't control the markets, but you can control your costs. More important, you can control your portfolio volatility."

"I'll get the check," said Jane.

Dick tapped on his contacts app. "Okay, Jane," he said, "What's the phone number of that financial advisor you've been using?"

But Jane was gone, having dashed off to the Ferrari dealership. Run, Jane, run!

Variance Drain Scenarios

For investors who may be interested in exploring the phenomenon of variance drain in greater detail, Table 4.1 shows six scenarios illustrating the accumulative impact of portfolio volatility on final wealth. In Scenario 1,

TABLE 4.1 Volatility and the Growth of Wealth

	Scenario 1	Scenario 2	Scenario 3	Scenario 4	Scenario 5	Scenario 6
Arithmetic Annual Return	10%	10%	10%	10%	10%	10%
Standard Deviation	0%	10%	20%	30%	40%	50%
Geometric Annual Return	10%	9.6%	8.3%	6.03%	2.58%	−2.42%
Starting Funds	$1,000,000	$1,000,000	$1,000,000	$1,000,000	$1,000,000	$1,000,000
Ending Funds	$2,593,742	$2,501,561	$2,219,353	$1,796,293	$1,290,725	$782,784
Total Period Return	159%	150%	122%	80%	29%	−22%

Source: Greycourt.

the portfolio grows at 10 percent per annum for 10 years with no volatility. (We can safely assume that this is impossible, but so is much of modern portfolio theory.) The terminal wealth of that portfolio is $2,593,742. To contrast an extreme example, consider Scenario 6, where the portfolio grows at 10 percent per annum for 10 years with a volatility of 50 percent. In this extreme-volatility scenario, the portfolio still boasts a 10 percent annual arithmetic return, but it actually loses money over the 10-year period, resulting in an ending value of only $782,784.

BEHAVIORAL FINANCE: ARE WE HARD-WIRED FOR FAILURE?

The findings of behavioral finance can make us feel that as investors we are doomed to fail. But human beings aren't automatons—we can become more self-aware and learn from our mistakes. This portion of the chapter briefly discusses some common behavioral failures and what we might do about them.[9]

We don't have to observe investor behavior for very long before concluding that human beings are hard-wired for investment failure. Large fortunes tend to disappear entirely in three generations. During bull markets investors lose all sense of perspective and load up on increasingly risky equities, as though prices could never go down. During bear markets investors give in to despair, selling out near the bottom, apparently convinced that equity prices are going to zero. Investors chase returns, piling into whatever sector or manager is hot, ignoring research showing that return-chasing behavior always ends in tears.

There is even an entire field of study—behavioral finance—devoted to the detailed analysis of how and why investors fail. Exotic-sounding concepts like "loss aversion" are really just academic jargon for investor behavior we see every day. These so-called "cognitive biases" lead us to behave in ways that are irrational, that is, that lead us into taking actions that are against our own interests.

It's very important for investors to recognize that we are optimized for wealth destruction, especially at inflection points in the capital markets (bull and bear markets). In effect, we seem condemned to own exactly the wrong portfolios at the peak of bull markets (i.e., too many stocks) and at the nadir of bear markets (not enough stocks).

The sequence of investor behavior always (always!) follows this pattern: As prices rise, investors enter a period of overconfidence, allowing equity exposures to exceed prudent levels. As more and more investors pile into the markets and brag about their great returns, "herding" behavior causes investors to own even more equities, as there now appears to be safety in numbers. Then, as prices begin to fall and wealth destruction takes hold, investors panic—at first individually and then, again, as a herd. Prices fall further and further and investors proceed to immortalize their losses by selling out.

Compounding this first round of wealth destruction is the next step in the pattern, where risk-seeking behavior has atrophied completely. Hapless investors, now sitting firmly on the sidelines (in cash), watch helplessly as the portfolios they used to own rebound powerfully. By the end of this cycle, capital has been destroyed on a massive basis.

Professor Odean on Behavioral-Inspired Wealth Transfer

Professor Terry Odean teaches at the Haas Business School at Berkeley. No one on the planet has studied individual investor behavior more closely than Odean, and what he has to say isn't pretty.

According to Odean, when an individual investor sells stock A and buys stock B, stock A outperforms stock B by (on average) 3.4 percent. In other words, the more stock ideas an individual investor has, the poorer he gets.[10]

And because there is always someone on the other side of these trades (institutional investors), individual investors are effecting a massive transfer of wealth from families to institutions. Odean and his colleagues once tracked every sale and purchase made on the Taiwan stock exchange for a year. Their conclusion was that every year, individual investors transferred an amount equal to 2 percent of the entire value of the Taiwan stock exchange to institutional investors.[11]

What Can We Do about It?

What is it about human beings, who in other aspects of their lives are capable of making rational decisions, that causes such wealth-destroying behavior? John Maynard Keynes once remarked that "markets are almost, but not quite, rational." True enough. But human investors are also almost, but not quite, rational. To be successful as investors we can't allow our emotions to dictate our actions. But this is very, very hard to do.

Here, for example, is how investors should behave: When stocks are cheap—near the bottom of bear markets—we would be near the top of our target equity range. When stocks are expensive—near the top of bull markets—we would be near the bottom of our range. When everyone else is buying, we would be sellers; when everyone else is selling, we would be buyers.

But ask yourself, is this the behavior you observe in other investors? Is it the behavior you observe in yourself? Of course not. If anything, we tend to do exactly the opposite. Human beings are rational, but not always: Our decision making is clouded and corrupted by our emotions. And the more powerful those emotions are—and greed and fear are right up there at the top of the heap—the worse our decision making will be. We are optimized for wealth destruction.

But all isn't entirely lost. There are steps thoughtful investors can take to minimize the likelihood of irrational action and to blunt its consequences. Michael Pompian's recent book addresses these very issues and is well worth looking into for investors who find their behavior chronically undermining their returns:[12]

- First, recognize the problem: Because we are emotional as well as rational creatures, we are prone to acting emotionally precisely when we should be acting rationally.
- Next, buy the right risk and keep it: If our comfort level suggests putting 65 percent of our assets in stocks, what in the world are we doing allowing that percentage to grow to 80 percent in a bull market or 40 percent in a bear market?
- Swim with a buddy: Find a friend, family member, or trusted advisor— someone whose money it isn't—who will watch your back, playing Devil's Advocate and holding you accountable for the emotional factors at play in your investment thinking and decision making.

- Study the past: Becoming familiar with the aftermath of bull and bear markets in the past will go a long way toward avoiding the "it's different this time" mentality.
- Own flight-to-quality assets: If you are spending 3 percent of your capital every year, consider setting aside 9 percent to 10 percent of the portfolio in laddered Treasuries. In a catastrophic bear market, you will have three years of spending in quality assets and at very little opportunity cost.
- Develop a crisis-management program: Decide now, while you are calm, exactly what you will do during the next period of market stress, whether that stress comes in the form of a bear or bull market. Write the program down, as well as the rationale for it. This step can help avoid the consequences of greed and fear, as well as avoiding troublesome behavioral responses such as framing, anchoring, and counterfactual thinking.

Before you know it, you'll be looking forward to the next market crisis!

EDITH AND THE HEADWINDS SHE FACES

> *If you swallow a toad when the market opens, you will encounter nothing more disgusting the rest of the day.*
> —Paraphrase of a remark attributed to the famous misanthrope, Nicolas de Chamfort (1741–1794)[13]

John Bogle, founder of The Vanguard Group and one of the wisest men in the business, once gave a speech titled, *Don't Count On It! The Perils of Numeracy*, in which he said, in part:

> *"My thesis is that today, in our society, in economics, and in finance, we place too much trust in numbers.* Numbers are not reality. *At best, they're a pale reflection of reality. At worst, they're a gross distortion of the truths we seek to measure."*[14] [emphasis in the original]

Oddly, nearly 20 years earlier, the eminent ecologist, Garrett Hardin,[15] had *bemoaned* our lack of numeracy:

> *"[L]iteracy is not enough ... we also need numeracy, the ability to handle numbers and the habit of demanding them. A merely literate person may raise no question when a journalist speaks of 'the inexhaustible wealth of the sea,' or 'the infinite resources of the earth.' The numerate person, by contrast, asks for figures and rates."*[16]

Far be it from me to choose sides between such towering *eminences grises*—let's just say that they are both right. Bogle is surely correct: Numerate investors have focused so hard on the gross return expectations developed by modern portfolio theorists that we have frequently missed the forest for the trees. But Hardin is also right: Frustration with investment results is all too often the result of innumeracy;, that is, our failure to appreciate the true import of the numbers we are looking at. The long and short of it is that investors who hope to preserve—much less grow!—their capital are faced with enormous challenges.

Let's follow Bogle's calculations,[17] as set forth in his speech, and see where they lead. Imagine an investor—we'll call her Edith—who at age 25 is the happy recipient of a $10 million inheritance from her grandmother.

Aside from being a very fortunate young lady, Edith is also no fool, having studied modern portfolio theory at Vassar. Edith decides that she would like to do the same for her own grandchildren one day—leave them a handsome inheritance. Noting that the long-term return on stocks is 11.3 percent,[18] Edith asks her family's longtime advisor, Mildew Trust Co., to invest the entire $10 million in stocks. A simple calculation tells Edith that, 50 years hence, when she is 75, she should be able to pass on to her grandchildren a trust fund *worth a cool $2.8 billion*. This should certainly earn her the distinction of Everyone's Favorite Grandma.

Unfortunately, Edith forgot a few things in her eagerness to generate terrific total returns and become Everyone's Favorite Grandma. Let's observe what is actually far more likely to happen to that wonderful sum of $2.8 billion.

The First Thing Edith Forgot: Variance Drain

Edith calculated her compound annual return on her trusty financial calculator, but she simply projected an 11.3 percent straight-line return. Alas, such returns don't happen in the messy real world of the capital markets.[19]

In other words, Edith isn't going to get an 11.3 percent return every year for 50 years. Sometimes her return will be better, sometimes worse. Specifically, assuming that her returns exhibit a standard deviation (S.D.) of 16, then two-thirds of the time her return is likely to fall between +27.3 percent and −4.7 percent. One-third of the time her return will be higher or lower than that.

And this variability in the return series—the price volatility that is inherent in owning equity securities—*will profoundly reduce her terminal net wealth*. Indeed, the greater the volatility of the returns the lower will be her terminal wealth, assuming that we keep the annual compound return constant.

If we assume, as we have, an average variability of 16 percent (roughly the S.D. of U.S. large-company stock returns over Bogle's measuring period), we find that the best Edith can hope for after 50 years of compounding is about $1.5 billion.[20] (Not to be an alarmist, but if the S.D. of Edith's returns turns out to be closer to 20 percent, as has been the case over longer periods of time with U.S. large-cap stocks, Edith's terminal wealth will be reduced further, to $1 billion. But let's hope for the best.)

We'll forgive Edith for this lapse—her grandchildren will still be billionaires—but variance drain is an issue to which too many investors (and all-too-many investment professionals!) don't pay enough attention.[21]

The Second Thing Edith Forgot: Inflation

As Bogle points out, over the past 50 years inflation has averaged 4.2 percent.[22] Therefore, the *real* rate of return on U.S. stocks is not 11.3 percent, but only 7.1 percent. Surely Edith doesn't want to leave her grandchildren worthless, inflated dollars, but real buying power. Alas, then, her original dream of leaving several billion dollars to her grandchildren has turned out to be a fantasy. The real value of her legacy is "only" $182 million. Even so, her grandchildren will be centimillionaires.

The Third Thing Edith Forgot: Investment Costs

Stock market indexes produce gross returns, but investors generate only returns that are net of the costs of obtaining them. These costs include investment management fees, brokerage commissions, spreads between bid and asked prices, and (something many investors overlook) market impact.[23] Bogle estimates that such costs come to at least 2 percent per year.[24] Although we are confident that Mildew Trust Co. could run that number up considerably higher, we'll settle for Bogle's number. Net of investment costs, therefore, Edith's return is likely to be about 5.1 percent. This brings her future grandchildren's inheritance down to $67 million. Well, even so, it's nothing to sniff at.

The Fourth Thing Edith Forgot: Taxes

If Edith had been born into life as a pension plan or charitable endowment, she could obtain her investment returns without worrying about having Uncle Sam as her investment partner. But as a taxpaying future grandmother, Edith must pay ordinary income tax rates on interest, dividends, and short-term capital gains, and capital gains tax rates on long-term gains. Bogle estimates that, over time, taxes eat up about 2 percent per year of investment returns.[25] This reduces Edith's annual returns to 3.1 percent and her grandchildren's inheritance to $25 million. A far cry from $2.8 billion, to be sure, but still better than a poke in the eye with a sharp stick.

The Fifth Thing Edith Forgot: Spending

A girl's gotta live somehow, of course, and though we don't know exactly how much of Edith's inheritance she will spend each year, we have some pretty good yardsticks to use for comparison purposes. The Internal Revenue Service, for example, requires private charitable foundations to spend 5 percent of their endowment values (on average), and many non-profit organizations also spend roughly 4 percent to 6 percent of their average endowment values each year.

Of course, these are largely[26] tax-exempt investors. But we also have the Uniform Principal and Income Act, which permits trustees to manage trusts as "unitrusts," adopting total return investment strategies and simply paying out to the income beneficiary a certain percentage of the value of the trust corpus each year. That percentage is fixed at 4 percent. Indeed, if a trustee wishes to pay out more or less than 4 percent per year it must seek court approval to do so. We harbor our private doubts about whether Mildew Trust Co. will spring for the unitrust idea, but we'll give them the benefit of the doubt and assume that they do. Her spending brings Edith's annual return down to—oops.

Edith's return has now moved into negative territory: −0.9 percent per year. In other words, instead of watching happily as her $10 million grows to $2.8 billion over the next half century, *Edith will be lucky to wind up with a bit over $3 million*, roughly 1/10 of 1 percent of what she hoped to get. Instead of Everyone's Favorite Grandma, Edith is likely to be remembered as That Old Witch Who *% ##@! Away Our Inheritance (this is a family publication).

WHAT SHOULD EDITH DO?

John Bogle has an answer to Edith's dilemma, and it will surprise no one who knows him: index funds.[27] Perhaps we can be forgiven for suspecting that Mr. Bogle would also view index funds as the cure for world hunger, the solution to the Arab-Israeli conflict, and a handy way to deal with killer asteroids. But in this case he's onto something. If Edith had used index funds instead of Mildew Trust Co., she would have reduced both her investment costs (index fund fees are very low and, given their relatively low turnover, generate lower frictional investment costs than do active managers) and her taxes as well (lower turnover translates into lower taxes).

Although we don't subscribe to Bogle's claim that the use of index funds will "reduce both investment costs and taxes almost to the vanishing point,"[28] if Edith could cut her cost- and tax-drag in half she would at least move her long-term rate of return back into positive territory. Adding 2 percent back to her bottom line annual return would bring her overall return to 1.1 percent and would allow Edith to grow her principal modestly and leave her grandchildren slightly more money than her grandmother left her.

But that's if everything else goes right, including Edith's ability to achieve an 11.3 percent annual compound return over 50 years. A far more likely outcome, we fear, is the one we reached a few paragraphs ago: Edith's $10 million inheritance will gradually diminish in value, not grow.

One reason we don't share Mr. Bogle's unlimited enthusiasm for index funds is that he was speaking about a retail investor—instead of starting with $10 million for purposes of his calculations, he started with $1,000—whereas we are speaking about families with a significant degree of affluence. Such families are almost always in far higher (and more complex) tax brackets than retail investors, and hence even the normal turnover and costs associated with the use of index funds will be problematic. Moreover, a U.S. large-capitalization index fund is hardly a clever portfolio strategy, nor one Edith—or any other investor—should adopt or stick with through thick and thin.

The point of all this is obvious: Investing capital successfully is a gigantic challenge. In fact, for families with significant capital, the stewardship of that wealth is almost certainly going to be the biggest challenge they will ever face. There may be *more important* challenges—raising happy and productive children, finding the right mate and making that relationship work—but we are largely programmed to undertake those challenges. Our everyday experience virtually from birth prepares us for those duties.

But almost no one is prepared to invest capital successfully. Our everyday experience is not only not on point, but is all-too-often positively counterproductive—because much about successful investing is counterintuitive.[29] Consider what Edith would have to do—and do it all right!—in order to grow her inheritance over a 50-year period:

- Edith would have to pay close attention to the problem of variance drain, by developing a sophisticated portfolio strategy that maximizes her investment returns while minimizing her risk (that is, the volatility of those returns). See the discussion earlier in this chapter.
- Because inflation is the insidious cancer of the investment world, quietly but effectively destroying wealth over time, Edith must anticipate this issue in her portfolio. She could permanently add assets to her portfolio

that tend to perform well during periods of unexpected inflation—real estate, commodities, inflation-protected bonds—but the problem with this tactic is that it will tend to bring down her long-term rate of return. See Chapter 13.

■ Like inflation, tax rates come and go, but like death, they will always be with us. Edith will need to adopt tax-efficient strategies *throughout* her investment portfolio, including:

■ Designing her asset allocation strategy using estimated after-tax (not pretax) returns, and adjusting expected correlations and volatilities as appropriate. Otherwise, she will not be deploying her assets efficiently. See Chapter 9.

■ Paying close attention to asset *location* issues. Putting the right investments in the wrong pockets can seriously compromise Edith's returns. See Chapter 19.

■ Developing tax-aware strategies in each asset class. A strategy that works in U.S. large cap, for example, will likely be suboptimal elsewhere in the portfolio. See Chapter 18.

■ Working with investment managers who exhibit proper awareness of the trade-offs between alpha generation and tax consequences. The production of alpha generally implies taking investment actions that will cause tax consequences for the investor. If the anticipated alpha isn't great enough to compensate the investor for the tax cost, the actions shouldn't be taken. See Chapter 18.

■ Aggressively harvesting tax losses throughout the year and across all managed accounts. See Chapter 18.

■ Edith will need to optimize (not minimize) her investment costs, primarily by (a) being aware of the damage such costs can cause to her portfolio, (b) allocating investment fees to asset classes and managers who actually have a chance to add value (and away from asset classes and managers who have little chance to do so), and (c) keeping portfolio turnover to a minimum. See Chapter 18.

■ If Edith is anything like the rest of us, her postinheritance lifestyle will be considerably more opulent than her preinheritance lifestyle. But although $10 million (or $100 million, or $1 billion) seems like a lot of money, there is no amount of money that profligate spending can't decimate over time. If Edith can keep her spending closer to 3 percent of her principal than 4 percent, she will have a far better chance to maintain and grow her wealth. See Chapter 21.

■ Finally, despite the many provocations Edith is likely to face over the course of half a century, she will need to stick to her long-term investment strategy with almost superhuman endurance.

CONCLUSION: PRESERVING WEALTH IS HARD SLOGGING

There is a Chinese parable about the sage who, having performed an important service to the empire, was asked by the emperor what he would like as his reward.

"All I ask," replied the sage, "is one grain of rice today, two grains tomorrow, four the next day and so on throughout the remainder of my poor lifetime."

"Ah," said the emperor, "surely you must ask for more than that!"

But the sage was firm in his modesty and the emperor agreed to the bargain. It was only a few months later that the emperor learned there was not enough rice in all of China to meet his obligation to the sage. Whereupon, recognizing that he had been evilly tricked, the emperor had the sage executed, bringing to a brutal but effective end this particular episode in the thrill of compound interest.

And that is precisely the point: Nothing compounds forever, or even for very long. Trees start from small seedlings but don't grow to the sky. Some species spawn thousands of offspring, threatening to overwhelm the earth, but few of these offspring live long enough to reproduce. Malthusians[30] have warned for more than two centuries that human population growth would quickly overwhelm the world's resources, causing the species to collapse. But it never happens: Between disease, famine, war, and economic and technological progress, the compounding never comes close to what a straight line projection would suggest.

Einstein is famously supposed to have remarked that, although the theory of relativity is certainly interesting, the most remarkable thing in the world is compound interest. But the truth is (talk about disagreeing with an *eminence grise*!) that the most remarkable thing about compound interest is how frequently its existence tends to be, as Hobbes said of the lives of the English poor, "nasty, brutish, and short."[31]

We have explored some of the reasons why the magic of compound interest rarely plays out in the lives of investors, but there are others as well: psychological factors, sociological issues, family dynamics, social and economic disruptions, the collapse of civil societies, and so on. But whatever the reasons, managing an investment portfolio in a taxable, family environment is the most formidable intellectual and psychological challenge Edith, or any other family, will ever face. The sad and simple fact is that most affluent families, faced with the challenges identified by Mr. Bogle and those just mentioned, will not grow their wealth over time, or even maintain it, but will watch helplessly as it disappears before their very eyes.

We are all so numerate these days that total return numbers trip lightly off our tongues. But those are sly devils as numbers go, Miltonesque Satans luring us into traps from which, unless we are very wary, there is no escape. And what escape there is involves not just a numerate understanding of how things actually compound and how they don't, but a very large degree of hard slogging, the paying of minute attention to the issues that count—if, that is, like Edith, we hope to pass along our capital intact to a future generation.

NOTES

1. One of the best books ever written about risk is Peter L. Bernstein's *Against the Gods: The Remarkable Story of Risk* (New York: John Wiley & Sons, 1998). It is highly recommended reading.
2. And, of course, luck. But Lady Luck always favors the bold.
3. If you could invest $1 million and compound it at 50 percent per year for 10 years tax free, your money would grow to $134,000,000. Venture capital profits aren't tax free, of course, but they are tax deferred (profits are generated many years after the investments are made) and almost always receive long-term capital gains treatment.
4. As discussed in Chapter 2, Andrew W. Mellon was probably the first American venture capitalist in the modern sense of the term. Mellon and his family and family bank provided the seed capital for such ventures as Alcoa, Koppers, Gulf Oil, and many other firms, as well, of course, as Mellon Bank itself (founded by Andrew's father, Thomas).
5. For this reason, purchases of *extremely* large blocks of a particular stock will often occur not on a stock exchange but in a negotiated transaction. In such a transaction the buyer(s) will often get a bargain, a true "quantity discount" relative to the price at which the stock is selling on the exchange. On the other hand, the seller will also get a bargain, because the discount he will give the buyer will be lower than the discounted price likely to result from the market impact of such a huge sale.
6. Even more extreme events are also characteristic of capital markets behavior, as I discuss later.
7. The only exceptions to this iron law of investment risk have to do with manager talent: A very few extremely talented managers appear to be able to generate excess upside price volatility (that is, excess positive rates of return) without concomitant downside price volatility. This trick seems to be easier to achieve in extremely inefficient sectors of the markets and where the manager is able both to buy stocks long and sell them short. But as we will see, it is extraordinarily difficult to identify these managers in advance. Moreover, adherents to the "strong" version

of efficient market theory would argue that most "talented" managers are really just lucky managers. If you flip hundreds of thousands of pennies, a very few, very "talented" pennies will come up heads 20 times in a row!

8. Several Nobel Prizes have been awarded for work in the field of behavior finance, including the 2002 award in economics, which went to Daniel Kahneman.

9. Special thanks to my partner, Jim Foster, for his contributions to this portion of the chapter, which originally appeared, in slightly different form, in my blog at www.Summitas.com.

10. As reported in *Forbes* magazine. See "The Average Investor Is His Own Worst Enemy," by David K. Randall (June 28, 2010).

11. Terrence Odean, Brad Barber, Yi-Tsung Lee, and Yu-Jane Liu, "Just How Much Do Investors Lose from Trade?" *Review of Financial Studies* 22, no.2 (2009): 609–632.

12. *Behavioral Finance and Investor Types* (New York: John Wiley & Sons, forthcoming, 2012). Pompian simplifies the complex world of behavioral investing so that investors and their advisors can get their arms around this large subject. He also provides clear guidance for how to avoid the behavioral traps that stand between investors and their financial goals.

13. Chamfort's actual remark was, "Swallow a toad in the morning and you will encounter nothing more disgusting the rest of the day."

14. John C. Bogle, *Don't Count On It! The Perils of Numeracy*, keynote address before the Landmines in Finance Forum of the Center for Economic Policy Studies at Princeton University, October 18, 2002.

15. Dr. Hardin is probably best known for his environmental parable, "The Tragedy of the Commons," *Science* 162 (1968): 1243–1248.

16. "An Ecolate View of the Human Predicament." This article appeared in McRostie (ed.), *Global Resources: Perspectives and Alternatives* (University Park Press, 1985). The essay was expanded into Hardin's book, *Filters against Folly* (New York: Penguin Press, 1985).

17. That is to say, I have applied the Bogle total return rates to a different set of dollars, just to make it more interesting.

18. Bogle, *Don't Count On It!* 5, note 2.

19. For another take on the important issue of variance drain, see Chapter 5.

20. Variance drain costs Edith 128 basis points of annual compound return, bringing her effective return (for net wealth purposes) down from 11.3 percent to 10.02 percent.

21. In adjusting our final wealth calculations for the variability of the returns, we have used the simple approximation: $C = R - \sigma^2/2$, where R is the mean return and σ is the variance in the return. See

Tom Messmore, "Variance Drain," *Journal of Portfolio Management* (Summer 1995): 106.

22. Bogle, *Don't Count On It!* 6, note 2.
23. Market impact refers to the fact that, because money managers tend to be huge investors, the mere fact that they are attempting to buy a stock will force the price of that stock up, substantially increasing the cost of the transaction. An identical problem occurs when the manager tries to sell a stock: The large sell order will cause the stock price to decline, reducing the sales proceeds. The combination of buying higher and selling lower has a huge impact on managers' abilities to produce competitive returns.
24. Bogle, *Don't Count On It!* 6, note 2.
25. Bogle, *Don't Count On It!* 6, note 2.
26. Private foundations pay a small excise tax on their investment income.
27. Bogle, *Don't Count On It!* 6, note 2.
28. Bogle, *Don't Count On It!* 7, note 2.
29. An entire branch of modern portfolio theory—behavioral finance—is devoted to studying the counterproductive actions people take when investing capital. In 2002 the Nobel Prize in economics was awarded to Daniel Kahneman for his pioneering work in "having integrated insights from psychological research into economic science, especially concerning human judgment and decision making under uncertainty," as the Royal Swedish Academy of Science said in its public announcement of the award. Much of Kahneman's work was done in partnership with Amos Tversky who, having died, was ineligible for the prize.
30. Thomas Malthus wrote his famous paper, "An Essay on the Principle of Population," in 1768.
31. Thomas Hobbes, *Leviathan* (1660). "No arts; no letters; no society; and which is worst of all, continual fear and danger of violent death; and the life of man, solitary, poor, nasty, brutish, and short."

CHAPTER 5

The Collapse of Ethical Behavior

Sadly, investors tend to have short memories. During the financial crisis that began in the summer of 2007 and didn't end until early 2009, thousands of investors were savaged by scandalous behavior by financial firms. But before the crisis disappears into the mists of history, let's take a look back at how the financial industry behaved. It's worth remembering.[1]

WHAT CAUSED THE CRISIS?

Most assessments of the 2007–2009 financial crisis identify as the source of the problem such issues as poor risk controls, too much leverage, and an almost willful blindness to the bubblelike conditions in the housing market. Well, maybe. These issues were certainly the proximate causes of the crisis we still find ourselves in, and if only one or two firms had drunk the Kool-Aid—a Drexel Burnham, let's say, or a Long-Term Capital Management—we could buy the usual nostrums as the full story.

But I suspect that the financial firms and their executives aren't quite so collectively stupid as this explanation would imply. I think there was something else going on, something that allowed intelligent people to persist in unintelligent behavior. In my view, poor risk controls, massive leverage, and the blind eye were really symptoms of a much worse disease: *The root cause of the crisis was the gradual but ultimately complete collapse of ethical behavior across the financial industry.* Once the financial industry came unmoored from its ethical base, financial firms were free to behave in ways that were in their—and especially their top executives'—short-term interest without any concern about the longer-term impact on the industry's customers, on the broader American economy, or even on the firms' own employees.

By a "collapse of ethical behavior" I mean exactly what I say—that the actions of many, if not most, of the large American financial firms (and of the many foreign firms that succumbed to the "American disease") would

strike an ordinary person as unethical—repulsive and scurrilous. But I also
mean something more specific to the long-term viability of the financial
industry, namely, the disappearance of any sense of fiduciary responsibility
to the ultimate client. Integrity and a sense of responsibility to the industry's
customers are at the core of what a financial industry must be all about;
otherwise, it's just a big Ponzi scheme.

AN UNSAVORY REHASH OF THE ETHICAL FAILURES

Painful as it is, let's take a look at some of the moral and ethical failures
of the financial industry, focusing on those that led directly to the current
financial crisis.

Ethical Failures in Subprime Lending

Back in the day, people obtained their mortgages from their local banker,
whom they likely knew personally. The banker held the mortgage paper on
his balance sheet, and hence cared very much whether the paper was good.
That was inefficient, of course, so matters began to evolve rapidly. By the
twenty-first century the system worked like this:

- Mortgage brokers developed to find borrowers. Because these brokers
  were paid on quantity ("How many mortgages did you bring me
  today?"), not quality ("How many *good* mortgages did you bring me
  today?"), and because they weren't carrying the paper on their own
  balance sheets, far too many of the brokers cared not at all whether
  the borrowers were engaging in thoughtful transactions or were being
  set up for heartbreak and penury. Once a mortgage was approved, the
  broker got paid and would never see the borrower again. To say that
  very large numbers of mortgage brokers behaved abominably is merely
  to state the obvious.
- Banks approved the mortgages after (maybe) reviewing the applications,
  but the banks had no intention of holding on to the paper. Instead,
  they needed to build leverage into their balance sheets, which meant
  getting this paper off the balance sheet as quickly as possible. (The paper
  was sold into mortgage pools that were in turn sold to unsuspecting
  investors.) Underwriting standards declined and eventually disappeared
  altogether. Did the banks care whether their shoddy practices resulted
  in lending money to people who couldn't possibly pay it back? Did
  the banks care what was likely to happen to the ultimate investors in
  this paper? Not likely. In fact, commercial banks scrambled to acquire

subprime lending banks so they could get ever more deeply into this seedy game.

- Because banks wanted to leverage their balance sheets (reusing their lending capacity over and over again), a market developed for pooled mortgages. Fannie Mae and Freddie Mac and the various megabanks and investment banks put these pools together and then sold them on to investors. Did the financial firms care about the quality of the paper they were selling, or the possible harm to investors who bought it? No, this was a volume operation: The more pooled vehicles the firms could form and the more they could reduce their costs (i.e., no actual checking on the quality of the paper), the higher the profits. What about the consequences for the end investors, many of whom were loyal, long-term clients of the financial firms?

- And what about the rating agencies, the last line of defense between a scamming industry and the ultimate investors? Turns out that conflicts of interest were so rife in the industry that at least one state attorney general is investigating the "symbiotic relationship" between the agencies and the banks and investment banks whose securities they were supposedly rating objectively. Were the rating agencies in the pockets of the financial firms, essentially selling their ratings to the highest bidder?

After a few years of this, is it any wonder that the subprime business blew up, destroying investor capital, wreaking havoc in the lives of overleveraged borrowers, and destroying confidence in the institutions, individuals, and regulatory agencies that not only allowed all this to happen, but in many cases actively cheered it on?

Ethical Failures among the Subprime Lending Banks

I think it likely that there is a special circle in hell reserved for subprime lending banks like Countrywide Financial, which were at the epicenter of the subprime collapse and at the epicenter of the ethical collapse. Looking back, it's clear that the main *raison d'être* of the subprime banks was to sell mortgage loans to people who couldn't afford them. Screaming ads were created to dupe people into applying for these mortgages, and new, highly misleading mortgage products were developed (teaser rates, Alt-A, etc.) to ramp up volume. Mortgage brokers were paid big fees to lure a steady stream of suckers into the scheme. There was a time when this would have been seen for what it was: predatory lending.

Strangely enough, prior to Countrywide and the rest, there had been a long and reasonably distinguished history of subprime lending in the United States. But here is the interesting point: Prior to Countrywide, lenders to less-than-prime borrowers employed *more* intensive underwriting, not *less* intensive underwriting, before making their loans. Loans to less creditworthy borrowers require more careful background checks, more complex structuring, different legal, collateral, and repayment conditions, and so on. Countrywide and others substituted volume for hard work, giving the entire subprime lending industry a bad name.

I single out Countrywide both because of the scale of its subprime lending activities and, especially, because of the egregious conduct of its CEO, Angelo Mozilo. Mozilo didn't build his huge personal fortune because he was smarter or harder working or more creative than other financial executives, nor even because he was luckier than others. He built it on predatory lending and by buying influence in high places. I described the predatory lending activities of Countrywide above, so let's turn to the sordid business of currying favor.

It is now clear that Countrywide attempted to suborn the support of key politicians, regulators, and other influential figures via a secret internal program (headed by loan officer Robert Feinburg, who became a whistleblower) that offered below-market terms on mortgages to individuals Countrywide wanted to curry favor with. This VIP-loan underwriting unit handled mortgage applications from what was known inside Countrywide as "Friends of Angelo;" that is, important figures Mozilo wanted to have in his pocket. The known list of "bribees" includes U.S. Senators, former Cabinet officers, Fannie Mae CEOs, judges, and many others.

Ethical Failures in Auction Rate Securities

To understand just how egregious the ethical failures were among the (many) financial institutions that sold Auction Rates Securities (ARS) to their clients, let's back up and look at the nature of ARS. The idea behind these securities was to create an instrument that would have a long-dated maturity but an interest rate similar to very short-term paper. This was attractive to municipalities and large nonprofit institutions that issued bonds, and it would also be attractive to individuals and institutions who wanted a cashlike risk level but a higher yield than cash. The way it worked was that a long-dated tax-exempt bond would be issued that would pay an interest rate determined by Dutch auctions held (usually) weekly or monthly.

Banks and investment banks eagerly structured such bonds on behalf of municipal clients, and even more eagerly hawked them to investors. Typically, an investor would receive a cold call from his broker, who would tout the exceptional benefits of ARS: "Safe as cash but with a higher yield!" The trouble was that ARS were "safe as cash" only so long as the periodic auctions were successful. If an auction failed, the issuer would pay a much higher penalty rate and the investor in the security would find that his funds were frozen. Some cash!

To ensure that the auctions wouldn't fail, the banks and investment banks agreed to support the auctions by stepping in if there weren't enough bids. In other words, regardless of what the fine print in the underwriting agreement said, the municipalities issuing ARS and the investors buying them clearly expected the banks to stand behind the paper. If there was no expectation that the banks would do so, then there could be no claim that the paper was safe. Thus, the ethical issue was clear from the outset: Either the banks had no obligation to support the auctions and hence the paper was very risky, or the banks did have such an obligation and the paper was safe.

I'm not suggesting that the financial firms intended to rip their clients off from the beginning, but I *am* suggesting that when the going got slightly tough (and after making big profits on ARS for years), the banks bailed, leaving their clients in the lurch. Specifically, the banks wanted to have their cake and eat it, too: Make money structuring the bonds and auctions and make more money selling ARS to investors, then abandon their clients when trouble first reared its head. The financial firms stood by and allowed ARS auctions to fail, causing issuers to pay egregious penalty interest rates and causing investors' funds to freeze up. Both the issuers and the investors were long-term clients of the banks.

Ethical Failures among the GSEs

GSEs are government-sponsored entities like Fannie Mae and Freddie Mac. They were[2]—let's face it—bizarre combinations of private corporations and federal bureaucracies. They were shareholder-owned corporations whose shares trade in the public market, but they were formed by the Federal government and their credit is backed by the government. The GSEs have been political footballs for many years, with (I simplify) Democrats defending them for their role in making housing affordable and Republicans vilifying them for usurping what should be the job of the private markets.

But let's sidestep the political heat and simply note that the role of the GSEs is simplicity itself: Using their government backing to borrow cheaply in the markets, the GSEs buy mortgage loans from banks, securitize these loans, and sell them to investors. Once the loans are off the banks' balance sheets, the banks can make more loans (thereby making mortgage loans more widely available). What a great racket! The investors who buy the mortgage-backed securities bear the interest rate risk and the taxpayers bear the default risk. What is it, exactly, that the GSEs bear? That's right—nothing! A 10-year-old could run Fannie Mae and Freddie Mac and not make a hash of it, to say nothing of, say, a GS-13 government bureaucrat. So how was it, exactly, that the CEOs of the GSEs screwed them up so badly?

The specific problem was that the GSEs tried to increase their profitability by not just buying loans, bundling them, and selling them, but also by holding billions of dollars worth of these mortgages on their own balance sheets. Anticipating how credit-challenged borrowers will behave, how housing prices will behave, and how these factors will affect the value of complex mortgage paper isn't a game for 10-year-olds or for government bureaucrats, and, as it turned out, it certainly wasn't a game for the ethically challenged CEOs of Fannie Mae and Freddie Mac (who leveraged these institutions' balance sheets 75-to-1). When the loans went bad, both the revenues and the balance sheets of the GSEs collapsed, and that was the end of them.

In any event, the more fundamental problem lay in the queer nature of these entities, half publicly held corporations and half federal bureaucracies, and in the ability of the senior executives to manipulate this hybrid nature to their own advantage. Thus, in their role as publicly held corporations the GSEs mainly behaved like government bureaucracies, and in their role as government bureaucracies they mainly behaved like publicly held corporations. The subprime debacle was a perfect example of this. When private firms began to make large numbers of loans to subprime borrowers, that should have been welcome news to a government bureaucracy—the private sector was stepping up to the plate, making housing more widely available, so there was no need to put taxpayer money at risk.

But the CEOs of the GSEs didn't see it that way. In their government bureaucrat role (making housing available) they behaved instead like private corporations, insisting that they couldn't lose market share. ("There goes the value of my stock options!") But in their publicly held corporation role, once subprime came unglued, the CEOs behaved like government bureaucrats, running to Congress for protection from the heat coming their way.

Indeed, because the mission of the GSEs was so simple, it's much more instructive to think of them not as players in the mortgage markets, but simply as get-rich-quick schemes for their senior executives. Thus greed-fueled executives like Franklin Raines, Leland Brendsel, Daniel Mudd, and Richard F. Syron made huge fortunes managing a completely risk-free operation. They hobnobbed with politicos in Washington to protect their sinecures and shamelessly pandered to public opinion with pious claims about their roles in keeping housing affordable. In fact, the GSEs under these executives so badly mismanaged themselves that the housing market has collapsed, thousands of homeowners have been thrown into the streets, and the taxpayers are about to be on the hook for billions of dollars to bail these blockheads out. Meanwhile, as noted, the executives got vastly rich.

The Contemptible Public Disclosures of Financial Firms

Publicly held firms in the United States have very strict obligations when it comes to making public disclosures. Among the more important obligations is to report material events in a timely and accurate way and to avoid making overly rosy claims about their business and financial condition. Failure exposes a firm and its executives to shareholder lawsuits and to SEC fines and penalties.

But was anyone listening to the public disclosures made by financial firms over the past year? Over and over again we were treated to impossibly optimistic statements from CEOs of financial firms, statements that were clearly designed to lure shareholders and customers into a false sense of security. Jamie Dimon of JPMorgan Chase told investors at the Investment Company Institute in May 2008 that the worst of the credit crisis "was 75 percent to 80 percent over." Lloyd Blankfein of Goldman told his shareholders at their annual meeting in April 2008 that "[W]e're at the end of the third quarter, beginning of the fourth quarter" of the crisis. At his own shareholder meeting, John Mack, then CEO of Morgan Stanley, said "You look at the subprime problem in the U.S., you would say we're in the eighth inning or maybe the top of the ninth." Even as the crisis was deepening toward the middle of 2008, Josef Ackermann, then CEO of Deutsche Bank, assured investors that the credit crisis was at the "the beginning of the end."[3]

Perhaps the best example of all occurred between December 2007 and September 2008 at Lehman Brothers. Late in 2007, Lehman's CFO assured the public that the firm was in fine shape and certainly wouldn't need to raise additional capital. The echoes of this breathtaking claim had barely died away when Lehman raised $6 billion (!) of additional capital, profoundly diluting the existing shareholders, who had just been assured that all was well. Despite frequent and ongoing assurances from Lehman's CFO and CEO that all was well, the firm continued to spiral downward, failing completely in September 2008. Were the Lehman executives, and those quoted above, simply delusional? Or were they engaged in something more disreputable; that is, lying to the public, to their customers, to their investors, and even to their own employees? Yet the regulators sat on their hands.

Shorting the Securities You Are Selling to Your Clients

Quite possibly the single most egregious example of unethical conduct in the financial industry was the practice of aggressively selling subprime debt-loaded mortgage paper to clients of a firm, while simultaneously and secretly shorting that paper for your own proprietary capital. The prime blackguard appears to have been Goldman Sachs, which noted in its 3Q07 quarterly report that, "Significant losses on nonprime loans and securities were more than offset by gains on short mortgage positions." It's possible—bizarre as it sounds—that this practice isn't illegal if you are an investment bank, but it is certainly disgraceful. If Goldman were, say, a registered investment advisor, and was selling subprime paper to its clients while secretly selling that paper short for its own account, the firm would be shut down by the regulators and its executives banned from the industry. But Goldman not only got away with this practice, but actively bragged about how smart it was.

Paulson Bernanke & Co. and the Conspiracy of Silence

The question naturally arises: While all this (and more) was going on, where was the U.S. government and its appointed regulators? Don't they exist to advocate the interests of consumers and investors against the combined might of the financial industry? And isn't it an important part of their responsibilities to head off trouble *before* it happens, rather than trying to clean up the mess afterward? And yet, from the beginning of the crisis in mid-2007 (and even long before), these folks have either been active cheerleaders for a financial industry whose actions should have been repulsive to them, or they have kept quiet and averted their gaze as one scurrilous activity after another paraded across the front pages.

Let's be clear—I'm not complaining about the actions PB&Co. took once the industry's unethical conduct began causing meltdowns of important companies. History will be the judge of that. But long before the companies collapsed, the Feds kept quiet and kept invisible. Where were they during the ARS scandal? It was the state attorneys general who knew a fraud when they saw it, while the Feds sat idly by. Where were the Feds when Goldman Sachs was secretly shorting mortgage debt it was aggressively selling to its customers? Where were the Feds when the GSEs were abusing their birthrights and mismanaging themselves into oblivion? Where were the Feds when financial firm CEOs and CFOs were lying to investors?

And where, most prominently, were the Feds while the financial firms were leveraging themselves into almost certain oblivion? PB&Co. claim to have been blindsided by the collapse of the entire investment banking industry, but if so it was an intentional refusal to see what was happening before their eyes. I have four words for them: Long-Term Capital Management (LTCM). Ten years ago LTCM overleveraged itself and so terrified the New York Fed that it organized a hasty rescue—not of LTCM and its investors, who were wiped out, but of the many other financial firms who had eagerly traded with LTCM on the way up and now didn't want to take their medicine.

We've had 10 long years to figure out what went wrong at LTCM and how to ensure that it wouldn't happen again. What were PB&Co. (and their predecessors) doing during those 10 years? They are like modern-day Rip Van Winkles, suddenly awakening in 2008, looking around and saying, "How could this have happened?"

A poor taxpayer might be inclined to think that the Feds cared far more about Wall Street than about Main Street as we were treated to the following spectacles:

- The bailout of Bear Stearns (taxpayers on the hook for at least $29 billion).
- The bailout of Fannie Mae and Freddie Mac (taxpayers on the hook for God-knows-what, but many billions).
- The banning of so-called "naked shorting"[4] *just for a handful of favored financial firms*, and eventually the banning of short selling for all financial firms in the United States (but not, of course, for nonfinancial firms).
- The opening of the Federal discount window for "dealers" (investment banks) for the first time since the Depression.
- The bailout of insurance giant AIG, by guaranteeing $85 billion of obligations. (This was later raised by another $38 billion—pretty soon we will be talking about serious money.)
- The $50 billion bailout of money market funds.
- The (so far) $700 billion bailout of every financial firm that has toxic paper on its balance sheet.

However important the TARP legislation might be, is it any wonder that public opinion was so solidly opposed to it that the House of Representatives at first voted it down?

HOW SCANDAL BECAME CRISIS

That large financial institutions ought to behave in an ethical manner seems perfectly obvious. But how bad behavior lay at the core of the current financial crisis may not be so apparent. I suggest that the medium of transmission from scandal to crisis followed two paths: loss of trust and abandonment of customers.

Trust

When a corporation behaves ethically, it might be functioning well or poorly, and it might be a good or bad firm to invest in, but at least we know how it will behave: It will obey the law, treat its employees respectfully, be honest in its public disclosures, honor its commitments, be a good citizen in the communities where it operates, and so on. But when a corporation (or, God help us, an entire industry) behaves badly, we have no idea what to expect. One day they are shoving mortgages down our throats and the next day you can't get a mortgage to save your life. One day they are standing behind ARS auctions and the next day they are nowhere to be seen. One day they are honestly disclosing their financial condition and prospects and the next day they are lying through their teeth. One day they are innocently selling us subprime paper and the next day they are quietly shorting that paper behind our backs.

Financial firms, much more than other firms, live and die on trust. The very definition of a bank is a firm that borrows short and lends long. A bank might take customer deposits—offering customers instant liquidity—and loan them to people who want 30-year mortgages. An investment bank might borrow in the overnight market and make trades that won't unwind for weeks or months. So long as people trust the financial firms, all is well. But once trust evaporates the jig is up—there is no way a bank can call in long-term assets to pay off the short-term demand.

Unethical behavior in the financial industry eventually became so widespread that trust evaporated—no one could possibly know what firms in the industry would do next, and so no one would play ball with anyone in the industry. This caused the failure of the weakest, most leveraged, least trusted firms, and it caused commerce to freeze up for firms that were stronger but still distrusted. Even inside the industry, banks wouldn't lend *to each other* because each believed that the other was lying about its own financial condition. Thus does a breakdown in trust lead directly to a financial crisis that cannot be fixed until trust—not just capital—is reestablished.

Customers

The disappearance of any sense of fiduciary responsibility to the financial industry's customers caused the industry to become unmoored. So long as financial firms felt an obligation to their clients, there were serious limits on how bad their behavior could become. But once they learned that customers could be treated badly and the only consequence was that profits went up, the industry went straight to hell in a handbasket.

Mortgagors, buyers of ARS, shareholders, bondholders, owners of subprime paper, and wealth management clients were all abandoned by the industry, and along with that abandonment went any limits on how the firms might behave. As I noted above, a sense of responsibility to its customers is the only legitimate reason for a firm to exist. Once the customers walk—and they have walked away from the financial industry in gigantic numbers—the industry is doomed.

WHY SUCH AN ETHICAL SWAMP?

Each of the scandals just described has been widely covered in the general and financial press. But what hasn't been so much commented on is the *pattern* of behavior, the cascade of scandal upon scandal, the consistency of ethical lapse unknown in any other industry.

I've spent considerable chunks of my professional career in other industries—law, business, the foundation world, and so on—so I can say from firsthand experience that the private moral character of financial industry professionals is no better or worse than that of people in any other industry. So why is the financial industry so prone to scandals, such a positive disgrace to American industry and the free market system in general? It's a bit of a mystery, to be sure, but here are some suggestions.

Hedge Fund Wannabees

Investment banks are, technically, broker-dealers, and for roughly a century the emphasis was decidedly on the broker aspect. A broker isn't a principal in a transaction, but an intermediary, a facilitator. If a Merrill Lynch broker convinced his customer to sell IBM and buy GE, he made a commission on the transaction but wasn't a principal in it. IBM, GE, and the customer could all go broke and the broker wouldn't be affected.

But by 1975, customers had had enough and commissions became negotiable. With the advent of competition, overall commission rates declined,[5] as did the revenue broker-dealers received from that source. In 1965, for example, broker-dealers earned 61 percent of their revenues from commissions, but by 1990 this had dropped to 16 percent.[6] Most of the wirehouses went out of business or fled for safety to banks and investment banks—Smith Barney to Citigroup, Paine Webber to UBS, Dean Witter to Morgan Stanley, and so on.

Because broker/dealers had to look elsewhere for revenues and profitability, they stopped being mainly brokers and became mainly dealers. Unlike a broker, a dealer is a principal, risking its own capital. There is nothing wrong with being a dealer, of course, but heeding the Wall Street axiom that "if some is good, more is better," the broker-dealers—now mainly dealers—began to add significant leverage to their trades. In the mid-1970s broker-dealers operated with leverage of about 6x. In other words, they had 16 cents of equity for every dollar of risk. But by 2006, broker-dealers were operating with about 30x leverage—they now had only 3 cents of equity for every dollar of risk.

In other words, broker-dealers had become very large hedge funds. Executives at broker-dealers had long envied the compensation earned by the best hedge fund managers, and eventually they succeeded in converting themselves into exactly that: gigantic, massively leveraged hedge funds. For example, in 2007 Goldman Sachs generated 68 percent of its revenue not from commissions or investment banking, but from proprietary trading.

As everyone knows, hedge funds are private partnerships, and if the manager of a hedge fund behaves stupidly—leveraging his fund 30-to-1, for example—his investors will get wiped out. But so what? It might be a private tragedy for the hedge fund manager and his investors, but it's hardly a matter for public concern.

One of the reasons the activities of individual hedge funds aren't matters of broad public concern is that hedge funds don't have *clients*, they have *investors*. But investment banks that are hedge fund wannabees *do* have clients, and unfortunately those clients are often on the other side of trades made by the banks' prop desks. If a hedge fund wants to short subprime paper, it might be a good or bad idea but it isn't an ethical issue. But when an investment bank shorts paper it is simultaneously selling long to its clients, the bank has sunk so deeply into a moral swamp that there is no getting back out. Moreover, as everyone knows, prop desks at banks routinely front-run client positions that the bank learns about precisely because these investors are clients of the firm's investment banking, wealth management, or capital markets groups.

Finally, unlike hedge funds, investment banks very much *are* a matter for public concern, in these very direct senses: Their shareholders include ordinary American investors (not just high-net-worth folks), and their activities are so vast, their influence on the broad economic world so crucial, and their interconnectedness so extreme that they can rarely be allowed to fail. Thus, American society finds itself in a world where "heads, the investment banks win; tails, the taxpayers lose." If the wild risks investment bankers take pay off, they make millions; if the risks collapse, taxpayers bail them out. It's not just a stupid way to run an economy, its morally abhorrent. If taxpayers are going to have to bail institutions out of their own cupidity, taxpayers need to set the rules under which those institutions can operate.

"When the Music Plays You Have to Dance"

With these memorable words, Chuck Prince, the former CEO of Citigroup, ran his company into the dumpster. Prince was saying, in longer words, something like this: "Look, pal, I know perfectly well that I'm stuffing my own balance sheet full of toxic waste and that all this nonsense can only end badly. But everyone else is doing the same thing and making tons of money doing it, so if I don't do it my board and shareholders will have my scalp."

Prince was possibly right—financial firm boards and shareholders were all enthusiastic participants in the let's-make-hay-today-and-to-hell-with-tomorrow follies. But did Prince ever stop to think about whether it was the right thing to do? Did his board pay him tens of millions of dollars to act like a lemming? Somewhere along the way, somewhere in all the muck of greed and breach of fiduciary obligations and the to-hell-with-the-customers attitude, Prince lost his moral compass. And he was in good company across the entire industry.

Compensation Follies

American industry in general has a serious problem with the compensation of its senior executives. Time after time, a CEO runs his company into the ground, devastating shareholders and employees, then glides off into the sunset, sheltered by his golden parachute.[7]

But bad as the general run of publicly held companies are, the financial institutions are much, much worse. Exactly why this should be so has been the subject of much commentary. It has been pointed out, for example, that whereas a typical corporation pays out about 25 percent of its gross revenues in compensation, financial firms can pay out as much as 60 percent.[8] But this can't be the full answer, because many firms in service industries pay out similar percentages of revenues in compensation (law firms, public accounting firms, consulting firms) but don't pay the scandalous compensation observed in the financial sector.

I think financial firms are driven by an unusual combination of circumstances: They are characterized in spades by the greed and short-term incentives that too-often dominate compensation at the top of other publicly held corporations. But they also have access to massive leverage, which magnifies both the upside of their risky behavior and also the downside. Thus, a run-of-the-mill public company CEO might use short-term tactics to boost his firm's quarterly earnings and therefore his compensation, only to see the earnings fall apart a few quarters later. He has already banked his winnings and laughs all the way to the bank. At financial firms, short-term tactics accompanied by massive leverage (thoughtfully made available by PB&Co. and their predecessors) produces huge short-term profits and huge short-term compensation. But when the wheel turns, it's not just that quarterly earnings sag—it's that the firm files for bankruptcy or is bailed out by the taxpayers.

The financial firms, which could have used cash flow to improve their products and services, or at least distributed it out in dividends, instead allocated that cash flow to compensation, especially for top executives. The contrast between the staggeringly high compensation paid to, and the breathtaking incompetence exhibited by, financial firm CEOs, is almost beyond belief. Stan O'Neal was paid $172 million at Merrill to drive the firm into the ground. James Cayne was paid $161 million to (reportedly) play cards, go golfing, and smoke dope while Bear Stearns collapsed. By the end of 2007, Richard Fuld had already made most of the mistakes that would destroy venerable Lehman Brothers, and for that he was paid a $45 million bonus in December 2007.

I wish I could argue that the greed and self-absorption of financial industry executives was a major cause of the financial crisis, but unfortunately I don't quite believe it. What I do believe is that the compensation follies complicated and prolonged the crisis in two ways. First, at the margin, the compensation practices in the industry represented a misallocation of capital, that is, away from improving products, services, risk controls, and so on and into the pockets of executives. Had the industry invested this capital more efficiently, it might have foreseen and thus avoided some of the more devastating problems it now faces.

More important, the greed of the financial executives so revolted the American public that policymakers' hands have been tied to some extent in dealing with the crisis. The TARP program was initially rejected by the House of Representatives precisely because enraged constituents opposed it in overwhelming numbers. When industry figures were summoned to appear before Congressional committees, we were treated to the spectacle of demonstrators holding up signs reading "Shame," "Cap Greed," and "Jail not Bail." Thus, as the Treasury, the Federal Reserve, and others tried to deal with the crisis, they faced consistent voter skepticism.

Conflicts upon Conflicts

I have elsewhere[9] detailed the conflicts of interest that permeate the financial industry, with an emphasis on the damage done to investors by these conflicts. But I might also speculate about the damage done to the ethical compass of people who have worked in conflicted institutions for their entire careers. If you know you are selling inferior in-house products to your customers, and if you observe that, time after time, you are richly rewarded for doing so, might you not, at the end of the day, forget that what you are doing is wrong?

Virtually all the top executives at America's financial firms have spent their entire lives living in a closed-architecture world. Is it any special wonder that they care so little about their clients? Just to pick one obvious example, in 2008 Citigroup removed Sally Krawcheck, the most prominent woman on Wall Street and the head of global wealth management at Citi. One key irritant between Krawcheck and Citi CEO Vikram Pandit was that Krawcheck (a former independent analyst at Bernstein) wanted the financial advisors at Smith Barney to operate in an open-architecture manner, offering the best possible products to their customers. Pandit, you will not be surprised to learn, wanted the advisors to stuff customer portfolios full of Citi products, good, bad, or indifferent.[10]

WHERE DO WE GO FROM HERE?

No one can doubt that excesses like too much leverage, poor risk controls, and a firm belief that housing prices could grow to the sky were the immediate cause of the financial crisis. But unless we are to believe in mass hypnosis—or perhaps that simply walking down Wall Street caused people to inhale stupid germs—the real question is why an entire industry collapsed at once, virtually every firm destroyed or badly crippled, the very face of the American financial sector changed unrecognizably in just a few months.

My suggestion here is that the common root cause of such destructive activity was the collapse of ethical behavior across the financial industry, and in particular the disappearance of any sense of fiduciary responsibility to the industry's customers.

Given the execrable conduct of the industry and its executives, one solution to the problem might be to tear the industry down and rebuild it according to very different principles and with very different people at the top. Few would put forth such a radical idea, of course. But I don't have to—it happened before our eyes. Almost as though an avenging Old Testament God had stormed down to wreak havoc on the unjust, the worst offenders in the industry—James Cayne/Bear Stearns, Dick Fuld/Lehman, Angelo Mozilo/Countrywide—were struck down, their firms gone from the face of the earth.

And vengeance has been wreaked on others in the industry as well, from Goldman and Morgan Stanley to WaMu, AIG, and Wachovia. Almost no one stood up for these firms and their now-beleaguered executives, because almost no one saw them as innocent victims of a financial crisis not of their making. Everyone saw the firms and their top people for what they were: greedy, hopelessly compromised, and getting pretty much what they richly deserved. To the extent that anyone advocated a bailout, it was solely to protect innocent bystanders, to minimize the externalities.

But of course there were many innocent victims of the crisis, and there will be more: hardworking employees who contributed nothing to the demise of their firms, but who lost their life savings and have dim prospects for similar employment elsewhere; innocent investors who had the simple misfortune to believe the CEOs and CFOs who assured them that recovery was just around the corner; homeowners who swallowed the industry's insistence that they could afford the houses they were buying; and all the rest of us, mired in a deep bear market and looking forward anxiously to the coming recession.

CONCLUSION: FIXING THE INDUSTRY

Alas, in the four years since the crisis came under control in the United States (it's still raging in Europe), little has changed. In early 2012, a Goldman Sachs vice president, Greg Smith, resigned publicly by publishing his letter of resignation in the *New York Times*. Smith said in his letter that "the environment [at Goldman Sachs] now is as toxic and destructive as I have ever seen it ... I truly believe that this decline in the firm's moral fiber represents the single most serious threat to its long-run survival."[11] Goldman may be the worst offender, but the other large banks aren't far behind.

At great expense to the taxpaying public, the banks have been yanked out of their own cesspools. But however urgent it may have been to preserve the financial system, the cost has been staggering, in both dollars and in ethical terms. It is patently clear that one doesn't convert rogue companies into model corporate citizens by merging them into each other or by converting them into bank holding companies.

Instead, I modestly propose the following three reforms:

1. The financial industry needs to adopt a laserlike focus on its customers and their welfare, in any event placing client interests far above the compensation interests of its executives.
2. The industry needs to eliminate its infamous conflicts of interest, and to avoid even the appearance of conflicts.
3. Finally, the industry needs to demand ethical behavior across the board from its executives and employees, even if it is sometimes inconsistent with short-term profits, and this behavior needs to be both exemplified and enforced by top executives.

Anyone who has watched developments in the financial industry over the past five years would likely find these suggestions to be Pollyannaish in the extreme. And no doubt top executives in the industry will be horrified. But in every other industry these behaviors are routine, ingrained in employees from their earliest years and demanded by top executives and boards of directors.

Emphasis on serving the customer is and has been for many years a mantra in most industry sectors. Ideas like Six Sigma, TQM, kaizen, quality circles, and the Toyota Production System are designed to help companies deliver the best possible products and services to their customers—an idea apparently unknown in the financial industry. As for conflicts of interest, they have been ruthlessly rooted out of most industries, including even the nonprofit world and the political world. But conflicts are mainly what the financial industry is all about: "No conflict, no interest."

But I remember back in 1987 when Paul O'Neill, later to be Secretary of the Treasury, became CEO of Alcoa. Alcoa was then a sinking, Rust Belt aluminum producer, its stock price long mired in the single digits.[12] If O'Neill had spent his career in the financial industry it's not hard to guess what he would have done: cut costs, cut customer service, demand longer hours from his employees. This would have raised quarterly earnings briefly, O'Neill would have cashed out, and when Alcoa sank even further into the muck he would have glided off into the sunset supported by his bright golden parachute.

But not being from the financial industry, none of this occurred to O'Neill. Instead, he focused his major attention on *worker safety*. At the time, Alcoa had one of the worst safety records in its or any other industry, and—guess what?—employees reciprocated by demonstrating a like concern for the firm and its customers. O'Neill demonstrated something else: that he cared about employees and their safety. Even low-ranking employees were given the power to stop production if they saw a safety issue. And the employees responded in kind, converting this sleepy also-ran into one of the most efficient, safe, and quality-conscious firms in the world. Profits soared, as did Alcoa's stock and the firm's reputation. Sure, O'Neill made a lot of money as Alcoa's CEO, but he earned it and he is as revered today among Alcoa employees as he was way back then.

Is anyone on Wall Street listening?

NOTES

1. This chapter is adapted from Greycourt White Paper No. 44: The Financial Crisis and the Collapse of Ethical Behavior (2008), available at www.Greycourt.com.
2. Postcrisis, the GSEs had to be nationalized.
3. See, generally, Jeffrey Goldfarb and Richard Beales, "It's Time to Feast on Crow," *Wall Street Journal* (July 21, 2008): C8. Regarding Lehman, see Floyd Norris, "Lehman's Assurances Ring Hollow," *New York Times* (September 12, 2008): C1, and "The Two Faces of Lehman's Fall:

Private Talks of Raising Capital Belied the Firm's Public Optimism," *Wall Street Journal* (October 6, 2008): 1.

4. Naked short selling occurs when a short seller fails to borrow a shorted stock before the settlement date.

5. Commission rates for small investors actually went up, but commissions for the major traders went down by more than half. Eventually discount brokerage firms arose to offer lower commissions to smaller investors as well.

6. "Eye on the Market," Michael Cembalest, JPMorgan Chase (September 10, 2008).

7. Even the best-parachuted CEOs outside the financial sector would envy Alan Fishman, whose golden parachute at WaMu entitled him to $19 million for serving as CEO *for 19 days* at the date WaMu failed.

8. James Grant, "Why No Outrage?" *Wall Street Journal* (July 19–20, 2008): W1.

9. Greycourt White Paper No. 24: A Modest Proposal: Let's End Conflicts of Interest in the Wealth Advisory Business (2003), available at www.Greycourt.com.

10. Eric Dash and Geraldine Fabrikant, "A High-Ranking Woman Is Out at Citi," *New York Times* (September 23, 2008): C7.

11. Greg Smith, "Why I Am Leaving Goldman Sachs," *New York Times* (March 14, 2012).

12. Adjusted for stock dividends and splits. Under O'Neill, Alcoa's stock price peaked at about $35/share.

CHAPTER 6

Finding the Right Advisor

We didn't underperform.
You overexpected.

—Financial advisor to his client

Not so long ago, finding an overall financial advisor was like falling off a log: Most families engaged the local bank trust department. A few larger or more sophisticated families might wind up at one of the national trust banks—Bessemer, U.S. Trust, Northern Trust, Wilmington Trust. But that was about it. It wasn't until about 30 years ago that even the very largest American families began to migrate out of the trust department backwaters and into a world that resembled what today we would call an open-architecture approach to wealth management.

But what a change a generation or two can make! Today, the problem for families is not lack of choice, but too many choices. The traditional banks and trust companies are still around, though many are unrecognizably changed. Investment banks, insurance companies, and brokerage firms have gotten into the business of advising wealthy families. Larger money management firms have begun to target substantial families. And, of course, there are the various open-architecture competitors that have come along in the past 10 or 15 years.

Given the huge range of choices, the primary challenge for families is how to narrow the field down to a manageable group of finalists. To help families make sense of the complex world of financial advisors, I will walk through the important subject of open-architecture advice, talk in some depth about the fastest growing advisory platform (the so-called "outsourced chief investment officer" model) and then move into some specific advice for finding the right advisor for your family.

OPEN ARCHITECTURE AS A DISRUPTIVE BUSINESS MODEL IN THE ADVISORY WORLD

One of the most important steps a family can take if it wishes to preserve and grow its wealth over time is, of course, to find the right advisor. For years this was difficult, bordering on impossible, because every firm in the advisory business was really just trying to sell something. But all this changed dramatically in the 1990s when open-architecture advisory services became available to families. To give families some perspective on this important—indeed, revolutionary—event, this chapter will describe the impact of open architecture not so much on families, but on the industry in general.[1]

What Is Open Architecture and Why Is It So Important?

Open-architecture financial advisors offer family investors objective, unconflicted advice because they have separated the business of giving advice from the business of selling proprietary investment products. This advisory platform has powerful appeal to investors.

Investors searching for advisors today will find that the open-architecture revolution has had a profound effect on the way that even the most traditional financial advisors now do business. Understanding the impact of open architecture can help investors make more informed decisions as they navigate their way through the financial services minefield.

A "disruptive business model" is one that blindsides existing competitors in an industry so completely that they are largely unable to defend against it, essentially ceding industry leadership to a new generation of firms. Disruptive business models were first identified in 1995 by J. L. Bower and Clayton M. Christensen in their classic 1995 Harvard Business Review article, "Disruptive Technologies: Catching the Wave." The theory of disruptive innovation has been described by Christensen, who has become the dean of disruption theory, like this:

> We view disruptive innovation as a dynamic form of industry change that unlocks tremendous gains in economic and social welfare. Disruption is the mechanism that ignites the true power of capitalism in two ways. First, it is the engine behind creative destruction.... Disruption allows relatively efficient producers to blossom and forces relatively inefficient producers to wither. This destruction, and the subsequent reallocation of resources, allows for the cycle of construction and destruction to begin anew, enhancing productivity, lowering consumer prices, and greatly increasing economic welfare.[2]

Examples of disruptive business models obsolescing existing competitors, even huge, powerful ones, are legion. Looking at the past, for example, consider Henry Ford's introduction of the assembly line into the auto industry, which eliminated dozens of competitors in one fell swoop; the introduction of the telephone, which nearly eliminated the telegraph (and marginalized then-powerful Western Union); the introduction of the table-top copier not by Xerox, IBM, or Kodak, but by Canon and Ricoh; the introduction of the personal computer, not by IBM or Digital (who had pioneered the minicomputer), but by dozens of theretofore unknown companies; the introduction of discount brokerage, not by the giant full-service firms but by Schwab and others (causing most of the full-service wirehouses to disappear).

Open Architecture in the Financial Industry

Open architecture is a disruptive business model that began to appear in the financial services industry in the mid-1990s. As is usually the case with disruptive models, open architecture was invented and launched not by the traditional competitors in the business—money managers, investment banks, traditional banks, and trust companies—but by theretofore unknown start-up boutiques. The existing firms had known since at least the mid-1970s that conflicted advisory models, in which conflicts of interest were endemic, were harmful to investors and needed to be replaced with a new model. Yet, like the dominant firms in other industries that had been brought to grief by earlier disruptive models, the dominant firms did nothing (or, as we will see, very little) while the aggressive new firms ate their lunch.

Why didn't the traditional financial advisors immediately embrace open architecture? There are numerous reasons, of course, but let's focus on the most important of them, using examples provided by Christensen.

Reason 1: Big Firms Can't Do Small Things When a disruptive business model is introduced, it is often a "stealth" model, introduced on such a small scale that even though existing competitors are well aware of it, its footprint is too small to be of interest. By the time it has become clear that the market for the new model is huge, it is too late for the existing competitors—the new firms own the business.

This situation has prevailed in the open-architecture world from the beginning. The global market for open-architecture services was simply too small to be appealing to the huge financial powerhouses that then dominated the advisory business. These firms weren't unaware of open architecture; they simply saw no reason to enter a business that couldn't possibly have a significant effect on their gross revenues or bottom lines.

Meanwhile, the open-architecture business has been "branded" by a group of still-boutique-sized firms that will likely own the market by the time the big firms have taken a serious interest.

Reason 2: Existing Competitors Often Have Outmoded Cost Structures Sometimes a new business model simply can't be adopted by existing competitors because their cost structures are too high. Sears Roebuck & Co. was an American retailing icon, for example, but its position was undercut by Wal-Mart's far lower costs.

Because profit margins had for decades been unusually high in the asset management business, cost structures in the industry also grew out of control. Enormous salaries were paid to people of very modest talents, and low-margin back-office tasks were conducted out of Class A real estate space in midtown Manhattan.

Open architecture disrupted this cozy world in at least two ways. First, by controlling costs, the open-architecture firms were able to operate profitably in a business the traditional firms had priced themselves out of. Second, open architecture disrupted the prevailing pricing model for asset management. In the pre-open-architecture world, any firm with a brand name could charge sky-high fees and get away with it. In the post-open-architecture world, only the most elite firms, those with the demonstrated ability to add value consistently across time, could hope to charge the kind of fees that used to be routine. In the post-open-architecture world, everyone else is a commodity.

Reason 3: Corporate Cultures Are Hard to Change If a new business model requires existing firms to change their culture in radical ways, it will be unlikely to happen. When Charles Schwab and the other discount brokers launched their disruptive business model, we might imagine that the old-line wirehouses would have quickly adopted the new model. But in fact the old-line firms couldn't change, and most of them disappeared.

Open-architecture firms and old-line financial advisory firms are both engaged in the financial advisory business, but their cultures could hardly be more different. The traditional model is all about asset gathering (sales), whereas open architecture is all about improving client investment performance. Changing the culture of the old-line firms would require changing the personnel, starting at the top and working all the way down the line.

Reason 4: A Large Installed Customer Base for the Old Products Is a Huge Obstacle Like firms in other industries that were undone by new, disruptive business models, traditional financial advisory firms have thousands of investors who like the product they are getting. Many traditional firms are listening to these customers and ignoring the "early adopting" customers, investors who have migrated to the open-architecture model. Because the old firms aren't actually losing clients, they have failed to notice that their businesses aren't growing nearly as fast as they should be growing. Eventually a tipping point will be reached when the existing customers of the old firms will suddenly see the light, demand open architecture, and abandon the old-line firms.

In the face of the open-architecture challenge, the traditional competitors have typically responded in one of the following ways:

Some competitors have left the business. The decisions by huge global firms like Citicorp and Merrill Lynch to exit the asset management business will seem astonishing to anyone not familiar with the open-architecture revolution. But to those who understand the current dynamics in the industry, it was clear that these huge firms simply could not both compete effectively in the business and also manage their conflicts of interest.

Some competitors have adopted the new model wholesale. A few firms, especially those who were already also-rans in the asset management business, have converted themselves to true open-architecture advisory firms, eliminating their proprietary products altogether.

Some competitors are still in denial. A few advisory firms still maintain that they can both advise investors effectively and also sell those investors proprietary products. This model is disappearing fast, but it is not completely gone.

Most competitors are straddling the fence. By far the most common response to the challenge presented by open architecture is to straddle the fence; that is, to continue to offer high-profit-margin proprietary products while also offering outside managers and products.

The Impact on Investors

What is the impact of all this change on investors searching for new advisors? The main challenge for investors is the turmoil that is roiling the industry as a result of the introduction of open architecture. In a free market economy, industry ferment is typically a long-term positive for customers, but in the short run confusion can reign. Here are a few suggestions for investors who may be searching for advisors in a transforming industry:

- Investors may find it prudent to avoid the few remaining closed-architecture firms. Although some of these firms are quite competent at managing their conflicts, the model is dying out and the best professionals are fleeing. The endgame for the best of these firms is life as a pure asset manager, with no advice offered.

- A healthy skepticism may be appropriate for firms that have recently converted to pure open-architecture platforms. Not only do most of these organizations lack experience offering investors strategic advice, manager recommendations, and consolidated performance reporting, but many of them will badly underestimate the challenges of managing an open-architecture business.

- The majority of firms—those now offering both open architecture and proprietary options—may appear to offer the best of both worlds, but in fact these firms tend to suffer from the objection cited above—lack of experience offering open-architecture products—and also to have an incentive to push higher-margin proprietary products even when superior open-architecture products are on the menu. Many of these firms haven't even invested in the infrastructure required to offer an open-architecture product, but have outsourced this activity.

- Pure open-architecture advisors have great surface appeal, but many of these firms are new, small, and untried. Due diligence and reference checking are required.

For investors willing to do their homework and conduct serious diligence on prospective advisors, the open-architecture era offers vastly greater choice and many attractive advisory models that possess fewer conflicts of interest than traditional models. But *caveat emptor* still prevails: Investors who fail to recognize the impact of open architecture on the industry are likely to come to grief.

THE OUTSOURCED CIO MODEL

Most family investors are familiar with the standard, nondiscretionary advisory model. The advisor—hopefully, an unconflicted one—makes recommendations and the family accepts or rejects them.

But over the past decade, and accelerating rapidly in the last few years, the so-called "outsourced chief investment officer" model for delivering financial advice has grown very rapidly.[3] (Note that some publications refer to this model as the OCIO model.) In the experience of many advisors, client requests for discretionary advice now outnumber client requests for more traditional nondiscretionary advice. The purpose of this chapter is to define what an outsourced CIO model is, identify why it has become so popular, distinguish its advantages and disadvantages relative to nondiscretionary advisory services, and suggest how families might think about choosing between the two models.

The Evolution of the Traditional, Nondiscretionary Model

Before we examine the outsourced CIO model, let's step back and take a look at the evolution of the more familiar nondiscretionary model of providing advisory services.

When investment consulting firms—the first "open-architecture" firms—appeared on the scene in the early 1970s, their clients were the huge pension plans and endowed institutions of the time: the IBM pension plan, Harvard University, the Ford Foundation. These large organizations boasted both in-house investment talent and investment committees populated by sophisticated professionals. They wanted to make all important decisions themselves, and therefore they looked to the consultants only for *recommendations*, especially regarding asset allocation and manager selection. In other words, investment consulting began, and remained for many decades, a nondiscretionary, advisory-only model for delivering investment advice. The consultants made recommendations, but the clients decided what to do.

Over time, other, smaller investors (pensions, endowed institutions and, ultimately, families) followed the lead of the big organizations and began to engage investment consultants to advise them on their portfolio needs. Because the consulting model had always been nondiscretionary, it continued to be nondiscretionary, even though these new clients were quite different from the traditional consulting clients: Typically, they lacked in-house investment talent,[4] access to sophisticated investment committees, and their asset bases were much smaller. These are, of course, related issues.

The possible weaknesses of the nondiscretionary model for these new clients tended to be disguised by the long and powerful bull markets that characterized most of the 1980s and 1990s. But matters began to come to a head around the turn of the century, when the Tech Collapse caught many investors off-guard. These investors had often ignored their advisors' advice to rebalance out of rapidly appreciating growth and tech stocks, and the collapse of 2000–2002 hit their portfolios very hard. It was at this point that clients began to consider the possible merits of asking their advisors to take discretion over their portfolios.

What had been a steady trend toward seeking discretionary advice became a virtual torrent following the catastrophic market environment of mid-2007 to early 2009. As noted above, today many advisors are seeing more requests for discretionary advice than for nondiscretionary advice.

And given the likelihood—in the New Normal investment environment—of lower returns and higher volatility, I expect the outsourced CIO model to be a trend that is here to stay.

Documenting the Trend toward the Outsourced CIO Model

According to a Casey Quirk study, just in the past four years fully outsourced assets from investors of all kinds have more than doubled.[5] The same study reported that U.S.-based institutions will outsource more than half a trillion dollars in investments by the end of 2012.

But it's not just institutional investors who are moving in this direction. According to a survey by the Family Wealth Alliance:[6]

- Approximately four in ten wealthy families have outsourced discretionary investment management and now use an outsourced CIO model.
- Among smaller family offices (those with $500 million or less in assets), two-thirds use an external advisor on a discretionary basis.
- A third of all single-family offices (SFOs) think they lack sufficient expertise to analyze investments themselves (up from 20 percent a year earlier). This rises to 50 percent for SFOs with $100 million to $500 million in assets.

It seems apparent that an ever-increasing number of "smaller" investors (those with assets below about $500 million) have concluded that the benefits of discretionary advice outweigh whatever the detriments might be.

What's Driving the Trend toward the Outsourced CIO Model?

The key investment issues all investors face are selecting and implementing the correct asset mix for the portfolio, instituting good governance and policy implementation practices, engaging capable managers, and monitoring the performance and risks of the portfolio. This seemed to be a manageable task in the 1980s and 1990s, but over the past decade it has become quite daunting. There are a variety of reasons for this complexity, including:

- Much more volatile and difficult capital markets.
- The perception that returns will be lower in the foreseeable future, and therefore the urgency of avoiding even small investment mistakes.
- Limited investment resources at the client level, combined with rising costs.

- The desire to add uncorrelated assets to the portfolio, especially in the nontraditional categories.
- Difficulty accessing best-in-class managers, especially hedge funds.
- Difficulty in fulfilling fiduciary obligations in the wake of greater scrutiny and regulation of financial activity.
- The overwhelming task of sorting through the plethora of financial instruments to determine the best fit for the portfolio.

More broadly, many advisors produced terrible results for their clients in 2008, and those advisors that were nondiscretionary tended to take refuge in their nondiscretionary status, ducking responsibility for the debacle: "I only made recommendations—you made the decisions." Clients want their advisors to step up to the table and accept responsibility for portfolio outcomes, and advisors are much more willing to do so if they have discretion.

It is also important to note that acting with discretion allows advisors to demonstrate the value of what they do in bottom-line dollars. Historically, investors have been willing to pay high fees to money managers and hedge funds (who, on the whole, subtract value from portfolios) but have insisted on paying low fees to investment consultants, who, on the whole, add significant value. By managing portfolios in a discretionary manner, formerly nondiscretionary advisors are able to demonstrate the value they add and, importantly, to get paid for it.

Finally, it is clearly the case that many investors who formerly took a firm, hands-on approach to the management of their portfolios decided, after 2008, that, "I give up! We're not very good at this and I need to outsource it!"

The Outsourced CIO Model Today

When investors talk about the outsourced CIO model, what they are referring to is the use of advisory firms to manage their portfolios on a discretionary basis, without seeking the clients' consent (at least within limits) to make changes. Overwhelmingly, the "advisors" clients are hiring are the same open-architecture firms that formerly operated on a nondiscretionary basis, but which have begun offering discretionary management as a result of client demand. These firms are basically using the same set of tools they have always used with clients—skills in asset allocation, manager selection, and performance reporting—but are simply exercising these skills on a discretionary basis.

How does the outsourced CIO model work? Although each firm has its own twists on the model, in general the outsourced CIO model works as follows.

Establishing a risk budget. Because risk is by far the most important issue associated with managing portfolios, the advisor will work with the client to establish a risk budget for the account. Typically, this risk budget will be built around the expected price volatility of the portfolio, but it may also incorporate such risk-management metrics as expected downside risk, maximum expected loss over a given period of time, value-at-risk, and so on. Ultimately, the risk budget will usually be expressed as a long-term, strategic asset allocation target with ranges around which the portfolio will be allowed to depart from the target. Except with the client's permission, the advisor may not stray from this overall portfolio design.

Return expectations. Returns will necessarily fall out of the decisions made about risk, but it is useful to express return expectations up front in any event.

Liquidity needs. This is both a real issue—some investors simply need more liquidity than others—and a perception issue: Some investors are more comfortable with more liquidity than others will feel they need. In general, the willingness to trade liquidity for increased return should be addressed.

Tactical positioning of the portfolio. Typically, ranges will be established that will allow the portfolio to fluctuate above or below the strategic targets, either as the result of market fluctuations or as the result of intentional tactical tilts imposed by the advisor. Again, except with permission, the advisor may not exceed these ranges.

Opportunistic ideas. One important way to add value to a portfolio is to allow the advisor to take advantage of occasional opportunities made available by dislocations in the capital markets. (Typically, these will be behaviorally driven dislocations, occasioned by greed or panic on the part of other investors.) The client and the advisor will agree up front on the percentage of the overall portfolio that can be allocated to such opportunities.

Manager selection. In general, manager selection will be left entirely to the discretion of the advisor. However, it is important that the client and the advisor agree on such key policy issues as the degree to which markets are efficient (and, therefore, the relative allocation to active versus passive management).

Diversification. The degree of diversification versus concentration is an issue that should be settled up front. This will include manager concentration issues.

Investment costs. Typically, clients and advisors will want to optimize costs (as opposed to minimizing or ignoring them). But if the client or advisor has a different view of investment costs, those views should be expressed up front.

Withdrawals from the portfolio. It's the client's money, of course, and in that sense all or part of the capital can be withdrawn at any time. But if wealth is to be maximized, there should be a clear understanding between the client and the advisor about the approximate size and timing of expected withdrawals, especially if they are to be large.

Tax management. For taxable accounts, the degree to which taxes will be managed, and the specific techniques that will be employed, should be addressed. Clients will differ on the relative importance they place on tax savings (a bird in the hand) versus the expectation of improved long-term returns.

Specific guidelines. If the client wishes to impose specific limits on the advisor's discretion (in addition to the broad limits described above), those limits should be specified: prohibited investments, quality guidelines for fixed-income securities, use of derivatives, socially responsible metrics, proxy voting, and so forth.

Performance reporting. Most advisors provide full quarterly reports with briefer monthly updates. If something more is desired, this will need to be negotiated up front. In discretionary accounts, some clients want to be notified every time a trade is made for their account, whereas others will be happy to wait for quarter end.

Unwinding trades. Most discretionary advisors will be willing to unwind any trade that makes a client uncomfortable, albeit at the client's risk. However, this issue should be made clear.

The written policy statement. All the above, plus any other topics of importance to the client or the advisor, should be memorialized in a written policy statement, which will become the "bible" for the advisor who is managing the portfolio.

Separate versus commingled accounts. Once the portfolio goes live, it may be managed as a separate account, or, depending on its size and the practices of the advisor, it may be commingled with other investor funds.

Advantages and Disadvantages of the Outsourced CIO Model

Like all advisory models, the outsourced CIO model presents both advantages and disadvantages. Following are the main issues.

Advantages of the Model   In deciding to engage an outsourced CIO, investors are seeking the following competitive advantages over investors who work with nondiscretionary advisors:

> *Reduced opportunity costs.*[7] In a nondiscretionary engagement, the advisor typically works on a quarterly cycle of issuing performance reports and making recommendations. (More frequent cycles tend to be cost prohibitive except for the very largest clients.) Thus:
> - On Day 1 the advisor formulates an investment idea.
> - Several weeks later, this idea is converted into a written recommendation for the client.
> - The recommendation, together with the quarterly performance report, is mailed to the client.
> - The client, who is abroad, eventually gets around to looking at the report and the recommendations.
> - A meeting or conference call is set up to discuss performance and recommendations, typically at least several weeks in the future, given everyone's busy schedules.
> - Following the meeting or call, the client takes the matter under advisement.
> - Eventually, the client approves, modifies, or disapproves the recommendation.
> - The advisor then implements the recommendation as-made or as-modified. We are now at Day 70.

No, this isn't the norm, but it's not an outlier outcome, either. Indeed, we've heard stories of clients who waited nearly a year to act on a recommendation. (We've also heard stories about advisors who formulate recommendations but then routinely wait three months to circulate them to the client base.) One very important advantage of the outsourced CIO model is that opportunity costs are virtually eliminated: The advisor formulates an investment idea and executes it almost immediately. Especially in the likely low-return environment of the New Normal, minimizing opportunity costs matters more than ever. For many investors, this one advantage of the outsourced CIO model will prove to be decisive.

A recent survey by Mercer showed that the need for speed in making investment decisions was the primary factor in the decision by institutions to engage an outsourced CIO: "A major reason for delegating those responsibilities is the desire for investment decisions to be made faster and with sophistication in volatile, fast-moving markets."[8] The same survey found that, "About one-third of the survey respondents take more than three months to make a decision on asset allocation or manager changes, while 11 percent take six months to a year."[9]

More sophisticated portfolio designs. If the client must make all decisions about the portfolio, the great likelihood is that the overall strategic asset allocation—which will, more than any other factor, determine the investment outcome—will be less sophisticated than it would be if the advisor is charged with the day-to-day management responsibilities. Unless the client is a skilled investment professional, the client's comfort zone regarding investment strategies is likely to be suboptimal.

Expanded opportunity set. As a corollary to the previous point, outsourced portfolios tend to include more asset classes, more tactical bets, more opportunistic ideas, and so on, thus offering a higher probability of capturing market inefficiencies for the client's benefit.

Focus on the primary mission or interests. Allowing families to focus on their core interests or other business, professional or philanthropic activities, and allowing institutions to focus on their core missions, is one of the advantages of the outsourced CIO model.

Enhanced fiduciary oversight. If the previous comments about opportunity costs, portfolio design, and expanded opportunity sets are accurate, fiduciary oversight may be enhanced by moving to an outsourced CIO model. In addition, of course, the outsourced CIO model ensures that professionals are managing the portfolio constantly, not once a quarter when the family or investment committee meets.

Intellectual capital. In a nondiscretionary engagement, once the client has indicated its lack of comfort with certain strategies, tactics, or managers, the advisor tends to simplify the recommendations it brings to the table going forward, either consciously or unconsciously. In a fully discretionary engagement, the client's portfolio benefits from the full intellectual capital of the advisory firm.

Eased diligence obligations. When the client is making the final manager selection decision, the client will often meet with the manager and/or conduct in-depth conference calls. After the manager is hired, the client may feel obligated to conduct periodic on-site visits, to hold regular calls, and so on. Many clients lack the time to carry out these diligence activities, and many others lack the skill to make them meaningful. Under the outsourced CIO model, the client delegates all this to the advisor, although the client can usually meet or speak with managers as desired.

Disadvantages of the Model   There are certainly disadvantages of the out-sourced CIO model, which will make it inappropriate for many investors.

> *Giving up control.* Although it is often merely an illusion (because most clients can't effectively second-guess advisor recommendations), many investors want more control over their portfolios than is possible in the outsourced CIO model.

> *Selecting a poor discretionary advisor.* It's very difficult to evaluate firms that are offering outsourced CIO services (see the following discussion), with the result that there is always the danger that a client will have turned its capital over to an incompetent advisor. Incompetent nondiscretionary advisors tend to do less damage to portfolios than incompetent discretionary advisors.

> *Forfeiting the benefits of open architecture.* Some outsourced CIO advisors use their own investment products (or products they are paid to use), rather than true arm's-length managers and products. As I note later, moving from a nondiscretionary open-architecture advisor to a discretionary conflicted advisor is a poor trade. The best possible trade for many investors would be to move from a conflicted nondiscretionary advisor to an open-architecture discretionary advisor.

> *Investment education.* One way for an investor to educate itself about portfolio management—and, therefore, to become a more effective client—is to participate meaningfully in the portfolio management process. Though outsourced CIO advisors also offer client education services, many investors will find there is no substitute for getting their hands dirty.

> *Reduced fiduciary oversight.* I have noted that in some cases moving from nondiscretionary to discretionary management can improve fiduciary oversight of portfolios. But if the advisor is a poor or conflicted one, fiduciary oversight can suffer.

> *Cost.* Most advisors charge more for discretionary advice, so if cost is an issue this factor could tip the scales in favor of the nondiscretionary model. However, many advisors are raising the price of nondiscretionary services, in part because in many cases they are nondiscretionary in name only. If the advisor is really making all the decisions, without meaningful client input, then the advisor is really responsible for the portfolio and should be paid appropriately.

Is the Outsourced CIO Model Right for Your Family?

Clients will likely have strong opinions about the appropriateness of the outsourced CIO model for their portfolios. However, in the following paragraphs I identify some of the motivating factors that lead family and institutional clients to migrate to the outsourced CIO model.

Family Investors   It's enormously difficult for families to attract and keep top-tier investment talent. It is nearly as difficult for a family to organize and maintain a high-functioning investment committee. Finally, most families made their money outside the financial sector and have little skill in managing liquid capital. These factors began driving families toward the outsourced CIO model earlier this century.

A more recent issue is the changing regulatory environment as it affects families and, especially, family offices. Recently passed legislation (the Dodd-Frank bill) eliminates the "small advisor" exemption from registration as an investment advisor, on which many smaller family offices relied. Although the legislation exempts family offices from registration going forward, it leaves it up to the SEC to define a "family office." One way for a family office to avoid any need to register with the SEC is to go out of the investment business altogether by granting investment discretion over their assets to an advisor who is already SEC-registered.[10]

Institutional Investors   Except for the smallest institutions, even institutional investors without in-house investment staffs have tended to engage nondiscretionary advisors and to work with those advisors through investment committees. In some cases this practice has worked well, but in many cases it has resulted in mediocre or worse investment performance, complicated issues surrounding the management of the investment committee, and serious opportunity costs associated with the quarterly meeting cycle of the committee.

Poor relative performance could be tolerated (or, rather, unnoticed) when market returns were well above historic norms, as during the 1990s. But in a low-return environment that is complicated by declining charitable giving and the need to refocus on core missions, institutional investors who cannot afford in-house talent might wish to rethink their nondiscretionary advisory relationships. Acting as a cofiduciary, the outsourced CIO advisor can bring many strengths to the relationship.

How to Select a Good Outsourced CIO Advisor

Evaluating potential candidates for an outsourced CIO mandate is fraught with all the complexities associated with evaluating any new financial advisor, but it also has a few wrinkles of its own. Here is a checklist of issues to focus on:

- It makes very little sense to trade in an open-architecture nondiscretionary advisor in order to retain a conflicted discretionary advisor.

All the problems with conflicts of interest apply in spades to out-sourced CIO advisors. Stick with outsourced CIOs who maintain a strict open-architecture platform.

- Many advisors advertising outsourced CIO services are simply respond-ing to client demand and have little experience or resources to support provision of these services. Tactical portfolio adjustments in particular can be dangerous if the advisor has little real investment experience.
- Is the advisor offering a one-size-fits-all approach? If so, run the other way. Especially when discretion is being given to an advisor, the overall portfolio design, risk level, and return expectations need to be tailored to the client's unique objectives and risk tolerance.
- Does the advisor have a clearly articulated investment process that is uniformly applied across all portfolios?
- How deep is the advisor's experience in public and private markets?
- How robust are the advisor's manager selection resources?
- Has the advisor put in place a sophisticated risk management process?
- Does the advisor have a culture centered on client relationship manage-ment? Even if the advisor is doing a good job, failure to communicate openly with clients can result in serious misunderstanding, as many hedge funds learned in 2008.
- Does the advisor maintain relationships with multiple service providers? Is the firm able to "unbundle" such services as custody, brokerage, banking, and so on?
- How deep is the performance reporting infrastructure? Are reports timely and accurate? Can the advisor offer customized reporting solu-tions?
- How transparent is the advisor with respect to underlying managers? Are manager profiles available to clients? May clients meet with or call managers used in their accounts?
- If the account is taxable, how much experience has the advisor had managing private capital? How actively are taxes managed and what techniques are used? It is unfortunately the case that most firms that offer outsourced CIO services have little or no experience managing taxable capital.
- If the account is institutional, does the advisor have expertise in asset/liability management?

It is certainly the case that the outsourced CIO model is not right for every investor. However, the rapid growth of the model indicates that it is here to stay. Investors who have not yet considered discretionary management might wish to take a look at the advantages and disadvantages of this approach to the management of their capital.

FINDING THE RIGHT ADVISOR FOR YOUR FAMILY

With an introduction to open architecture and the outsourced CIO as background, let's move on to the specific challenge of finding the right advisor for your family.

Dimensions of the Problem to Focus On

Though every family will have its unique needs, most families will find it useful to focus on the two main dimensions along which advisors fall. These are what we might call the "bundled-versus-unbundled" spectrum and the "open-versus-closed architecture" spectrum. Finding the right place for your family on these two dimensions will very substantially simplify the challenge of finding the right advisor.

Bundled versus Unbundled An advisor who bundles its services is mainly selling convenience, simplicity, and one-stop shopping, but at the cost (usually) of quality and family knowledge (we'll discuss why in a moment). At the extreme "bundled" end of the spectrum, the advisor might already have in place such services as custody, brokerage, asset allocation, money management, performance reporting, fiduciary services, and a broad range of "softer" services some families will need, such as check-writing, intergenerational counseling, and so on. These services might all be performed by the advisor itself, or some or all might be outsourced.

At the extreme "unbundled" end of the spectrum, an advisor is mainly selling best-in-class services across the board, but at the sacrifice (usually) of simplicity. An unbundled provider will wait until it understands the family's needs before recommending custodians, brokers, asset allocation strategies, money managers, and so on. Even performance reporting can be outsourced these days.

Extreme bundled advisors tend to be closed architecture, whereas extreme unbundled advisors tend to be open architecture, but that is not universally true. In particular, as we move along the spectrum from completely bundled to completely unbundled, we will encounter every possible variety of bundling and unbundling mixed up with every possible variety of open and closed architecture.

Open versus Closed Architecture A purely closed-architecture advisor will employ a service platform that relies on its own in-house capabilities, sometimes across the board, sometimes only in money management. A purely open-architecture advisor, on the other hand, will employ a service platform that offers no products of its own. Instead, it will search for the best and most appropriate products for its clients across the board. As with the bundled-versus-unbundled dimension, advisory firms can fall anywhere along the spectrum from completely closed architecture to semi-closed architecture, and from semi-open architecture to completely open architecture.

To illustrate how we might approach the problem of locating the optimal position on the bundling and architecture dimensions, let's look at the experience of an individual family, the Schulbergs.

The Schulberg Family

In 2005, the Schulberg family had liquid assets of $23 million. In absolute terms, of course, that was a large sum of money. But as a percentage of the total wealth of the family, the liquid assets were dwarfed by the value of the family's operating business: a regional cable television company that was growing very rapidly and was already worth, in 2005, an estimated $100 million.

What Business Is the Family In?   In looking at the range of advisory options available to it, and in trying to reduce the sheer number of possibilities to a manageable few, the Schulberg family asked itself two very simple questions (the answers to which, however, are not always simple). The first question was, "What business are we in as a family?"

Because the ultimate destiny of the Schulberg family would be far more dependent on how well the family managed the cable TV business than on how well the family managed its liquid wealth, the family sensibly concluded that it was in "the business of running a business." It was important that the family apply most of its time and talents to the cable business to ensure its success. That didn't mean that the family would ignore what was happening with the liquid assets, but it did have important implications for the kind of advisor the family would need.

Because the family would have little time to devote to the management of its liquid assets, the Schulbergs realized that they needed an advisor that fell toward the "bundled" end of the business. Such an advisor would take most of the complexity and most of the time-consuming activities associated with wealth management off the family's shoulders, leaving the family free to focus on operating the business. This one important decision eliminated many possible competitors for the family's advisory business.

How Does the Family Feel about Conflicts of Interest?   In terms of the open-versus-closed architecture spectrum, the Schulbergs asked themselves a second question: "How do we feel about conflicts of interest?" Some families will be very sensitive about conflicts, seeing them as going to the very heart of the issue of trust, without which no advisory relationship can flourish. Other families will see conflicts as an inherent part of the advisory business, and as an issue to be managed, not avoided.

The Schulbergs fell into the former category, partly because, in the early 2000s, the family had experienced a brush-up with conflicts of interest in the investment banking business. The family's investment banker had recommended that the cable TV company issue junk bonds as a way to gain access to the financing it needed to propel its growth. This turned out to be good advice, except for one problem: Another unit in the investment bank was buying up smaller issues of junk bonds (like those issued by the Schulberg's company), gaining leverage over the company and trying to force a sale of the company or a buyback (at a premium) of the bonds.

This experience had sensitized the Schulbergs to the dangers of conflicts of interest, and consequently they decided to limit themselves to the "open-architecture" end of the advisory spectrum. This decision also eliminated many competitors and, combined with the family's decision about bundling, allowed the family to focus on a very small group of appropriate advisory firms. It was to this limited group of four or five firms that the Schulbergs sent a request for proposal (RFP) designed to assist them in distinguishing the strengths and weaknesses of these few remaining competitors.

Defining (and Redefining) the Definition of the "Right" Advisor   Ultimately, the Schulbergs selected a firm that offered what it called "outsourced chief investment officer" services. This firm bundled most of the services the Schulbergs would need to manage their $23 million: asset custody, asset allocation, manager selection, and performance reporting. All the family needed to do was review the periodic performance reports to monitor the portfolio. The advisor was also mainly open architecture in the sense that it selected providers of these services in a best-in-class manner, taking nothing of value from any vendor.

All went well for seven years, at which point the Schulberg family sold its cable television company for cash and stock. The family could simply have continued with its existing advisor, but the Schulbergs didn't become wealthy by allowing inertia to dictate their fate. Instead, the family convened a series of family meetings, including the family's key advisors, at which it reasked the two key questions: "What business are we now in as a family?" and "How do we now feel about conflicts of interest?"

Obviously, the family's situation was now—mid-2011—quite different than it had been in 2005. Back then, the family had been deeply involved in building a strong regional cable TV business. Now, the Schulbergs were sitting on a pile of cash and securities—including a concentrated position in the acquiring company's stock—of nearly $300 million dollars.

Family Intellectual Capital   Thus, when the Schulbergs reasked themselves the question, "What business are we in as a family?" the answer was quite different. The Schulbergs were now no longer in "the business of running a business," but in the "business of managing liquid wealth." These are very different activities, and the consequences for the Schulbergs were momentous.

Earlier in the chapter, I mentioned that bundled advisors offer simplicity at the cost of family knowledge. During the almost eight years that the Schulbergs' liquid wealth had been managed by its bundled advisor, the Schulbergs had learned almost nothing about the business of managing wealth. Their investment results had been satisfactory, but the family's advisor had made all the decisions and therefore the results in terms of the family's human capital had been unsatisfactory, indeed.

The family knew nothing about the role of an asset custodian, knew nothing about how brokerage was handled in their account (the answer to this would not please them), understood nothing at all about the very complex business of selecting money managers, and they viewed the asset allocation process as a black hole. The Schulbergs reviewed their performance reports regularly, but exactly what those reports meant had never been very clear to them. In effect, the family had become an intellectual ward of their advisor during those years.

At the time, that sacrifice in the family's intellectual capital had been worth it—the Schulbergs had been focusing on larger issues and their liquid wealth had been mainly a sideshow. But now the management of the liquid wealth was the entire ball game for the Schulberg family—screw that up and it would all be over. What the Schulbergs badly needed was to become as good at managing liquid wealth as they had been at managing a cable TV business. And just as it had taken many years for them to learn the ropes and become adept at the one business, it would also take many years to become adept at the other. But the family needed to start learning right away.

Consequently, the Schulbergs decided to terminate their bundled advisor and to engage an advisor whose services would be as unbundled as possible. The family had a lot to learn, and the best way to start the learning process was to participate with a good, unbundled advisor in making decisions about every aspect of the wealth management process.

"Conflicts Really Matter Now"   Even before the cable business was sold, the Schulbergs were sensitive to the issue of conflicts. But back then advisor conflicts would at least compromise only a small portion of the family's wealth. Now financial conflicts of interest would go right to the heart of what the family needed to do. As a result, the family was now much more focused on identifying advisors who were located on the extreme open-architecture end of the open-versus-closed architecture spectrum.

Gathering Names

As I mentioned above, the choices available to families like the Schulbergs have grown like kudzu. But this is where the process of narrowing the advisory choices down to those that are likely to be most appropriate comes in. The Schulbergs knew that they wanted an unbundled relationship, and they knew that they wanted an open-architecture relationship. Hence, they were in a position to be specific when they asked around for recommendations.

The sources for advisory recommendations used by the Schulbergs were the ones most families would use. They spoke to their legal and tax advisors, their bankers and trustees, and families in similar circumstances. They also used the resources of intermediary membership organizations such as the CCC Alliance in Boston, the Family Office Exchange in Chicago, the Family Wealth Alliance (also in Chicago), and the Institute for Private Investors in New York. CCC, FOX, the Alliance, and IPI have had long relationships with many different types of advisors, and also have had the benefit of feedback from their family members about which advisors do what, who is doing a good job and who isn't, and so forth. Finally, the Schulbergs spoke to members of their regional family office networking group.[11]

Note that another route the Schulbergs could have taken was to engage one of the firms that specialize in finding appropriate advisors for families. Although it may seem odd to pay someone to find an advisor you will then have to pay, the advisor selection process has become so complex that for very large families this route may make a lot of sense. The main challenges here are (a) how to find the right search firm (there are a few good ones and a lot of bad ones), and (b) keeping control of the process (discussed in the next section).

When the family had a list of four or five advisory firms that met its unbundled/open-architecture requirements and that came highly recommended, they were ready to circulate an RFP (request for proposal) to those firms.

The RFP Process

Until about a decade ago it was almost unheard-of for a family to use an RFP as a tool in its advisor selection process. But as families have become more serious about engaging advisors who are both appropriate and first rate, it was natural that they would borrow a tool from the institutional world. Still, the RFP process is fraught with dangers and difficulties. Let's examine some of the major pitfalls.

The Problem of Mimicking Institutions Unfortunately, by the time families began to use RFPs, the institutional RFP process had become seriously calcified. Initially, institutional investors such as pension plans and endowments used the RFP process as a sensible and focused tool that was part of a larger process designed to identify an appropriate financial advisor (typically a pension consultant). But by the time families began to use RFPs, and to look to the institutional world for models, the RFP process was often a sham. There are only a limited number of serious pension consultants in the United States, and after a couple of decades everyone knew everything about all of them. Thus, the RFP process was little more than an attempt to demonstrate diligence where none actually existed: Institutions already knew which firm they were going to engage long before they sent out the RFP.

As an example, I know of one public pension plan that has religiously distributed an RFP to consulting firms every three years since at least the mid-1980s. But that pension plan is still working with the same consultant it was working with in 1985. It's possible, of course, that in every case the plan trustees carefully evaluated their existing consultant against others, and that in all six searches they concluded that the existing consultant was the best choice. But given the fact that the existing consultant and its personnel have changed unrecognizably over those 18 years, and given the regular and loyal payment of campaign contributions the consultant has made to the public officials who appoint the trustees of the pension plan, we might be forgiven for being suspicious.

In point of fact, the RFP process in the case just mentioned is and for many years has been a joke. And this is true of all-too-many supposedly honest advisory searches in the pension plan world, and, increasingly, in the endowment world (which, like families, mimicked the pension plans' use of RFPs). As far as families are concerned, the important point of this is that no one in the institutional world has given much thought to the RFP process for many years. Therefore, simply mimicking the institutional approach is unlikely to prove useful and may actually lead families into trouble.

The RFP Is Only a Tool Even the best-designed RFP has to be viewed not as a magic bullet but as one tool among many to be used in identifying an appropriate advisor. In the institutional world, the RFP often represents the entire diligence process, except possibly for the final "beauty contest," at which the two finalists present. Because most pension plans are seriously understaffed on the investment side and have trustees (policemen, firemen, teachers, bus drivers, political appointees) who know nothing about the investment process, this may be the only way they can proceed. But for families, where their own private capital is at stake, using the RFP as the only—or even as the principal—tool in the advisory selection process is a serious mistake.

Instead, the family process should begin (as described previously) by asking the key questions that will dramatically narrow down the field of possible advisors to a few who are likely to be appropriate. The family should then seek comments about those advisors from people in the business who are likely to know them: money managers, other families, other financial institutions, FOX, IPI, and so forth. Only then should they begin to think about using an RFP.

Preparing the RFP   Referring back to our friends the Schulberg family, we will recall that the family had narrowed its advisory search to a small handful of firms that offered unbundled, open-architecture services. The family had asked around to get informed feedback on this group of firms, and that feedback had eliminated one of the firms. (That firm had recently been acquired by a larger firm and, in the process, the firm's founders had left.) The Schulbergs were ready to prepare an RFP to the four remaining firms. There were a number of mistakes the family could have made in preparing the RFP, including those discussed below.

> *Possible mistake #1: Copying an institutional RFP.* This is almost always a gigantic mistake, partly because no one in the institutional world has taken the RFP process seriously for many years, and partly because institutions are very, very different from families. After examining a few samples of institutional RFPs, the Schulbergs tossed them in the circular file, thereby dodging this particular bullet.

> *Possible mistake #2: Copying another family's RFP.* Though this is not as big a mistake as copying an institutional RFP, it is still a mistake. No two families are alike, and even families with identically-sized asset bases can have wildly differing investment needs. Tempting as it was to take this shortcut, the Schulbergs were unable to find a family RFP specifically seeking unbundled, open-architecture services, so they were able to dodge this bullet as well.

> *Possible mistake #3: Allowing themselves to be "gamed" by the advisors.* Like money managers, financial advisory firms can be divided into those whose business success is based on giving sound advice and those whose business success is based on asset gathering. If families aren't careful—if they don't control the process tightly

themselves—they will find that they have been "gamed" by advisors who are far better at the RFP process than families are. Most families will be lucky (well, unlucky) to send out one or two RFPs in an entire investment lifetime. Advisory firms receive hundreds of RFPs every year. What the family doesn't want is to find that it has have engaged a firm that is good at responding to RFPs, rather than a firm that is good at giving advice.

Possible mistake #4: Making the RFP too detailed. In the course of constructing an RFP, it's always a temptation to ask just another few questions, to bore in just a little more specifically on this point or that point, to ask this or that question in several different ways. Families can easily convince themselves that they are simply exercising their stewardship obligations, making certain that they aren't overlooking anything of importance. If the family is working with outside advisors in the search process (legal, tax, etc.), those advisors will all want to demonstrate their own knowledge and diligence by suggesting numerous areas of inquiry. Soon, counting subparts and sub-subparts of questions, we will find that we have created the Frankenstein Monster of All RFPs, with several hundred questions.

Keep in mind that we are sending this RFP not to one firm, but to several. No two firms will answer any of our questions, much less all, in the same way, or will even approach their answers in the same way. What we will receive back for our efforts will be thousands of pages of completely incomprehensible, radically inconsistent, totally incompatible responses. We will now have to engage McKinsey & Co. to make sense of it all (and McKinsey will charge us far more than the advisor would have charged us).

If we keep in mind that the RFP process is simply one of many tools we are using to find the right advisor, we will recognize that what we need to do is focus the RFP on a few key areas that are of intense concern to us. At this stage of the process we are not interested in the esoterica of how Advisor A (versus Advisor B versus Advisor C versus Advisor D) balances turnover versus tax lot accounting in assessing the tax-awareness of money managers. Instead, we want to focus on key differentiating features of the advisors we are looking at evaluating.

In the case of the Schulbergs, the family's main concerns focused on these issues:

- Which services are bundled and which are unbundled?
- What kinds of financial and nonfinancial conflicts of interest exist at each of the advisory firms?

- Which professionals would be assigned to the Schulberg account?
- How would the family's fees be calculated?
- How would the advisor's success or failure be measured?
- How was the portfolio design process approached at each firm?
- How did each firm identify, evaluate, and monitor money managers recommended to their clients?
- What kinds of performance reports would the family receive?
- And probably the most important kinds of questions, designed to get at whether or not the advisor knows anything about *investing*. Astonishingly, families regularly fail to inquire into this issue, resulting in engaging an advisor who doesn't really bring positive harm to the portfolio but who has no idea how to make money. Families ask, "How many analysts do you employ?" apparently unaware of the fact that most analysts are engaged in doing low-level diligence on money managers. Families ask, "How many managers do you follow?" as though quantity weren't the enemy of quality. Instead, a family should assess a financial advisor they way they (or their advisor) would assess, say, a multistrategy hedge fund. No one much cares how many analysts a hedge fund has, but only how good they are and how well they are being trained working under senior portfolio managers. No one cares how many opportunities a hedge fund manager is looking at, but only the quality of those opportunities. Other useful questions might fall along these lines: What is your process for identifying interesting investment opportunities? How well structured is that process? Do you implement your ideas yourselves or via external managers (or both)? How do final decisions get made about which opportunities will be pursued? How do you size opportunities? Unfortunately, few families ever ask such questions.

There were a million other things the Schulbergs could have asked about in their RFP, but each additional area of inquiry would, in fact, have compromised their ability to focus on the key factors that were of most importance. Later, when the field has been narrowed to two final firms, the Schulbergs will inquire orally or in writing into these other issues. In other words, the Schulbergs recognized the RFP for what it was: merely one tool among many in a well-designed advisory search process.

Where Is the Sample RFP?

In other chapters I have given examples of forms I discuss in the text: investment policy statements, spending policies, manager guidelines, and so forth. So where is the sample RFP? I have in my files dozens of examples of RFPs, some of which I consider to be quite well done, very focused, and useful to the families who circulated them. Why not attach one or two samples to this chapter?

The reason is that I want to emphasize the point that *there is no such thing as a "good" RFP in the absence of detailed knowledge about the family that is conducting the search*. Sure, there are better and worse ways of inquiring into specific issues, but that's a detail. The important point is that a terrific RFP for the Schulberg family might well be a terrible RFP for the Greene family, and vice versa. The time we devote to custom designing our own RFP will be time very well spent, because it will require us to focus on those few areas that we really care about. And by keeping the RFP focused, we will also be able to make sense of the results we receive, even if we are sending the RFP out to five or six firms.

Final Diligence

Once a family has received and reviewed the responses to its RFP, the next step is to conduct telephone conferences with each of the firms that are still in the running. The point of these calls is simply to go over responses that weren't completely understood by the family, or responses in which the advisor seemed to have missed the point.

Next, if at all possible, family members should visit each of the remaining competitors in their home offices. It might be the case, for example, that the individual professional(s) to be assigned to the family's account might be terrific—very people-oriented, very charming, very experienced, and knowledgeable. But who is working behind these people? If the home office is staffed by former brokers and insurance salesmen whose sole mission in life is to improve the profitability of the firm's accounts, we should probably know about that before we sign up. If the RFP response is warm and fuzzy, but the home office is clearly an impersonal bureaucracy, that is also something the family should know. If the individuals we have met are organized and focused, but the home office is disorganized and confused, that is likely to say something important about the experience the family is likely to have as a client of the firm.

Finally, the family should invite *no more than two* firms to meet with all important family members and any key outside advisors. *The family*—not the advisory firms—should prepare the agenda for these meetings, and that agenda should focus on the issues that are most important to the family.

Why meet with no more than two firms? Two reasons. The first is that if the family has truly done its diligence well, it should be able to identify the top two candidates at this point. If there are still four or five firms under serious consideration, the family simply hasn't done its job. The second reason is that having more than two firms present to families will only generate massive confusion. It's reasonably easy to compare Firm A with Firm B. But start adding Firms D, E, and F and everyone's head will be spinning. If a decision is made at all, it will be made out of sheer exhaustion.

Where Does Diligence Leave Off and Psychodrama Begin?

For families looking to engage an overall advisor for the first time, or when families have worked with an advisor but new family members have been charged with replacing that firm, the decision can be excruciatingly difficult. After all, we are talking about turning the hard-won family fortune over to people who are essentially strangers. Not only that, but we are not buying a technology, we are engaging specific human beings with whom we will be working. Many people who are otherwise decisive find "personnel" decisions to be very difficult. On top of everything else, most people would rather discuss their sex lives than their personal financial affairs with a stranger.

This difficulty tends to play itself out in the form of endless diligence, as families inquire ever-more-intensely into ever-less-important issues. They eliminate firms from consideration for reasons that are, objectively speaking, silly. Anything to avoid or postpone making a decision. It's all perfectly understandable, but also perfectly deadly. Short of engaging a completely incompetent or fraudulent advisor, the worst decision a family can make is to do nothing. Even a marginally competent objective advisor, though he or she might not grow our wealth at the rate we were hoping for, will at least stand as a bulwark against the kinds of bad decisions that will destroy our wealth.

Recognizing that advisor decisions can be difficult ones to make, it may help families who are having trouble bringing their search to a conclusion to ask exactly what it is that they fear.

What's the worst that could happen? Realistically speaking—again, short of engaging incompetent or fraudulent advisors—there are only a few serious mistakes we can make in our advisor search process.

> *Possible mistake #1: Engaging an advisor who pushes narrow strategies.* Some advisors—mainly, but not exclusively, closed-architecture firms—advocate strategies that are very narrowly focused on individual asset classes and/or individual investment styles (hedge funds, for example). Many of these narrow strategies would be imprudent per se in most fiduciary portfolios, and as families we should heed that message.

> *Possible mistake #2: Engaging an advisor who possesses conflicts of interest we can't manage.* Even families who are not terribly sensitive

to conflicts of interest can easily underestimate the consequences of those conflicts. Around the turn of the century, conflicts of interest among accountants, corporate executives, stock analysts, and such were well understood by investors who nevertheless lost billions of dollars. The problem was that those investors didn't quite realize just how badly they could be hurt by conflicts. Some conflicts don't get properly managed because we don't know they exist (i.e., we haven't done our diligence). Some conflicts don't get properly managed because families underestimate their danger t(i.e., they placed ourselves on the wrong end of the open-versus-closed architecture spectrum). And sometimes families simply overestimate their level of sophistication relative to the financial services professionals who are bringing their conflicts to the table. If a family has doubts about its ability to recognize, manage, or understand conflicts of interest, the best course is to engage advisors who don't have them.

Possible mistake #3: Not engaging an advisor at all. This is the biggest mistake of all. Families are often quite experienced, sophisticated, and smart. But those smarts will have been honed in a world quite different from the investment world. Just because a family has been wildly successful at business, real estate, oil and gas, technology, or whatever, doesn't have any implication at all for their ability to compete successfully in the world of capital markets. As I mentioned above, even a moderately competent advisor can serve as an important shield against the horribly bad decisions that can devastate a family's wealth. Competent advisors, properly selected for our needs, will virtually ensure the preservation of our wealth across the generations.

CONCLUSION: FOCUSING ON A FEW KEY VARIABLES

Wealthy families face a plethora of challenges as they seek to identify the financial advisor that's best for their family. The advisory business has become ever more complex, offering a myriad of platforms, megafirms, and boutiques, conflicted and unconflicted models.

In this chapter I've tried to organize this cumbersome process by focusing on a few key variables that will profoundly affect a family's advisory experience. Those variables are open architecture versus closed architecture, discretionary versus nondiscretionary mandates, and bundled versus unbundled services. Within each of these choices, there are blended options—semi-open architecture, for example, or firms that bundle a few services but not all services.

Finally, I've given the example of the fictitious Schulberg family, and how its own evolution as a family affected its advisory needs.

A family without an advisor is like a ship without a rudder. But a family with a bad (incompetent, venal, conflicted) advisor is probably in even worse shape. Thus, difficult as the advisor selection process is, it needs to be taken seriously.

NOTES

1. This portion of the chapter is adapted from Greycourt White Paper No. 38: Open Architecture as a Disruptive Business Model (2006), available at www.Greycourt.com. The paper appeared in slightly different form in *The NMS Exchange* 7, no. 1(August 2006): 7, and was subsequently published as Chapter 8 in A. Srikant and C. Anand, eds., *Disruptive Technologies: Concepts and Application* (Hyderabad, India: Icfai University Press, 2006).
2. Clayton Christensen, Sally Aaron, and William Clark, "Disruption in Education," from the EDUCAUSE 2001 Forum for the Future of Higher Education.
3. This portion of the chapter is adapted from Greycourt White Paper No. 49: The Outsourced CIO Model (2010), available at www.Greycourt.com. The paper was subsequently published, in slightly different form, as "The Outsourced Chief Investment Officer," *Investments & Wealth Monitor* Featured Article (May/June 2011). Special thanks to Margaret Towle for her contributions to the original paper.
4. A recent NACUBO-Commonfund study of smaller endowments indicates that only 11 percent of funds between $100 million and $500 million employed in-house CIOs. See *2009 NACUBO-Commonfund Study of Endowment Results*. The percentage for families is far lower.
5. "The New Gatekeepers: Winning Business Models for Investment Outsourcing," (Casey Quirk, 2008).
6. "Inaugural 2009 Single-Family Office Study," Family Wealth Alliance. The study is available for purchase from the Family Wealth Alliance.
7. "Opportunity costs" refers to the price movement that occurs between the time an investment idea is formulated and the time it is executed.
8. See Greg Saitz, "Investors Cite Need for Speed as OCIO's Appeal," Fundfire (March 16, 2012).
9. Ibid.

10. The final SEC rules (all 52 pages of them) on whether or not family offices need to register can be found at 17 CFR Part 275 [Release No. IA-3220; File No. S7-25-10].

11. Many large cities have informal (or, sometimes, more formal) groups of families that meet periodically to network and discuss matters of mutual interest. These groups often go by cute acronyms such as CAFE (Cleveland) and PALS (San Francisco).

CHAPTER 7

Making Family Investment Decisions

When you come to a fork in the road, take it.

—Yogi Berra

In some families one family member—usually the patriarch or matriarch—makes all the investment decisions. This is simplicity itself—until it's time to pass the torch to the next decision maker, which is when things get very sticky. At the opposite extreme, some families involve practically every family member in the decision-making process. This is highly inclusive, but tends to result in very slow decision making, or often none at all.

In the long run, human capital is far more important than financial capital, for the simple reason that if the former is frittered away the latter will soon disappear. As long as the family's human capital flourishes—through the education of family members and their deepening experience managing wealth in a serious fashion—the stewardship of the family's wealth will be in sound hands.

If it were simply a matter of forming a family investment committee and then letting it take its course, every family would have one and every family would maintain its wealth indefinitely. It is unfortunately the case, however, that all too often investment committees become part of the problem, not part of the solution. In the next section of this chapter we will examine why it is that investment committees so often fail to accomplish their missions, and what might be done about it. I will then take a look at the costs of slow decision making (opportunity costs), and, finally, will ask the very large question whether we are even capable of making sound investment decisions.

THE FAMILY INVESTMENT COMMITTEE TODAY

Many families (along with virtually all pension plans, charitable foundations, and endowed institutions) use investment committees to provide oversight of the management of their investment portfolios. Unfortunately, history has shown that most investment committees do a poor job of stewarding the assets entrusted to them. There are many reasons why the investment committee has proved to be such an unreliable tool. Let's take a look at some of them.

The Origin of the Investment Committee

The investment committee originated not out of the investment world but out of the world of board governance. Most boards, rather than acting at all times as a "committee of the whole," delegate much of their important activity to committees—smaller groups of board members that are really subcommittees of the "committee of the whole." This process of delegation improves the efficiency and productivity of a board, and has been enthusiastically supported by good governance groups such as the Association of Governing Boards of Universities and Colleges (known as the AGB).[1]

The trouble is that the investment committee is fundamentally unlike other board committees. Virtually any board member, no matter what his or her professional background, can be a productive member of such committees as nominating (sometimes called the committee on trustees), executive, advancement, buildings and grounds, presidential search, and so on. Our general experience of life and business suit us well for service on these committees. Even the finance committee, although more typically requiring some technical knowledge of accounting, bookkeeping, and financial statements in general, can be easily mastered by anyone with a desire to do so.

But successful service on an investment committee requires knowledge so specialized and experience so extensive that it will be a rare board that can produce even one or two such people, much less an entire committee-full. This is a point that is usually ill-understood by boards and board chairs, who generally appoint to the investment committee anyone with a generalized background in "finance." Hence, investment committees typically include accountants, attorneys, bankers, investment bankers, brokers, and similar professionals, none of whom is likely to possess the specialized skills and experience required to design, implement, and effectively monitor an investment portfolio for a substantial pool of capital. That experience would include a sound understanding of modern portfolio theory, asset allocation, manager selection, performance monitoring, and a host of other skills that are very narrowly distributed through the population of any governing board. When families establish investment committees, they tend to follow the institutional model, placing on the committee individuals who are unlikely to possess the appropriate skills.

Hence, the first and fundamental reason investment committees fail is that the demands placed on them are fundamentally incompatible with their capabilities. The demands on investment committees are different from the demands on other board committees, yet the investment committee is assembled and operated as though it were no different than any other board committee.

Committee Dynamics

Anyone who has served on a governing board is familiar with the often-dysfunctional internal dynamics of committees. Virtually all board committees consist of volunteers devoting their time to board work as a philanthropic endeavor. Hence, committees of such boards necessarily operate largely by consensus. No one wants to make waves or offend anyone else. Decisions almost always reflect the lowest common denominator, because to do otherwise would necessarily offend some committee member. (And that member may be the largest financial contributor to the organization!) Unless the committee chair is highly experienced in managing committees and a good leader, committee meetings will meander here and there, wasting large amounts of time on side issues, running out of time to deal with more pressing matters. Family investment committees operate according to identical dynamics. Indeed, because families don't exactly qualify as charitable enterprises, the challenge of attracting good people and motivating them to do a responsible job is especially perplexing.

In the operation of some committees, this dynamic is something less than disastrous. On the nominating committee, for example, lowest-common-denominator thinking is often the best way to ensure collegiality among board members. Fighting to nominate an individual who is actively disliked by another board member is likely to lead to disruption, not improved productivity. But in other committees the unavoidable process of committee dynamics and decision-by-committee can be devastating, and this is decidedly the case with the investment committee. Successful management of a large pool of capital requires incisive thinking; a willingness to go against the grain of perceived wisdom; and an ability to behave counterintuitively, avoid acting on the basis of short-term events, and take the long view.

But, as currently operated, it is virtually impossible for the voting plurality of an investment committee to act in any of these ways, much less all. Instead, investment committees engage in woolly thinking (often because they are not experienced in the management of capital), tend to follow the conventional wisdom in adopting investment strategies, fail to recognize that much of the process of successful investing is counterintuitive, and typically act (usually in at least a mild state of panic) in reaction to short-term market events that will quickly reverse themselves, whipsawing the investment portfolio.

Making an Impact

The natural desire to contribute, to make an impact, means that even when investment committee members are acting on the best possible motives, their impact on the performance of the portfolio is likely to be negative. Consider, for example, an investment portfolio that has been designed and implemented in a first-rate manner. The best thing an investment committee can do with such a portfolio is to leave it alone, perhaps rebalancing it on occasion. But no member of an investment committee wants to be perceived as lazy or lacking in ideas or motivation. As a result, even if each member of the committee tosses out his or her idea only once a year, the aggregate effect is that the portfolio will find itself constantly being rejiggered. This is the opposite of a sound approach to portfolio management.

ATTEMPTS TO DEAL WITH THE PROBLEM

Given the many defects of the investment committee as an investment instrument, families (and institutions) have come up with a variety of "fixes." In this section I will describe the main approaches to taming investment committees, as well as the pros and cons of each "fix."

Asset Allocation Guidelines and Investment Policy Statements

The usual approach to controlling investment committee behavior is for the full governing board or family to adopt asset allocation guidelines and a written investment policy statement, within whose parameters the investment committee is expected to act. Asset allocation guidelines and policy statements are essential tools in the management of capital, but as instruments for the control of investment committee behavior they are wholly inadequate. The reason is simple: Whenever an investment committee wants to act outside the constraining bounds of a written guideline or policy, the committee simply changes them (or, worse, ignores them). And who is to enforce compliance with these strictures? If the committee simply ignores the restraints, who will know about it? If the committee asks the board to change guidelines or policies, who on the board is going to argue with the investment committee, who are, after all, the anointed experts on such things?

Using Outside Experts to Populate the Investment Committee

Some large-endowed institutions and many wealthy families have given up on the in-house investment committee in favor of an outside investment committee or board of advisors populated by experts selected for their skill and experience in the management of large pools of capital. At Yale University, for example, chief investment officer David Swensen has recruited a sizeable group of experts who serve on what is called the Yale Corporation Investment Committee. Only three of the Investment Committee members need be Fellows of the Yale Corporation, Yale's governing board. There are currently 11 members of the Investment Committee. In other words, instead of accepting full responsibility—and the associated time commitments—of board membership, these experts focus exclusively on the management of the Yale endowment.

Clearly, Yale and the many families who use boards composed of outside experts believe that this approach is far superior to the more traditional investment committee approach. Unfortunately, experts on the caliber of those used by Yale are few and far between (and typically expensive), making it impossible for smaller institutions and families to mimic the Yale approach.

The Separate Investment Management Corporation

Some very large investors—Harvard University, Princeton University, the University of Texas—have abandoned the investment committee approach altogether. Instead, they have established separately incorporated management companies charged with the responsibility of managing the institutions' endowments. These management companies employ many—sometimes, hundreds—of highly compensated investment professionals, and they have typically produced results that are far superior to those achieved by part-time, in-house investment committees. Unhappily for smaller investors, the investment management corporation is not a serious option for anyone managing less than about $5 billion.

THE FAMILY INVESTMENT COMMITTEE, TOMORROW

Like well-crafted riddles, capital markets events are usually perfectly comprehensible after the fact. But while they are happening there is so much "noise," so much emotional resonance (and dissonance), that we can't make out what will later become clear. Most events in the markets, however important they may seem at the time, are merely noise, and attempting to act in reaction to them is a very sound way to reduce our wealth.

Thus, it was perfectly obvious in the late 1990s that equity valuations had become disconnected from reality. The "justifications" for those prices—it's a whole new paradigm; things are different this time—were specious on their face. But there was so much noise and confusion going on, and the short-term pain of missing out on the almost daily price appreciation was so much more intense than the longer-term prospect of a market crash, that perfectly sensible people continued to pay higher and higher prices for stocks that were pretty obviously (but retrospectively!) worth only a tiny fraction of those valuations.

Even events that are truly substantive are often not actionable in a way that will improve returns. The valuation disparity between growth and value stocks, for example, became compelling in the mid-1990s, but anyone who attempted to profit from that disparity was hammered by the continued, almost mystical, appreciation among growth and technology stocks. In other words, it is often possible to "know" that valuations in one sector or another are attractive, but it is never possible to know when the value will be recognized.

Thus, the challenge for investment committees is to maintain their discipline and patience when everyone else has long run out of both. Yet, as noted at length above, investment committees are ill-equipped to act in a disciplined manner or to demonstrate patience in the face of capital markets provocations. As we have seen, traditional attempts to control dysfunctional committee behavior—written investment policy statements and asset allocation guidelines—don't work, and alternatives to investment committees—committees of outside experts and separate investment management corporations—are beyond the reach of most families and institutions. So what can be done? One promising option is the investment committee operating manual.

The Investment Committee Operating Manual

Most very wealthy families have little choice but to manage their capital by using the traditional vehicle of the investment committee. Moreover, most families have little choice but to populate those investment committees with individuals who, however competent in other areas, are likely to have little experience in the management of large pools of capital. The point of using an investment committee operating manual is to build on the strengths of the traditional investment committee—namely, common sense and a desire to contribute to the sound risk-adjusted growth of the portfolio—while avoiding many of the defects of the traditional investment committee approach described previously.

The companion website (www.wiley.com/go/stewardshipofwealth, password: curtis2012) includes samples of many kinds of policy statements, including a sample investment committee operating manual.

OPPORTUNITY COSTS: PRUDENCE VERSUS RETURNS

There is, unfortunately, a trade-off between the soundness of investment decisions made by a family and the speed with which those decisions must be made to be effective.[2] All too often, in other words, there is a conflict between a family's desire to be prudent in its decision making and the family's desire to achieve competitive returns.

In the fiduciary world, over the course of several hundred years, standards of fiduciary prudence have become ever more process oriented and ever less outcome oriented. The main reason for this is that, under traditional trust doctrine, a trustee was absolutely liable for almost any loss of principal: "Traditional trust doctrine caused ultimate liability for losses to the trust to sit like a devil on the shoulder of every trustee."[3] As a result, trustees typically invested only in gold-plated investments, such as gilts (debt securities issued by the Bank of England).

The traditional rule was very much outcome-oriented: Allow the capital to decline in value and you will be held liable. Interestingly, this situation began to change when trustees in the United States found that there was no domestic counterpart to gilts: Bonds issued by the new United States were too risky! This circumstance "encouraged the majority of American fiduciaries to direct their investments toward promoting nascent industrial enterprises"[4] in the United States, and this in turn caused American courts to revisit the absolute liability rule that applied to English trustees. The new American approach looked to process, rather than outcome.

Prudence versus Returns for Trustees

In the remarkable case of *Harvard College v. Amory*, the Supreme Judicial Court of Massachusetts rejected the English doctrine of strict trustee liability, adopting instead the so-called "prudent man rule," which was not *outcome*-oriented ("Did the capital lose value?") but *process*-oriented ("Did the trustee behave responsibly?"):

> *All that can be required of a trustee to invest is that he shall conduct himself faithfully and exercise a sound discretion. He is to observe*

how men of prudence, discretion and intelligence manage their own
affairs, not in regard to speculation, but in regard to the permanent
disposition of their funds, considering the probable income, as well
as the probable safety of the capital to be invested.[5]

In other words, Justice Chase was saying, "Don't look at the investment
result. Look, instead, at whether or not the trustee was proceeding sensibly."

The Harvard College case proved to be a flash in the pan, however, as
other jurisdictions refused to follow it. Courts, to say nothing of beneficiaries, weren't all that interested in how procedurally prudent trustees were
being; they were interested in keeping their capital intact.

By the end of the American Civil War, therefore, U.S. trustees were
pretty well limited to investing in government bonds and mortgage-backed
corporate debts. Invest in anything else and trustees found themselves
absolutely liable for any diminishment of value. Indeed, by the 1880s, many
states had adopted "legal lists," that is, lists of securities trustees were
permitted to buy (mainly fixed-income debt instruments and bonds).

Gradually, however, things began to change, which is to say that
they reverted back to the process-oriented "prudent man rule" first laid
down in the early nineteenth century. The development of the modern,
postindustrial economy vastly complicated trustees' lives, squeezing them
between beneficiaries who wanted higher returns and fiduciary rules that
limited trustees to bonds. Of course if trustees were going to shoot for the
higher returns available in equity securities, they were sometimes going to
fall short. Something had to give.

At roughly the same time, and impelled by roughly the same developments, modern portfolio theory (MPT) arose. Whereas traditional trust
doctrine required trustees to avoid risky investments, MPT taught investors
to profit by them. MPT distinguished between systematic (or market) risk,
for which an investor was compensated, and specific (or residual) risk,
which must be diversified away. MPT argued that a true understanding of
diversification would allow investors to add risky assets to a portfolio while
actually reducing (or at least not increasing) overall risk levels.

Today, the Restatement (Third) of Trusts articulates the "prudent
investor rule," whose main feature is that—as in Justice Chase's formulation
back in 1830—we are asked to look not at how the capital performed but
at how the trustee behaved. Here is the core of the rule:

The trustee is under a duty to the beneficiaries to invest and manage
the funds of the trust as a prudent investor would, in light of the
purposes, terms, distribution requirements, and other circumstances
of the trust.

> *This standard requires the exercise of reasonable care, skill, and caution, and is to be applied to investments not in isolation but in the context of the trust portfolio and as a part of an overall investment strategy, which should incorporate risk and return objectives reasonably suitable to the trust.*[6]

Nowhere, I note, does the prudent investor rule suggest that a competitive return on the capital should be any part of the analysis.

Prudence versus Returns for Families

Let's assume for the moment that, in the fiduciary context, it makes sense to elevate process over outcome—otherwise, trustees would shrink from taking risk, as they did for centuries. Outside of the fiduciary context, in the world of private family capital, legal liabilities are very different and therefore the relative emphasis I place on process versus outcome should also be different.

Yet, when we look at how wealthy families behave, we find that they are also encouraged to elevate process over outcome. Pressed by well-intentioned financial advisors, family investors who aren't fiduciaries in any legal sense have gone to great lengths to draft mission statements and investment policy statements, have laboriously created investment committees, and have encouraged inclusiveness by bringing in the ideas and concerns of many different family units and generations. These families are, in effect, mimicking the behavior of legal fiduciaries by focusing mainly on the procedures that will be used to make investment decisions.

Just as a thought experiment, let's consider whether this obsession with process is entirely wise.

Families and their advisors are spending so much time on process because they believe that sound, prudent procedures will inevitably lead to good investment outcomes. But will they? Certainly they don't in the fiduciary arena. Every corporate trustee in America, for example, is deeply schooled in prudent processes, yet the vast majority of them underperform, say, the Vanguard STAR Fund,[7] a simple, inexpensive option that costs a small fraction of what trustees charge and beats the pants off almost all of them.

I'm not arguing for dysfunctional family investment procedures. Certainly it's true that families with alarmingly dysfunctional behaviors almost always experience bad outcomes. However, it's also true that many families who have developed extremely thoughtful, highly prudent, thoroughly inclusive procedures find that their investment returns are far below par.

What's going on here? The simple answer, I suggest, is that these families have overlooked the importance of opportunity costs. Technically, "opportunity costs" refers to market price movement that occurs between when somebody comes up with an investment idea and when they get around to executing it. In rapid-fire computer trading strategies, thousands of trades are executed on a split-second basis to try to take advantage of small and fleeting price disparities. The opportunity costs associated with the loss of even a second or two can mean the difference between a profit and a loss.

In a more typical situation, good advisors' investment ideas tend to be good ones when they're formulated, but those ideas will degrade in value over time, as other, less insightful investors belatedly pick up on the idea. What was a good idea on January 1 tends to be a less good idea on January 15 and tends to be a bad idea in March.

Sound, thoughtful family decision-making processes are crucial to holding a family together, especially during stressful periods of time, and they go a long way toward enabling families to keep their legacies intact. But if the procedures are ignoring opportunity costs, the game may not be worth the candle: Nothing breaks up a family more quickly than poor investment performance.

Ask yourself if your family makes investment decisions like this: Investment ideas are communicated to your family by your advisor; your family takes these ideas under advisement; the ideas are forwarded to the family's investment committee; Uncle Ralph, who hates hedge funds, weighs in from his safari in Africa; somebody checks the policy statement and notices that not enough notice has been given to younger generations to review the recommendations; Uncle Ralph will return from safari next month, so why rush into a decision he's likely to oppose? And so on.

Like it or not, every day we spend being prudent is a day that our returns go down, because our investment ideas are going stale while we are waiting to implement them. Add these opportunity costs up over the days and months and years and we have a seriously underperforming portfolio.

Ah, you are thinking, but by intensely reviewing my advisor's recommendations, I'm weeding out the bad ones, and that will offset the opportunity costs. If that's the case, you need to fire your advisor. Looking back over 30 years of working with families, I observe two things. First, families almost never disagree with a good advisor's recommendations—they just implement them too slowly. Second, on the rare occasions when families overrule advisors, the families are usually wrong, thereby compounding opportunity costs with bad investment decisions.

The problem has to do with the respective skill sets of families and advisors. Just as it's true that a lawyer who represents himself or herself has a fool for a client, a family that thinks it knows more about investing than its advisor needs a new advisor. Family members often believe that they aren't doing their job unless they review and discuss every action *ad nauseum* before allowing their advisor to implement it. This ignores the realities of the marketplace and, especially, it ignores the relative skills and experience of families and investment professionals.

Striving for Prudence *and* Returns

For wealthy family investors, there is a serious tension between two important aspects of the investment process: on the one hand, following thoughtful, sensible procedures and, on the other hand, achieving good investment returns. How might I reconcile these tensions?

The critical issue, I suggest, is to identify what it is that families do best and what it is that investment professionals do best, then assign those tasks appropriately.

Many of the most critical activities associated with the management of private capital have no particular time pressure associated with them. For example, establishing an appropriate risk level for the capital is the single most important thing a family can do. That task requires a lot of soul searching by family members and a lot of discussion among family members and between families and advisors. Ultimately, all of this work results in a policy statement in which the key risk metrics are written down. Once this has been accomplished, all the family has to do is to review the policy regularly.

Similarly, the family needs to monitor investment performance, but short periods of performance are mainly irrelevant, so there is little time pressure associated with performance monitoring.

Finally, the family should always be striving to improve its understanding of the investment process and capital markets, but educational sessions, outside speakers at family meetings, and so on are not time sensitive.

Note that most of the issues I would assign to the family not only address broad-but-critical issues, they also address principal/agent issues. No matter how good your advisor is, the interests of an advisory firm and the family whose principal is being invested can never be identical. By carefully considering the long-term strategic issues associated with wealth management *and writing them down in a policy statement*, the family will have gone a long way toward aligning its own interests with those of its advisor.

By the same token, issues such as manager selection and replacement, tactical moves in the portfolio, and implementation of opportunistic ideas have serious opportunity costs associated with them and should be left in the hands of the professionals—subject, of course, to the family's investment policy statement and to the family's obligation to monitor the advisor's performance. If an advisor takes an action in violation of the policy statement, it must be undone at the advisor's risk. Even if the action doesn't violate the family's policies, but simply makes the family uncomfortable, the advisor should reverse the trade at the family's risk. (Both of these events should be extremely rare.)

As noted in Chapter 6, many families avoid opportunity costs by outsourcing the investment function to an outsourced chief investment officer. Note that complete outsourcing is not required. All that is required is that the various activities that make up the total management of the family's portfolio be allocated between the family and its advisor appropriately.

A good working example is offered by very large institutional investors, such as endowments, pension plans, and sovereign wealth funds. Best practices at such institutions allocate investment responsibilities between the institution's board (or investment committee) and the institution's in-house investment staff exactly as suggested above: The *board* sets long-term risk targets and investment objectives and policies, and establishes strategic asset allocation guidelines. The *staff* selects managers, negotiates mandates, shifts the portfolio tactically within the bounds set by the institution, and implements opportunistic investments (again, within the limits established by the policy statement).[8] By analogy, the family is the board and the advisor is the investment staff. This allocation of responsibilities is illustrated in Table 7.1.

TABLE 7.1   Investment Decision Making

	Sovereign Wealth Fund	Process-Obsessed Family	Optimized Family
Risk Metrics	Board/Investment committee	Board/Investment committee	Board/Investment committee
Objectives/Policies	Board/Investment committee	Board/Investment committee	Board/Investment committee
Long-Term Asset Allocation	Board/Investment committee	Board/Investment committee	Board/Investment committee
Tactical Allocation	Staff	Board/Investment committee	Advisor
Opportunistic Investments	Staff	Board/Investment committee	Advisor
Manager Selection	Staff	Board/Investment committee	Advisor
Security Selection	Staff/Outside managers	Outside managers	Advisor/Outside managers

Source: Greycourt; World Economic Forum.

CONCLUSION: FOCUSING ON WHAT FAMILIES DO BEST

The investment decision-making process that works best will certainly differ from family to family. But there are some characteristic issues families face when making investment decisions, and by paying attention to these issues, family investment outcomes will be much improved.

In particular, I've tried to address such issues as the all-too-often dysfunctional investment committee and the poorly understood tradeoff between prudence (process) and returns. I've cited the typical decision-making process of the big sovereign wealth funds as a model for families to imitate, substituting independent advisors for in-house investment staff.

Most important of all, I suggest that families focus their activities on what they do best: on the broad, 80,000-foot issues associated with family cohesion and the critical issues that matter most to the long-term health of the family's capital, especially risk and asset allocation strategy. Day-to-day, week-to-week, month-to-month investment decisions should be in the hands of a capable advisor.

Families who best address the challenges associated with investment decision making will find that they have succeeded in having their cake and eating it, too: They will keep their families intact, and they will keep their capital intact.

NOTES

1. The AGB publishes a variety of useful information about the management of endowment portfolios. See, for example, John H. Biggs, *The Investment Committee*. The booklet is available on the AGB website, www.agb.org.
2. This portion of the chapter is adapted from Greycourt White Paper No. 51: Prudence Versus Returns (2011), available at www.Greycourt.com.
3. W. Brantley Phillips, Jr., "Standards of Prudent Investment under the Restatement (Third) of Trusts." *Washington & Lee Law Journal* (Winter 1997).
4. Ibid.
5. 26 Mass. 446, 465 (1830). In the Harvard College case, the trustees had invested in the stocks of manufacturing and insurance companies, which declined in value.
6. "Restatement (Third) of Trusts," §227.
7. Ticker VGSTX. STAR is a fund of Vanguard funds with no extra fee at the fund of funds level. Except for its preposterously low non-U.S. exposure, it's a nifty option.
8. See, for example, *The Future of Long-Term Investing*, World Economic Forum (2011), 25.

CHAPTER 8

Trusts

It is better to have a permanent income than to be fascinating.
—Oscar Wilde

The subject of trusts is a massive one. A fellow named Austin Wakeman Scott Jr. first published his monumental *Scott on Trusts* in 1939. Last we looked (it was a long time ago) the reference work ran to some 12 volumes—6,837 pages!—of small print. In this chapter I will only touch on some of the main points investors will want to consider as they establish and manage their trusts.[1]

OPEN-ARCHITECTURE TRUSTS

The basic problem with the trust business is that it is operated almost entirely for the benefit of the banks, rather than for the benefit of the beneficiaries. In 1928, a few years before being appointed to the United States Supreme Court, Benjamin Cardozo articulated the standard that governed fiduciary conduct: "A trustee is held to something stricter than the morals of the market place. *Not honesty alone, but the punctilio of an honor the most sensitive*, is then the standard of behavior [emphasis supplied]."[2]

But the "morals of the market place" dominate the trust business today. According to the Center for Fiduciary Analysis, litigation against trustees is rising at the astonishing rate of 22 percent per year compounded.[3] Just to mention a random example, virtually every institutional trustee invests assets for which it serves as trustee in its own mediocre investment products, rather than in the many superior, less-expensive, best-in-class products readily available everywhere.[4] What should be an obvious, actionable, and surchargeable breach of fiduciary duty is in fact the everyday reality. Doesn't it seem obvious that a trustee who engages in self-dealing by using only its own investment products should become a guarantor of performance? Dream on.

To understand how what should have been an enterprise entirely devoted to the interests of trust beneficiaries should have deteriorated into such a hopeless, swampy morass, it will be necessary to revisit the history of the common-law trust, which is not as musty as it might sound.

A BRIEF, UNCONVENTIONAL (BUT WICKEDLY ACCURATE) HISTORY OF THE COMMON-LAW TRUST FROM THE CLIENT'S PERSPECTIVE

The common-law trust as we know it arose in the late Middle Ages as a blatant tax-avoidance scheme,[5] but it proved to be so flexible and valuable that it has persisted to this day. Frederick W. Maitland, perhaps the greatest of the legal historians, went so far as to claim that:

> *Of all the exploits of equity the largest and the most important is the invention and development of the trust. ...This perhaps forms the most distinctive achievement of English lawyers.*[6]

Maybe so, but roughly three centuries before English lawyers had ever heard of the trust, Islamic law had developed the *waqf*, a device that is uncannily similar to the trust. Indeed, in the ninth century an Islamic legal scholar (and lawyer), Abu Bakr Ahmad b. Amr b. Muhayr al-Shaybani al-Khassaf (known, not surprisingly, as al-Khassaf) wrote an entire treatise on the *waqf*, recently translated,[7] in which he cited more than two centuries of Islamic trust law and addressed such contemporary-sounding issues as, "Will a trust over which the grantor retains powers be treated as part of his estate when he dies?"

For several hundred years after the trust was either invented or reinvented in England, the business of managing trusts was pretty straightforward and largely a family matter. Trust assets were mainly land (or, later, gilt securities), and the income therefrom was passed along to the beneficiaries. Trustees were family members or friends or maybe the family solicitor. Life was simple.

But as the world became more complicated, trust assets became more complex to manage, exceeding the capacity of family members to deal with them, and as a result the potential liabilities of trustees expanded. Moreover, family members had a nasty habit of dying off, causing unwanted turnover in the trustee ranks. Enter the institutional trust company, which promised to bring professional management to complicated trust assets, to deflect liability away from the family, and to stay alive indefinitely. In addition, because the early trust companies were local institutions, they tended to know the settlor and the beneficiaries and were in an ideal position to make informed, yet impartial, exercises of discretion as necessary.

At first, these developments were all to the good—professional management of the trust assets, a corporate deep pocket to sue if anything went wrong, and a trustee blessed with perpetual life no doubt seemed like godsends. But somewhere along the way a wrong turn was made. We would describe this wrong turn as having been navigated somewhat as follows, using the main selling points of the institutional trustee to make our arguments.

Professional Management

Because an important selling point of the institutional trustee was its ability to bring professional management to trust assets, early corporate trustees managed the assets themselves. Naturally, then, when most trust assets came to be in the form of marketable securities, corporate trustees held themselves out as experts in the management of those securities.

That may have been all well and good for a while—certainly the trust institutions managed assets better than the families or their lawyers would likely have done. But around 1970 there occurred a sea change in the way investment portfolios were managed. I've gone into great lengths about this elsewhere,[8] so suffice it to say here that by at least 1980 the management of securities portfolios had become a well-established and highly competitive business, and institutions that called themselves corporate trustees simply weren't among the competitive players.[9] At this point, corporate trustees that managed trust assets in-house were no longer acting in the interests of beneficiaries, but in their own interests. They should simply have gotten out of the investment management business—or gotten out of the trust business—because persisting in both was inimical to the interests of the trust beneficiaries they were supposedly serving.

But there was a slight problem—over the years, fees from investment management activities had come to dwarf fees from more traditional fiduciary duties. To say that this constituted a gigantic conflict of interest is merely to state the obvious. "Open architecture" was, and largely remains, a swear word among corporate trustees, except for the very largest trusts. The morals of the market place, indeed!

Deep Pockets

The notion that if something went wrong beneficiaries could sue the institutional trustee and expect a significant recovery was a nice one in theory, and indeed so many trusts are so abysmally mismanaged that corporate trustees lose lawsuits with great regularity. But the reality today is that institutional trustees go to extraordinary lengths to protect themselves—and in the process to disadvantage beneficiaries—from liability. Most of this occurs behind the scenes, as it were, buried in the fine print of state trust laws, over which the banks have enormous influence. The rest of it occurs in the remarkable acrobatics corporate trustees go through to avoid anything remotely smacking of an exercise of discretion (see below), or anything remotely smacking of incurring any risk in order to carry out settlor or beneficiary interests.[10]

Perpetual Life

Here, at least, we might expect the institutional trustee to live up to its billing—corporate entities do indeed have indefinite lifetimes. But, again, the real world has intervened with a vengeance, as the local banks that historically handled most trust business have been gobbled up by larger and larger banks until, today, the trust industry is very highly concentrated in a few hands. Even beneficiaries of relatively large trusts find that they are relegated to calling a toll-free number whenever they need a trustee's attention. On top of this, turnover among corporate trust employees is notoriously high, and it is the individual turnover—and the destruction of family privacy that goes out the door with it—that is as infuriating as the institutional turnover.

Sound Exercise of Discretion

When most corporate trustees were local institutions, they were generally able to exercise discretion as necessary in an impartial and informed manner, as mentioned above. But today, on the rare occasions when a corporate trustee can be arm-wrestled into making a decision, that decision is made by an anonymous group known as the "trust committee," whose main role seems to be to protect the institution at all costs, especially including sacrificing the interests of the beneficiaries.

DOWN WITH THE BUNDLED TRUST! UP WITH THE OPEN-ARCHITECTURE TRUST!

Given the hopeless and infuriating state of the trust business these days, families could be forgiven for taking to the barricades and demanding that the entire 1,000-year edifice of the common-law trust be pulled down so that we can start over. Of course, I am aware, with Anatole France,[11] that it is rarely the wealthy families who are manning the barricades. And yet families are in effect dismantling the bundled trust as we speak, replacing it with what I have dubbed the open-architecture trust. At its core, the open-architecture trust asks the simple question: For each activity that has historically fallen under the heretofore bundled umbrella of the trust, what is the best practice today? Let's ask—and answer—those questions for ourselves.

Activities Required to Operate a Trust

The operation of a trust requires that the assets be held in safekeeping, that the assets be capably managed, that tax issues be addressed and tax returns be filed, that administration and bookkeeping be handled, and that there be in existence a fiduciary capable of making decisions that cannot legally be made by settlors, beneficiaries, or other disqualified persons. These activities can be bundled together and carried out by one institution, or they can be unbundled and evaluated separately, determining what the best practice might be in each case and pursuing that practice unless the cost is prohibitive. Let's examine each of these activities separately.

Safekeeping of Assets   Trust assets must be safeguarded, and in the usual case that means holding securities in a custody account that is segregated from the bank's own assets and therefore not reachable by the bank's creditors in the event—relatively common these days—that the bank should fail. If this were, say, 1970, keeping the assets "safe" might be all that was required of a trust/custodian bank (most trustees bundle custody with all the other activities). But these days custody is a highly competitive, vastly complex business in which perhaps 10 or 12 institutions globally are even in the running. This is because the custody business is capital intensive (banks must be willing to invest huge sums of money in their technology platforms just to stay even) and low margin—even world-class custodians typically charge only a few basis points for custody. Yet modern custodians must be capable of handling a dizzying variety of securities traded on a global basis and must also offer such complex services as partnership accounting, securities lending, transition management,[12] and so on.

For these reasons, most trust banks' custody platforms are not just not best in class, they are often "worst in class," based on technology that is decades old. An interesting observation is that when professionals of large trustee banks leave to launch their own boutique trust companies, they almost never use their former employers' custody platforms—they know far too much about them.

Thus, the best practice for custody of trust assets is straightforward: Unbundle this activity and engage the best independent custodian at the best price available. For most trusts, there will be no more than a small handful of institutions that are appropriate candidates for the job.

Management of Trust Assets These days the overwhelming bulk of trust assets consists of cash and securities. And as we noted above, most institutional trustees bundle asset management with other trust services. But as with the issue of custody, corporate trustees are not merely not best-in-class money managers, they are mostly "worst in class." Open-architecture firms evaluate thousands of managers before selecting the best to add to their recommended list, and we do this on a straight-up, objective basis. Yet trustee-based investment managers are unrepresented to the point of invisibility on most open-architecture platforms.

Thus, the best practice for management of trust assets is to unbundle this activity and to select the asset managers independently of whoever the fiduciary might be. Typically, this is done by establishing an investment committee made up of trustees, but often not even including the corporate fiduciary. (See The Nitty-Gritty of Establishing Open Architecture Best Practices Trusts, following.) The investment committee then selects the actual managers, usually with the advice of an investment consulting or similar firm.

Tax Issues For simple and smaller trusts, the institutional trustee may be perfectly capable of advising on tax issues and of preparing and filing the tax returns. But for more complex trusts, tax issues should be unbundled and handled by competent tax counsel. In any case, tax returns can be prepared by outside tax advisors and then reviewed and filed by the trustee, or prepared and filed by the trustee on its own. The complexity of the trust's needs, including the need for partnership accounting,[13] should determine whether tax issues are bundled or unbundled.

Trust Administration Trust administration is a relatively straightforward proposition. It encompasses such tasks as ownership of the assets, bookkeeping, preparing trust statements, making distributions to beneficiaries, paying bills, maintaining bank accounts, and so on. The fiduciary normally bundles these activities ("ownership" must be bundled), but there is no reason why most of them couldn't be outsourced in appropriate circumstances.

Fiduciary Matters The fiduciary sits at the core of the trust relationship and should obviously be selected with great care. Therefore, the selection of the fiduciary should be based on a trustee's direct fiduciary skills, almost without reference to any other services the trustee might offer. Although occasions requiring the exercise of serious fiduciary discretion are typically rare, when they do arise they are likely to be sensitive and important.[14] Typical candidates for the role of fiduciary are trusted individuals (albeit raising the succession issue), distribution committees (see The Concept of the Directed Trustee, next), boutique trust companies,[15] traditional institutional trustees who are willing to unbundle trust services, and private trust companies.

The Nitty-Gritty of Establishing Open-Architecture Trusts

Establishing an open architecture trust is relatively straightforward, but there are a few key issues to focus on, including the concept of the directed trustee, controlling costs, and the deductibility of expenses.

The Concept of the Directed Trustee A key to the successful use of the open-architecture trust is the ability—under the language of the trust instrument or under the trust law of the state in which the trust is domiciled—to "direct" the trustee.[16] For example, management of the trust's assets might be vouchsafed to an "investment committee," and the trust institution will be "directed" to follow the instructions of the committee as to investment matters.[17] (Note that the trustee can be "directed" for some purposes—asset management, for example—but not for other purposes—making discretionary distributions, for example.) The investment committee might engage an advisor, such as an investment consulting firm, to assist it in designing the portfolio, selecting and monitoring money managers, reporting on investment performance, and so forth.

Similarly, discretionary decisions over distributions to beneficiaries might be lodged in a distribution committee, which itself might be subdivided into a family distribution committee that handles normal distribution issues and an independent distribution committee (with no disqualified members) to handle more sensitive, legally restricted decisions about distributions.

When a trust operates with an investment committee and a distribution committee, the corporate trustee becomes an administrative trustee, whose responsibilities are largely limited to owning the trust assets, physically making distributions to beneficiaries, preparing trust statements, signing the tax return, and similar administrative and ministerial activities. In a sense, the administrative trustee's most important role is to take direction from the trust committees.

Large institutional trustees who normally bundle asset management with other trust services will often agree to serve in an unbundled, best-practices trust structure, so long as (a) the trust is a very large one, or

(b) they can be directed to accept the decisions of investment committees and distribution committees. Many boutique trust companies are organized to do business mainly as directed trustees.

Isn't an Open-Architecture Trust Complicated?   Not really. Keep in mind that even if you take your trust business to a traditional, bundled provider, you will be dealing with completely different individuals for every key activity. The trust officer assigned to your account will be different from your investment officer, who will be different from the tax guy, who will be different from the folks in the custody group, and so on. With the open-architecture trust, instead of dealing with several different individuals selected for you by the bank, you will be dealing with several different individuals selected by you because they are competent and cost efficient.

What about Costs?   A carefully designed open-architecture trust will almost certainly be less expensive than the usual bundled trust structure. The main reason is that the client negotiates fees across the board in an open-architecture trust structure, rather than waking up years down the road to find that embedded fees in the bundled trust (for asset management, for example) have eaten up all the returns. In addition, under an open-architecture trust structure, each provider has no conflict of interest, and hence they will be watching each other. If the investment advisor's fees are too high, the outsourced tax advisor will happily point this out, and vice versa. If custody and reporting services are deteriorating, the investment advisor will cheerfully bring this matter to your attention—and vice versa. None of this happens in a bundled environment.

Deductibility Issues   Families sometimes express reluctance to unbundle their trust relationships because, historically, trustees' bundled fees have been deductible as ordinary and necessary business expenses, whereas some unbundled expenses (such as asset management fees) are subject to the "2 percent floor." This is penny-wise and pound-foolish, but in any event even if it was once an advantage of bundled trusts, it won't be for long. Following the United States Supreme Court decision in *Knight v. Commissioner of Internal Revenue*,[18] it is expected that the Treasury department will issue regulations requiring bundled trustees to unbundle their fees, even if they don't (or won't) unbundle their services.

The Rise of Beneficiary Rights

Suppose you are the beneficiary of an existing trust that you wish were an open-architecture trust but unfortunately isn't. Under common law you were basically up the creek without a paddle: There was little a beneficiary—or even a grantor—could do to remove or replace a trustee. Once a trustee was appointed it became the legal owner of the trust property with full authority over it. Only a gross breach of the trustee's duties could be grounds for its removal.

But the times, they are a-changing! Many states are adopting (in whole or in part) the Uniform Trust Code, which acknowledges, to a far greater degree than common law, the rights of beneficiaries and grantors. Often, for example, a beneficiary's rights can be protected only by removal of the existing trustee or by requiring the trustee to unbundle an activity that it is able to carry out only in mediocre fashion. For example, the Uniform Trust Code permits a trustee to be removed for "unfitness, unwillingness or persistent failure ... to administer the trust effectively."[19] Commentary by the drafters of the Code suggests that a "persistent failure" may "include a pattern of mediocre performance, such as consistently poor investment results."[20]

I believe that the natural evolution of court decisions in Code states (and, by analogy, in non-Code states) will be to require trustees to unbundle activities they are not very good at: custody and asset management especially.

If I Was a Big Trust Institution

If I was a big trust institution I would be very nervous about the increasing use of open-architecture trusts, directed trusts, private trust companies, the rise of the beneficiary rights movement, and so on. It would seem that the world was ganging up on me.

But, actually, trust families are simply mounting an intervention: trying to get the trust institutions' attention before it's too late. The open-architecture trust is one of those disruptive business models that seem to come out of nowhere and then one day own the business.[21] There are, after all, lots of reasons a family would want to work with a large institution as trustee, so long as it could pick and choose the activities it wanted and could go elsewhere for the others.

I don't blame the big banks for wanting all the business, but I actually believe that they would be better off in the long run by playing the open-architecture trust game: Their liability would be significantly reduced as a directed trustee; they wouldn't have to mess around with the complex business of custody unless they were good at it; they would likely get some of the asset management business; their relationships with their trust clients would be far happier; and the trust relationships would be much "stickier" than they are now, which is very good for profitability.

At the end of the day, if the big trust institutions don't become more flexible, the bundled trust business will go the way of the closed-architecture business; that is, it will evolve from the dominant business model to a besieged backwater. But if those institutions do become more flexible, both they and the families they work with will be a lot happier and more productive.

Note that most newer *private* trust companies (PTCs) operate on open-architecture principles, selecting portfolio management services by engaging the best managers available (see the following discussion). More recently, some old-line trust companies with public charters have begun to offer open architecture, or (more commonly) semi-open architecture approaches. In other words, these firms are willing to accept fiduciary responsibility without bundling it with asset management (although most bundle it with custody services). These offerings vary widely and need to be examined with care—the skill set and experience required to operate successfully in an open-architecture format are not easily acquired. But for families who need trust services, want open architecture, and cannot form their own private trust companies, open-architecture trust companies may be worth looking at.

Semi-Open Architecture Trusts

An option that is growing very rapidly is for families to convince their trust banks to allow them to operate in a semi-open architecture manner. Under this arrangement, the family's trust bank continues to serve as trustee and custodian, manages some portion of the trust, and allows the balance of the asset base to be managed by best-in-class managers selected by the client (and approved by the bank). Given the consolidation that has taken place in the banking industry, and especially on the trust side of the bank business, many families will find that their trusts have ended up at an institution that actually has something approaching a best-in-class investment product. Often this will be bonds, because fixed income is an asset class that thrives in a large, institutional environment.

Even if the family bank appears to have no products remotely approaching best-in-class quality (a distressingly common occurrence), a family can often structure a fixed-income portfolio that the bank will manage to strict guidelines, resulting in a bond portfolio that, though it will be unlikely to outperform, will at least rarely underperform dramatically. A final option when there is no place else to hide is to allow the family bank to manage equities on the condition that all equity exposure managed by the bank be in index products. These will likely be very expensive index products, when they exist at all, but what the family will give up in fees will be more than made up for in avoided underperformance.

PRIVATE TRUST COMPANIES

For very large families—those with liquid assets at least over $100 million—the private trust company (PTC) can make a great deal of sense. Such families are already likely to have significant infrastructure in terms of a family office, hence the incremental cost of setting up a PTC can be minimal. And because a PTC vastly simplifies many of the jobs the family needs to do—including complex accounting and reporting and providing ongoing trusteeship and administration of family trusts—the true net cost can easily be negative.

Until the late 1980s, when the Rockefeller family established a PTC, virtually all substantial families used the services of a commercial trust company or the trust department of a commercial bank. That option was never particularly desirable (aside from the poor quality of the investment performance, leaving sensitive family decisions to the trust committee of a corporate entity unrelated to the family was especially problematic), but with the massive consolidation of banks, leaving most American communities with no true local trust company, it has become unacceptable for any family that can afford another option.

The main advantage of the PTC is that it can provide fiduciary services directly to a family. Other forms of family office organization can support individual trustees or work with commercial trust companies, but they lack trust powers. A family that forms a PTC can thus avoid having to deal with an unaffiliated fiduciary and can, if desired, avoid ever having to burden any family member or friend with the risks of serving as an individual trustee. In addition, of course, a PTC is by its nature a far more private operation than a commercial trust company.

Until recently, PTCs were problematic for many families as the result of legal barriers in most states. For example, for centuries trust companies had been required to serve the needs of a broad public in order to obtain a charter. Only a few U.S. jurisdictions permitted the formation of a trust company designed to serve only one family, and those jurisdictions tended to be remote from population centers. These geographic and legal barriers boosted costs to a point where most PTCs formed before 1995 had to work with other families in an attempt to spread the costs of the operation. (Even the Rockefeller PTC became a multifamily office.)

Beginning in the mid-1990s, however, states began to understand the need for PTCs. By 1997, the Conference of State Bank Supervisors had promulgated the model Trust Modernization Act, which authorized PTCs on a reciprocal basis.[22] As of this writing, according to John P. C. Duncan (probably the leading legal expert on PTCs), 30 states have adopted the model Act or versions of it, including Connecticut, Illinois, New Jersey, New York, Ohio, Pennsylvania, Virginia, and Texas. Notably missing are California (California is always notably missing), Florida, Maryland, and Massachusetts.[23] With so many states jumping on the bandwagon, many families will find it possible to charter a PTC in a favorable jurisdiction (for example, one with a low minimum capital requirement) but to have the main office in their own town. On the other hand, if most of the family's existing trusts are in one state, it may be prudent to establish the PTC in that state. Courts will look more favorably on a petition to replace a trustee if the new trustee is domiciled in the same state.

TOTAL RETURN TRUSTS

Most trusts are designed to pay "income" (mainly interest and dividends) to one set of beneficiaries, while the "principal" (the original corpus of the trust plus any undistributed appreciation) accrues to the benefit of another set of beneficiaries. From the time the concept of the trust was first developed until about the 1950s, trust assets tended to produce far more income than capital appreciation. The long-term result was typically that early income beneficiaries fared well, but later income and principal beneficiaries fared poorly. (The decline of the English aristocracy was prominently fueled by this quiet phenomenon.) All that began to change half a century ago, and by the end of the twentieth century many sensibly invested trusts were yielding well under 2 percent. Today, therefore, the problem has reversed itself. Sensibly invested trusts—that is, those with predominantly equity-oriented portfolios—tend to appreciate handsomely over time, but they produce little in the way of current yield in our low-dividend, low-interest-rate environment.

Properly drafted trusts can easily deal with this problem by providing both a floor and a ceiling for payouts to current income beneficiaries. But what about the hundreds of thousands of trusts that were drafted years ago? State legislatures, under pressure from the legal and financial community and from income beneficiaries, have grappled with this issue, and roughly half the states now address it in one of two ways: via the Uniform Principal and Income Act (UPIA) or through unitrust legislation.

The Uniform Principal and Income Act

The UPIA, adopted in 1997, allows trustees to adjust distributable income by transferring principal to income or income to principal as required to achieve fairness between income and principal beneficiaries. The UPIA applies only to trusts that calculate the payout to beneficiaries by reference to net income. The UPIA, or a version of it, has been adopted in 24 states and another three or four have the Act under current review.

Under the UPIA approach, a trustee can invest the trust assets in any manner that is prudent, without regard to how much net income the trust will generate. Then, if the income is so low as to be unfair to the income beneficiaries, the trustee can make an adjustment by transferring principal to income and making a larger income distribution. If the income is so high as to be unfair to the ultimate principal beneficiaries (an unlikely situation these days), the trustee can transfer income to principal and make a smaller distribution. A provision added to the UPIA in 2000 limits trustee liability for making good-faith adjustments.

Unitrust Legislation

Another approach, adopted by fewer states, permits trustees of net-income trusts to convert those trusts to unitrusts. In a unitrust, distributable income is specified as a percentage of the trust assets as those assets appreciate or depreciate annually. Hence, a trustee can invest the trust assets in any manner that is prudent, then pay out a specified percentage of the trust value without regard to whether the payout includes income, principal, or both.

Note that a few states, notably New York, have adopted both approaches, giving trustees the choice of which to pursue.

The IRS View

The Internal Revenue Service has issued proposed regulations that endorse both the unitrust and UPIA models. Hence, the IRS will honor total return approaches to all trusts, including such trusts as marital trusts and generation-skipping trusts, in states that have adopted total return legislation. Importantly, the IRS provides a safe harbor only for total return payouts between 3 percent and 5 percent.

Total Return Trusts in States without Total Return Legislation

Newly drafted trusts can adopt total return approaches regardless of state laws. But what about older trusts domiciled in states that have not adopted total return legislation of any kind? There are two possible solutions for these trusts:

1. *Resorting to discretionary principal distributions.* Many net-income trusts authorize the trustee, in its discretion, to make principal distributions to income beneficiaries. Some trustees, particularly if they feel that they may otherwise lose the business, will use their discretionary power to distribute principal to augment low income distributions. If a trustee is recalcitrant, many trusts permit the trustee to be removed and replaced by an institution with a more modern outlook.
2. *Moving the domicile.* If necessary, the domicile of a trust can be moved to a jurisdiction that permits a total return approach. Court approval may be required.

The desire to have a trust managed on a total return basis is, of course, only one of many considerations in judging a trustee's performance. However, my experience has been that trustees who refuse point blank to explore approaches that make simple common sense are likely also to be undesirable from many other points of view.

CONCLUSION: LET'S GET REVOLUTIONARY

The financial industry in general is stacked against investors, but nowhere is the stack higher than in the trust business. This unfortunate situation wasn't designed-in by the industry, it was simply a byproduct—collateral damage, as it were—of the vast and accelerating consolidation in the banking industry.

But that doesn't mean that families are stuck with whatever the industry offers. Instead, there are many better solutions, from unbundling trust activities into what I've called open-architecture trusts, to using private trust companies, to finding those needle-in-a-haystack regional trust companies that offer best-in-class fiduciary services that are family friendly.

What families *shouldn't* do is settle for the status quo. *Wealthy families of the world, unite!*

NOTES

1. Parts of this chapter are taken from Greycourt White Paper No. 48: Best Practices Trusts (2010), cowritten with my partner, Thomas R. Moore. The paper is available at www.Greycourt.com.

2. *Meinhard v. Salmon*, 164 N.E. 545 (NY 1928).

3. Thrupthi Reddy, *How Not to Get Sued* (April 1, 2005). Available at registeredrep.com/mag/finance_not_sued/. Ms. Reddy was a senior editor at *Trusts & Estates* magazine.

4. At least one trust company, which manages almost all trust assets in its own mediocre products, was recently quoted as bragging that its clients trusted it because "we have no conflicts of interest." Such is the sad, deluded state to which corporate trustees have fallen.

5. Following the Norman conquest of England in 1066, all land on the island was confiscated in the name of the Crown. The king then parceled it out to his lords, who passed it on to their own vassals and so on, via the process of subinfeudation. Obligations, including heavy taxation and severe restrictions on the sale and use of the land, flowed from the bottom up: from the serfs to the higher vassals to the lower and higher lords and so on, up to the king. Because these obligations applied to the holder of legal title, the common-law trust—which divided legal title from beneficial use—was a kind of trick to avoid many of these obligations, especially taxes. In 1535 Henry VIII convinced Parliament to enact the Statute of Uses (a "use" is a trust), which collapsed legal title and equitable use back into each other. Henry's purpose was to destroy the monasteries, which, to avoid the Statutes of Mortmain (1279 and 1290), were all held in trust. (I know, it's complicated, but it gets better.) Henry dissolved the monasteries, all right, but most other trusts persisted via a nice bit of sleight of hand: Trusts were now created by making a grant in fee simple "unto and to the use of A in trust for [i.e., for the use of] B." Because a use upon a use had not been contemplated by the Statute of Uses, the Statute was held not to apply to these clever trusts.

6. F. W. Maitland, A. H. Chaytor, W. J. Whitaker *Equity: A Course of Lectures*, Cambridge: Cambridge University Press (1936).

7. Gilbert Paul Verbit, *A Ninth Century Treatise on the Law of Trusts*, Bloomington, IN: Xlibris (2008). It is a matter of considerable dispute whether the trust was independently invented by English common law or whether Crusaders returning from Arab lands brought the idea back with them. See, for example, Monica M. Gaudiosi, "The Influence of the Islamic Law of Waqf on the Development of the Trust in England: The Case of Merton College," *University of Pennsylvania Law Review* 136, no. 4 (April 1988): 1231–1261.

8. See Greycourt White Paper No. 24: A Modest Proposal: Let's End Conflicts of Interest in the Wealth Advisory Business (2003), available at www.Greycourt.com.

9. There were many reasons for this, but the main one was that bank and trust company cultures and compensation practices were inherently incompatible with superior securities management.

10. One of the most common issues involves holding concentrated securities positions. I'm not a fan of concentrated positions, but when the enterprise is a family company there can be very important reasons to be flexible about such holdings. Institutional trustees, on the whole, aren't.

11. "The law, in its majestic equality, forbids the rich as well as the poor to sleep under the bridges."

12. Most of these issues are discussed elsewhere in this book. See Chapter 22.

13. There are a (very) few institutional trustees that handle tax accounting for partnerships competently. For all others, partnership accounting should be unbundled and outsourced.

14. A common example would be a request by an income beneficiary for a principal distribution. Principal distributions are often permitted by the trust instrument, but are usually surrounded with qualifications. Only a completely independent fiduciary can make such decisions.

15. The rise of the boutique trust company is an important phenomenon. Typically launched by trust professionals who are refugees from the large institutional firms, these boutiques are usually located in and associated with a specific jurisdiction (Delaware, Nevada, South Dakota) that has abolished the Rule Against Perpetuities and has adopted other family-friendly laws and regulations. Other boutiques are regional firms not attempting to take advantage of a particular trust situs but simply designed to be much more user-friendly.

16. If your trust doesn't contemplate the use of a directed trustee, it is usually possible to have the trust language reformed (in court). If the state of your trust's domicile doesn't acknowledge directed trustees, it is usually possible to move the domicile to a more modern state.

17. For example, the South Dakota provision covering directed trustees: "Any excluded fiduciary [i.e., a directed administrative trustee] is also relieved from any obligation to perform investment reviews and make recommendations with respect to any investments to the extent the trust advisor has the authority to direct the acquisition, disposition or retention of any such investment." SDCL Sec. 55-1B2.

18. 552 US 1 (2008). Following Knight, and in light of proposed regulations issued by the Treasury department, most fees paid by trusts (bundled or unbundled) will be subject to the 2 percent floor; in particular, custody fees and investment advisory fees. For trustees who bundle services under a single fee, the trustee must unbundle the fees and use a reasonable method to allocate the single fee between the costs subject

to the 2 percent floor and those that are not (trust accountings, filing of tax returns, etc.).

19. Uniform Trust Code §706(b)(3).
20. Uniform Trust Code §706 (Comment); Restatement (Third) of Trusts Section 37, comment e (Tentative Draft No. 2, approved 1999).
21. See Chapter 6, especially the discussion of open architecture as a disruptive business model.
22. In other words, the Act allows a PTC chartered in one jurisdiction to maintain a full-service trust office in any other jurisdiction that has adopted the model Act or a similar measure.
23. Duncan, John P. C., "The Private Trust Company: It's Come of Age," *Trusts & Estates* (August 2003): 49ff.

Three

The Rich Get Richer

The Nuts and Bolts of Successful Investing

Assuming they start with roughly equal talent, great football teams are great because their strategies are better than those of other good football teams—their vision of the game is superior. But football teams have to be good before they can be great, and being good means mastering the rudiments of the game—the blocking and tackling without which even the greatest game plans cannot be carried out.

And so it is with managing a substantial investment portfolio. Whether a family's investment activities turn out to be great or not will depend on many factors, including the level of talent and vision the family can deploy. But every family can—and must—be good at the task. And being good means mastering the rudiments of the game—the nuts and bolts of the investment process.

Mastery in this sense doesn't mean mastery at a professional level. I don't expect that many families will read Part Three and promptly go into the business of advising wealthy families on their investment portfolios. But families need to master the nuts and bolts sufficiently to know when they are being competently advised; to ask the key questions; to carry out, in other words, their stewardship duties.

Part Three begins at the beginning—with the question of how taxable investment portfolios are designed—and proceeds through the various steps in the investment process roughly in order:

- Designing taxable investment portfolios.
- Adding value to family portfolios.
- Working with money managers.
- Investing in U.S. and non-U.S. equities.
- Investing globally.
- Investing in real assets.
- Investing in fixed income.
- Investing in hedge funds.
- Investing in private equity.
- Working with money managers.
- Managing investment-related taxes.
- Asset location, implementation, and portfolio transition.
- Performance monitoring and rebalancing.
- Investment policy statements.

Part Three ends with a long chapter that discusses a variety of investment challenges that seemed, for one reason or another, not to justify full-chapter treatment: asset custody, concentrated stock positions, establishing a family office, family investment partnerships, spending, asset protection planning, and soft dollars.

Because this section of the book is likely to be of most interest to other financial advisors, I have sprinkled throughout the text a series of Practice Tips, based on my own experience working with wealthy families over more than 30 years. I hope my colleagues in the industry will find these to be useful in their own practices, and that they will therefore avoid many of the mistakes I've made over the years.

CHAPTER 9

Designing Taxable Investment Portfolios

Asset Allocation for the Private Investor

I was particularly struck by David Hume's argument that, though we release a ball a thousand times, and each time, it falls to the floor, we do not have a necessary proof that it will fall the thousand-and-first time.

—Harry Markowitz

The stock markets are a trap for logical investors because they are almost, but not quite, reasonable.
—Paraphrase of a remark by G. K. Chesterton[1]

From earliest times, mankind has attempted to diversify the risks it faced. Shippers in ancient Egypt consigned their goods to several boats and sent them off at different times, presumably to avoid encountering the same storm (or perhaps the same pirates). In the Middle Ages traders sent their goods to the same destinations overland and by sea. The Rothschild dynasty's famously early and accurate news of world events (used by them to trade with very great effect[2]) was made possible in part because the family depended on more than one method of communication: fast, proprietary ships, but also couriers and even carrier pigeons.

In the first half of the twentieth century, modern investors intuitively understood the principle of diversification. We knew that owning two stocks rather than one would reduce our risk, and that owning 10 stocks would reduce risk still further. Moreover, we understood that owning both stocks and bonds would effect a dramatic reduction in risk, albeit at a similarly dramatic reduction in our returns.

But this was what we might call, in hindsight at least, "naive" diversification. It was naive because, while it often worked, investors misunderstood the underlying principle of diversification; namely, that what was important was not simply owning more than one security, but *owning securities that are not perfectly correlated in their pricing behavior.*

Consider investors who owned both Worldcom and Global Crossing—they fared little better than investors who owned one or the other of those hapless companies. Or consider investors who owned 10—or 50—dot-com stocks; they were clobbered in the tech collapse virtually as badly as if they had owned only one dot-com. Finally, as noted, investors who added bonds to their portfolios did indeed achieve risk reduction, but they also suffered a proportionate return reduction.

THE MARKOWITZ REVOLUTION

It wasn't until the middle of the century that Harry Markowitz, then a young, unknown professor at the University of Chicago, had the fundamental insight that it was correlation that mattered. In a then-little-noticed article published in a then-obscure journal,[3] Markowitz not only demonstrated that correlation mattered (or "covariance" as he put it); he went far beyond that insight to show that by paying attention to correlation investors could create portfolios that reduced risk without necessarily reducing returns. Indeed, in some cases (such as adding international stocks to a U.S. stock portfolio) risk could be reduced while returns actually *increased.* And in every case in which portfolios were sensibly constructed, risk could be reduced faster than returns declined. Markowitz was the Einstein[4] of the financial world, revolutionizing the way we thought about risk and return and making possible all the subsequent advances that have come to be known as modern portfolio theory.

This astonishing idea took more than 20 years to be adopted in the design of actual portfolios. Part of the delay had to do with the inherent time lag between ideas generated in the academy and the adoption of those ideas in the real world. But there was another problem; namely, the cost and unsophisticated nature of computing power. Consider how portfolios are designed using Markowitz's insights.

Asset allocation à la Markowitz seems deceptively simple. We need only know the future risks (expressed in terms of the standard deviation of returns) and returns for each asset class we wish to work with, as well as the future correlation of each asset class with each other asset class. This data is programmed into a computer which then chugs away, looking at all possible combinations of these assets.[5] The computer program, which is an "optimizer," is trying to identify those asset combinations that are optimal, that is, which produce the most return per unit of risk. Depending on how much risk we are willing to take, there may be many optimal portfolios available to us, and those will fall along the familiar efficient frontier curve. Possible portfolios that fall below the efficient frontier line are undesirable in the sense that they produce less return for the same risk. Portfolios that fall above the efficient market line are theoretically impossible.

PROBLEMS WITH MEAN VARIANCE OPTIMIZATION

Whenever there is a major bear market, investors begin to question everything. In particular, following the Financial Crisis of 2007–2008, many families decided that mean variance optimization (MVO), the main tool for designing investment portfolios for decades, simply didn't work.

Certainly MVO was overhyped by advisors, who should have been using MVO techniques simply as "what if" modeling exercises, not to design final, real-world portfolios. But now that the crisis is several years behind us and the markets have largely recovered, let's take a calmer look at the problems presented by MVO.

Computational Power

This process is known as mean variance optimization, or MVO, and so far, so good. But there are serious problems here. The first problem is that there are many, many possible asset combinations to be looked at. If, for example, we wish to consider including 10 asset classes in our portfolios, our optimizer will have to search through almost 33 million possible portfolios even before it begins to think about changing the *percentages* of each asset.[6] Even as recently as the early 1970s it required a computer the size of a large room, two days of computational time, and tens of thousands of dollars to run one mean variance optimization. In other words, the delay in adopting Markowitz's ideas was not entirely due to intransigence on the part of real-world investors.

Oddly, however, the unavailability of cheap, massive computational power was in some ways a blessing for investors. Without access to simple optimization tools, investors relied on reviewing portfolio combinations that had been developed by large financial firms and academic institutions, then applied their own judgment to the application of those portfolios to their own circumstances. In other words, they had little choice but to be thoughtful about the underlying theory of mean variance optimization.

Today, however, investors face a very different and, probably, more intransigent problem. MVO calculations are now simplicity itself.

Optimization programs are inexpensive and investors have access to massive and cheap computational power. These days any laptop computer carried around by a college freshman can run an optimization in a few seconds. But as a result, investors have come to rely on the machine, rather than to consider the underlying theory in a thoughtful way. Let's consider ways in which the machine might produce results that are dangerous to our wealth.

Garbage In, Garbage Out

I mentioned, earlier, the three inputs needed to conduct an MVO exercise: future risks, returns, and correlations for each asset to be included in the optimization. The trouble is, we not only don't know what these values are, we don't really have any idea what they are. This is partly because we can't foresee the future. If we could, we wouldn't be wasting our time designing our portfolios—we would simply pick the stock that is going to be the next Google and load up on it. But we can't.

The best work on asset class risks, returns, and correlations, for example, has been done by Ibbotson Associates, whose annual *Ibbotson Stocks, Bonds, Bills, and Inflation Yearbook* gives values for asset class data on a quarterly basis from 1925 to the present. Yet, when Ibbotson Associates attempted to issue projections for *future* asset class returns, their estimates were so bizarrely off the mark that the firm soon stopped issuing forward projections altogether.

But our inability to predict the future isn't the only problem—we also can't know the past. That may seem like an extraordinary remark, especially considering that I have just cited the excellent Ibbotson data. But the problem is one of definition—what past are we talking about? If, for example, we are talking about the returns on stocks since 1925, then we will get one answer. If we are talking about returns in the post-World War II period, we will get another answer. If we are talking about returns over the past 20 years, we will get still a third answer. Which of these (or many other) pasts is most likely to resemble the future? We can't know, of course.

But if we can't know the future and don't know the past—that is, if we are putting garbage data into the optimizer and are therefore certain to get garbage advice out of it—what good is mean variance optimization?[7] The answer is that, if used thoughtfully and with a clear sense of its limitations, MVO can lead investors toward portfolios that are more efficient and more appropriate for their needs than any other approach known to the financial world. But for MVO to play this role, our financial advisors must work exactly at the cutting edge of knowledge in this area.

The Challenge of Developing Thoughtful Data Inputs

If we are working with competent financial advisors, they will not use purely historical returns in their MVO calculations. Instead, they will adjust past returns to meet the conditions existing in the capital markets today and over our effective time horizons as investors. Future returns are extremely sensitive to starting values, and therefore, in particular, advisors must give serious thought to the valuations of assets at the time the MVO exercise is being undertaken. Advisors, frankly, tend to be very bad at this exercise, for two reasons. The first is that it is an enormously difficult task—if we really knew which assets were undervalued and (especially!) when those undervaluations were going to be reversed, we would be far wealthier than we are. The second reason is that most advisors are sales-oriented, not advice-oriented, and hence they are far better at telling investors what they want to hear than they are at giving their honest opinions about important matters.

Consider MVO analyses performed in the late 1970s—clearly, they should have taken into account the very low valuations of most equity securities at that time. And consider MVO analyses performed in the late 1990s—clearly, they should have taken into account the very high valuations of equity securities at that time. Instead, most portfolios designed during those periods of time used long-term historical returns (or something close to them) and performed miserably. Investors in the 1970s found themselves seriously *under*exposed to stocks just as the greatest bull market in U.S. history was starting. Investors in the 1990s found themselves seriously *over*exposed to stocks just as one of the worst bear markets in history was starting.

In addition, in thinking about the investment environment going forward, family advisors must consider not some generic time period that is convenient to the advisory firm, but the family's own actual investment time horizons. Thus, for example, the advisor might believe that, over the next decade, U.S. large-cap stock returns will reflect essentially their long-term averages. But if the family's real investment time horizon is 5 years, not 10, the advisor's opinion is largely irrelevant. If a family hopes to experience any investment success, they will want to work with advisors who can tailor their MVO inputs to the family's actual needs, rather than employing a central-office approach where one size fits all.

Multivariate Modeling

Virtually all modeling now being performed by advisors to create client portfolios looks nothing like real-world capital markets. The key problem is that single-period optimizers assume that the expected risks, returns, and correlations that are programmed into the optimizer will not change, even over long periods of time. In fact, risk levels, returns, and correlations vary, sometimes quite dramatically, over time. Markets can be calm or volatile, correlations can change overnight as markets move from risk-off to risk-on, and returns vary hourly. Skewness and kurtosis vary over time.

What is needed, but what is generally not available, is a multivariate input model that represents multivariate processes with time-varying joint distributional properties, that applies to a wide variety of dependence structures, and that allows the representation of many time series. While a few firms are working on designing such systems, most advisors continue to use overly simplistic modeling that generates portfolios that will not be robust under real-world scenarios.

Taking Taxes into Account

Family investors can't spend gross returns. Like it or not, Uncle Sam is our investment partner, as are the governor and, very often, the mayor. Because that is the case, why do advisory firms persist in conducting MVO analyses using pretax returns? The answer is that that's the way it has always been done. The first investors to use (and pay for!) MVO analyses were pension plans and large endowed institutions. When advisory firms began to seek private clients they didn't bother to adjust their analyses to reflect the singular nature of family clients—the most singular feature being that private clients pay taxes and institutional clients don't.[8]

Even if the tax consequences of all investment assets were the same, advisors who use pretax MVO analyses with private investors would be seriously misleading those clients. Assuming nontaxable and taxable investors with identical risk tolerances, the returns achievable by the former will be substantially higher than those achievable by the latter. In other words, private investors will either have to accept lower returns than institutional investors owning the same portfolios, or they will have to own different and more risky portfolios to achieve the same returns.

But the tax consequences of owning different investment assets are in fact *not* the same for private investors. Consider this question: Would you rather own a well-performing hedge fund that returns 15 percent per annum or a poorly performing private equity partnership that returns 15 percent per annum? If you are an institutional investor, the answer is that you would prefer to own the hedge fund—it is less risky and has better liquidity than the private equity partnership, yet generates the same return.

But if you are a *family* investor, the answer is likely to be quite different: You would probably prefer to own the private equity partnership. Why? Because the hedge fund will generate its 15 percent return primarily through short-term capital gains, while the private equity fund will generate its 15 percent return primarily through long-term capital gains. Most wealthy investors will pay high taxes on the hedge fund gains, but much lower taxes on the private equity gains. Hence, the question can be rephrased as follows: Would you rather get 12 percent per year or 9 percent per year?[9]

We can conduct a similar analysis with essentially every asset we might wish to use in our portfolios. We would notice, for example, that "value" stocks will generate much of their return through dividend payments, while growth stocks will generate much of their return through long-term appreciation. We will note that real estate and oil and gas investments offer tax advantages to families. And so on.

The point of all this is simple—our advisors need to conduct their portfolio design studies using *after-tax* returns, not pretax returns. The result of such an approach will be that different assets will be used in different proportions than would be the case if the studies were performed using pretax data—and the portfolios thus designed will be efficient and appropriate for taxable investors, as opposed to nontaxable institutions.

PRACTICE TIP

One obvious problem with designing investment portfolios to be keenly tax aware is that taxes aren't static. Especially in a world where governments at all levels are wallowing in debt, taxes are going to change, sometimes dramatically. And when they change, the responsive changes in our portfolios cause tax drag!

The lesson of this is that portfolios should be tax informed, but not tax driven. All the savings—and more—created by tax-driven portfolios can be lost when tax laws change.

Monte Carlo Simulations

In the process of designing our portfolios, financial advisors generate a substantial collection of modern portfolio theory statistics about the characteristics of various possible portfolios. These statistics are useful to advisors, but they are hardly useful to investors. What we need to see is the range of possible outcomes for various portfolios in dollars—and, preferably, in after-tax dollars. Such outcomes are developed using Monte Carlo[10] or similar simulations. These simulations begin with a portfolio starting value, then run many iterations based on the risk, return, and correlation characteristics of the portfolio.

Monte Carlo simulations are not perfectly accurate for several reasons. A principal reason is that what the computer is actually doing is taking a portfolio, holding it for a one-year period, and seeing what the outcome looks like. It then runs the initial portfolio for another one-year period and looks at that outcome, and so on. In the real world, our portfolios change every year and it is the range of outcomes associated with those changed portfolios that matter. Note that in reviewing Monte Carlo simulations, we will want to observe the range of outcomes for short, intermediate, and longer time periods. Because negative outcomes rise much more slowly than positive outcomes over time, if we look only at longer term periods we might be tempted to select a portfolio that will, in all likelihood, prove too risky for us over shorter term periods. It is therefore important that we look at each portfolio over a range of time periods.

The Problem of Fat Tails

Many natural events occur in a similar pattern; namely, a range of outcomes clustered around a long-term average outcome: the height of trees, the weight of smallmouth bass, visits of birds to a sanctuary. If you live in a region that, on average, receives 40 inches of rain in a year, the actual pattern may show that, two-thirds of the time, annual rainfall lies between 30 inches and 50 inches. A statistician would tell you that the mean rainfall in your area is 40 inches with a standard deviation (S.D.) of 10. Rainfall results therefore distribute themselves along the familiar bell curve.

Knowing this, we can calculate that, 95 percent of the time, rainfall in the area will be between 20 inches and 60 inches—two S.D.s. It might be *climatically* possible for rainfall in the area to be as low as 5 inches or as high as 75 inches, but those outcomes would be *statistically* almost impossible. We would not expect to observe such outcomes even over many centuries, and hence it doesn't pay us to prepare for or anticipate them in any way. (The so-called 100-year flood is really just the most remote of the possible outcomes, the one that falls in the 95th percentile, or two S.D.s. above the average.)

The returns produced by the capital markets also distribute themselves in bell curve fashion. But there is a crucial difference between capital markets and natural phenomena. The example of rainfall is an example of natural behavior largely uncompromised by human interaction. But securities prices don't somehow magically change from time to time—they change only in response to the action of human beings in buying and selling them. And human behavior, as we all know, is at best complex and at worst truly bizarre. We can behave with calm resolution one moment and panic along with the rest of the crowd the next moment.

The result is that the bell curve distribution of capital markets performance is not shaped exactly like a bell curve. Instead, it's shifted slightly to the left and is characterized by so-called fat tails: Extreme outcomes, good and bad, are far more common than statistics would suggest.

Thus, if the mean return on U.S. large-capitalization stocks is 10 percent and the S.D. is 20 (both roughly right over very long periods), then we would almost never expect to see annual losses of more than about −30 percent; that is, more than two standard deviations below the mean return. Indeed, if we experienced such a loss even once in a lifetime of investing we could consider ourselves to be relatively unlucky.

In fact, however, extremely poor and extremely good returns are far, far more likely to occur than a pure statistical analysis would lead us to believe. When Eugene Fama did his doctoral thesis on price movements of the Dow Jones Industrial Average, he discovered that for each stock in the index there were many more days of extreme price movements than would occur in a normal distribution. Random distribution couldn't explain these outliers:

> *If the population of price changes is strictly normal, on the average for any stock ... an observation more than five standard deviations from the mean should be observed about once every 7,000 years. In fact,* such observations seem to occur about once every three to four years."[11] (Emphasis supplied.)

Or consider the breathtaking market collapse that occurred over two days in October of 1987, an event that would have been statistically unlikely to occur "had the life of the universe been repeated one billion times."[12]

Investors thus face a curious dilemma. On the one hand, we have carefully constructed our portfolios using the best modern portfolio theory techniques, employing the necessary[13] assumption that market events will occur in a normally distributed fashion. On the other hand, we know from examining the actual data that some market events—namely, very bad portfolio performance[14]—will occur far more often than a normal distribution would lead us to expect. We have, in effect, succeeded in controlling a mathematical version of risk—normally distributed price volatility—but we have not adequately addressed the real risk that investors face: the risk that we will depart from our sound strategies in the face of unexpectedly poor results, thus incurring permanent losses of capital.

Price volatility matters, to be sure, and not just in the world of financial theory. Given our druthers, most of us would prefer to obtain a handsome long-term rate of return with little or no price volatility along the way. But we have to live in the real world, and in that world we must choose between, on the one hand, low price volatility and low returns and, on the other hand, high returns and higher price volatility. Given that reality, most investors can get used to price volatility *so long as it stays within an expected, reasonable range*. It is not price volatility itself that causes us to flee from sensible long-term strategies—it is unanticipated, apparently irrational price volatility.

BEST PRACTICES IN DESIGNING INVESTMENT PORTFOLIOS FOR FAMILIES

Now that we've reviewed the asset allocation process in a general way, along with some of the issues associated with it, let's take a look at how the best advisors and families approach the challenge of designing thoughtful asset allocation strategies.

What Are the Objectives for the Portfolio?

While most institutional portfolios have similar objectives,[15] the objectives for family portfolios can be radically different. It is therefore crucially important that families and their advisors discuss the family's goals, dreams, fears, and so on so that the objectives of the portfolio will accurately reflect the family's wishes.

At the end of the day, for the bulk of their portfolios, most families will want to focus more on the return *of* their capital than on the return *on* their capital. It's not that high returns are unimportant—it's that private capital is *irreplaceable*. Most families who have accumulated a great deal of liquid wealth are no longer in the wealth-producing phase of their family history. Indeed, the reason they have the liquid wealth is because they have sold the family business.

Contrast this with institutional capital. If a university endowment experiences dismal returns and its capital has shrunk relative to inflation, the university will simply gear up its advancement office and mount a capital campaign. If a pension plan performs poorly, the sponsor company will simply be required to inject capital into the plan. But if a family's wealth shrinks or disappears, it can't be replaced—it's gone forever.

This is what people mean when they say that family investors tend to focus on "capital preservation," or when they say that institutional investors are "relative return-oriented" while family investors are "absolute return-oriented." If the equity markets are down 30 percent and an institution's equity portfolio is down 28 percent, the institution has outperformed relative to the indexes and is, at least theoretically, satisfied. But a family whose equity portfolio is down 28 percent is unlikely to be satisfied, theoretically or otherwise.

Note, also, that unlike institutions, families often hold their wealth in radically different "buckets" and these buckets may have very different objectives. To take a simple example, imagine a family whose patriarch and matriarch have plenty of wealth to satisfy their needs over their lifetimes. They may wish to own a relatively low-risk portfolio. On the other hand, that same family may have established a generation-skipping trust (GST) that has no current spending demands on it and which is intended to benefit generations that haven't yet even been born. The portfolio for the GST may take a much higher-risk approach.

Because the process of understanding a family and its objectives is so crucial, it can take many months and many conversations to get it right. Advisors who rush into the job of designing a portfolio are likely to find that they have incorrectly understood the family's needs, and/or that the family has misstated those needs. Getting this process right takes time.

Current Claims versus Growth Claims on a Portfolio

One useful way of thinking about the initial steps of portfolio design is to ensure that the portfolio is built to satisfy—on a prudent basis[16]—both current and future claims on it.[17]

Current claims include the family's spending needs, including taxes, plus any additional lifestyle needs such as travel, philanthropy, and so on. *Future* claims (or growth claims) require that the portfolio will maintain the family's purchasing power (that is, net of inflation) over time, net of taxes and all fees and costs, and will also likely include the family's desire to *enhance* its financial status on a net-net basis.

Looked at in this way, we can see that the family is exposed to three primary risks. The first and most urgent risk is that the family could fail to meet its spending needs. The second risk is that the family's lifestyle might not be maintained over time: Even if their income stays the same, its purchasing power will decline in the face of inflation. Finally, the family could overcome those two risks but still fail to enhance its wealth across the generations. This last risk is the most difficult to overcome, not least because it is decidedly the case that families tend to compound faster than capital.[18]

Matching Portfolio Assets to Each Type of Risk

Risk #1—ensuring that the family can meet its current spending needs—requires that the family own an appropriate amount of capital preservation or "protective" assets, assets that will throw off income and tend to hold their value even in a broad and deep financial crisis. These assets will include cash, United States Treasury securities, TIPS,[19] and, as appropriate, portfolio hedges executed through puts, calls, and collars. Extremely safe municipal bonds might also fall into this category, although most municipal securities won't qualify, because in a deep financial crisis cities and states will find their income impaired. And, unlike the Federal government, they can't print money.

Risk #2—maintaining the family's lifestyle net of inflation over time—requires that the family own an appropriate amount of "market" or growth assets. These assets include global equities, bonds other than Treasuries, cash that is held for optionality[20] reasons, hedge funds of funds, diversified real assets (including commodities), and hedge funds.

Risk #3—the serious challenge of increasing a family's wealth over time net of all costs—requires the family to invest in "aspirational" assets. Aspirational assets include venture capital, buyouts, individual hedge funds, distressed illiquid investments, concentrated real estate, and similar investments.

As everyone knows, investment assets generally offer return characteristics that are consistent with the risks assumed. Thus, cash is a very safe investment but it returns less than inflation (after tax) over time. Venture capital returns can be very high, but the risk associated with venture investments is extreme. Thus, the more capital preservation assets we put in a family's portfolio, the lower the overall portfolio return will likely be. The more aspiration assets we include in the portfolio, the higher the risk will be.

It is at this point that modeling becomes important. In effect, the optimizer is told what percentage of income and aspirational assets to hold and then it simply optimizes for the growth portion of the portfolio. By specifying the income assets, we ensure that the family's current spending needs can be met. By specifying the aspirational assets, we at least give the family some hope for growing its wealth dynastically. The optimizer will specify the best combination of growth assets that will keep the family capital growing with inflation.

PRACTICE TIP

Obviously, the asset allocation selected for a client's portfolio has to be right. But very nearly as important is the way an advisor *frames* the issues and *discusses* the process with the client.

All too often, asset allocation strategies seem to the client to have emerged from an incomprehensible black box. The family might implement the strategy—what choice do they have?—but that doesn't mean they understand the first thing about it, or why it was selected, or how it is likely to perform over time. As a result, the strategy will be abandoned at the first sign of trouble—the very worst-case outcome for a family (and also for the advisor!)

As noted previously, I recommend talking to the family about asset allocation not in modern portfolio theory terms, but in terms of current and future claims on a family's capital. This is something family members can understand, even if they've never bought a stock or bond.

TRADITIONAL ASSET ALLOCATION MODELING

Financial advisors have traditionally begun the asset allocation process by assuming that there is a regular relationship between risk and return. For example, we would start with cash (the lowest-risk, lowest-return asset), then add an increment to compensate us for the risk of buying the next-riskiest asset, and so on. Consider Table 9.1.

TABLE 9.1 Building-Block Approach to Developing Return Expectations

Asset	Incremental Premium	Next-Riskiest Asset	Expected Return on Next Asset
Cash	Term premium	Inflation-linked bonds	Unknown
Inflation-linked bonds	Inflation premium	Government bonds	Unknown
Government bonds	Default risk premium	Corporate bonds	Unknown
Corporate bonds	Real estate premium	Listed real estate	Unknown
Listed real estate	Equity risk premium	Stocks	Unknown

Source: Greycourt.

And so on. This approach is accurate enough in a general way: Over very long periods of time cash will be the least risky and the lowest-return asset, while equities will return much more but also but with substantially more risk. But no one knows what the value of the incremental premiums should be. Even the equity risk premium, probably the most important source of return, is unknowable. Scholars have debated the value of that premium and their estimates for it range from 0 percent to 7 percent.[21]

And note that the uncertainty of the estimates gets worse as we go out along the risk spectrum: Because all the estimates are linked, errors can compound as we go along. Certainly, 30 years ago no one was predicting that bonds would outperform stocks, but that is what has happened. Maybe 30 years is simply too short a time period to make such a calculation, but note that three decades is longer than the typical investment lifetime for a member of a wealthy family.[22]

MODERN ASSET ALLOCATION MODELING

For these and similar reasons, many advisors have jettisoned the traditional approach and moved to an approach championed by Fischer Black and Robert Litterman (known as the Black-Litterman model).[23] Black-Litterman is an alternative method for estimating the inputs needed for portfolio optimization. Instead of estimating forward-looking risks, returns, and correlations, Black-Litterman relies on equilibrium models to determine the inputs.

Thus, Black-Litterman lets the markets themselves tell us what returns are, creating a market equilibrium portfolio using capital asset pricing model (CAPM) techniques. Black-Litterman presupposes that if everyone in the market had the same views about valuations, the demand for various assets would exactly equal their supply. Thus, global market capitalizations tell us what we need to know about returns, except for the process of applying our own views to that mix. As Black and Litterman put it in their original paper, "Our approach allows us to generate optimal portfolios that start at a set of neutral weights and then tilt in the direction of the investor's views."[24]

An example of this tilt would be to compare (for example) Robert Shiller's CAPE (cyclically adjusted price-earnings) ratio to current P/Es. The Shiller P/Es are "normalized" by dividing the real (i.e., inflation-adjusted) price level of the S&P 500 index by the moving average of the preceding 10 years of real reported returns by S&P companies.[25] At the time of this writing, current P/Es seem reasonable, at about 15x. But CAPE suggests that on a normalized basis, P/Es are actually well above 20x. Because the long-term average for normalized P/Es is about 16x, this suggests that stocks may in fact be well overvalued.

Whether stocks are cheap or expensive can't be known in advance, but an investor or its advisor will likely have an opinion, and that opinion, using the Black-Litterman approach, will drive the stock allocation in the investor's asset allocation strategy.

PRACTICE TIP

Using Black-Litterman to design portfolios represents a very large advance over older approaches, but it should also be said that Black-Letterman isn't for sissies. For many years after the approach was first proposed—and many articles written about it—it was still maddeningly difficult to figure out how to design a real-world portfolio using Black-Litterman techniques.

Fortunately, Thomas M. Idzorek, of Ibbotson Associates, has authored "A Step-by-Step Guide to the Black-Litterman Model."[26] It's recommended reading for any firm wishing to migrate from traditional asset allocation models to a more sophisticated model.

SATISFYING PORTFOLIO CLAIMS *PRUDENTLY*

Recall that I said that claims against the portfolio must be satisfied on a prudent basis. What I am thinking about is that the *path* of a portfolio's returns matters a great deal. Imagine a six-foot tall nonswimmer who is determined to cross a pond he knows to have an average depth of three feet. The critical question for our nonswimmer isn't the *average* depth of the pool, but the *deepest* depth. If the pond is 100 feet across, and there is a 30-foot stretch that is 15 feet deep, our nonswimmer is doomed.[27]

A family can also be doomed even if the long-term average return on its portfolio is satisfactory, because there could be a very bad stretch in the markets that drives the portfolio value and the family's income below critical limits. Thus, a portfolio can end up, many years in the future, achieving the family's long-term return objectives, but the family (or the portfolio) won't be around to see it. The portfolio ultimately achieved its goal, but it was a failed portfolio because along the way it allowed the family's wealth to fall below the minimum level that enabled the family to live the way it wishes to live.

PRACTICE TIP

Asset allocation isn't the sexiest part of an advisor's job, and as a result it's easy to give it short shrift. Especially for advisors who have been in the business for a very long time, it's easy to imagine that we know better than the client how best to structure the portfolio. But in fact there is no one best way to design an investment portfolio for a family—everything depends on the family itself.

It's important to get the family talking about the nature of the risks it faces with its capital, to ask the right questions, and, especially, to listen to the answers.

CONCLUSION: ART VERSUS SCIENCE

Designing investment portfolios—and especially portfolios for taxable investors—is more art than science. But it has to be done: We have to have a structure to guide the investment of our capital, and that structure has to be fundamentally related to the risks we will be facing as we invest. Traditional mean-variance optimization was a way of getting at these issues, and over the years other approaches have been suggested as well, including the Black-Litterman process I have highlighted.

In the future, there will no doubt be newer and perhaps better approaches to the challenge of portfolio design. But the industry will never develop a fail-safe approach that works for everyone because the markets are full of uncertainty. What matters is the thoughtfulness of the process itself.

NOTES

1. Chesterton's actual remark was, "Life is a trap for logicians because it is almost, but not quite, reasonable.
2. Perhaps the most famous example of the Rothschild family trading on early knowledge of world events occurred in connection with the Battle of Waterloo. Nathan Rothschild, then head of the English branch of the family, learned early in the day that Wellington had defeated Napoleon and that English securities would rise dramatically when the news was broadly known. You might imagine that Rothschild would use that news to buy. But he knew that Waterloo was a once-in-a-lifetime opportunity

and he intended to make the most of it. Therefore, he began quietly to sell. Word gradually spread across the floor of the exchange that the Rothschilds were pulling out of the market. Astute traders began to sell also, assuming that Wellington had lost. Rothschild accelerated his selling and soon the exchange was in a panic. Finally, with prices at preposterously low levels, Rothschild swept in and bought, making a vast fortune in a few hours.

3. "Portfolio Selection," *Journal of Finance* 7, no. 1 (March, 1952): 77 ff. Markowitz's breakthrough ideas about portfolio design actually had their origin in his earlier insight about the possibility of applying mathematical methods to the capital markets. It was from this inspiration that all else followed.

4. Like Markowitz, Einstein was virtually unknown when he published his seminal papers on the photoelectric effect, the special theory of relativity, and statistical mechanics. Indeed, he was not even a practicing academic, but an obscure clerk in the Zurich patent office.

5. Notice that the computer is not trying to solve a complex equation. Instead, it is conducting an iterative process of looking at each portfolio and discarding those that produce inferior results.

6. Modern mean variance optimizers employ algorithms designed to reduce—drastically—the number of asset combinations that must be reviewed. See, for example, Markowitz's own work on the fast computation of mean-variance frontiers in his book, *Portfolio Selection: Efficient Diversification of Investments* (New York: John Wiley and Sons, 1959), Appendix A. In addition, financial advisors almost always constrain the optimizer—by, for example, requiring that recommended portfolios have minimum or maximum exposures to certain desired assets.

7. There are many other problems with using MVO and similar asset allocation techniques. See, e.g., Gregory Curtis, "Asset Allocation," in *J.K. Lasser Pro Expert Financial Planning: Investment Strategies from Industry Leaders*, edited by Robert C. Arffa (New York: John Wiley & Sons, 2001), 327–345. But the best and most popular book on the subject of asset allocation is Roger C. Gibson's *Asset Allocation: Balancing Financial Risk*, 3rd ed. (New York: McGraw-Hill Trade, 2000).

8. Private foundations do pay a small excise tax.

9. Yes, private equity is typically a riskier asset class than hedge, but even on a risk-adjusted basis most families would prefer the private equity return.

10. The name is unfortunate, as it connotes gambling. However, as we all know (I hope!), gambling statistics are biased in favor of the house,

while Monte Carlo simulations produce a straight-up, unbiased series of possible outcomes.

11. Eugene F. Fama, "The Behavior of Stock-Market Prices," *Journal of Business of the University of Chicago* 38, no. 1 (January 1965).

12. These calculations were prepared by Jens Carsten Jackwerth and Mark Rubinstein, "Recovering Probability Distributions from Option Prices," *Journal of Finance* 51, no. 5 (December 1996): 1,612. Yale Professor Benoit Mandelbrot has calculated the odds of the three major daily market declines in August 1998 at 1 in 500 billion, and the odds of three large declines in July 2002 at 1 in 4 trillion. See Benoit Mandelbrot and Richard L. Hudson, *The Misbehavior of Markets* (New York: Basic Books, 2004), 4.

13. Necessary because mean variance optimization is a mathematical technique, not a psychoanalytical technique.

14. Our portfolios will also experience unexpected and very good performance, but we are unlikely to complain about that.

15. Many institutions, for example, state the objectives for their endowment portfolios roughly like this: "The objective of the endowment is to provide a steady and growing stream of revenue to support the institution's operations and mission." There will also be metrics around this broad statement, such as, "The stream of revenue, and the return on the portfolio, should grow faster than inflation net of all costs over a long period of time."

16. The issue of prudence is discussed later. See Satisfying Portfolio Claims Prudently.

17. This discussion is indebted to the insightful work of Ashvin B. Chhabra, whose signature article in *The Journal of Wealth Management* should be required reading for anyone involved in designing portfolios for family investors. See "Beyond Markowitz: A Wealth Allocation Framework for Individual Investors," *The Journal of Wealth Management* 7, no. 4 (Spring 2005): 8–34. I have departed from Chabbra's terminology somewhat, given the nature of the audience for this book. I am also indebted to my partner at Greycourt, Jim Foster, who contributed substantially to this discussion.

18. Estate taxes also represent a significant headwind, albeit one that can be substantially reduced via competent estate, tax, and trust planning.

19. Treasury Inflation Protection Securities, which are Treasury bonds designed to pay a real (adjusted for inflation) yield.

20. In other words, cash held now but which is expected to be invested when interesting opportunities present themselves. Portfolios that are too illiquid lack optionality.

21. See Brett P. Hammond, Jr., and Martin L. Leibowitz, "Rethinking the Equity Risk Premium: An Overview and Some Ideas," *The Research Foundation of the CFA Institute* (2011). Hammond and Leibowitz review the literature and come up with 19 estimates of the equity risk premium, ranging from 0 percent to 7 percent.

22. That is, family members typically succeed the prior generation by assuming stewardship of the portfolio when they reach their mid-40s and their parents are in the mid-60s. They will maintain oversight of the family's capital for about 20 years and then pass the mantle to the next generation. Thirty years' worth of upside-down capital markets returns means that an entire generation will have failed in its stewardship duties.

23. The background of the Black-Litterman model and how it is used is described on the website www.blacklitterman.org. See, also, Guangliang He and Robert Litterman, "The Intuition behind Black-Litterman Model Portfolios," available at SSRN: ssrn.com/abstract=334304.

24. Fischer Black and Robert Litterman, "Global Portfolio Optimization," *Financial Analysts Journal* (September–October 1992): 28–43.

25. Reported earnings are averaged in order to control for business cycle effects. See John Y. Campbell and Robert J. Shiller, "Valuation Ratios and the Long-Run Stock Market Outlook," *The Journal of Portfolio Management* (Winter 1998).

26. Thomas M. Idzorek, "A Step-By-Step Guide to the Black-Litterman Model, Incorporating User-Specified Confidence Levels," (working paper, draft of April 26, 2005, available on numerous websites).

27. I am indebted for this analogy to Chhabra, "Beyond Markowitz", note 17.

CHAPTER 10

Adding Value to Family Investment Portfolios

Price is what you pay. Value is what you get.

—Warren Buffett

Over a very long period of time, the greatest value will be added to a portfolio by the long-term asset allocation strategy the family and its advisor have selected. That's one reason it's so important to get asset allocation right.

But once the allocation strategy has been settled on, there are numerous other ways in which a family and a good advisor can add value. In this chapter we'll briefly discuss those value-adding techniques.

MOVING FROM THE CURRENT STRATEGY TO THE NEW STRATEGY

When a family has just experienced a major liquidity event and is mainly invested in cash, or when a family has engaged a new advisor who has recommended a different strategy than what the family has been using, the question will arise: How do we move from our current position to the new strategy?

The answer depends mainly on market valuations at the time the new strategy has been selected. If it's 1999 and the equity markets—especially the growth and tech sectors—are selling at all-time highs, it would be very foolish to move quickly to a fully invested position in stocks. Sure, the markets could continue to run for a while, and if the family isn't fully invested they won't fully participate in the run-up.

But this is a minor problem—after all, the family is already rich. On the other hand, if the family jumps heavily into extremely rich equity markets, it will be vulnerable to a price collapse—and such a collapse did in fact occur in early 2000. For a family that has spent an entire lifetime—or several lifetimes—building its wealth, losing a substantial chunk of it right out of the box is a devastating event.

Instead, the family will be better advised to move slowly into the equity markets, probably not moving above its minimum equity targets and also focusing on undervalued sectors like value stocks.

On the other hand, if it's mid-1974 or early 2009 and the markets are in the tank, moving to a fully invested equity position rather quickly can make sense. Even if the markets continue to decline for a while, the stocks will have been purchased at attractive valuations and the family can be assured that any losses will be made up.

PRACTICE TIP

Moving to a new strategic target when the markets are in a screaming bull phase or a frightening bear phase isn't complicated (though it can be nerve-racking). But suppose you, the advisor, are agnostic or uncertain about the markets. For example, in late 2011 and early 2012, there were both attractive and unattractive aspects of stock prices. P/Es were relatively low, corporate profits were high, and balance sheets were strong. The U.S. economy seemed to be slowly growing again. On the other hand, there were serious concerns about a blowup in Europe and/or a war with Iran, and Shiller CAPE ratios suggested that stocks might be seriously overvalued.[1]

In cases of uncertainty, my suggestion is to keep firmly in mind how long it took the family to get rich. In one case I began advising a family that had sold a business that took three generations to build. It was early 2001 and I didn't know whether the bear would continue or whether markets would improve. My inclination was to invest the family's capital very slowly—over three or even five years. Although the family members weren't experienced investors, they were concerned about taking so long to get to a fully invested position.

So we compromised. I took $100 million (a fraction of the family's total wealth) and invested it immediately in the long-term strategy I had developed but was reluctant to fund. The rest of the capital remained in cash and bonds, along with a few opportunistic bets and some absolute return-oriented hedge funds. Although the fully-invested $100 million portfolio didn't do very well, it helped the family understand what investing was all about and how complex the risks can be. Meanwhile, the main bulk of the family's capital preserved its value and we accelerated the investment program as the markets recovered in 2003.

ADDING VALUE THROUGH MANAGER SELECTION

Although selecting good managers is the first thing most investors think of when talking about adding value, the sad fact is that in almost all cases managers will *subtract* value from the portfolio. I have devoted an entire chapter to the subject (and the perils) of the manager selection process, so I won't repeat that here.[2] Instead, let's simply assume that selecting managers who will outperform net of all costs *in the future, while they are managing our capital* (rather than in the past, when they weren't), is extraordinarily difficult.

So how can manager selection add value? First, select your managers with care. Although it's very difficult to identify managers who will outperform, it's not so difficult to identify managers who are extremely competent, reasonably priced, and who invest in predictable ways.

Second, adopt a skeptical attitude. Unless you are very certain that a manager will add value, your default position should be to index. I don't necessarily mean index in the Vanguard S&P 500 Index Fund sense, because capitalization-weighted indexes present serious issues. But passive and structured products should always represent the default option.

Third, try not to think about individual managers as representing permanent positions in your portfolio. Instead, think about managers as arrows in your quiver of value-adding techniques that can be used opportunistically, as appropriate. For example, consider the case of a manager who uses a defensive style, buying only high-quality companies and raising cash when he doesn't like the looks of the market. I may have no idea whether that manager will outperform over a long period of time, but I can be pretty certain that he will outperform in treacherous market environments. If that's the kind of market I expect, that's the kind of manager I want. Once markets recover, I may not be so enthusiastic about that manager.

The same thing is true, for example, of a manager with a value bias. If value stocks have been on a tear, I can be pretty certain that my value manager isn't going to do too well over the next cycle. I should probably reduce my exposure to him.

Fourth, size your managers appropriately. Your largest positions should normally be in passive products like tax-aware index funds or structured funds. Around that position we can build "satellite" positions in managers whose styles—very different from index or "closet" index funds—give them a chance to outperform. But these positions won't typically be as large as the passive position.

Finally, think countercyclically. If I know a manager is very competent, and if I observe that he has underperformed in recent years, I can be pretty sure he will outperform over the next market cycle.

PRACTICE TIP

When you first begin working with a new client, it's very important to begin the education process with the family about managers. Falling in love with managers and focusing on them as the main hope for adding value is a rookie mistake. And because most families are rookies when it comes to the investment process, this is a very common error.

No matter how good a job you do in selecting managers, many of them will disappoint you. Therefore, if you live and die in your client's eyes on manager selection, you will have a very short lifespan.

One way to help get the client's focus off managers is to emphasize the many other ways in which you can add value to the portfolio. Hence this chapter.

ADDING VALUE BY TACTICALLY REPOSITIONING THE PORTFOLIO

Many investors are so terrified by the sin of "market timing" (which certainly can't be done successfully) that they shy away from any sort of tactical positioning. This is a mistake, and it's especially a mistake in family portfolios, which are far more sensitive on the downside than on the upside.

When an asset allocation strategy has been established, it will have targets for each asset category but will also have defined strategic ranges; that is, upper and lower limits within which the portfolio will be allowed to fluctuate. After all, you can't rebalance back to the target every day!

For example, suppose the strategic target for exposure to U.S. small-company stocks is 8 percent. The strategic range might be 6.5 percent to 9.5 percent. How does an investor know whether to be at target or at the minimum or maximum exposure?

The answer is that it depends on where market valuations currently stand in relation to where valuations have been historically. If small-cap stocks are selling today at valuations that are well above long-term norms, an investor would be well advised to move toward the lower limit of the strategic range. On the other hand, if small-cap stocks are selling well below their long-term valuations, the investor might do well to move toward the upper end of the range.

This isn't market timing because the tactical moves never extend beyond the strategic ranges that have already been approved. And there has to be *some* thoughtful way for an investor to position the portfolio within the range. That thoughtful way should be valuation based.

Note that the most common reason tactical positioning fails has to do with the timing of the move. The mere fact that prices in some sector are above the norm doesn't mean they won't go even further above their norms—and stay there a long time. (And the same on the downside.) For this reason, families and their advisors shouldn't undertake tactical moves unless they are guided by a detailed and thoughtful outlook on the markets and on each sector that might be subject to tactical repositioning.

PRACTICE TIP

Many families, having read over and over that market timing doesn't work, will be skeptical that tactical positioning can add value. It's a reasonable position for a family to take, especially with a new advisor who has no track record with the family.

If you are the new advisor, you can do two things to help build street cred with the family. First, make *small* tactical decisions early in the relationship. Even if the family is skeptical that you will add value, they won't object to a small repositioning.

Second, focus on tactical shifts that are *capital-preservation* based. In other words, when prices in some sector of the market are well above normal, back off on that allocation. Because the family likely has a capital-preservation bias anyway, they are more likely to go along with a defensive repositioning—and more likely to forgive you if you're wrong!

ADDING VALUE THROUGH OPPORTUNISTIC INVESTMENTS

However bad the markets are, there are always pockets of opportunity somewhere. And even during bull markets, when sensible investors won't buy expensive stocks, there is likely to be something cheap if you look hard enough.

In 1999, when tech and growth companies were selling at outrageous multiples, value stocks were going begging,[3] as were nontech small-caps and real estate investment trusts. In 2007–2008, when the credit crisis was in full bloom and markets were on the verge of their worst collapse in a generation, they were practically giving away closed-end bond funds.

Unfortunately, though, too many advisory firms seem brain-dead when it comes to finding nuggets of gold in a mountain of dross. Once, when I was serving on the investment committee for a well-known university, a committee member asked the university's advisor if he had any interesting investment ideas. "Well," said the advisor, "I saw in the *Wall Street Journal* that the smart money is buying blue chips."

The reason so many advisors wouldn't know an opportunistic investment if they tripped over it is simple—most advisors aren't investors. They are consultants, brokers, client service professionals, and so on. There may be a small army of analysts somewhere in a back room, but those people are (a) too young to understand investment value, and (b) focused on manager diligence, a very different thing.

For institutional investors, this may not be a big issue. Many institutions have their own in-house investment staff, and virtually all have investment committees, often full of savvy investors. Also, many institutions actively avoid making opportunistic investments, for fear they won't work out. The institutional mind-set tends to be to get to the target asset allocation and stay there by rebalancing every quarter. As many people have noted, institutions would rather fail conventionally than succeed unconventionally. Still, because rebalancing necessarily involves selling high and buying low, it works reasonably well over time.

Unfortunately, it doesn't work well for families, who have to pay taxes (and higher transaction costs) every time they rebalance. Because families can't take as much advantage of the magic of rebalancing as institutions, families need other arrows in their quiver, and one of these arrows should be opportunistic investment ideas.

That means, of course, that families need to engage an advisor who isn't brain-dead when it comes to sniffing out interesting values. But how can a family find such an advisor? I've devoted a separate chapter to the important question of hiring the right advisor, so I'll cut to the chase here. You hire a good investor by asking good investment questions during the interview process.

Unfortunately, most families ask questions like, "How many analysts do you employ?" These families are apparently unaware of the fact that most analysts are engaged in doing low-level diligence on money managers. Families ask, "How many managers do you follow?" as though quantity weren't the enemy of quality.

Instead, consider assessing a financial advisor they way you would assess, say, a multistrategy hedge fund. No one much cares how many analysts a hedge fund has, but only how good they are and how well they are being trained working under senior portfolio managers. No one cares how many opportunities a hedge fund manager is looking at, but only the quality of those opportunities.

And those are the kinds of questions a family should be asking of potential advisors. What is your process for identifying interesting investment opportunities? How well structured is that process? Do you implement your ideas yourselves or via external managers (or both)? How do final decisions get made about which opportunities will be pursued? How do you size opportunities?

Unfortunately, few families ever ask such questions.

PRACTICE TIP

One extremely important aspect of opportunistic investment is its role as a morale-booster during difficult market environments. When it seems to your client that everything is going to hell in a handbasket, that's the best time of all to show up at a client meeting with an interesting opportunity. Even if the family isn't going to put a lot of capital behind the idea, the mere fact that there are ways to make money in such a headwind will help cheer the family up and make it far more likely that they will stay the course.

So though it's true that investment opportunities can be found in almost any market environment, opportunities that you can show your client during the market's darkest hours are worth their weight in gold.

ADDING VALUE THROUGH MONITORING AND REBALANCING

This should go without saying, but careful monitoring of investment portfolios pays ongoing dividends. (See Chapter 20, which goes into some detail on this subject.) Note that this doesn't imply taking frequent actions in a portfolio. Indeed, the default position should also be *not* to act, because so many investment mistakes happen as a result of knee-jerk or emotional decision making. But thoughtful monitoring will identify areas that need to be watched carefully. Is your small-cap growth manager shooting the lights out even though the small-growth benchmark is stalled? Maybe he's a very smart guy—but maybe he's jumped aboard a tech bandwagon that's going to run off a cliff.

I mentioned rebalancing earlier, but will reiterate it here: Frequent, by-the-numbers rebalancing might work for institutional investors, but it doesn't work for families. Instead, rebalancing must be done in a thoughtful and tax-sensitive (and cost-sensitive) way. Strategic bands around target allocations should be wider for families than for institutions, and even when an allocation is out of guideline, the costs associated with rebalancing need to be assessed against the benefits. Rebalancing is important, because it is directly associated with the risk level of the portfolio. But taxable investors can also go broke rebalancing.

CONCLUSION: WE NEED ALL THE VALUE-ADD WE CAN GET

Given all the headwinds they face (see Chapter 4), families need to exploit every opportunity to add value to their portfolios. While the value we can add will sometimes be modest, every basis point counts. Paying attention to portfolio transitions, manager selection, tactical repositioning, investment opportunities outside the core allocation, and monitoring and rebalancing of the portfolio will help keep the capital growing net of costs, taxes and inflation.

NOTES

1. Shiller's CAPE (cyclically adjusted price earnings) "normalizes" P/E ratios by dividing the real (i.e., inflation-adjusted) price level of the S&P 500 index by the moving average of the preceding 10 years of real reported returns by S&P companies. See Chapter 9.
2. See Chapter 17.
3. During that strange era a very fine value firm, Sanford C. Bernstein, was so weakened that it was acquired by a very ordinary growth firm, Alliance Capital.

CHAPTER 11

Investing in U.S. and Non-U.S. Equities

*In investing money, the amount of interest you want should
depend on whether you want to eat well or sleep well.*
                                        —J. Kenfield Morley

Once their portfolios have been properly designed, many investors (and, alas, many advisors) immediately move on to the selection of money managers. This is almost always a mistake, because it confounds two allied but distinct issues. Evaluating and selecting managers is one of these issues, of course (see Chapter 17). But a preliminary issue exists; namely, what are the optimal *strategies* that should be pursued in the asset classes that are to be included in the portfolio? Once asset class strategies have been identified, the manager selection process will be much simplified.

In this and the next few chapters I will discuss best practices for investing in the main asset classes wealthy families employ in their portfolios: domestic equities, non-U.S. equities, fixed income, hedge funds, private equity, and real assets.

Every type of investment asset comes fully accessorized with its own investment challenges, as well as different tax, risk, return, correlation, and other characteristics. And every investor comes fully accessorized with his or her own individual objectives, time horizons, tax issues, and judgments about alpha versus risk premium.

Before families turn their attention to the hiring of money managers, they need to give careful consideration to the characteristics of the asset classes they propose to use and to their own specific needs and points of view. They can then structure investment strategies that maximize advantages and minimize disadvantages. Strategies that might be appropriate for nontaxable investors, for example, might be wholly inappropriate for taxable investors. Strategies that are appropriate for the U.S. large-cap sector might be inappropriate for the international sector, and so on. Once these strategies are in place for each asset class the family plans to include in their portfolio (based on the asset allocation strategy they have selected), the strategies will themselves point us toward a very small subset of the huge money manager population that is likely to be of interest.

Let's now take a look at strategies that are likely to prove productive for taxable investors in each of the main traditional asset categories: U.S. large- and mid-cap stocks, U.S. small-cap stocks, international stocks (including international small-cap and emerging markets), and fixed income.

U.S. LARGE- AND MID-CAPITALIZATION STOCKS

The first thing to notice about U.S. large- and mid-capitalization stocks, that is, stocks in companies whose names are likely to be familiar to us, is how extraordinarily efficient this category of assets is. These companies are so large and important to the U.S. economy, so many money managers and investors are buying and selling them, and so many analysts are following them, that it is virtually impossible for any one money management firm to gain *and sustain* a competitive advantage over its peers.

When we consider the burdens that managers bear—management fees, trading commissions, spreads between bid and ask prices, the market impact of their trading activity[1] and the opportunity costs associated with making buy and sell decisions[2]—it's easy to understand why it is so difficult to find U.S. large-cap managers who will add to our wealth beyond what we could obtain by investing passively through index funds, exchange-traded funds (ETFs), structured funds, or passive, tax-aware funds.

As a result, many family investors will find that the most attractive approach to the U.S. large-cap sector will be to create a core position with a passive, tax-aware manager, and then supplement that position with more modest commitments to boutique or hedge fund managers selected for their ability to deliver after-tax alpha. A passive, tax-aware manager is simply a management firm that, rather than attempting to own securities that will outperform the index, attempts instead to make intelligent trade-offs between matching the index performance and minimizing investor taxes.

The best way to understand how passive, tax-aware management works is to compare it with purely passive investing, as through an index fund. If we buy an index fund, my manager will purchase a portfolio of securities designed to replicate the performance of the benchmark index, typically the S&P 500 stock index. The manager will simply hold those securities passively until the makeup of the index changes. (Periodically, Standard & Poor's will remove some stocks from the index and add others in an attempt to keep the index current and representative.) The manager will then sell those stocks that have been removed from the index and buy the stocks that have been added.

That selling and buying activity will cause me to incur taxes, even though we have done nothing but passively own the index fund. Worse, over time and assuming the stock markets go up, my interest in the index fund will be worth far more than our tax cost basis. When we wish to sell my interest, we will face a big capital gains tax bill. Some investors who have owned index funds for decades have built up such huge embedded gains that the tax cost of selling the account becomes prohibitive—the investment is frozen, even though it may no longer be appropriate in purely strategic terms.

A passive tax-aware manager starts out in the same way as an index fund, purchasing a portfolio of securities designed to replicate the performance of a benchmark index.[3] However, the manager then begins to tax-manage the account. Every day, some stocks in the index will appreciate in price and others will decline. When individual stocks have declined sufficiently in price to justify the costs of the trade, the manager will sell them, "capturing" the losses. The manager will then either wait 31 days[4] and buy the stock back or, more commonly, replicate the position derivatively. Over time, the manager will have created a basket of losses that can be used to offset the inevitable gains that occur when the makeup of the index is changed. More important, by capturing losses consistently, the manager is ensuring that there will never be a huge difference between the tax cost basis of the account and its market value. Thus, the investor can liquidate the account without incurring a large capital gains tax.

The main downsides of passive, tax-aware investing are the costs of trading and the increased tracking error against the benchmark caused by the tax-management of the account. "Tracking error" simply refers to the difference in the performance of the account and the performance of the benchmark index. A true index fund should evidence extremely small tracking error, while a tax-managed index fund will inevitably show slightly larger tracking error. However, the savings in taxes will almost certainly compensate the investor for this downside. The goal of a passive, tax-aware manager is not to outperform the index on a gross basis, but to outperform it on an after-tax basis.

Once the passive, tax-managed core position is in place—typically 50 percent to 75 percent of the entire U.S. large-cap stock allocation—we can then turn to filling out our large-cap position by hiring the best managers we can find. Recognizing that persistent outperformance in the large-cap space is extraordinarily difficult, we will tend to look for such managers among boutique firms and hedge fund managers (see Chapter 17). Even if we make mistakes, as we are likely to do, we will at least have reduced the impact of those mistakes on our net wealth.[5]

PRACTICE TIP

As I've noted elsewhere (see Chapter 17), some clients are "manager junkies," investors who seem mesmerized by money managers and who believe that selecting great managers is the key to investment success. Such clients can be very difficult to deal with, as they are constantly chasing hot managers and insisting that their advisors hire this manager or that manager.

A cursory look will usually disclose that the manager the client wants to invest with simply happened to be in the right place at the right time recently, and will soon be in the wrong place at the wrong time. But it can be very difficult to convince the client of this.

A useful strategy with such clients is to structure the equity portfolio in a core-and-satellite manner, with a passive, tax-aware core. Around this core we can engage "satellite" managers, that is, managers who will be entrusted with much smaller portions of the client's portfolio.

This strategy allows us to honor the client's wishes, even if we are skeptical about the manager. If the client proves to be right and the manager performs well, we can always increase the allocation to that manager. In the more likely event that the manager disappoints, at least he will have done so with less of the client's money.

U.S. SMALL-CAPITALIZATION STOCKS

In stark contrast to the efficient nature of the large- and mid-cap stock markets, the small-cap sector is intensely *inefficient*. There are thousands of small companies in scores of different industries, scattered all across America and frequently located in smaller, out-of-the-way communities. Investment banking firms cannot make much money on these firms, and hence investment analysts don't cover them. The only way to learn anything useful about such companies is to engage in very hard work: traveling to their locations and talking directly to the management teams, the suppliers to the companies, the customers of the companies, and the competitors of the companies. This isn't what most people think of as fun, and consequently managers who are willing to do it end up in the possession of information about small companies' prospects that is of considerable value, because it is not widely known. Indeed, history shows that, over time, smaller capitalization stocks significantly outperform larger capitalization stocks.

But before we leap to the conclusion that families should load up on small-cap stocks, let's look at the dark side of this picture. The first negative is the high price volatility historically associated with owning small-cap stocks. As we know from reading Chapter 4, investment assets that exhibit high price volatility must produce much higher returns than low volatility assets to achieve the same terminal wealth. Hence, the higher historic returns of small caps are to some extent negated by their higher price volatility.

The second problem with small caps is that, even if they ultimately produce returns superior to large caps, they can go for very long periods of time (e.g., virtually the entire 1990s) without doing so. Small cap investors, in other words, must be prepared to be patient.

Finally, there is a body of thought that argues that the superior return historically produced by small-cap stocks is a product of the fact that small-cap indexes (such as the Russell 2000 stock index) are not traded. Trading smaller securities, it is argued, is so expensive that it completely negates the superior returns offered by the asset class. A representative example is a memorandum sent by Aronson Johnson Ortiz, a (large-cap) money management firm, to its clients and friends in the spring of 2003. AJO commissioned Wilshire Associates to examine trading costs and returns across different capitalization sectors of the stock market. Wilshire concluded that the largest quintile of stocks by capitalization returned, between 1974 and 2002, only 13.0 percent, versus 17.6 percent for the smallest quintile. However, Wilshire also estimated round-trip trading costs for the largest quintile of 31 cents, or 0.8 percent of the average share price of $41. By contrast, Wilshire estimated round-trip trading costs for the smallest quintile of stocks to be 91 cents, or an astonishing 6.1 percent of the average small-stock share price of $15. This caused small-cap returns, on a net basis ("Real World Returns," in AJO's terms), to fall below large-cap returns, 11.5 percent to 12.2 percent.[6]

There is clearly something to this argument. Commissions and spreads on smaller company stocks are much higher than on larger, highly liquid stocks. But the crux of the issue is market impact. Many small companies have limited stock issues and quite small floats.[7] As a result, when a large money manager attempts to purchase a useful position in such a company, its interest causes the stock price to rise significantly. Similarly, when a manager believes that a small company stock has reached its full potential, the manager's desire to sell the stock seriously depresses its price. Unless the manager is very careful, the trading costs incurred in buying and selling a small-cap stock will completely offset the superior return of the stock.

My own view falls somewhere in between the argument that "small caps will always outperform in the long run," and the argument that "the small-cap effect is completely illusory." A small group of small-cap managers have mastered the art of trading smaller company securities, accumulating positions very slowly over time, and liquidating positions slowly and carefully. They limit turnover severely and will avoid even attractive stocks if they cannot find a way to trade them efficiently. These managers can deliver significant alpha, even net of their trading friction. On the other hand, the notion that we can simply invest in smaller stocks and sit back and watch our wealth increase is clearly delusional.

PRACTICE TIP

A perfectly sensible strategy in the small-cap space would be to ask our passive, tax-aware manager (see the earlier discussion under U.S. Large- and Mid-Capitalization Stocks) to manage our client's money not against the S&P 500—a pure large- and mid-cap index—but against, say, the Russell 3000, which includes smaller-cap stocks. That will give the client roughly a 7 percent to 8 percent exposure to small caps on a passive basis. We can then consider increasing that exposure by identifying one or two boutique or hedge fund managers who specialize in small caps and in whom we have great confidence.

A final issue to keep in mind in the small-cap space is that there is a huge difference between small-cap value and small-cap growth. A small-cap growth company may be a budding technology company that could either become the next Microsoft or the next Wang (which went bankrupt). A small-cap value company is likely to be making iron castings in Duluth. These are very different enterprises, needless to say, hence when we look for small-cap managers we will probably want to diversify our exposure between growth and value.[8]

INTERNATIONAL DEVELOPED COUNTRY STOCKS

Most of what was said above about small-cap stocks goes equally well—except more so—for international equities. The sector is a vast and inefficient one, hence manager skill and hard work can pay off handsomely. On the other hand, trading costs (and custody costs[9]) can be very high, bleeding away much of the advantage of international investing. Fortunately, as free market economic systems gradually spread throughout the world, the most bizarre and inefficient local market practices are fading away, to be replaced by trading institutions and mechanisms that look more like those in the United States and Europe. This is, however, a slow process, as older, inefficient players continue to exercise enough political clout to slow their own march toward oblivion.

There are many criticisms of international diversification. Some investors believe that international diversification is unnecessary, pointing to the very high correlations between the U.S. markets and international developed country markets that have persisted in recent years. Other investors concede the long-term benefits of international diversification, but point out that during very negative periods in the U.S. markets the international markets are also highly likely to be weak, rendering international diversification useless just when you need it most. Finally, some investors, even those who recognize the benefits of international diversification, simply distrust foreign markets (and foreign governments) and advocate gaining international exposure mainly through American Depository Receipts (ADRs).[10] Let's examine these criticisms one by one.

International Diversification Is Unnecessary

It is certainly true that, from time to time, the correlations between U.S. equity markets and foreign equity markets increase. But to argue from this that international diversification is unnecessary is to drive by looking in the rearview mirror. Correlations among equity markets change slowly over time, but they are not monodirectional. During some market periods—especially those that are powerfully directional (up or down)—correlations will increase and we will conclude that international diversification provides no benefits. But no sooner will we eliminate our international exposure than—*voilà!*—correlations will move the other way and we will have lost the benefits.

It can, to be sure, be maddening to own international stocks during periods when they are both underperforming U.S. stocks and providing little diversification (as was the case during much of the 1990s). But because it is impossible to time correlation changes and investment return leadership, the only way to gain the long-term benefits of international diversification is to own international equities as a permanent core position in our portfolios. Thus, in constructing those portfolios we should establish a range for international exposure and remain near (but not below) the bottom of that range when correlations are high. As correlations decrease, our exposure to international stocks will typically rise of its own accord and it will now be our job to keep that exposure near (but not above) the top of the range.

Just When You Need It, Diversification Doesn't Work

This is, alas, all too true, at least if we think of our need for diversification as a short-term requirement. When the U.S. equity markets collapse, we can be pretty certain the international markets will also collapse. But if we wish to succeed as investors, we simply have to accept the fact that we cannot design portfolios that are both bulletproof and wealth creating. If we try to do so, we will end up failing as investors, mainly by consistently buying into markets at the top and selling out of them at the bottom. Bad markets—bad markets globally—are simply a part of the investment experience, just as bad periods are a part of any good marriage. The only way to make our portfolios bulletproof is to put all our money in U.S. Treasury bills and become slightly poorer every day.

PRACTICE TIP

It's understandable that clients become annoyed when diversification doesn't seem to be working. During global market crises, correlations do in fact go to one.

An important point to communicate to your clients is that diversification isn't designed to work at all times and under all conditions. It's not a short-term fix for volatile markets. The point of diversification—including, especially, international diversification—is to reduce the *long-term price volatility* of our investment portfolios. The reason for reducing portfolio volatility over the long term is that, the more volatile our returns, the lower our terminal wealth will be. (See the discussion of variance drain in Chapter 4.)

Thus, it is precisely when our clients don't seem to need it—when the price volatility of our client portfolios is being modestly suppressed by our international diversification—that diversification is doing its job. Yes, it would be nice if collapsing U.S. markets were always offset by rising international markets (or vice versa), but it doesn't happen that way. More important, it isn't necessary for it to happen that way for diversification to work its wealth-creating magic for our clients.

It's Easier and Safer to Gain International Exposure by Investing in ADRs

It's easier and safer, to be sure, but it's also mainly a waste of time. ADRs are issued mainly by gigantic multinational foreign corporations whose prospects are affected in the main by exactly the same factors that affect the prospects of gigantic multinational domestic corporations. Buying ADRs of BP isn't going to gain us any more diversification than buying ExxonMobil. There is nothing wrong with buying ADRs if we think the issuer is a good investment bet, but there is no point in buying them to obtain international diversification.

The Bottom Line

The best way to gain international diversification for most family investors is to look for international equity managers who are truly exposing their portfolios to regional, national, and even local factors. Some of these managers will be focused on smaller-capitalization companies whose prospects are inherently more likely to be dominated by nonglobal factors, while others will be buying larger-capitalization companies focused heavily on local and regional foreign markets. Owning these kinds of companies will, over the long term, tend to provide both diversification against a U.S. stock portfolio and also slightly higher returns—one of the few "free lunches" in the investment world.

As with U.S. managers, some international managers will tend to have a growth bias and some will have a value bias. If our portfolios are large enough, we may wish to gain exposure to both types of managers. However, international managers can also be classified as top-down or bottom-up in their approach, and this taxonomy is likely to prove more useful to us in diversifying our international exposure.

A top-down manager tends to observe conditions in global regions and countries and to decide which of those locations are likely to offer the most attractive investment prospects. Only then does the manager begin to look for individual companies in those regions. A bottom-up manager tends to look for the best companies regardless of where they may be domesticated, and then only secondarily will the manager make sure it is diversified regionally and by country. While the long-term results of these two types of managers will be similar, over intermediate periods of time, top-down and bottom-up managers will exhibit quite different return patterns, justifying diversification between those two approaches when possible.

EMERGING AND FRONTIER MARKETS

Emerging and frontier markets are where most of the excitement is in international investing. Because they are growing much faster than the developed world (at this writing, they represent about 8 percent of global market capitalization), there are more opportunities to make money—but also more opportunities to lose it.

Emerging Markets

It's useful to think of emerging markets as being analogous to U.S. microcap stocks. The sector is very inefficient, and hard work—and shoe leather—can pay off. On the other hand, with emerging markets you not only have to do serious work on individual companies, you also have serious geopolitical risk. Many investors in emerging markets are "hot money," people who have piled into the sector because recent returns have been strong. But when the market turns, these people bail out quickly, driving the markets down even further. Capital flight is a huge problem for emerging economies.

Because of the many challenges associated with emerging markets, many people either index[11] this sector or they go in the opposite direction, gaining their exposure via long/short hedge funds that typically exhibit huge tracking error against the MSCI Emerging Markets Index. There is, in other words, a lot of skepticism that traditional active managers can add much value in emerging markets, and it's a skepticism that I share.

While every long-term investor should have something like an 8 percent to 10 percent position in emerging markets, it's important not to go overboard in this sector. Even if it's true that the emerging economies will continue to outgrow the United States, Europe, and Japan, that doesn't necessarily translate into higher returns. And given the enormous price volatility these markets exhibit, it especially doesn't translate into greater wealth.

Consider, for example, that the United States grew much faster in the nineteenth century, when it was an emerging market, than it did in the twentieth century, when it was a developed market. But the returns during both periods were quite simple—you just had a lot more volatility along the way in the nineteenth century.

Okay, that's old news. But before you join the emerging market bulls, here are a few other things to keep in mind:

- First, everyone on the planet knows that the emerging economies are growing far faster than developed world, that their stock exchanges are generally fairer than they have been in the past, and that the emerging countries have broadly managed their economies better than the developed countries in recent years (albeit largely by accident). So guess what? The good news is already priced into the emerging markets—you can only make money on a risk-adjusted basis if those markets do even better than everybody thinks they will do. This seems unlikely. Second, there is no necessary correlation between a region's rate of economic growth and the investment returns of investors in the region. Price is everything. I already mentioned the example of the United States. But consider Asia versus Latin America in the first decade of the twenty-first century: Asia experienced much faster growth, but Latin American returns were three times as high.

- Third, note that there is a technical problem with emerging market stocks. Companies in emerging economies are growing rapidly, and, to fund that growth, they issue stock financings that invariably dilute existing shareholders—who are thereby "cheated" out of the returns they might have expected.
- Finally, a powerful analogy can be made with the tendency of boring stocks to outperform exciting stocks. Because investors tend to overestimate the potential of growth stocks (seduced by their concededly rapid growth and sexy products) and to underestimate the potential of boring value stocks, value stocks have significantly outperformed growth stocks over a very long period of time. Keep this in mind the next time you are tempted to pay up for rapidly growing, sexy emerging markets stocks.

Frontier Markets

If emerging markets are an exciting place to invest capital, I hardly know what to say about the so-called frontier markets. Although the term "frontier markets" is now 20 years old, it has really been only in the last few years that investors have discovered this obscure sector.[12]

A market falls into the frontier category for any of several reasons. For example, it might be very small (in terms of market capitalization), there may be trading or ownership restrictions that disqualify the market for inclusion in the MSCI Emerging Markets Index, and liquidity will tend to be poor. Note that not all frontier markets are poor: Kuwait, Qatar, and the United Arab Emirates are wealthy countries and they represent the largest component of most frontier markets indexes.

Some frontier markets will be reasonably familiar to most people (Argentina, for example), but most nations that fall into the frontier category will make the typical investor's skin crawl: Bangladesh, Botswana, Estonia, Nigeria, Pakistan, Serbia, Sri Lanka, and Vietnam.

There are basically two reasons to consider investing in frontier markets. The intuitive reason is that some—perhaps many—of these markets will gradually evolve in a positive direction, becoming more like emerging markets. Getting into such markets early, while prices are still discounting all the uncertainty, can pay off.

The second reason has to do with the possibility that frontier markets add diversification to global equity portfolios, improving the efficiency of portfolios and roughly offsetting other risks the frontier markets bring to the table. This advantage hasn't been conclusively demonstrated, but it seems plausible.

In any event, frontier markets allocations in family portfolios should be small. Altogether, frontier markets represent only 3 percent of global equity market capitalization (but note that they are roughly twice that large in terms of GDP).

Most investors will gain access to frontier markets via index funds or ETFs, but beware of huge tracking error. Mutual funds are another option, because careful country selection can add value, but keep in mind that liquidity is by definition low and costs very high.

For the most sophisticated investors, hedge funds and hedge funds of funds may be the best option. But even here it's important to keep in mind that it's nearly impossible to short individual securities listed on frontier markets, and that shorting ETFs or indexes is fraught with basis risk.[13]

PRACTICE TIP

Whether we're talking about emerging markets or frontier markets, the question will arise: What kind of benchmark should we use for this sector of our client's portfolio? Obviously, the benchmark will have a powerful effect on the managers or investment products we use and on how we will feel about our managers' performance.

One interesting option for these markets is to select a *fundamentally*-weighted benchmark. Suppose, for example, we choose a version of the emerging markets or frontier markets index that is not capitalization-weighted, as most indexes are, but GDP-weighted. Such an index will result in ever-larger allocations to the fastest-growing economies, which is more or less what we would like to see.

CONCLUSION: EQUITY SECURITIES ARE AT THE CORE OF MOST PORTFOLIOS

Long equity securities will constitute the central core of most family investment portfolios, allowing the capital to grow along with the global economy and, with hard and careful work, adding value beyond the inherent beta of these securities. To maximize the value of a long equity exposure, family investors will need to look beyond the familiar Blue Chip stocks that were once deemed sufficient. Non-US stocks, emerging markets stocks, and even frontier markets stocks should be considered. The opportunity set for family investors is very broad, and families should take advantage of those opportunities.

NOTES

1. "Market impact" refers to the fact that when someone buys or sells a stock, that very activity affects the price of the stock. When a manager buys, the increased demand causes the price of the stock to rise slightly, meaning that the management firm pays more for the stock than the market price before it placed its order. Similarly, when a manager sells a stock, that activity depresses the price of the stock slightly, causing the manager to receive less for the stock than the prevailing market price before it placed the sell order.
2. Opportunity cost refers to the loss of value that occurs between the time a manager decides to buy or sell a stock and when the transaction actually occurs.
3. Note that clients often include low-cost-basis securities in these types of portfolios, hoping that tax harvesting elsewhere will allow the low-basis stocks to be diversified over time at a low tax cost.
4. Investors cannot simply sell a stock on day one and buy it back on day two—the so-called "wash sale rule" prohibits such purely tax-motivated selling. The rules require investors to wait a minimum of 31 days before buying back the same stock they have just sold. There are, however, many ways to maintain essentially the same investment exposure without actually owning the stock—by buying a very similar stock, for instance, or buying an exchange-traded security that is highly correlated with the stock.

5. See Chapter 18 for a discussion of the use of directional (long/short) hedge funds as the high-alpha component of a U.S. large-cap asset class strategy.

6. Aronson Johnson Ortiz, "Small Cap Stocks Are *Sometimes* Cheap but They're *Always* Expensive," quarterly letter, April 24, 2003 (emphasis in the original).

7. "Float" refers to the amount of a stock issue that is actually traded. Many smaller companies, even publicly held ones, are owned primarily by one family or by the management team. As a result, only a portion of the stock actually floats; that is, is available for purchase.

8. An increasingly troublesome issue for small-cap managers is the crowding-out factor caused by hedge fund activity in the small-cap space. A few long-only small-cap managers have actually exited the business because hedge funds were, in their view, causing chaos in the pricing of small-cap stocks.

9. See the discussion in Chapter 25.

10. American Depository Receipts are securities issued by foreign companies that trade on U.S. stock markets. A foreign company that wishes to list its ADR in the United States must comply with certain rules, mainly regarding U.S.-type financial disclosure and financial reporting.

11. When I say "index," I include highly structured approaches such as those used by Dimensional Fund Advisors (DFA), although these are not traditional index products.

12. The term was first used in 1992 when International Finance Corporation began to produce data on markets even smaller than the emerging markets. The first investable index wasn't launched until 2007, when Standard & Poor's introduced the Select Frontier Index (which included 30 of the larger companies based in 11 frontier countries) and the Extended Frontier Index (150 companies from nearly 30 countries). Today there are several rival frontier markets indexes and ETFs.

13. "Basis risk" refers to the possibility that when a manager attempts to hedge an investment position, the long position and the offsetting short position may not experience price changes precisely in the opposite direction from each other.

CHAPTER 12

Investing Globally

The world is round.

—Eratosthenes (225 B.C.)

The world is flat.

—Indicopleustes (550 A.D.)

The world is round.

—Galileo Galilei (1610)

The world is flat.

—Thomas Friedman (2005)

The overwhelming majority of families are inappropriately diversified versus the global equity opportunity set. And because this is so, and so inappropriate, I propose to spend a considerable amount of time on the case for global investing.[1]

Not so long ago, it was routine for advisors to recommend allocating, say, 35 percent of a portfolio to U.S. large- and mid-cap stocks, 10 percent to U.S. small-cap stocks, and 15 percent to all non-U.S. stocks. In other words, only 25 percent of the overall equity portfolio was invested outside the United States, even though more than half the global equity market is non-US.

This huge home country bias reflected mainly inertia from the days when the U.S. equity markets dominated the world. But those days are long gone—beginning with the collapse of the Soviet Union and the adoption of free market economic models virtually everywhere. Today, the United States represents less than half the total global equity capitalization, and that percentage is highly likely to continue to shrink, as emerging economies like China, Brazil, India, and Russia grow rapidly.

Thus, if by "global investing" we mean looking for the best stocks on a global basis, regardless of where the company is domesticated, then global investing is a very rare phenomenon. American investors, even experienced investors, tend overwhelmingly to own U.S.-centric portfolios. Are investors really intending to make such a huge bet against foreign stocks? Probably not. But if not, why the low exposure to international equities?

WHY GO GLOBAL?

The arguments for global investing are reasonably familiar to everyone—they proceed from the undoubted rapid integration of the world's economies and financial markets since the collapse of the Soviet Union (and with it, collectivist economic ideas)—but perhaps they bear repeating briefly. Here are the main points.

> **The world has become a very small place.** Today we can e-mail someone halfway around the world, call him to let him know we need a quick response, conduct final discussions through instant messaging, text-message over a final comment, then fax over the signed contract, all as simply as doing business with the fellow down the street. And when the initial prototype is ready for review, our supplier in Bangalore can FedEx it to us and we'll have it the next morning. Instantaneous communications push the idea of global investing in many ways large and small, but the main thrust of modern telecommunications is that our fear of things foreign dies out quickly in the glare of familiarity and habit.

> **Everyone's a capitalist.** For those of us who were already in midcareer when the Soviet Union collapsed in 1989, it seemed as though one day half the economies in the world were centrally managed and the next day none of them were. That's an exaggeration, of course—witness Cuba, Venezuela, parts of the Middle East and sub-Saharan Africa, and even China, to a larger extent than its boosters want to acknowledge. But it is certainly true that the demise of the Soviet Union caused—if only by example—most of the world to turn to free market economies of one kind or another. As a result, the world is a more stable, more friendly, more understandable, and more investable place than it ever was before.

It's harder and harder to tell a U.S. company from a foreign company. Coca-Cola is headquartered in Atlanta, but it gets far more than half its revenue, and even more of its profits, from non-U.S. operations. Is Coke an American or foreign company? When Lenovo acquired IBM's personal computer business, it was headquartered in Beijing. Lenovo is incorporated in Hong Kong and its stock is listed there. But its CEO is based in Singapore, its Chairman is based in Raleigh, North Carolina, its CFO is in Hong Kong, its human resources head is in Seattle, and global marketing is managed out of India. An increasing number of U.S. companies have decided to reincorporate in an offshore jurisdiction to escape what they view as noncompetitive U.S. regulatory practices. Foreign or domestic? Indeed, there seems to be an increasing push for one worldwide accounting standard, making domicile distinctions not just increasingly irrelevant but almost prehistoric. Finally, many companies in the United States and elsewhere, regardless of where their sales and profits come from, have integrated their design, manufacturing, and distribution processes worldwide. And these are not just the global multinationals, but so-called "platform" companies everywhere.

Many foreign economies seem to be better managed than the U.S. economy. In the bad old days, international investing in general, and emerging markets investing in particular, was only for investors with very strong stomachs. Many foreign economies were abysmally managed, local juridical systems were highly suspect, and currencies were widely manipulated. But today, having apparently learned their lessons, a remarkable number of foreign economies are well managed and robust, evidencing smaller budget deficits, lower trade deficits, and even more stable currencies than in the United States.

Foreign companies are now as well managed as American companies. The world is a very competitive place, and foreign companies that may once have sought senior corporate executives only from among the nomenklatura have long since wised up. Cultural differences still exist in the corporate world, but it would be very difficult to say with assurance that the United States has any decided advantage in the quality of our corporate leadership—if only because American management practices have been so widely emulated.

The quality of foreign markets has improved substantially. Given that I am talking about the buying and selling of securities, the efficiency, honesty, cost, transparency, liquidity, and legal protections of foreign stock markets are obviously of central importance. And here the news is mostly good. No foreign bourse can rival the New York

Stock Exchange in these metrics, but many come close and all have improved—and continue to improve. Even in the emerging countries, stock markets are fairer and more rational than ever before, and in the developed economies there is now little to complain of.

The BRICs[2] really matter. In the old days, outside the United States there was Europe and a few emerging economies. Europe was mired in a quasi-socialist quagmire and the emerging economies were mainly good places to lose lots of money. Today, though, Europe has made great strides and, as noted above, many emerging countries could teach the United States a thing or two about managing an economy. But the real story is one that didn't even exist a decade ago: Brazil, India, and China (Russia is more problematic) are gigantic and hugely productive societies that are not merely emerging from long backwardness but may one day replace the United States as the world's largest economy. Investors who aren't exposed to these and other rapidly emerging economies simply have their heads in the sand.

The world is growing faster than the United States. The U.S. economy, despite its gargantuan size, often seems to have the vibrancy, the resilience, and a variety of growth characteristics that make it look more like an emerging market than like, say, Western Europe. But on the whole, the non-Western world is growing much faster than we are, and with that sort of growth come many and varied opportunities for investors.

Home-country bias incurs serious opportunity costs. As noted above, more than half the global equity market capitalization lies outside the United States. Ignoring more than half the opportunity set in a game as competitive as that of investing simply makes no sense. In addition, of course, stock valuations outside the United States are often more attractive than those in the United States. And although investors normally attempt to access these valuations by changing their U.S./non-U.S. allocation, some commentators point out that that is a clumsy approach by comparison with the "real-time asset allocation" available to global investors.

WHY STAY HOME?

It's frankly difficult to find sensible arguments for a home country bias. Most of the reasons investors overweight U.S. stocks have to do with fear, discomfort, lack of experience, and inertia. The one argument for a home country bias that I hear from investors I (otherwise) respect goes something like this: I am domiciled in the United States and must discharge my liabilities in U.S. dollars. Therefore, a portfolio overweight in U.S. dollar-denominated assets makes sense for me.

Well, maybe. But this argument doesn't carry as much water as you might think. For one thing, outside the marketable equity portion of most investors' portfolios, almost all assets are U.S.-dollar denominated (fixed income, private equity and real estate, for example), thus reducing the need to focus on dollar-denominated equities. For another, diversifying into non-dollar-denominated assets adds only a small amount of short-term volatility to our returns (currency fluctuations tend to even out over time), while adding a very large amount of diversification. Thus, our net risk is probably reduced.

Given all the arguments favoring a global approach to equity investing, and the paucity of arguments against it, why shouldn't we simply accept global equities as an asset class that should replace domestic equities and international equities in our asset allocation strategies? The answer, it turns out, is that global investing is a great idea in theory, but its advantages begin to dissipate along the potholed road of actual practice.

GLOBAL INVESTING IN THE REAL WORLD (OR, MAYBE, REAL INVESTING IN A GLOBAL WORLD)

Let's take a look at just a few of the more serious challenges faced by an investor who wishes to adopt a global investing approach.

Is "Global Equities" an Asset Class?

When thoughtful investors design portfolio strategies, they begin with the concept of an asset class. By mixing and matching different asset classes in a sensible way—that is, taking advantage of less-than-perfect correlations among the asset classes—they are able to build portfolios that optimize return per unit of risk. I don't wish to get bogged down in the debate over what constitutes an asset class, but for portfolio construction purposes it is generally useful to divide investment assets into smaller, rather than larger, categories. For example, using as building blocks for a portfolio such categories as U.S. large-cap stocks and U.S. small-cap stocks makes more sense than trying to design a portfolio around one huge asset class called "U.S. equities." By using the finer definitions, families can tailor the portfolio to their needs much more carefully, and they are also likely to end up with a better-diversified portfolio.

Extending this thought to global equities, I would make the same comment: The term is too broad, too encompassing, to be of much use in the design of investment portfolios. It incorporates all the domestic asset classes mentioned above, as well as non-U.S. large-cap equities, non-U.S. small-cap equities, emerging markets equities, and even frontier markets. If an investor simply turns all the securities over to one global equities manager, what chance is there that that manager will create an efficient portfolio? The answer, of course, is "little to none."

Of course, one argument for investing globally is that correlations among world markets have become so high that the former usefulness of asset class distinctions like U. S. and EAFE (Europe, Australia, and the Far East) no longer matter. Certainly it is true that correlations between the S&P and EAFE have risen from roughly 0.40 in the early 1980s to roughly 0.80 in the first decade of the twenty-first century, driven by the collapse of the sponsor of socialism in 1989. But U.S./non-U.S. correlations have always followed long, cyclical patterns, and it is not yet clear that today's high correlations represent a whole new paradigm. For example, the correlation today between the S&P 500 and the MSCI Emerging Markets Free Index is also very high—roughly 0.75. Does anyone expect that high correlation to persist long term?

Is It Possible to Succeed as a Global Equity Manager?

Theoretically, if a manager is talented, the larger the opportunity set the better his returns should be. But the opportunity set for global equities is so vast that very, very few investment organizations can possibly amass the resources required to succeed with the strategy. Moreover, the firms that do possess those resources tend to be the kind of organizations (i.e., very large ones) in which stock-picking talent has not traditionally blossomed. As a result, many firms that offer global equity products stick to index or enhanced index products, rather than attempt active management in so vast a sector. Thus prospective global investors must ask themselves these questions:

- Do I only want an indexed approach, and if so, why not get it by, say, mixing the Russell 1000, Russell 3000, MSCI EAFE, and MSCI Emerging Markets indexes, which allows me to specify my asset allocation strategy?
- Do I really want to be a captive client of a very small handful of megafirms that have the resources (at least theoretically) to invest on a global basis?

- Because global equity portfolios (other than enhanced index portfolios) tend to hold only a tiny subset of the entire MSCI World index, am I willing to live with the very large tracking error these portfolios are likely to generate?

We might also keep in mind that for decades, the name of the game in beating the MSCI EAFE was getting the Japan bet right—Japan represented so much of the EAFE that overweighting Japan when it underperformed, or underweighting Japan when it outperformed, was death to a manager's performance. Consider how much more true this is of the decision to over- or underweight the United States.

Can a Global Manager Outperform in the U.S. Portion of its Portfolio?

Research has overwhelmingly suggested that even highly diligent managers in the U.S. large-cap sector will have difficulty outperforming the index net of their fees and other costs. If this is the case, then what possible reason is there to believe that a global manager—distracted by the need to evaluate thousands of securities across dozens of countries—can outperform in the U.S. large-cap sector? Isn't it more likely, in fact, that a manager preoccupied with picking stocks all over the world will be even less likely to outperform in the highly efficient U.S. market? And won't this undercut the rationale for going global?

Do the BRICs Really Matter as Much as We Think?

The growth and influence of the Chinese and Indian societies—along with Brazil—has certainly been spectacular, and we can all be forgiven for being rather transfixed by it all. But we shouldn't make the mistake of projecting straight-line growth in these economies.

On the subject of straight-line projections, I frequently read things like this: "Growth in the Chinese economy has averaged 14 percent per year and therefore China will control 50 percent of the global economy in 30 years." Possibly, of course, but highly unlikely. In the first place, the annual growth rates that are so casually bandied about really represent the growth rate of the large Chinese cities, not of the country as a whole. When you add in the (dismal) growth rate of the Chinese countryside you come up with a much lower number.

I discuss China in Chapter 1, but don't forget that it's a totalitarian country, and no command economy has ever made the transition from agrarian to industrial to modern postindustrial economy. The Chinese Communist Party has to give up power and democratize if it wants to keep growing the economy, but if the CCP gives up power, what will hold China together?

India, of course, has the opposite problem. It's "the world's largest democracy," and a fractious one at that, deeply divided along ethnic, religious, and caste lines and with a massive and growing population of desperately poor citizens who are barely being touched by the rapid progress of the educated elite. The only way we know of to move a society from undeveloped to developed is to install the necessary infrastructure—roads, power, basic manufacturing, and so on—exactly what the Soviet Union and China produced and exactly what India lacks. And without a command-and-control government like China's, India is unlikely to have the necessary infrastructure any time soon.

China, like the USSR, kept its people impoverished for decades while it built the infrastructure it needed through brute force. But as a democracy, India can't follow suit. The global economy isn't interested in what India can produce in two decades; it's interested in what India can produce today—which, given its educated elite, means services. But as far as I know, a service economy won't carry India as far as it needs to go without vast improvements in its basic infrastructure.

Brazil utterly dominates South America, being the largest country in both land mass and population—indeed, Brazil's population is larger than that of all the other countries of South America combined. Nonetheless, it's only about two-thirds the size of the United States and vastly smaller than China and India. And like most of South America, Brazil has suffered for centuries without a large middle class—in Brazil, you were either phenomenally rich or dirt poor.

More recently, Brazil's middle class has begun to grow, an enormously positive development. But the country is still very much a work in progress. Brazil's economy is mainly dependent on natural resource production and agriculture, it lacks control of its waterways (and in any event they run in the wrong direction), and the natural geography of the country impedes development.

In my view, Russia doesn't even belong in the same category as the other three countries. Although it is the largest country in the world by far in terms of land mass, its population is less than half that of the United States and is 50 million people smaller than Brazil. In addition, Russia's population is rapidly aging, its economy is more a kleptocracy than a free market, and democracy in any real sense has yet to take hold.

Don't get me wrong—the growth in the BRICs is real, and rapid improvement in living standards in the world's most populous countries is the most important story of the past half century. The question is whether that growth, and the investment opportunities it makes possible, can possibly keep up with the current optimistic expectations.

What about Investing in Multinationals?

Many investors argue that the main benefits of global investing, without many of the downsides, can be obtained by investing in global, multinational companies, regardless of where they are domesticated. That would be nice if it were true, but at the end of the day a portfolio of multinationals turns out to be mainly a U.S. domestic portfolio. Of the 50 stocks in the Dow Jones Global Titans 50 index, for example, fully 28, representing 62 percent of the market capitalization, are U.S. companies.[3] Moreover, the multinationals portfolio tracks the Dow or S&P 500 very closely, meaning that it offers little diversification.

The Challenge of Stock-Picking in "Non-Nonsynchronous" Markets

In the most developed stock markets, stock behavior tends to be nonsynchronous; that is, the complement of stocks traded on those markets don't tend all to move in the same direction. In the United States, for example, in most weeks roughly 58 percent of the stocks move in the same direction. By contrast, in China more than 80 percent of the stocks move in the same direction.[4] In non-nonsynchronous markets, why pay an active management fee to a global manager when an ETF would be a lot less expensive?

Thinking Nonmonolithically

Although I have tended to talk in this book—for simplification purposes—as though global equities consisted of only two subcategories, U.S. and non-U.S., in fact the world is vastly more complex than this. U.S. equities includes large-cap, mid-cap, small-cap, microcap, hedge, venture capital, buyouts, and the large group of quasi-equity investments that includes mezzanine, distressed, turnarounds, and so forth. Non-U.S. equities includes EAFE, emerging markets, global small-cap, hedge, venture capital (in the UK and Israel), buyouts (in Europe), and so on. Accessing this vast and diverse opportunity set through a global equity manager, even among long-only asset classes, would be, to say the least, challenging.

PRACTICE TIP

Periodically—and regularly—I hear that this or that sector of the market has "decoupled" from market sectors with which it was traditionally more correlated. For example, historically, when the United States got a cold, emerging markets caught pneumonia.

Recently, for example, it has been argued in some quarters that the emerging markets have decoupled from the United States. The rationale suggests that, as an outlet for emerging markets goods, the United States and Europe have been replaced by burgeoning middle classes in China, India, and Brazil, so that the United States could fall deeply into recession without significantly affecting the emerging economies. There is something to all this, to be sure—if nothing else, many emerging countries have far sounder economies these days.

But keep in mind that the decoupling arguments are usually made by someone with an ax to grind—someone selling the product that has supposedly decoupled. As an advisor, don't fall into this trap. Decoupling very rarely happens, because the factors that cause markets to be "coupled" change with glacial slowness. Some day, no doubt, the middle classes in emerging economies will possess the buying power of the middle classes in the United States and Europe—but that day is far, far away.

In the meantime, advisors should cast a very skeptical eye on decoupling arguments.

CONCLUSION: THINK GLOBALLY, ACT LOCALLY

Thinking globally. Beginning the equity allocation process by looking at global equity market capitalization makes all the sense in the world (pun intended). Here is an exercise investors might try. Assume our investor has 35 percent of his entire portfolio in U.S. large-cap stocks, 5 percent in U.S. small-cap stocks, 15 percent in international stocks and 5 percent in emerging markets stocks. Of the 60 percent of the portfolio in equities, then, our investor has 40 percent (67 percent of the equity exposure) allocated to U.S. and 20 percent (33 percent) allocated to non-U.S., compared to a market weighting of (roughly) 45 percent U.S. and 55 percent non-U.S.:

	Investor's Portfolio	Global Market Cap (rounded)
U.S. equities	67 percent	45 percent
Non-U.S. equities	33 percent	55 percent

Now we might ask ourselves why we are so smart that we can make a huge, 22 percent bet against non-U.S. stocks? What is it we know that gives us confidence to make such a sizable bet? Would we do so elsewhere in our portfolio? If not, we should probably take steps to bring these two allocations closer together.

Acting globally. I have discussed above the challenges associated with using a global manager for our equity portfolio, but of course it's possible to do so, with these being the main choices:

Option #1—Engage an active global equity manager. Here the main challenge is that there are so few firms that have the global resources required to demonstrate ongoing competence in such a challenging endeavor. Thus, if our client adopts Option #1 they will be taking very substantial organizational risk: If the manager blows up or substantially underperforms, so will the client—big time.

Option #2—Engage a "core plus" global equity manager. Many large firms—global banks and investment banks in the main—offer so-called "core plus" strategies. These firms have decided that active management in this area is far too challenging, and so they manage global money by indexing most of the allocation and then "porting" return from a short-term bond portfolio into the indexed global equity portfolio. If all goes well, these managers will deliver the return on a global benchmark—the MSCI All Country World index, for example—plus a few points of return from the bond portfolio. Of course, all does not always go well.

Option #3—Engage a pure index manager. This is the simplest approach to a global equity exposure, but it means that roughly 60 percent of the overall equity portfolio cannot outperform.

My skepticism of global equity management notwithstanding, I see no reason why adventurous investors shouldn't dip their toes in the global equity market by engaging one of the managers described above. A global manager would therefore be managing money alongside more traditional domestic and foreign managers, and this in itself presents complications in terms of maintaining our asset allocation strategy and in judging relative performance. But it's not impossible, and may be worth the trouble just to gain experience with a global manager.

Most likely, the slowly increasing population of quality global equity managers will be used by sensible investors as satellite managers who provide useful manager diversification, given that they are working with a different opportunity set than pure domestic or pure non-U.S. managers.

Acting "locally." By acting "locally" I mean implementing the globally designed portfolio in the traditional way: by engaging domestic and international specialist managers. Thus our globally designed, locally implemented portfolio might look something like this:

Long Equity Asset Allocation

	Investor's Current Portfolio	Global Market Cap	Investor's New Portfolio
U.S. equities	67%	45%	45%
Non-U.S. equities	33%	55%	55%

Portfolio Implementation (Long Equities)

	Subtotal (% of Equity Alloc)	Total (% of Equity Alloc)
U.S. large-cap passive	35%	
U.S. small-cap active value	4%	
U.S. small-cap active growth	6%	
U.S. total		45%
EAFE active value	10%	
EAFE active growth	10%	
Non-U.S. small-cap	5%	
Emerging markets core	20%	
EM Asia ex-Japan	10%	
Non-U.S. total		55%

If you were to inject a global equity manager into the portfolio, you would likely take that manager's allocation out of the U.S. large-cap passive and EAFE active allocations, roughly equally.

Given the very fundamental changes in the economic organization of the world that followed the collapse of the Soviet Union, and how rapidly those changes have evolved over the ensuing two decades, I agree wholeheartedly that a conceptually global approach to equity investing makes sense. I have argued, however, that implementing a global approach using global equity managers remains problematic and it is likely to remain so for many years to come. "Think globally, act locally" is likely to be the preferred strategy for most U.S.-based and non-U.S. based investors.

NOTES

1. I am indebted to my now-retired partner at Greycourt, John G. Mebane, for his many contributions to this chapter, which originally appeared as Greycourt White Paper No. 42:Global Investing: An Idea Whose Time Has Come? (January 2008), available at www.Greycourt.com.
2. Brazil, Russia, India. and China.
3. The UK has nine companies, Switzerland four, and Japan two. No other country has more than one.
4. Michael J. Schill, "New Perspectives on Investing in Emerging Markets," The Research Foundation of CFA Institute (2006).

CHAPTER 13

Investing in Real Assets

Real assets are those that, in contrast to financial assets, are actually tangible. But more important than their tangibility is the pattern of their typical returns. Real assets tend to perform well at crucial periods of time—periods of rapid, unanticipated inflation—when virtually all other investment assets tend to perform very poorly. Because high inflation—and even moderate inflation—is the principal enemy of families wishing to preserve their wealth, it will be a rare family that should not have at least some exposure to real assets.

REAL ESTATE

The most common real asset is real estate;[1] indeed, real estate is the largest single asset class in the world. Properly structured real estate portfolios will exhibit low correlations to equity and fixed-income assets, will provide a strong ongoing yield, will appreciate slowly but consistently, and will perform well during the periods of unanticipated inflation referred to earlier. It's a pretty compelling portrait, marred only by the fact that, over long periods of time, real estate will tend to underperform stocks, and therefore there are modest, but real, opportunity costs associated with allocating too much money to real estate.

Real estate can be further broken down into two core groups, residential and commercial. The latter includes many different sectors, including retail, industrial, multifamily, office, hospitality (hotels and resorts), and raw land. Except for raw land, real estate must be "created," and therefore real estate assets will fall along a continuum, depending on where they fall in the stages of value creation:

- Entitlement—The property is in the process of being planned and approved, but no construction has yet occurred.
- Development—The property has been approved and is being prepared for construction.
- Construction—The structures are being prepared for occupancy.
- Lease-up—The buildings are largely completed but not fully occupied.

- Stabilized—For commercial property, this means the property is fully leased and operational. For residential housing, it means the property is sold out, and responsibility for things like maintenance of the common areas and operating the homeowners' association is transferred from the developer to the homeowners.

Leverage

It's important to understand that the use of debt (or leverage) is a core aspect of real estate investing. Leverage can magnify returns, but it can also magnify losses. Many real estate developers are hooked on leverage, and as a result they prosper mightily during good times and frequently go bankrupt in bad times.

In the late 1980s and early 1990s, the United States headed into a downturn and the capital markets shut down to real estate developers. In response, Wall Street invented the concept of a mortgage-backed security, or MBS. The premise of an MBS was that a bank would lend money to a borrower to buy a building, and the bank would then sell the loan to investors. In addition, the bank prioritized the loan so that investors could buy higher or lower in the capital stack depending on their risk appetite.

This created a new source of capital for real estate buyers, because banks no longer had to hold the mortgage on a property, compromising their capital ratios. Instead, they could sell the loan in the open market. Unfortunately, MBSs created a moral hazard, because the banks that made the loan no longer bore the risk on the mortgage.

Why Invest in Real Estate?

Real estate generally provides a slow and steady return to investors, and over long periods of time it will typically underperform other risk assets. I say "generally" because, just like other asset classes, real estate is susceptible to occasional bubble phenomena (1985–1993, 2003–2008, etc.). This usually occurs when other asset classes are out of favor and access to capital is cheap and easy.

So why invest in real estate? The main advantages of including a real estate allocation in your portfolio are that real estate tends to move in a different direction from the rest of the market, thus offering good diversification, and that real estate acts as a natural hedge against unanticipated inflation.

Correlation to other asset classes. Historically, real estate has been relatively uncorrelated to the main traditional assets found in most family portfolios: stocks and bonds. The main reason for the lack of correlation is the illiquid nature of real estate: Unlike highly liquid securities, investors cannot generally make buy and sell decisions when they want to.

Inflation protection. Real estate also acts as an inflation hedge, much like other real assets (see the following). When inflation is rising (or expected to rise), investors tend to bid up real estate both because it's a tangible asset and because landlords tend to be able to raise rents as their own costs rise.

How to Invest in Real Estate

Assuming that an allocation is going to be made to real estate, families will have many possible strategies available to them. Among the more prominent are:

REITs. Public, open-end real estate investment trusts (REITS) operate much like mutual funds. Investors buy shares in the REIT, which in turn uses the money to invest in actual properties, mortgages (or mortgage-backed securities), operating real estate companies, or other REITs.[2] The advantages of REITs are their liquidity and their frequent high yields. Disadvantages include REITs' higher correlations with equities (especially small-cap value stocks).

REOCs. Real estate operating companies (REOCs) differ from REITs in that investors are buying into a real estate company's business model where real estate is the core business. Examples of REOCs would be hotel chains, large-scale home builders, and major commercial developers. Another major difference between REITs and REOCs is the tax treatment. REITs receive special nontax status: In exchange for distributing at least 90 percent of their income to shareholders, they are able to pass through the income free of corporate income tax. However, this also limits their reinvestment opportunities, and REITs therefore tend to trade mainly on their yield.

Open-end funds. Many firms offer open-end real estate funds; that is, partnerships or LLCs that are always open to new investors (though sometimes with quarterly windows) and that usually offer some form of liquidity after an initial lockup period.

Closed-end funds. Closed-end funds are similar to open-end funds in that they raise capital from investors and then redeploy that capital in broad or narrow real estate investments. Unlike open-end funds, however, closed-end funds do not continue to accept new capital from investors. Once the fund is raised it closes and thereafter focuses on managing the portfolio. An advantage of closed-end funds is that the partners are not constantly distracted by the need to raise funds—they can focus on making money for their investors. A disadvantage is that, because all the capital is raised at once, the fund may find that it has bought into the market at a bad time. Investors may find, therefore, that closed-end funds make more sense for targeted investments in specific sectors of the real estate market that are believed to be currently undervalued.

Mortgage-backed securities. As mentioned above, mortgage-backed securities offer another way for investors to participate in real estate investing. In fact, however, most buyers of MBSs are looking at the securities as a type of fixed-income investment. And, indeed, MBSs act much more like a bond (and, technically, they are bonds) and have similar risk-return characteristics as corporate bonds and other fixed-income assets.

Private investments. Private investments in real estate usually require a greater amount of capital and are therefore limited to investors with deeper pockets than a typical REIT investor. Private real estate investments come in many forms and allow investors to choose their type of investment based on their risk and return appetite:

- *Direct ownership.* Probably the most common way to gain real estate exposure is simply to buy properties directly. More American families have created their wealth through direct real estate investing than in any other way. On the other hand, this is also the most difficult and most dangerous strategy.
- *Joint venture.* In a joint venture, an investor will partner with someone who has experience in direct real estate ownership. The investor relinquishes day-to-day control of the asset to the operating partner but retains authority over major decisions (refinancing, disposition, etc.). The risk is somewhat lower than direct ownership but the success of the investment still relies heavily on the outcome of a single investment, which in turn relies on the capabilities of the operating partner.
- *Private partnership or fund.* Like private equity deals, multiple investors invest in a pool that is managed by a general partner who has extensive experience in direct ownership. Investments tend to be passive, meaning even major decisions are delegated to the general partner. Investors usually share profits disproportionately with the general partner: Investors may put up nearly all of the capital but receive only 50 percent to 80 percent of the

profits. However, the investors will normally get their money back first, and in many cases an additional amount (usually called a "preference"). Real estate funds are the recommended approach for investors who are not experienced in real estate development but who want to have an allocation to the sector.

- *Fund of funds.* A fund of funds is simply a fund that invests in underlying real estate funds or partnerships. A fund of funds enables investors with limited capital to build a diversified portfolio of private real estate properties. As with private equity funds of funds, real estate funds of funds will charge a management fee and may even charge an incentive fee, and that's on top of the fees being paid to the underlying managers. But the fees can be worth it for investors who cannot build a high quality allocation in any other way.

Over time, a well-structured and well-diversified real estate portfolio should generate attractive risk-adjusted returns for families, often in a tax-advantaged and inflation-protected manner. As a result, allocations in the 5 percent to 15 percent range are common in family portfolios.

PRACTICE TIP

Families should be careful not to buy into any risk asset when it is overvalued, of course, but this is especially the case with real estate. Real estate cycles can be very long, and if we put our clients into highly leveraged real estate near the top of the cycle, the result are highly likely to be very, very poor.

When core real estate isn't attractive, however, there are often many interesting opportunities to invest in distressed or niche properties or paper. These investments will tend to be smaller than core investments, but they will allow our clients to keep a hand in the real estate bucket until real estate prices become attractive again.

OIL AND GAS

Whether a family will have a significant allocation to oil and gas[3] tends to depend on where the family is located. Wealthy families in Texas and Oklahoma, for example, are more likely to own oil and gas than to own real estate. Similar families in New York or Florida may well have no oil and gas exposure at all.

Even more than with real estate, managing a successful oil and gas portfolio requires that a family be willing to "be in the business," to learn the arcane jargon and (often) slippery practices in the industry that can lead amateur investors astray. Once a family decides to make a commitment to the asset, there are many strategies available: buying royalty interests; buying pieces of producing wells; investing in low-risk, low-return drilling partnerships; investing (speculating?) in wildcat drilling; buying up leases; investing in operating companies, and so on.

Aside from specific oil and gas investments, virtually every investor already has a position in oil and gas, and usually a complex one, because almost every portfolio will hold stocks with an obvious connection to the oil and gas business. For example:

- The major integrated oil companies that produce, transport, refine and distribute petroleum
- Independent producers
- Pipeline companies
- Oilfield service companies
- Manufacturers of the capital goods used in production, transportation, distribution, and refining

Just as important, most portfolios include a large number of companies that consume energy and would be hurt by a sharp rise in oil prices. (Even the major integrated oil companies buy crude.) Thus, a focused investment in energy, as opposed to the generalized exposure most investors already hold, could serve as a source of increased return to the portfolio, as a hedge against the impact on the portfolio of rising oil prices, or both.

I will discuss a number of practical ways to invest in energy, but at every stage it is important to consider whether a particular strategy is likely to produce a return that is partly independent of oil prices, to provide a hedge against rising prices, or both. For example, an independent exploration and production company is certainly affected by changes in the oil price, but it creates value primarily by finding and lifting petroleum. At the other extreme, a futures contract on oil will have little intrinsic return, and its performance will be dominated by changes in the oil price.

Value Creation Mechanisms

When investing in a high-energy-price environment, it is important to identify valuation mechanisms other than the hope that energy prices will go even higher. Across the energy industry, there are common mechanisms by which companies create value, and the investment strategies described below employ these mechanisms in various combinations. Understanding how value is created in energy investing makes it much easier to understand the investment strategies.

- Buying reserves "smart." Every company claims to buy cheaply, but the reality is that some firms have repeatedly demonstrated an ability to buy smart. This is a value-add in a normal environment and critical in a high-price environment.
- Making production improvements. For this strategy to succeed, three things must be true:
  - The seller actually has undermanaged or mismanaged it's property
  - The buyer actually has skills greater than the seller
  - None of the other bidders have factored the same opportunities into their bids
- Creating an aggregation premium. An operator may gain some markup in the value of assets simply by aggregating small properties into a package that would be more attractive—more economically efficient—to a group of larger companies.
- Engaging in development drilling. Many companies in this category plan some infill or step-out drilling. This can be a conservative value-add, but sellers and competing bidders usually take into account the potential for such drilling. "Infill drilling" means drilling new wells between existing producing wells. "Step-out drilling" means drilling new wells outside of, but very close to, a cluster of existing producing wells.
- Exploration. This is the romantic part of the oil and gas business, and the ultimate in value creation: discovering previously unknown reserves and putting them into production. Exploration is an inherently risky activity, and it can be very hard for an investor to evaluate exploration skill. Organizations with a good track record in one locale may not prove as skilled when working in an unfamiliar province, with different geological formations, or with new exploration technologies. Most family investors have little access to true exploration deals, and that is probably a good thing.

Hedging to Protect Value

Buying or creating petroleum reserves in a high-price environment has obvious risks, and many operators are unwilling to commit to projects that depend on high-priced oil. There is a "producer price curve" that is different from, and lower than, the forward market prices for oil and gas. (This curve is not published, but with some work can be derived from industry deal prices.)

Operators will sometimes buy petroleum reserves and hedge the price of some future production, enough to ensure at least a return of capital. It's important for an investor to know whether and how much an operator is planning to hedge and to be comfortable with that strategy.

Investing Strategies

The strategies described below are the basic building blocks of the currently available investment strategies.

Drilling programs. Many investors have been offered participation in drilling programs. These are usually partnerships organized by a drilling organization in order to raise capital to drill in a limited geographical area. This activity once was tax driven, but is less so now. The terms are often "retail," that is, unfavorable to investors, and the limited geographical focus concentrates risk. Returns depend on the exploration and operating skills of the operator, and few investors have the ability to evaluate these skills. Investment decisions are often based on casual character judgments and recommendations from friends. The risks are mitigated somewhat by the fact that many of these programs are very conservative from a geological point of view, commonly drilling infills or cautious step-outs from existing producing fields.

Exploration and production buildups. Private equity is raised not just to buy petroleum reserves but also to build a company in the process. Value is created through the reserve aggregation process described next, but also through creation of a business enterprise capable of repeating that process. There is usually a sponsoring organization assisting in the process. Some of these have gone on to become publicly traded companies.

Production aggregators. These firms buy, aggregate, and operate oil and gas production on behalf of clients, most often large institutions. They come to market periodically to raise capital through discrete funds. They do development drilling, but they are intended to be low risk. They act as a portfolio hedge by creating a long-term ownership position in the commodity. They also provide current return from operations. They are usually well diversified.

Royalty pools. Royalties are the right to receive a share of the selling price of oil and gas, usually at the wellhead. The royalty owner does not contribute to the costs of drilling and has almost no control over operations, including the decision to drill wells.

Purchase of royalty rights from mineral owners. This is done through funds offered to investors. The pool will attempt to diversify its investments across multiple regions and geological ideas. Success will depend on the pool operator's judgment about the quality and longevity of production from developed properties, the prospects for future drilling on undeveloped properties, and the skills of the operators of the properties.

Private equity funds. There are a number of funds that invest in or alongside operators who employ one or more of the four basic value-creation mechanisms. Across a fund's portfolio all of the mechanisms would be employed to some degree, with the least emphasis on exploration. The fund managers often bring a lot of experience and sophistication to these investments, significantly supplementing the operators' own skills. They can assist with everything from financing to exit strategies.

Private equity funds of funds. It is possible to invest in a fund of funds that will aggregate some of the best private equity funds working in energy and natural resources. These operate much like other private equity funds of funds. Typically they would invest in many of the firms previously identified. Most of these funds of funds include nonenergy resources, particularly timber. A 30 percent exposure to timber would not be unusual.

Commodity funds. Some investors seek a pure exposure to oil and gas commodity prices, less for any inherent return (there is little) than for inflation protection and for the effect that commodities have on a portfolio that is rebalanced periodically. Commodity investing is discussed later.

Sector funds, long only or long/short. There are many energy sector mutual funds and separately managed accounts. There are also long/short hedge funds focused on stocks in the energy sector. Portfolios will include major integrated companies, independent exploration companies, oilfield service companies, and other energy and nonenergy resource companies. There are also index funds for the energy sector.

Energy master limited partnerships (MLPs). MLPs, publicly-traded limited partnerships, consist primarily of energy infrastructure companies, such as pipelines and intermediate processors of oil and gas. (A few hold timber or other assets.) MLPs were originally created as a way for integrated companies to spin out and "monetize" assets that provided steady cash flow but were unappreciated and undervalued by securities analysts. The partnership structure allowed this to be done tax efficiently. (Qualified MLPs do not pay tax at the partnership level.) MLPs were originally viewed as repositories for depreciating assets, but have proven to be normal industrial companies. Their managements have also proven to be surprisingly entrepreneurial, growing their businesses through acquisitions and even new construction. Oddly, MLP prices have displayed zero correlation to oil and gas prices and instead behave like yield instruments correlated with interest rates. In this and in their tax structure, they resemble real estate investment trusts.

Recommendations

An investor's choice of an energy investment strategy depends first on the role the investment will play in that investor's portfolio. For example, if the investor has a strong conviction that oil prices are headed higher, then a commodity fund heavy in oil and gas futures would be a good choice. Another investor might choose the same strategy for a more conservative reason; for example., to offset the impact that increasing oil prices would have on a concentrated ownership in a particular privately owned or publicly traded company.

Here are some sound ways to build an energy portfolio:

Core strategies. Most investors will be looking for a way to participate in the oil and gas business with a reasonable balance between participation in rising prices and some downside protection. The private equity funds and funds of funds serve best in this role. Though they will benefit from continued price increases, they also have available the widest array of techniques to create value independent of prices. The price hedging many funds employ provides reasonably good downside protection but leaves some price upside for the investor.

Satellite strategies. A larger investor can supplement this core exposure with direct investments in some seasoned individual funds engaged in value-added production aggregation or royalty pooling.

Hedging strategies. An investor seeking to minimize the negative portfolio impact of rising energy prices can do so using the commodity funds, private equity investments in unhedged (or minimally hedged) production aggregators, or through derivatives.

Absolute return strategies. Strategies such as energy hedge funds and MLPs can play a useful role in a portfolio independent of oil and gas prices. The energy hedge funds, for example, may represent a fresh source of returns in the somewhat overdone hedge arena. The point is to understand the investment need, then meet it with an appropriate strategy.

PRACTICE TIP

In addition to its general role in a portfolio, oil acts as a sensitive reflector of global fears. For example, as this chapter was being written the world was focused on the possibility of war between Israel and Iran, possibly involving a blockade of the Strait of Hormuz and even the involvement of the United States in the war. Oil prices spiked, although other assets—including other commodities—barely budged.

Of course, a possible stoppage in Hormuz was a special issue for oil, given that roughly 20 percent of the world's oil passes through the Strait. But this is typical behavior during any sort of serious global crisis. If the crisis looks like war, oil prices will spike. If it looks like global economies will be disrupted, oil prices will collapse.

As a result of oil's sensitivity to major international events, it's possible for a financial advisor to address client fears by buying oil stocks (or an ETF) or by selling or shorting oil-sensitive securities. This will typically be a better approach than making major changes in the portfolio.

COMMODITIES

Commodities,[4] when viewed in isolation, display an unfavorable balance between risk and volatility. Nevertheless, commodities improve the overall performance of a well-diversified portfolio. This happens because of the very low correlations between the performance of commodities and other asset classes.

To realize the benefits of a commodity allocation, we must be prepared to rebalance periodically in a disciplined way. This means, for example, that we must be prepared to sell down a commodities position as oil goes from $40 to $147.50 and be prepared to buy back in as oil goes from $147.50 to $40. This can be a challenge organizationally and behaviorally. In addition, of course, we will need to carefully manage the tax impact of rebalancing.

It is possible that an investor might have a fundamentally bullish view of demand for commodities based on predicted scarcity, anticipated demand from emerging economies, and so on. That would suggest a buy-and-hold strategy very different from the portfolio-based strategy examined in this chapter. In order to pursue such a strategy, the investor would have to conclude that (a) a paradigm shift has occurred that is strong enough to overcome the tidal pull of mean reversion and (b) other investors have not already reached the same conclusion and moved prices to a level reflecting that bullish view.

This section of Chapter 13 focuses on (a) the role of long indexed positions in commodities which are designed to mirror the broad commodities market, and (b) an exploration of the interaction of such a position with the balance of a family's portfolio. Given the myriad possibilities, I will not attempt to present an optimal investment strategy in this space.

In addition to long commodity indexes, there are several other ways to invest in the commodity space. Many of these are oriented to oil and gas investing (previously discussed), and the strategies can take the form of a private equity approach, highly directional commodity trading accounts, or hedge strategies.

Sources of Return from Commodities Investing

Although it seems to contravene common sense, commodity returns are almost unrelated to commodity prices. Instead, returns in the commodities sector result from the interplay between the actions of hedgers of commodity prices and the investors who facilitate the hedging process. Many producers of commodities find it difficult to manage their businesses without knowing reasonably well in advance what price they will receive.

A soybean farmer, for example, may wish to lock in a price for his crop in June to hedge against the possibility of a decline in prices by the time the crop is harvested in October. Assume that the spot price of soybeans in June is $6.00/bushel. The expected future spot price in October, which incorporates all known information about the soybean market, might be $6.50/bushel. But the futures price will be lower than the expected future spot price because market players who are willing to facilitate the farmer's hedge will only do so if they are paid a risk premium.

This phenomenon, in which the futures price is lower than the future spot price, is called backwardization and it is the usual state of the futures market. In the usual case, then, a seller of futures will earn a positive return measured by the risk premium. Occasionally, the spot price is below the futures price, a phenomenon known as contango.

One reason it is important to understand the actual source of returns in commodity investing is that an investor who is exposed to spot prices of commodities may find that the return series for commodities futures is actually quite different.

The Commodities Indexes

Two indexes dominate the commodity sector: the Dow Jones-UBS commodity index (DJ-UBS) and the S&P Goldman Sachs commodity index (GSCI). The GSCI data extends back to 1970, whereas the DJ-UBS began in only 1998. The difference between them is significant, and although we might prefer one over the other for investment purposes, they are both excellent tools for analyzing the commodity sector.

The GSCI is composed of 24 commodities, which can broadly be organized into five core groups: energy, industrial metals, precious metals, agriculture, and livestock. The GSCI is world production–weighted by normalized units produced over the last five years. This is the equivalent of a market capitalization–weighted index that focuses solely on production.

The DJ-UBS is composed of 19 commodities. In contrast to the GSCI, this index is weighted by combining production and liquidity over the most recent five-year period. Liquidity is measured by the volume and dollar value of contracts traded. The liquidity matrix is used to counter potential underestimation of the economic significance and potential investment value of storable commodities such as precious metals. Perhaps more important, the index includes a cap of 33 percent on any related commodity grouping (such as energy) as well as a floor: Each commodity must represent at least 2 percent of the index in order to be included.

The energy sector completely dominates the GSCI index, sometimes approaching an 80 percent weighting, with crude oil and Brent Crude accounting for most if this. The DJ-UBS index caps energy at a 33 percent weighting. By limiting the energy sector in the DJ-UBS, the other sectors become much more significant to the performance of the index. One might argue about how meaningful liquidity factors are, but I believe they are quite meaningful, as the amount of trading in a period can be just as indicative of importance and demand as physical production. In any event, the core benefit of the DJ-UBS index from an investment perspective is that the energy cap offers the index much better diversification across the commodity space.

Historical Risk, Return, and Sharpe Ratios

Table 13.1 examines historical return and risk using the GSCI and a range of other asset classes using common index proxies over the last 30 years (1979–2009). As shown in the chart, commodities have generated a return lower than bonds with a risk level higher than stocks over the period. Obviously, bondlike returns and equitylike risk make for an unattractive

TABLE 13.1 Commodities, Risk and Return

	Index	Annualized Return	Annualized Risk
Commodities	GSCI	6.3%	19.3%
U.S. Large-Cap	Russell 1000	10.3%	15.6%
Bonds	Barc Govt/Credit	8.5%	6.1%

Source: Greycourt.

TABLE 13.2 Correlations between Commodities and Other Assets

	U.S. Large-Cap	International Dev.	Bonds	Real Estate
1979–2009	0.13	0.19	0.00	0.14

Source: Greycourt.

stand-alone investment and certainly pose a significant hurdle to inclusion of the asset class in a mean-variance optimization study.

Historical Correlations

Table 13.2 focuses on correlations between commodities (using the GSCI) and other asset classes.

Obviously, correlations between commodities and other asset classes are extremely low—and this is the key to the use of commodities. It's rare to find asset classes that are so uncorrelated, and therefore the use of commodities as a risk reducer suddenly becomes interesting. More on this follows.

Some Thoughts about Historical and Prospective Commodity Returns

Note that the 30-year measurement period I've evaluated may significantly underestimate the future return potential of the commodities asset class. At the evaluation period's inception the United States was in a high inflation environment with commodity prices elevated. The middle period saw a strong dollar policy and relatively low constant inflation accompanied by a period of extremely low commodity prices. At the end of the period we observed a run-up in commodity prices under the threat of future inflation, but the final one and a half years experienced an unprecedented reversal as we experienced a credit crisis and the specter of deflation.

Going forward, commodity returns could prove to be higher. We can construct a prospective return for commodities using the following components:

- I begin with the inflation-adjusted (real) returns to commodities since 1933: 0.5 percent.
- To this I add the rate of inflation since 1933: approximately 4 percent.
- To this I add an estimate of the return on the collateral for the derivative commodity positions. The 3-month Treasury bill rate since 1933 has averaged 4 percent. Our prospective outlook is 4.5 percent.
- The assumed total return for a long commodity index is therefore 0.5 percent + 4 percent + 4.5 percent = 9 percent

I want to emphasize these points:

- The small inflation-adjusted return of 0.5 percent ascribed to commodities is generally considered to be the premium received by investors in futures contracts for their willingness to take on the price risk of the contracts.
- Obviously, the prospective return will be heavily influenced by future inflation, as it is a strong driver of commodity returns and is also correlated to the Treasury bill rate, which will be earned on invested cash. Together, these factors could bring the potential inflation sensitivity of a commodities holding to the ~2x level.
- If we consider that the 1979–2009 return of the GSCI has been 6.29 percent and the 3-month Treasury bill return for the same period has been 5.93 percent, we can conclude that commodities have actually suffered a negative real return during this period: The return to the futures was 0.36 percent, while inflation was much higher over the period.

The Role of Commodities in a Diversified Portfolio

Table 13.3 examines the role of a commodities exposure (DJ-UBS) in low- and higher-risk portfolios. From the negative efficiency gain numbers we see for the low-risk portfolio, we can conclude that adding commodity exposure to more conservative portfolios is unwise. Adding commodities decreases return slightly and increases risk significantly—a lose-lose outcome. It seems clear that the low-risk nature of the portfolio causes the additional risk introduced by commodities to overwhelm the benefits of low correlation.

However, as we move to the growth portfolio, the use of commodities becomes more interesting. Adding commodities even up to the 15 percent

TABLE 13.3 The Role of Commodities in Portfolios

	Low Risk Portfolio			Growth Portfolio		
	Return	Risk	Eff Gain	Return	Risk	Eff Gain
Portfolio	6.04%	5.67%	—	7.14%	11.85%	—
With 5% commodities	6.04%	5.68%	−0.19%	7.08%	11.53%	+1.15%
With 10% commodities	6.04%	5.78%	−2.03%	7.03%	11.26%	+2.18%
With 15% commodities	6.04%	5.95%	−5.01%	6.97%	11.04%	+2.88%

Source: Greycourt.

level produces a more efficient portfolio. I find this especially compelling given that the time period being evaluated has not been particularly strong for commodities.

It should be noted that the impact of commodities on a portfolio is dampened by the drain that taxes impose on both return and volatility. Only at very marginal contribution expectations, however, would taxes impact the decision of whether or not to include a commodities allocation.

Effects of Rebalancing

The long-term returns to commodities are not spectacular: This is simply not an asset class where investors should expect to earn high real rates of return over the long term. The asset class is also very volatile, as was evidenced by high standard deviations and very lumpy periodic returns. The periodic returns tend to be cyclical and to correlate with inflation expectations. Though the uncorrelated nature of the asset class lends itself to a risk mitigation role in a portfolio, volatility is a challenge.

What this suggests is that, in order to maximize the utility value of a commodity allocation and harvest the volatile returns, investors must rebalance more frequently than in other asset classes. The world adjusts and reprices assets quickly: Culling gains on the commodity allocation is important to avoid reversion.

The Impact of Extreme Events

Monte Carlo analysis seeks to employ a large number of random trials in order to explore the probabilities of one or more defined outcomes. The drawback to Monte Carlo is that it draws from a defined distribution. Knowing that a commodities allocation has the primary function of reducing portfolio risk, we know that in portfolios where it is desirable to hold such an allocation, Monte Carlo analysis will reflect the lower modeled risk levels with a narrower distribution of outcomes for a given target return.

Qualitatively, the volatility and the cyclical nature of commodities make them very sensitive to changes in global growth and inflation expectations (rate of return on a futures contract) and interest rates (cash held as collateral). As noted above, it would make sense to use a strict rebalancing strategy to mitigate the impact on the portfolio of downside fluctuations and to cull gains made from upside moves.

Summary

My analysis suggests the following:

- Commodities primarily exert a positive effect on a portfolio by decreasing the overall portfolio risk.
- Commodities exert the majority of risk benefit on a portfolio through their low correlation against the other asset classes, as opposed to providing a compelling risk/return as a long-term stand-alone investment.
- Due to the inherent volatility in the commodities asset class, its ability to improve the risk/return trade-off improves in more risky and volatile growth-oriented portfolios.
- Historic long-term returns for the commodity asset class from the 1979–2009 period are not compelling, but the DJ-UBS provides substantially better risk/return than the GSCI, albeit with slightly higher correlations.
- With respect to the returns generated in the 1979–2009 period, a case could be made that the measurement period was uniquely unsympathetic to commodities returns and may not be representative of returns in future periods.
- The advantages of a commodities allocation are slightly dampened in taxable family portfolios, but only at the margin.

CONCLUSION: THE USE AND MISUSE OF REAL ASSET EXPOSURE

Enthusiasm for real assets comes and goes over the years for reasons that are sometimes rational and sometimes not. For example, investors who believe in Malthusian principles will tend to see human population growth and its associated resource use as inevitably driving up prices of real assets. Investors who fall into the Julian Simon school of thought will tend to see human ingenuity as driving down real asset prices over time.

I don't intend to get myself in between these two groups, both of whom make strong points. Suffice it to say that whoever is right, the effect tends to occur over periods of time much too long to be of much use in investing capital.

On a shorter-term basis, real asset enthusiasts point to the emergence of rapidly growing middle-income populations in the emerging markets, arguing that the buying power of this group will inevitably drive up prices. Others point out that in the short term the production of many commodity-like assets is elastic, as technological improvements keep prices more under control than not, and that in the long term, the middle classes in Asia and Latin America won't be "emerging" any more.

PRACTICE TIP

Investing in commodities can improve the performance of family portfolios, especially those at the more aggressive end of the risk spectrum. Unfortunately, there are many behavioral problems with commodity allocations.

As noted above, disciplined rebalancing is required, and many families will find it very hard to sell down their commodities positions when prices are rocketing upward. As a result, they will be dramatically overexposed to the sector when the inevitable collapse comes.

In addition, it can be very difficult for a family to remain patient with a commodities allocation that appears, in isolation, to be a very low-returning sector. The advantages of diversification and lowered volatility are very important, but hardly very visible.

If as an advisor you want to put commodities into a family portfolio, you may find it necessary to act not merely as an investment advisor, but also as a family counselor.

NOTES

1. I am deeply indebted for this portion of the chapter to Eric Haskel's excellent paper on real estate investing. See Greycourt White Paper No. 47:Investing in Real Property (2009), available at www.Greycourt.com.
2. Vanguard offers a mutual fund that is a REIT index fund. Other mutual funds also specialize in investing in real estate–related companies—the Third Avenue Real Estate Value Fund, for example.

3. With thanks to my partner, Mark J. Laskow, whose excellent paper on this topic very much informed this portion of the chapter. See Greycourt White Paper No. 37:Investing in Oil & Gas (2006), available at www.Greycourt.com.
4. Special thanks to my partners at Greycourt, Mark Laskow and Chris Fineburg, for their assistance with this portion of the chapter.

CHAPTER 14

Investing in Fixed Income

Fixed-income markets—bond markets—tend to be efficient, meaning that it is difficult for any manager to produce sustained outperformance. They tend to be low returning, net of inflation, meaning that there is little wealth-creation potential to be had in the sector. Finally, they tend to be "boring," with little in the way of the spectacular peaks and valleys that characterize equity markets.

Instead, fixed-income markets tend to follow broad secular trends as interest rates rise over the course of many years (the 1970s, for example), then decline slowly over the course of many more years (the 1980s and 1990s, for example). As a result, we might expect to find that investors have such markets well in hand and that we can safely focus our advisory attention on the gamier equity side of client portfolios.

In fact, however, my experience is that investors tend to make at least as many mistakes on the bond side of their portfolios than they do on the equity side, probably because, for the reasons just mentioned, investors don't pay enough attention to fixed income. Granted, mistakes in bond portfolios tend to be less disastrous for investors than mistakes elsewhere, but foolish deployment of our capital is always harmful to our wealth, whether the harm occurs in brief, spectacular fashion (as with equity mistakes) or slowly and largely invisibly (as with bond mistakes).

MISTAKES BOND INVESTORS MAKE

Let's examine some of the typical mistakes we make in our fixed-income portfolios, and then we'll turn to best practices in this sector.

Employing Managers Who "Cheat"

Given the extraordinary efficiency of the bond markets, especially on the taxable side, it's surprising to observe how many bond managers claim to have outperformed the indexes. Closer examination almost always discloses, however, that the managers have exposed their clients to significantly more risk than was embedded in the index, and it was the added risk that explains the outperformance, not the managers' skill. Adjusted for risk, these managers will usually be found to have underperformed.

Let's look at how a typical taxable bond manager "outperforms," by observing the fictional firm of Wily Bond Management.

Wily manages taxable bond accounts for institutional investors and for families who have private foundations or large IRA accounts. Its typical benchmark is the Barclay's Aggregate bond index, a very broad long-intermediate index. Over the past 10 years, Wily has outperformed the Barclay's Agg, and this fact is naturally trumpeted in its marketing materials. Looking at this record, many investors have hired Wily, and Wily's business is growing and profitable.

But a closer look at Wily's performance discloses what is not disclosed by the firm's sales staff: Wily has subjected its client accounts to considerably more risk than is contained in the index, and it is that increased risk, pure and simple, that accounts for Wily's so-called outperformance. In fact, controlling for the risk it has taken, Wily has actually underperformed the index by a considerable margin.

How does Wily take on more risk than the index? In at least three or four ways. First, Wily has exposed its clients to greater *duration*[1] risk. Over the past 10 years the average duration of the Barclay's Aggregate bond index has been about 3.8 years, whereas the average duration of the Wily portfolios has been about 4.1 years. Over time, longer-duration portfolios will outperform shorter-duration portfolios, albeit with greater price volatility along the way. This is what has happened to the Wily accounts.

Second, Wily has exposed its clients to greater *credit* risk. The average credit quality of the index is AA, but the average credit quality of the Wily portfolios is A–. Though this may not seem to be a big deal, lower-credit-quality bond portfolios naturally tend to return more than higher-quality portfolios for the simple reason that investors demand more return to take on the increased risk of default.

Third, Wily has exposed its clients to greater *optionality* risk. Many corporate bonds are callable; that is, under certain conditions the issuer can redeem the bonds long before they are scheduled to mature. Naturally enough, companies tend to call their bonds when they can replace them by issuing new bonds at lower interest rates. For the unhappy investors, this means that we have received our money back exactly at a time when we don't *want* it back—because we will have to reinvest it at lower yields. Issuers of callable bonds pay a very small premium for the privilege of being able to call those bonds, and Wily has taken advantage of that by buying a far higher percentage of callable bonds than is represented in the index.

Finally, Wily has exposed its clients to benchmark risk in other ways—by owning more structured products (mortgage-backed and asset-backed instruments, for example) than are present in the index, by overweighting certain sectors of the index, and so on.

There is nothing inherently wrong with anything Wily has done with its client portfolios, *except for the singular omission that none of it was disclosed to the clients*. Thus, Wily has achieved outperformance against the index, but it has not achieved something far more important—risk-adjusted outperformance. Nor is this a hypothetical problem for investors.

If we look at Wily's aggregate performance over the past 10 years, we do, indeed, see long-term outperformance against the Barclay's Aggregate (though not risk-adjusted outperformance, of course). But if we look, instead, at each individual account Wily has managed over that time period, we observe problem after problem. Investors look at Wily's aggregate performance and hire the firm, looking no further. Things go along well enough for a period of time, but then suddenly the risk embedded in the Wily portfolios jumps out and bites us.

Perhaps it is an unexpected jump in interest rates that harms the Wily portfolios much more than we expected (and much more than the index was harmed, as a result of its shorter duration). Perhaps slowing economic conditions have caused several of the weaker credits in the Wiley portfolios to be downgraded or—horror of horrors!—to default. (The index will experience downgrades, too, but at a less frequent pace, as a result of its higher average credit quality.) Perhaps rates have fallen and many issuers have called their high-yielding bonds, forcing us to go out and buy lower-yielding bonds to replace them (the index will also have experienced calls, but fewer of them due to its lower optionality).

Yes, investors who stayed the course with Wily for the entire 10-year period will actually have beaten the index, albeit with many unhappy surprises along the way. But there will actually be few such investors. Many more investors hired Wily, were unhappily surprised by the risks that bit them, then fired Wily, poorer but wiser. We don't want to be one of those investors, and so we need to look much deeper before we hire bond managers who claim to have outperformed.

PRACTICE TIP

Perhaps because bonds are such a low-returning asset class, the temptation for an advisor is to try to juice up the sector in one way or the other. But there are good and bad ways to do this.

The good way is to find a niche bond manager who is actually doing something different from everyone else and who therefore stands a chance of producing real, risk-adjusted outperformance. If you go in this direction, *make sure you are straight with the client* about what the manager is doing and what the risks are.

The bad way is to hire a bond manager who cheats and hope he doesn't (and you don't!) get caught. Remember that even though bond mistakes typically don't result in losses as big as mistakes elsewhere in the portfolio, you can never forget that this is your client's sleep-well money. Even a smallish loss can infuriate a client who is taken unaware by duration, credit, or optionality risk.

Paying Too Much for Bond Management

Whereas some investors are being penny-wise and pound-foolish (by hiring brokers to build their bond portfolios or by doing it themselves), other investors are simply paying way too much to have their fixed-income portfolios managed. Keep in mind that the long-term expected return on an intermediate bond portfolio, net of tax (or using tax-exempt bonds) is going to be on the order of 5 percent. Yet, according to Morningstar, the average intermediate bond fund has an expense ratio of 1 percent and charges an average load of 0.83 percent. That's nearly 2 percent in the first year, or roughly *40 percent of the long-term expected return.*

Even the great Bill Gross, probably the best bond manager who ever lived, has trouble overcoming the high expense ratios of the retail versions of the PIMCO bond funds. As Morningstar puts it, "fees are simply too high to recommend some [of PIMCO's retail] share classes—no matter how good the management."[2]

EMPLOYING BEST PRACTICES IN BUILDING BOND PORTFOLIOS

The world of bonds may seem like a simple place, compared to equities and alternative assets, but it's actually a very complicated asset class. Consider that it includes government bonds, corporate bonds, municipal bonds, high-yield bonds (corporate *and* municipal), and cash management, as well as the whole other world of foreign sovereign and corporate bonds and Yankee bonds.

Let's look at some of the best practices associated with successfully navigating the world of fixed-income securities.

Building Laddered Bond Portfolios

Because bonds deliver relatively little in the way of return, and are used by investors mainly to produce income and to control portfolio risk, one way to keep bond management costs down is to ladder our fixed-income portfolios. If, for example, we want to build a $1 million bond portfolio with an average maturity of five years, we might simply buy the following bonds:

	Dollar Amount	Maturity
Bond #1	$100,000	2012
Bond #2	$100,000	2013
Bond #3	$100,000	2014
Bond #4	$100,000	2015
Bond #5	$100,000	2016
Bond #6	$100,000	2017
Bond #7	$100,000	2018
Bond #8	$100,000	2019
Bond #9	$100,000	2020
Bond #10	$100,000	2021

This gives us a $1 million bond portfolio with an average maturity of five years. Each year, one of our bonds will mature and we will use those proceeds to buy the longest maturity needed to maintain our five-year average maturity. (In 2012, for example, we will use the proceeds of Bond #1 to buy a $100,000 bond maturing in 2022.)

The advantages of this laddered approach are considerable. First, the cost is minuscule, particularly if, as we should, we are using U.S. Treasury notes and bonds.[3] Second, because a bond matures every year, we have fairly short liquidity if we should need it. Third, because we are buying bonds over a long period of years, we are averaging in to interest rate changes. Finally, because we are planning to hold each bond until it matures, we can't experience a capital loss in our bond portfolio.

But laddered bond portfolios are not entirely without their complications. In the first place, they should only be used in circumstances where the use of U.S. Treasury securities is appropriate. These securities are the safest paper available and they are not callable. (The U.S. Treasury does, from time to time, attempt to repurchase its notes and bonds on the open market.) Some investors build laddered bond portfolios out of corporate or municipal bonds, but this is dangerous, because many of these securities are callable—defeating the purpose of holding them until maturity and reinvesting at the then-prevailing interest rates—and because nobody is watching the credits of the issuers. (Ah, you say, you plan to confine your fixed-income ladder to the best investment grade bonds. Well, the next time you find yourself thinking along these lines, here is a useful corrective. Repeat to yourself this phrase: "Enron, WorldCom, Global Crossing; Enron, WorldCom, Global Crossing....")

In the second place, owning a laddered bond portfolio requires iron discipline in not abandoning the ladder in the face of disquieting conditions. In a rising interest rate environment, for example, there will be paper losses in the laddered portfolio and you may be tempted to sell out of some of the bonds and replace them with higher-yielding securities. This will almost surely prove to be a double mistake: You will lock in your loss on the sold bonds and rates will continue to rise on you, causing you to lose money even on your newly purchased bonds.

Similarly, in a declining rate environment your bonds will show gains and you may be tempted to capture those gains before rates rise and they disappear. Again, this is almost certain to prove a foolish strategy: Rates will continue to decline and you will simply be destroying your income stream. In short, the whole thesis underlying laddered fixed-income portfolios is the impossibility of foreseeing the direction or rapidity of interest rate changes or the shape of the yield curve.

Owning Only High-Grade, Noncallable, Long-Term Bonds

Many investors believe that the only fully justifiable excuse for owning bonds—which, after all, impose substantial opportunity costs on portfolios as a result of their low real returns—is as a hedge against the outbreak of deflation. Deflation is a very serious economic condition in which prices actually decline in real terms.[4] About the only investment assets that will perform well in a deflationary environment are long-term, high-grade, noncallable bonds: for example, 30-year U.S. Treasury bonds.

Actively Managing Municipal Bonds

Most wealthy investors will keep the greatest part of their bond portfolios in municipal bonds, which are (currently, anyway)[5] free of federal taxation. Unlike Treasury securities and corporate bonds, the municipal bond sector is complex and inefficient, and fairly cries out for competent active management. That said, we have to keep firmly in mind that the municipal sector embraces a particularly unattractive set of issues: It is complex and difficult to succeed in the sector, it is essentially impossible to add wealth to our portfolios no matter how well we do in the sector, and yet the sector represents an essential asset class for most families.

Regarding complexity, consider that the municipal sector includes general obligation (GO) issues floated by all 50 states; issues floated by thousands of cities and towns; issues floated by tens of thousands of special-purpose districts, hospitals, and airports; issues floated by water authorities; prefunding issues; and on and on. The creditworthiness of these many entities is always suspect and is always changing.[6] There are also odd seasonal issues associated with the municipal sector that must be dealt with, as certain issuers tend to come to market at certain times and as certain large holders of munis tend to liquidate those holdings at certain times. Finally, munis are susceptible to all the interest rate dynamics that bedevil other sectors of the bond markets. In short, individual investors who imagine that they can intelligently assess this world, and then continue to monitor it, are simply kidding themselves.

The best way to manage a substantial municipal bond portfolio is not to give our money to a muni bond manager and hope they do well. Instead, we (and our advisors) should develop a detailed set of objectives and guidelines and insist that our muni bond manager abide strictly by them. The objectives will typically address the relative priority among capital preservation, liquidity, and income. The guidelines will also specify a target average duration for the bond portfolio (either an absolute target or, more commonly, a target set in relation to the municipal bond index we wish to have our money managed against); maximum and minimum durations for individual securities in the portfolios; minimum average credit quality for the overall portfolio; minimum credit quality for individual issues in the portfolio; maximum exposure to individual issuers (allowable exposures will differ depending on the perceived creditworthiness of the issuer types); use of leverage in the portfolio; employment of derivative securities; the amount of cash permitted to be held; and how the performance of the portfolio will be monitored and evaluated.[7]

In other words, in looking for competent municipal bond management firms, what we are really looking for is sophistication in the sector, intense tax awareness, sufficient volume to keep trading costs down, willingness to work as our agent,[8] and strong internal control and management systems that will give us confidence that the manager can actually comply with our guidelines. Simply looking at past investment performance is less of a priority.

PRACTICE TIP

I've placed on the website (www.wiley.com/go/stewardshipofwealth, password: curtis2012) a sample of guidelines for actively managed bond portfolios (municipal and taxable). For substantial municipal bond accounts, this is really the way to go and it's worth spending some personal capital explaining to your client why that is so.

But take the guidelines as examples only—every account will need to be customized for your client's state and federal tax bracket, AMT status, risk level, and so on. Most very large municipal bond managers will have standard guidelines, but never, never accept these as is. Start with your own guidelines and then negotiate with the manager from there.

One final issue associated with municipal bond investing has to do with whether we should insist that all bonds in our portfolios be tax-exempt in the state where we pay income taxes. The trade-off here is higher after-tax income versus the increased risk that arises from having all our bonds concentrated in one state. Tax rates in some states are so high that most investors in those states will find it prudent to accept the concentration risk (California, Massachusetts, and New York, for example). Even in these states, however, it will sometimes pay to buy out-of-state bonds, and hence that flexibility should be given to our municipal bond manager.

In most other states, however, it will generally pay us to accept slightly reduced after-tax income in order to avoid highly concentrated bond port-folios. Assume, for example, that our muni bond portfolio is yielding, on average, 4 percent. Assume that the state income tax is 6 percent. If all our bonds were exempt from tax in that state, our net after-tax yield would be 4 percent. If *none* of our bonds were exempt from tax in that state (but were only exempt from federal tax) our after-tax yield would be 3.76 percent. Given that we can buy many in-state bonds that are fully tax exempt and still build a nationally diversified bond portfolio, our actual after-tax yield is likely to be much closer to the 4 percent that is maximally possible. And given the damage that can happen to our portfolio as the result of a series of downgrades (or, horrors, defaults) resulting from negative regional economic factors, we will generally be better off with a nationally diversified portfolio that has, perhaps, a state-of-residence focus.

Actively Managing Corporate Bonds

Most everything we have said thus far about managing municipal bond portfolios can also be said about managing corporate bond portfolios. The main difference is that the corporate bond sector is more efficient, hence fees should be lower. Aside from that, however, most of us will be better off either indexing in this sector or insisting that our corporate bond manager manage our account to our exact specified guidelines.

Indexing can be accomplished via, for example, the Vanguard Total Bond Market index fund. For bond portfolios over $250,000, Vanguard charges only 17 basis points (17/100 of 1%) per year. Larger portfolios can use the Vanguard Institutional version of the fund, which charges only 10 basis points, or can have their bond portfolios custom indexed by a large financial institution. There are also exchange-traded funds that offer indexed corporate bond management.

Bond accounts managed according to our own guidelines should be handled by bond managers who possess the systems and controls required to ensure that those guidelines are adhered to, and who manage sufficient bond assets to ensure reasonable trading costs. As emphasized above, we will want to work with a bond manager who is buying and selling bonds as our agent using other dealers, not with a brokerage firm selling bonds to us out of their own inventory.

High-Yield Bonds

I have put the discussion of high-yield bonds in the Fixed Income chapter because, legally speaking, high-yield bonds are in fact bonds—they pay a fixed coupon. But in virtually every other way, high-yield bonds are far more analogous to equity securities.

For example, high-yield bonds experience price volatility that is more akin to that of stocks than to that of bonds. In addition, the use of the proceeds raised by issuers of high-yield bonds is typically for longer-term corporate activities that would normally be funded by issuing equities, except that the company is not strong enough to be of interest to the equity market. Finally, astute investors treat high-yield bonds more like stocks in terms of how they spend, or don't spend, the return.

Most bond investors spend most of the return their bonds generate—the coupon payments—but most stock investors spend, if anything, only dividends paid on their stocks and often not even that. Because virtually all the return on high-yield bonds comes from their unusually high yields, investors who spend the entire yield will achieve a zero return (a negative real return) on their high-yield holdings. Hence, smart investors will tend to spend only a small portion of the yield on high yields, or spend none at all.

The term "high yield" is, of course, a euphemism. The traditional term for bonds issued by non-creditworthy companies is "junk." The term was not changed in an effort to be Politically Correct—a disease happily almost completely absent from the financial services world—but for sales reasons. Investors who wouldn't touch a "junk" bond will snap up a bond that is described as having a "high yield." It is, however, a useful corrective to keep in mind that, although bonds in this sector do indeed have high yields, they are in fact junk bonds.[9]

Bond ratings were created by credit rating agencies to assist investors in evaluating the credit quality of the issuers of bonds. The highest credit rating, AAA, is enjoyed only by the most creditworthy firms. As a result of their high standing, these firms have to pay interest on their bonds that is only slightly higher than the interest paid on U.S. Treasury securities with similar maturities. This difference between Treasury yields and yields on other bonds is referred to as the yield spread. Junk bonds—those bonds rated below BBB—are considered speculative grade by the ratings agencies and must pay much higher rates of interest in order to have any chance of selling their bonds. Hence, their spreads are much wider.[10] (Bonds rated D are already in default.)

Junk bonds entered center stage in the capital markets with Michael Milken and Drexel Burnham Lambert in the 1980s. That episode ended in scandal and in the collapse of many of the lower-rated companies Milken had championed. Nonetheless, the notion that weaker firms should have access to capital was an attractive one, and many of the innovations launched by Milken survived his own troubles. Today, the junk bond market is thriving, and many firms that simply would not have survived in the capital-starved pre-Milken world have grown into pillars of the corporate community.

Junk bond managers range all over the lot, from managers who dip only slightly below investment grade (their portfolios will have average ratings of BB or BB−) to managers who deal in the true heart of junk bond land—the C credits—to managers (many of them organized as hedge funds) who deal in seriously distressed securities, many of which are already mired in bankruptcy proceedings.

Because the junk bond sector is highly cyclical, there are only two intelligent ways to play the junk bond game for most family investors. The first is to create a permanent allocation to junk (say, 10 percent) and to rebalance religiously back to that allocation whenever it is exceeded or whenever the actual allocation falls below the target. This disciplined rebalancing will introduce a countercyclical effect into the junk bond portfolio, causing us to sell junk when the bonds are outperforming and to buy junk when the bonds are underperforming. Over time, this will provide a nicely enhanced return to our portfolios and will inject considerable diversification.

A more sophisticated approach is to buy junk on an opportunistic basis, that is, whenever spreads significantly exceed their long-term norms, and to sell junk when spreads return to their long-term norms. This approach will provide higher returns, but it is difficult, both technically and emotionally, to implement.

MANAGING CASH

Managing cash may appear to be simplicity itself, but in fact managing very large amounts of cash—as in very large family portfolios or where cash has been received following a liquidity event—can be complex and, indeed, agonizing. True, the returns that are possible on cash investments, especially net of tax, are piddling. Yet, we are reminded of Henry Kissinger's remark about faculty disputes being so bitter precisely because the stakes are so small: Mismanaging cash investments rarely proves to be a complete disaster, but the failure to eke out a tiny increment of return above some benchmark can cause investors to suffer agonies wholly disproportionate to the actual harm.

Middle-income investors have a simple answer to the problem of investing cash—send it to a money market fund. But if the amounts are very substantial, that is unlikely to be the optimal strategy. In the first place, most money market funds are uninterested in receiving gigantic sums of new money from wealthy investors, especially in a declining-rate environment. The problem of investing all the money can reduce the already-low rates of return on the fund, rendering the money market fund uncompetitive versus its peers. Taking $1 billion in cash from one investor can cost the fund many more billions of dollars as other investors flee the resulting depressed returns: In a declining-rate environment the new money must be invested at current interest rates, which are, by definition, lower than past rates, and this brings down the average return of the entire fund.

Finally, although money market funds are used to dealing with "hot money"—investors who are constantly moving from fund to fund to get the highest interest—they are unwilling to take in very large sums from one investor who is likely to pull it out soon. In other words, it is much more difficult for a large cash investor to "roll down the yield curve"[11] than it is for smaller investors.

Investors deploying large sums of cash will typically be better-off creating their own "money market fund" by engaging one or more managers who will purchase and sell individual financial instruments that comply with precise guidelines. The companion website (www.wiley.com/go/stewardshipofwealth, password: curtis2012) includes a sample of cash management guidelines.

PRACTICE TIP

Given the uncertain world we now live in, with the United States having lost its AAA status and with no solid ideas on the table for how the country plans to reduce its debt load, it may be useful for a financial advisor to consider advocating global diversification even for the cash portfolio. This can be especially important if the cash balance is quite large.

In short, though managing cash may seem simple, it can actually be quite complex and surprisingly emotional. By structuring a separate account arrangement with strict guidelines, investors are likely both to fare better and to sleep better.

PRACTICE TIP

Here's a cautionary tale about managing cash.

A few years ago a California family sold its business for more than $1 billion. The family members were extraordinary business managers, but they had little experience in investing. Recognizing that they couldn't simply send a billion dollars to a standard money market fund, and wanting to get institutional diversification to minimize counterparty risk, they divided the money into thirds and gave one-third each to two commercial banks and one investment bank.

The two commercial banks invested the money as expected, in a conservative, customized money fund. But the investment bank opted for a much more aggressive approach, placing most of the money in auction rate securities. An auction rate security is a debt instrument with a long-term nominal maturity but with an interest rate that is reset periodically via a Dutch auction. When the markets became difficult in early 2008, most of the auctions failed, and the family lost nearly $300 million.

The next time you think managing cash is a no-brainer, keep this example firmly in mind.

CONCLUSION: FIXED INCOME IS UNDERAPPRECIATED

The bond allocation in a family investment portfolio serves many purposes. It provides a relatively steady stream of income. It provides stability to the portfolio, controlling volatility within parameters acceptable to the family. It can serve as a comforting, low-risk segment of the portfolio, allowing the family to spend down the bond portfolio while waiting for a bear market in stocks to recover. (Some risk-averse families will keep three to five years' worth of spending in a laddered portfolio of Treasury bills, notes, and bonds.) And on top of this, over the past 30 years bonds have out-returned stocks!

Thus, although many investors are hopelessly bored by bonds, they play an essential role in the portfolios of almost every family, and learning something about the sector is well worthwhile.

NOTES

1. Duration is a more accurate measure of the interest rate sensitivity of a bond portfolio than the more commonly used "maturity," because duration includes all cash flows coming in from the bond, including interest payments and principal repayments. Thus, a bond with a ten-year maturity and a 5 percent yield will have a much shorter duration (and hence will be much less susceptible to interest rate changes) than a bond with a ten year maturity and a 3 percent yield.
2. Eric Jacobson, "Still a Leader Worth Following," Morningstar Fund Analysis, (February 10, 2012) available at http://analysis.morningstar .com/analystreport/far.aspx?t=PTTDX&region=USA.
3. Commissions on the purchase of U.S. Treasury securities are very small, and can be avoided altogether by using the Treasury Direct program. Because we are planning to hold all our bonds until they mature, there will be no commissions on sales.
4. Deflation is not to be confused with disinflation, a propitious condition in which the rate of inflation is declining.
5. The Obama administration has proposed to tax municipal bond interest.
6. As this chapter was being written, both Harrisburg, Pennsylvania and Jefferson County, Alabama (Birmingham) had declared bankruptcy.
7. The guidelines will also give tax information about the investor. While most municipal bond investors will be in the highest federal and state tax brackets, family investors increasingly fall under the provisions of the Alternative Minimum Tax. AMT taxpayers will sometimes find that tax-exempt bonds will be appropriate and that sometimes taxable bonds will be appropriate. Our municipal bond manager must therefore possess capabilities in both taxable and municipal securities.
8. In other words, buying and selling bonds through dealers on our behalf, not selling bonds to us as a broker would do.
9. Okay, okay, some companies that technically fall into the junk bond category, especially the upper echelons of junk (BB rated bonds, let's

say) are hardly "junk companies." Some simply happen to be in an industry that is temporarily out of favor, while others are going through a rough period financially but are fundamentally sound. Most issues of junk bonds, however, are highly speculative investments.

10. In the fall of 2002, spreads between Treasuries and junk bonds reached their widest gaps in history. This was, to say the least, a propitious time to buy junk bonds.

11. This phrase refers to the phenomenon just noted: A money market fund that purchased many of its investments when rates were higher will still own those investments until they gradually mature. Thus, the interest rate offered by the fund will be higher than the interest rate investors could get by buying similar investments today. The fund's yield will gradually decline, of course.

CHAPTER 15

Investing in Hedge Funds

Buying stocks long is to selling stocks short what touch football is to Iwo Jima.

—Dave Barry (paraphrase)

Because most taxable investors have a strong capital preservation orientation, and because many hedge funds also have a capital preservation aspect to their activities, it is hardly surprising that hedge fund investing has proven to be extremely popular among affluent families. In the past 20 years, hedge fund investing has gone from a fringe activity practiced by obscure gnomes to the most rapidly growing of all investment opportunities.[1]

Today, there are at least 8,000 hedge funds in existence, and probably more than 10,000. Note that this is far more than the number of stocks listed on the New York Stock Exchange. In an average year, hedge fund managers generate more income than all the mutual funds registered in the United States. Indeed, what used to be exclusively the province of wealthy and institutional investors is now hot retail territory. "Retail" hedge funds of funds offered by large financial institutions and requiring very low minimum investments are sprouting everywhere, and there are also mutual funds that invest in hedge funds or that attempt to replicate hedge fund strategies.

Why are hedge funds so hot? Partly, of course, it's the mystique that surrounds hedge funds. They are exclusive, nontransparent, and engage in exotic kinds of investment strategies. Families who invest in hedge funds feel that they are somehow special, that they have gained access to an esoteric sector where wonderful things can happen.

This is mainly nonsense, but there are in fact good reasons to consider investing in hedge. One important reason is that, at least among the best managers, hedge funds have produced very good risk-adjusted performance over long periods of time. Exhibiting roughly bondlike price volatility, the best hedge funds have nonetheless produced equitylike returns, a feat that seems to fly in the face of modern portfolio theory. In addition, although hedge funds performed poorly in the dreadful market of 2008, declining about 20 percent, long equities declined more than twice as much.

As a result, although most people still think of hedge funds as an alternative investment, the category has become very much mainstream. It is a rare wealthy family these days that doesn't maintain a healthy allocation to hedge.

WHAT IS A HEDGE FUND?

The President's Working Group on Financial Markets, which looked into the causes of the failure of Long-Term Capital Management, defined a hedge fund as "a pooled investment vehicle that is privately organized, administered by professional investment managers, and not widely available."[2] This is about as unhelpful a definition as one could wish for, but it does make the point that hedge funds are very hard to define. Many hedge funds don't hedge at all, for example, and some are quite widely available.

The first hedge fund, so far as we know, was established half a century ago by Alfred Winslow Jones, a former financial reporter. If Jones had $100 to invest he would invest it all in the stock market. He would then borrow another $30 and invest that as well. Then, in order to "hedge" the risk of the leveraged $30, Jones would sell $30 worth of stocks short. His idea was that if his stock picks were very good he would make far more money than a typical long-only investor: He would make money on his long positions, of course, but he would also make money from his leverage and his short positions. If his picks were only "good," he might lose money on his short positions but make it up on his long and leveraged positions. His only real danger, aside from incompetent stock-picking, was a very bad down market, in which case his long and leveraged positions would overwhelm his short positions. (This actually happened to Jones in 1969–1970.)[3]

Today a hedge fund can be defined as any investment vehicle organized as a partnership in which the manager shares in the profits and in which (speaking very generally) the manager invests in marketable securities.[4] (In other words, private equity funds don't count.) The manager may or may not sell short; he may or may not employ leverage; he might be buying equity securities or fixed-income securities or currencies; he may specialize in a specific niche or market sector, or he may migrate from niche to niche and sector to sector. The only way to know what a hedge fund is doing is to speak at length with the manager and to check everything he or she says.

TYPES OF HEDGE FUNDS

Speaking very generally, hedge funds can be categorized as directional funds (so-called macro funds and most long/short funds) and absolute-return-oriented or ARO funds (sometimes called nondirectional funds or market-neutral funds). Hedge funds, however, are not truly nondirectional or market neutral.

Most directional macro funds employ few or no hedging strategies, but simply make bets on their specific ideas, whereas long/short funds are mainly similar to long-only managers except that they also sell stocks short, thus reducing (but not eliminating) their exposure to broad market trends. Many hedge funds fall easily into these broad categories, but some do not.

Hedge funds can also be categorized according to the kinds of investment strategies they follow. Following are some of the many examples of strategies a hedge fund might focus on:

> *Convertible security arbitrage.* Many companies issue convertible securities—securities that are convertible into another company security at a stated price. Depending on the characteristics of the company, the price volatility of the securities, the relative price level of the securities, the level of interest rates, and other factors, the two securities will tend to trade in a price relationship with each other that can be ascertained. If the securities are trading outside this range, the difference can sometimes be arbitraged at a profit.

> *Distressed debt.* Most investors are familiar with high-yield bonds— lower-rated bonds that must offer a much higher yield than traditional bonds. Hedge funds tend to work even lower down in High-Yield Land, buying all or parts of bond issues that have already defaulted and that are mired in bankruptcy proceedings. This sector of the distressed debt market tends to be highly inefficient. Not only must the hedge fund manager accurately estimate the issuer's ability to reorganize and make good on the bonds (or at least pay more for them than the hedge fund paid), but the hedge fund must assess the complex legal rights of the parties to the bankruptcy proceeding and estimate when (if ever!) the company will emerge from bankruptcy. Very often, distressed debt investors

find that they must get proactively involved in the bankruptcy proceedings or even in the management of the company in order to realize value.

Event-driven. These are mainly[5] merger arbitrage hedge funds. When a merger is announced there will always be at least some degree of doubt about whether the transaction will actually close. As a result, if the buyer is offering $27 a share, the seller's stock price will remain somewhat below $27 until the transaction actually closes. Arbitrageurs who study the potential acquisition carefully can buy the seller's stock long, sell the buyer's stock short, and make a profit when the transaction closes—a profit that is largely independent of the direction of the market (because the arbitrageur has hedged his position).

Long/short equity. This is the classic hedge fund, buying stocks long that the manager believes will rise in value and selling stocks short that the manager believes will decline in value. As noted elsewhere, this promising-looking strategy is much more difficult to implement successfully than it looks—especially on the short side.

Short-selling. Short sellers are increasingly rare for a good reason: When a long-only or long/short manager performs poorly, he simply underperforms; when a short seller underperforms he goes bust. When we buy a stock long, we limit our risk to the price of the stock—it can only go to zero. But when we sell a stock short our risk is theoretically unlimited.

Global macro. These hedge funds scour the investable universe for compelling opportunities, then make (often staggering) bets on them. The manager might be shorting the kroner or trying to dominate the silver market, and might be leveraging those bets as well. These funds are not for the faint of heart. Global macro managers are especially drawn to currency and interest rate trading. In more recent years, observing the increasingly poor results of the traditional global macro players, managers in this space have opted to take many smaller bets, rather than a few larger ones.

Multistrategy. As the name implies, multistrategy hedge funds move their capital around among strategies depending on where they are finding value and opportunity. If opportunities in event arbitrage (or arb) have dried up, a multi-strategy manager might move capital to distressed debt or convertible arb. Given the level of difficulty involved in outperforming in any single strategy, imagine the difficulties posed by performing well in many different strategies. Multistrategy funds are therefore relatively rare and tend to be very large—large enough to employ specialist managers in several different disciplines.

PRACTICE TIP

A special problem with multistrategy hedge funds (multi-strats) is that, too often, they represent less an investment strategy than a business strategy. Most multi-strats began life as convert arb funds. But convert arb is a seasonal strategy: When it works it works, and when it doesn't it doesn't. And when it doesn't, investors redeem. As a result, many convert arb managers morphed into multi-strats. But do they know anything about investing outside the convert arb space? And has the founding manager spread equity around in a fair way? If the founder runs 50 percent of the book but has 80 percent of the economics, take your client elsewhere.

Hedge funds, especially directional funds, are not, strictly speaking, a separate asset class. Hedge fund managers are buying and selling the same kinds of investment assets as long-only managers—they are just employing different techniques. It is true, to be sure, that the risk-return profile of a well-diversified group of long/short hedge funds will be quite different from that of a well-diversified long-only portfolio, and therefore it is important to evaluate directional hedge exposure independently. But this doesn't make directional hedge a separate asset class: A leveraged exposure to the Nasdaq will have a very different risk-return profile from a long-only exposure to the Nasdaq, but no one would consider it a separate asset class. It is better to think of most hedge funds—the so-called long/short, or directional funds—as alpha strategies[6] that can complement the long-only strategies in our portfolios.

Nondirectional hedge funds—more properly called absolute return-oriented funds, or ARO funds—on the other hand, do tend to exhibit more of the characteristics of a separate asset class, at least when we invest in a diversified portfolio of ARO strategies. These strategies tend to be uncorrelated—or loosely correlated—to the broad markets.

CHALLENGES FOR HEDGE FUND INVESTORS

A few years ago advisory firms faced an uphill battle trying to convince investors to add hedge fund exposure to their portfolios. Today the problem is almost the opposite—when an advisor first encounters new clients they are as likely to have too much hedge fund exposure (or the wrong kind of exposure) as to have not enough. Whether investors are drawn to hedge funds for their return potential, whether they are fleeing debacles in other capital markets or whether they are simply seeking prudent diversification, the problems today are too much haste, too little caution, and diligence that is too superficial.

Probably the main challenge for investors in hedge funds going forward is the one just mentioned: the popularity of hedge fund investing. The more money that pours into a sector, the more difficult it will be for managers to add value. Vendors in the hedge fund business will argue that, though some strategies are naturally capacity constrained—merger arbitrage, for example—others are not.[7] Long/short equity managers and fixed-income arbitrage managers play in markets that are measured in the trillions of dollars. Hence, so the argument goes, even a manager with several billion dollars under management will represent only a tiny drop in the vast ocean of opportunities.

But this is the wrong measure. In U.S. large caps, the question isn't whether or not any individual manager has a lot or a little money to work with. The question is how much money, and how many players, are at work in the sector. As more and more managers engage in long/short equity or fixed-income arbitrage, the information available to everyone in those sectors will expand, leaving even talented managers with little room to run.

More broadly, we should assume that all alpha-based strategies are inherently capacity constrained. The most talented managers may develop many more good ideas than less talented managers, but less talented managers are exceptionally good at copying successful strategies. Hence, as more and more players enter a field, the half-life of good ideas declines precipitously. In addition, although there may be trillions of dollars invested in global equities and fixed income, the subset of those markets that have value to be exploited is far, far smaller. Managers who identify value and act on it will find that their activities are much more conspicuous than we would imagine if we think only about the aggregate size of the equity and bond markets.

Let's examine some other challenges faced by prospective investors in hedge funds.[8]

Survivorship bias. Earlier, I cited the extraordinary returns achieved by hedge funds over the past 10 years. But that data is highly suspicious, not least of all because of the phenomenon of survivorship bias. This phrase refers to the fact that only the most successful hedge fund managers have survived for the 10-year period we are measuring. Less-successful managers long ago went out of business, and their demise has imposed a kind of double-whammy on reported returns. First, because they are no longer in business and reporting their results, the (poor) performance of failed managers has been removed from the historical record, dramatically raising the reported performance of the surviving managers. Second, because they are no longer managing money, failed managers are no longer turning in those lousy returns, which would continue to bring down the averages.[9] In other words, the actual returns achieved by investors in hedge funds over the past 10 years are far lower than the actual returns achieved by the *surviving* managers over that period. In the Lake Wobegon world of hedge funds, all managers are above average.

Volatility and risk. When investors and their advisors design portfolios, they tend to use volatility as a proxy for risk. But in the hedge fund world, price volatility does not capture anything like all the risks embedded in the sector. Specifically, volatility ignores the liquidity risk inherent in hedge fund investing, as well as the risk of fraud or other misconduct. Most hedge funds offer only quarterly liquidity, though some impose one-year lockups or even longer. For an investor who needs or wants cash, even a quarter can be an eternity. Fraud, although rare, is hardly unknown among hedge fund managers, and when it happens, the consequences for investors in the affected funds can be truly disastrous. The long and short of this is that investors who look only at hedge fund volatility in designing their portfolios will almost certainly end up with an overexposure to the sector: The apparently attractive combination of low risk (volatility) and high returns will cause hedge funds to dominate the optimizer, resulting in "optimal" hedge fund exposures that are far higher than is prudent.

Skewness and kurtosis. As noted above, most hedge funds do not constitute a separate asset class—they simply represent an alpha strategy. Hence, the use of traditional modern portfolio theory tools to design hedge fund portfolios (standard deviation, correlation, expected return) simply will not work. The problem, in technical terms, is that the hedge fund world is characterized by skewness and kurtosis. Translated into English, this means that (a) hedge fund returns don't occur in a normal, bell-shaped distribution the way returns occur in equity markets, and (b) the likelihood of very bad outcomes is very high. Among other things, hedge funds occasionally blow up for all sorts of reasons, resulting in the loss of all or most of the fund investors' capital. But it is also important to keep in mind that, although adding hedge funds to a traditional portfolio will typically reduce the dispersion of outcomes, it will also increase the likelihood of a negative outcome.[10]

A diluted manager talent pool. Fifteen years ago only the most talented managers could hope to be successful in raising money for a hedge fund. These days, however, there is so much demand for hedge fund exposure that it seems as though anyone with a high school diploma can successfully set up a hedge fund. Many newer hedge fund managers do not even have investment track records—they may have been financial analysts, for example. Even those with direct investment experience often have no experience selling stocks short or employing other hedging strategies. Short selling is a nerve-racking activity in which potential losses are unlimited and potential gains limited. Other problems with new managers include inexperience managing their own businesses and inexperience managing complex back-office challenges.

Too much capital coming into the business. Very few investment strategies can preserve returns when massive amounts of capital pour into the business, and hedge fund investing is no exception. Some of the new capital in the hedge fund world emanates from investors who are thoughtful and experienced, but who must invest so much capital (in order to have any impact on the returns in their gigantic portfolios) that they simply cannot do a good job of putting the money to work. Other capital is coming from sources that have precious little experience investing in hedge funds and who are proceeding with such undue haste that it is clear they are simply exploiting the public's sudden appetite for hedge exposure. A particularly worrisome development involves the advent of so-called "capital guaranteed" products. Many European banks (and, recently, some American banks) have raised large amounts of capital from inexperienced investors via this tactic, under which the financial institution guarantees investors that they will not lose money in hedge funds if they keep their money invested for some minimum period of time, usually five or six years. Other structured products—typically levered—are also being offered, as well as the retail products described earlier.[11]

Tax inefficiency. For taxable investors, this may be the biggest issue of all: The gross returns of hedge funds have to be adjusted for their tax inefficiency. And note that this inefficiency can be huge, because, for most funds, almost all the return is generated in the form of short-term capital gains and ordinary income.[12] There are techniques that can be used to shelter hedge fund gains or convert them into long-term gains, but these techniques bring their own complex challenges.[13] Managing hedge fund tax issues is a very complex subject, but suffice it to say here that no hedge fund belongs in your portfolio unless its after-tax results are satisfactory relative to the risks being taken. This is true of all investments, of course, but few are as tax-disadvantaged as hedge funds.

Lack of transparency. For investors who are used to tracking their portfolio results on a frequent basis, the lack of transparency that characterizes hedge fund portfolios is likely to provide a whole new experience. What is transparency all about?[14] Transparency refers to the ability of an investor in a hedge fund to understand what the manager plans to do, how he plans to do it, and whether he is actually doing it. Without transparency, investors can't understand the nature of the risks they are taking, and hence cannot, for example, hedge those risks by investing with managers using other strategies.[15]

Conflicted prime brokers. In a typical separate account money management arrangement, cash and securities are held by a bank acting as custodian. The manager has only a limited power of attorney to direct the investments in the account, but cannot remove funds from the account. The investor is the bank's customer, not the manager. If anything even remotely fishy is going on in the account the bank will notify the investor immediately. Hedge fund accounts, however, are not custodied in the usual sense. Instead, the funds reside with a "prime broker," typically an investment bank or brokerage firm that serves as global custodian, broker, lender (via margin loans), vendor of derivative transactions, and even fund-raiser for the hedge fund. The customer is the hedge fund, not the investor. Prime brokers play so many roles, have so many conflicts of interest, and earn such large profits for their firms that they cannot be counted on to blow the whistle on shenanigans committed by hedge fund managers with whom they work.

Hedge fund advantages are also disadvantages. In the upside-down world of hedge funds, virtually every advantage claimed by the industry also represents a potential disadvantage for investors. For example, Jonathan Lach lists the following burdens hedge fund managers are able to avoid (relative to other money managers): "excessive capital under management, benchmark objectives, diversification requirements, daily liquidity, and significant organizational time demands."[16] Lach is right, and these are in fact important advantages of hedge funds. But many investors will view all but the first and last[17] of these not so much as burdens to be avoided but as important risk controls. Or consider the "advantage" that many hedge fund managers have much of their own money invested in their funds. This is certainly an advantage in the sense that such a manager is likely to pay close attention to the business. But that is a different issue from the question of whether the manager's interests are aligned with the investor's—they typically aren't. If a manager has much of his net worth invested in his fund while a typical investor has only a modest portion of his net worth invested in the fund, the interests of manager and investor are structurally misaligned from the beginning. Moreover, manager and investor may have different time horizons and may have very different feelings about leverage, downside risk, long and short exposures, and so on.

High fees. Hedge fund managers charge annual fees of 1 percent to 2 percent, plus (usually) 20 percent of any profits. Some managers are worth every penny of this, but they are rare, indeed. In other words, there is nothing inherent in the hedge fund format[18] to justify such fees—only talent justifies them. Investors who don't aggressively seek out talent are likely to be disappointed in their hedge fund returns in part because too much of the return is going to the manager.

Mischievous fee structures. Hedge funds often have both a hurdle rate and a high-water mark. The hurdle rate means that the manager cannot get any part of his 20 percent share of the profits until the fund has exceeded some preset annual rate of return—8 percent, for example. The high-water mark simply ensures that, once a loss has been incurred in a fund, the manager cannot receive his 20 percent share of the profits until the loss has been recovered. Both elements of the fee structure are perfectly fair, but they can easily combine to produce odd incentives. Consider a fund with a 1 percent annual fee, an 8 percent hurdle rate and a high-water mark provision. The fund starts with $100 million in year one, rises to $200 million in year two (a hell of a year, to be sure), declines to $150 million in year three, and rises to $175 million in year four. In year four, the fund is not yet back to its high-water mark of $200 million. In addition, the manager has failed, over years two and three, to earn the 8 percent hurdle rate. Moreover, as the hurdle rate piles up and the high-water mark looks more and more unattainable, the manager is faced with receiving nothing but his 1 percent annual fee for many years. He didn't go into the hedge fund business to earn a 1 percent fee, so what does he do? As Roland Lochoff puts it, "It is not uncommon for a fund to fall so far underwater that the chance of ever reaching the high water mark is improbable. It simply pays the hedge fund manager to go out of business and start afresh with a new name."[19] In other words, heads he wins, tails we lose.

PRACTICE TIP

It's worth mentioning that this very issue—high-water marks causing more mischief than help—is bedeviling hedge fund investors now. As this chapter is being written (early 2012), it's estimated that more than 65 percent of hedge funds remain below their high-water mark as a result of poor returns in 2008.[20] Five years is a long time to go without receiving an incentive fee, and even many good funds are beginning to lose top talent or even to consider shutting down and reopening.

Thus, as you look at hedge fund managers, check carefully into the high-water mark issue. If a fund is only a few points below its high-water mark and otherwise seems stable, it may not be an issue. But for funds that are still way below the high-water mark, it's probably best to keep your distance.

High tracking error. Investors who have traditionally focused on tracking error to monitor their managers will be sorely disappointed with hedge funds. It is virtually impossible to create a benchmark that will be useful for monitoring a hedge fund portfolio. As a result, whatever benchmark is used, tracking error will be impossibly high—so high as to be largely useless as a manager-monitoring tool.[21]

Correlations increase just when you need them not to. Over long periods of time, hedge funds have demonstrated low correlations to the equity and fixed-income markets. Unfortunately, during liquidity crises (August 1998, the summer of 2002, 2007–2008, for example), the correlations between hedge funds and marketable securities increase dramatically—just when you most need the diversification. In other words, hedge funds provide diversification over the long run but not over the short run.

Selling beta as alpha. Investors can buy beta cheaply—via index funds, exchange-traded funds, futures, and so on. Alpha is expensive, and properly so, because it is so rare. Hedge funds charge very high fees because they claim to be delivering alpha. Some, surely, are doing so, but most are simply expensive beta shops. Bridgewater Associates once measured the performance of managers in seven popular hedge fund strategies against the performance that would have been obtained by naively replicating the systematic risks taken by the managers. They found that the naive strategies typically outperformed the average hedge fund manager.[22] To take a simple example, instead of investing with merger arbitrage hedge funds, an investor could simply buy the top 10 acquirees during any given year and sell the top 10 acquirers short. That investor will likely have achieved a return that is higher than the aggregate returns of merger arb hedge funds.[23]

The difficulty of ongoing monitoring. It is difficult to perform enough diligence on a hedge fund to justify investing in it. But, unfortunately, that is far less than half the battle. Investors in hedge funds find themselves in hot water not so much because of the lack of up-front diligence—though there is a lot of that going around—but because of the almost complete lack of ongoing diligence. It is hardly an exaggeration to say that most investors' ongoing diligence is limited to checking their returns. But an ongoing understanding of exactly what our hedge fund managers are doing, why they are doing it, and how well they are doing it is critical to avoiding disasters. It is exceptionally rare for a hedge fund manager simply to blow up with no warning whatever. More typically, there were alarming red flags flying for months or years before the blowup, but most investors weren't paying attention. Some of those red flags should have been identified in up-front diligence—a checkered regulatory or personal history, for example. Others show up only months or years later. An example would be suspiciously good or consistent performance versus other similar hedge fund managers (think Bernard Madoff.) Another would be an increase in leverage or other kinds of risky behavior. Ongoing diligence conducted at a level of detail that matters virtually requires (a) spot-checking position-level detail for each manager (though not necessarily in real time), and (b) a staff with the trading sophistication to understand what the trades mean. The group of investors who can't perform this sort of diligence includes virtually all private families and family offices, virtually all investment consulting firms, and, alas, most hedge funds of funds.

In the face of all these challenges, it is inevitable that, as has always been the case with private-equity funds, performance dispersion among hedge funds will widen until, unless we are invested with top quartile funds, we should, like Yogi Berra, have stood in bed.

PRACTICE TIP

If you have a client who is a hedge fund junkie, life as an advisor can be very difficult. The basic problem with investors who are fascinated by hedge funds is that they are never able to build a true best-in-class hedge fund portfolio. Instead, they are so excited by the latest hot manager or so delighted that they've gotten into a supposedly closed fund that the portfolio soon fills up with very average funds. One way to help break the client of this habit is to start showing the performance of the individual hedge funds not just in after-fee terms, but in *after-tax* terms. Only the very best hedge fund managers will produce good risk-adjusted performance on an after-tax basis.

BUILDING A FIRST-RATE HEDGE FUND PORTFOLIO

Given all the difficulties of investing successfully in hedge funds, investors have resorted to various and sundry strategies designed to improve the odds. Let's take a look at the main strategies used by hedge fund investors.

> *Designing a separate hedge fund portfolio.* A great many investors have built what they think of as separate hedge fund portfolios that are designed to improve their overall returns, but that aren't thought of as playing a particular role in the overall investment portfolio. The trouble with this approach is that, if we don't have an expectation for exactly how the hedge fund portfolio is supposed to behave, how can we know whether it is working for us or not? The notion that it doesn't really matter as long as the hedge fund portfolio is performing well is naive. No hedge fund portfolio, however well designed, will always perform well. Thus the question is always before us: When the hedge fund portfolio isn't performing well, is it still playing a worthwhile role in our overall portfolio? We need to know the answer to this question, but too many investors aren't even asking it.

> *Using long/short hedge funds as the high-alpha component of an asset class strategy.* One of the best uses of hedge funds, especially

directional funds, is as the high-alpha portion of an equity strategy. We could decide to index a core position in U.S. equities, then build a satellite position using long/short hedge funds. One difficulty with this strategy is that hedge fund managers tend not to keep doing what they were doing when we hired them, with the result that our overall U.S. equity exposure will tend to behave in quixotic ways.

Using hedge funds of funds. All but the very largest families will likely find that the safest strategy in the hedge fund space is to build a core hedge fund exposure by investing in a hedge fund of funds. Yes, this adds yet another (often substantial) layer of fees to the already burdensome fee structure. But a best-in-class hedge fund of funds will perform at least the following services for investors:

- Instant diversification among hedge fund styles, hedge fund managers, and different levels of risk.
- A risk-return profile designed to deal with the issues of skewness and kurtosis mentioned previously.
- Extensive up-front investment and operational diligence on hedge funds and their professional staffs, including intensive background tests.
- Perhaps most important of all, the fund of funds will conduct serious, thorough, ongoing monitoring of every hedge fund in the portfolio (as well as any hedge funds the fund of funds is considering investing in). Given the lack of transparency and forthcomingness of many hedge fund managers, this ongoing diligence process is extremely expensive and time-consuming.

Alas, it is also true that the great majority of hedge funds of funds either can't or don't provide high-quality ongoing monitoring of their managers. Of the more than 1,000 hedge funds of funds available to investors, no more than a few score are worth their fees. It is, in other words, nearly as difficult, though perhaps not as dangerous, to identify best-in-class hedge funds of funds as it is to identify the best individual hedge funds. Intense diligence will be required before engaging such a fund of funds.

Using nondirectional hedge funds. Nondirectional or absolute-return-oriented (ARO) hedge funds exhibit more of the characteristics of a separate asset class, at least when combined into numerous ARO strategies. Typically, then, the best practice with ARO funds is to create a separate allocation to these strategies. A well-balanced group of ARO funds (accessed in the case of most family investors via an ARO hedge fund of funds) should exhibit volatility roughly similar to that of bonds but should generate returns more similar to those of stocks. But don't be fooled by the low volatility. ARO hedge funds pack plenty of risks, even though volatility measures don't necessarily pick up those risks.

Using multistrategy hedge funds. Most individual hedge funds focus on one investment strategy, or perhaps two related strategies. Some funds, however, are so-called multistrategy hedge funds. These funds tend to engage in a variety of strategies, many of them unrelated to each other. The senior professionals overseeing the multistrategy fund will allocate capital among the various strategies depending on where they see value in the marketplace. Thus, if spreads have tightened in the distressed debt markets, the multistrategy fund might reduce the capital employed in that strategy and move it to, say, convertible arbitrage. In a sense, then, multistrategy funds can sometimes stand in for funds of funds, offering strategy diversification within one investment partnership. Investors should keep in mind, however, that executing many different strategies successfully will severely tax all but the very best multistrategy funds—and many of those will be closed or will demand very high minimum investments.

Using tax-efficient strategies. High-taxed short-term capital gains and high fees (especially at the fund of funds level) have led some sophisticated families to rethink hedge fund investing from the bottom up. Rather then viewing hedge funds as an alpha opportunity, these investors have consciously decided to forgo potential alpha in favor of certain tax savings. These strategies involve gaining derivative exposure to a hedge fund index, typically via a structured note whose value is linked directly to the performance of the index. These linked notes should be treated for tax purposes as forward purchase contracts, with all profits deferred and converted to long-term capital gain once the one-year holding period has been met. Linked notes usually have weekly liquidity and can be purchased in lots as small as $50,000. No K-1s or 1099s are issued and the notes are DTC eligible, which means they can be custodied along with the client's other assets. As an extra bonus, investors in the notes need not meet the superqualified investor standards required by many hedge funds and funds of funds. Although this will not be an issue for most family investors themselves (the requirement is $5 million in investable assets), many substantial families will have family foundations that do not meet the $25 million (assets) standard for a qualified purchaser, and hence will be frozen out of many funds. It is important to remember that, as with any structured product, there is counterparty risk: The party selling the structured note—usually a large bank or other financial institution—could possibly go bankrupt before paying us off.

CONCLUSION: SHOULD ANYONE BUT YALE INVEST IN HEDGE FUNDS?

We got them steadily depressin', low-down mind messin', workin' at the hedge fund blues.
                                              —With apologies to the late Jim Croce

David Swensen, as almost everyone knows, is the extraordinarily successful manager of the Yale University endowment. In Swensen's first book, *Pioneering Portfolio Management*,[24] published in 2000 and addressed to institutional investors, hedge funds were portrayed as playing an essential role in reducing portfolio risk and in gaining access to the most talented managers. So it's no surprise that Yale has a big exposure to hedge funds.[25]

But in Swensen's second book hedge funds seemed to have disappeared from the face of the earth. In *Unconventional Success*,[26] addressed this time to the individual investor, Swensen mentions hedge funds only in passing, mainly complaining about their fees. What gives?

Obviously enough, the first decade of the twenty-first century has been a rough one for the hedge fund industry. Returns have been disappointing, at least compared to what investors were expecting (and compared to what many hedge fund managers were projecting). The Securities and Exchange Commission (SEC) has decided to get tough on hedge funds, forcing them to choose between registering with the SEC or imposing long lockups on their investors. A steady stream of frauds and blowups have occurred in the industry—Bernard Madoff being Exhibit A—giving everyone a black eye.

I yield to no one in my skepticism of many of the players in the hedge fund business, and earlier in this chapter, I've not been shy about expressing my reservations. But let's try to strike a middle ground, because wealthy families are neither the institutional investors Swensen addressed in his first book nor the retail investors he addressed in his second. It's important to be aware of the challenges and disadvantages of investing in hedge funds, but it's also important to keep the advantages firmly in mind.

When people like David Swensen criticize hedge fund investing these days, it's worth taking the man seriously. After all, investors might ask themselves, if David Swensen says to avoid hedge funds, why am I so smart?

It's a good question. In fact, I agree with much of what Swensen has to say about hedge funds and funds of funds. In an interview in the *New York Times*, following the publication of his second book, Swensen was quoted as saying, "Funds of hedge funds generally aren't a good investment for the unsophisticated investor."[27] Hard to quibble with that. It isn't even controversial. After all, we know from a Dalbar paper[28] that between 1983 and the end of 2000—the best U.S. bull market of all time—while the S&P 500 was returning an average of 16.3 percent per year, the typical equity investor achieved only 5.3 percent. And just to rub it in, while long-term bonds rose 11.8 percent, bond investors got only 6.1 percent.

We can hardly expect investors who can't manage stock and bond portfolios to be great hedge fund investors. And because most hedge funds of funds don't even begin to earn their extra layer of fees, suggesting to unsophisticated investors that they invest in funds of hedge funds is almost certainly doing them a disservice.

The key point here is that Swensen's advice about hedge funds—and my advice about hedge funds—differs depending on the nature of the investor. Here, in a (largish) nutshell, is how I would put it.

> *Category #1—Investors acting on their own.* As noted above, my advice to these investors is nearly[29] identical to Swensen's: Don't try this at home. Most hedge fund portfolios I've seen that have been assembled by individual investors are flat-out frightening. They tend to be undiversified, there tends to be no ongoing diligence on the managers (and precious little up-front diligence), and no thought at all has been given to how the hedge fund exposure fits with the rest of the portfolio.

> *Category #2—Investors who are captive clients of product vendors.* When I speak with investors who are captive clients of large, product-selling financial firms (large banks and investment banks, for example), I tend to hear something like this: "Sure, the firm's products may not be best-in-class, and sure, they might be over-priced, but [insert here name of voracious bank] wouldn't endanger its reputation by pushing truly awful products." To which my response is, "What are you smoking?" Financial firms that have been disciplined again and again by federal regulators for engaging in everything from outright fraud to conspiring with the likes of Enron are hardly going to draw the line at pushing a lousy investment product.

> *Category #3—Investors working with objective advisors.* Okay, I'm blowing my own horn here, but the hard fact is that investors who are working with competent, objective advisors are far more analogous to very large institutional investors than they are to the investors described in Categories #1 and #2. Open-architecture advisors act as a kind of private investment office for their clients,

searching for the best hedge funds and funds of funds, ensuring that appropriate diligence is done on them (and continues to be done long after the funds are bought), avoiding conflicts of interest themselves and refusing to do business with funds of funds that have embedded conflicts, and so on.

There is no gainsaying the fact that the hedge fund community has had a difficult time since the turn of the century, and that it has become a target for criticism by the knowledgeable and the clueless alike. Nor can I quibble with the claim that hedge fund investment activities are often (though hardly always) complex, opaque, and secretive. But the bottom line is the same as it usually is: Investors who are poorly or corruptly advised are likely to come to grief, and the more complex the investment sector the more grief they are likely to come to. Investors who are well advised, however, fall into a completely separate category and should stop worrying.

NOTES

1. "From Infamy to Fame—The Rapidly Changing Landscape of the Hedge Fund Industry," *Advent Client News*, Advent Software, Inc. (2nd Quarter 2002): 1.
2. The President's Working Group on Financial Markets, *Hedge Funds, Leverage, and the Lessons of Long Term Capital Management*, 1999.
3. I am indebted to James Grant, an infinitely provocative financial writer and investor, for this description of Jones's hedge fund, A.W. Jones & Co. James Grant, "Yes, But," *Forbes* (June 10, 2002): 220.
4. Of course, many of the securities purchased by hedge funds are highly illiquid. Because a hedge fund manager deals in marketable securities, that doesn't mean that his portfolio can be accurately marked-to-market every day.
5. Event-driven hedge funds also invest in other special situations that are expected to dramatically change the financial or operating conditions of a firm.
6. "Alpha" is simply a measure of risk-adjusted return.
7. "While one must admit there are capacity issues in some sectors, a careful strategy-by-strategy review suggests this is not a concern for the bulk of the hedge fund industry." R. McFall Lamm, Jr. and Tanya E. Ghaleb-Harter, *An Update on Hedge Fund Performance: Is a Bubble Developing?* Deutsche Asset Management research monograph (September 1, 2001): 3.

8. Interested investors may also wish to look into Simon Lack's controversial attack on the hedge fund industry, *The Hedge Fund Mirage: The Illusion of Big Money and Why It's Too Good to Be True* (New York: John Wiley & Sons, 2012). For an earlier but similar take on the industry, see Daniel Quinn Mills, *Wheel, Deal, and Steal* (Upper Saddle River, NJ: Pearson Education, 2003).

9. Jonathan Lach refers to "the tailwind of survivorship bias." See Jonathan Lach, "Investing with Wolves: Classic Hedge Funds—Better than Equities," *The Journal of Wealth Management* (Fall 2002): 75.

10. See, for example, "10 Things That Investors Should Know about Hedge Funds," *The CFA Digest* 33, no. 3 (August 2003); Gaurav S. Amin and Harry M. Kat, "Hedge Fund Performance 1990–2000: Do the 'Money Machines' Really Add Value?" *Journal of Financial and Quantitative Analysis* 38, no. 2 (June, 2003). Professor Kat has been a vocal opponent of the mindless use of hedge funds, and his many writings on the subject, though somewhat technical, are well worth looking into. Kat is the director of the Alternative Research Centre at the Cass Business School in London.

11. "Democratize the hedge fund business? Sure, and as long as we're at it, let's democratize the New York Philharmonic. We'll all play first horn." Grant, "Yes, But," note 284.

12. See, for example, James R. Cohen, Jeffrey S. Bortnick, and Nancy L. Jacob, "Tax-Efficient Investing Using Private Placement Variable Life Insurance and Annuities," *The Journal of Private Portfolio Management* (Winter 1999) and Majed R. Muhtaseb, "To Outperform the Market: Get Out of It!" *The Journal of Wealth Management* (Fall 2002). These authors suggest that roughly 80 percent to 90 percent of hedge fund returns are generated in the form of dividends, interest, and short-term capital gains.

13. For example, hedge funds can be placed in tax-exempt accounts, such as IRAs or charitable foundations. Hedge funds can also be wrapped in onshore or offshore insurance products.

14. "Hedge fund transparency is like pornography—it is hard to describe, but you know it when you see it." Mark Anson, "Hedge Fund Transparency," *The Journal of Wealth Management* (Fall 2002): 79.

15. I don't mean to suggest that hedge fund investors need to have full position transparency on a regular basis. I do suggest that many hedge fund managers offer so little in the way of tactical and risk transparency that investors would be better off avoiding such managers altogether.

16. Lach, "Investing with Wolves," note 10, 77.

17. Even these characteristics can be viewed as disadvantages. Hedge funds can avoid having excessive capital under management by closing to new investors. But this means that, just about the time a sensible investor has concluded that the manager knows what he is doing, it's too late to get in. Organizational time demands are certainly a bugaboo for long-only managers associated with large institutions, but organizational supervision also tends to reduce the kind of fraud and mismanagement that occurs in the hedge fund industry.

18. Some would argue with this view. R. McFall Lamm, Jr., for example, argues that, "Conceptually, the long-only manager faces a constrained optimization problem [that is, he can only buy long; he can't sell short], while the equity hedge manager is unconstrained." R. McFall Lamm, Jr., "How Good Are Equity Hedge Fund Managers?" *Alternative Investment Quarterly* (January, 2002): 21. Conceptually, yes, but the execution challenges facing the unconstrained manager make it likely that only the most talented managers will be able to use the unconstrained vehicle to full advantage.

19. Roland Lochoff, "Hedge Funds and Hope," *The Journal of Portfolio Management* (Summer 2002): 92.

20. "Quitting While They're Behind: Some Hedge Funds Are Throwing in the Towel," *The Economist* (February 18, 2012).

21. Lamm Jr., "How Good Are Equity Hedge Fund Managers?" 21.

22. Bridgewater Daily Observations (February 17, 2004).

23. Ibid., p. 4.

24. *Pioneering Portfolio Management: An Unconventional Approach to Institutional Investment* (New York: Free Press, 2000).

25. *Ibid.*, Chapter 8.

26. *Unconventional Success: A Fundamental Approach to Personal Investment* (New York: Free Press, 2005).

27. Geraldine Fabrikant, "Hedge Funds Work for Yale, but Will They Work for You?" *New York Times* (November 27, 2005): BU 5.

28. "Quantitative Analysis of Investor Behavior" (2001).

29. Swensen's attitude toward individual investors is almost bizarrely paternalistic. He believes, for example, that hedge funds of funds should be legally banned and that all but the largest institutional investors (e.g., Yale) should be barred by law from investing in hedge funds. Such a deal for Yale!

CHAPTER 16

Investing in Private Equity

Whereas public equity refers to securities we can buy on the open market, private equity (PE) refers to interests in businesses that are privately held.[1] In other words, these are businesses that are culturally similar to the businesses that made most wealthy families wealthy.

Families invest in such businesses by buying limited partnership interests in ventures managed by individuals who are skilled in acquiring, improving, and growing such businesses. If the business being acquired is a mature enterprise, probably a spinout from a larger company, we are investing in a buyout. If the business is quite new and untested, we are investing in a venture capital deal. We can also invest in mezzanine deals (loans to middle-market companies) or distressed deals (companies in need of a turnaround).

PE is very much a skills-based business, and the skills required for success are not broadly available. One important result of this fact is that only a small percentage of the PE deals being marketed are worthwhile. And as true as this is in buyouts, it's even more true in venture. Thus, if you are interested in investing in PE, keep these three words firmly in mind: access, access, access.

The reason we want to invest only in the best partnerships is that the average PE partnership produces returns that are roughly in line with those of long-only equity managers. This dramatically undercompensates investors for the leverage, risk of loss, and illiquidity of PE investments, which can take 10 years (or a lot more) to play out. According to FLAG Capital Management, top quartile PE partnerships—that is, those whose investment results place them in the top 25 percent of all partnerships—outperform average PE funds by 1,500 basis points (15 percent) per year.[2] Clearly, those are the funds families will want to invest in, but gaining access to them is almost impossible for most family investors. PE funds tend to prefer large institutional investors as limited partners, believing that family investors tend to be less sophisticated and more fickle. Lack of access to the best PE firms is the main reason that most family investors in private equity don't earn returns anywhere near what they need to compensate for the risks they have taken.

Like it or not, then, the first rule of PE investing for most family investors is to invest via a best-in-class PE *fund of funds*. Families tend to hate funds of funds, but the best of them (granted that there aren't many good ones) will bring many benefits to justify their extra layer of fees. However, the key benefit is the one just mentioned: access to the best partnerships, a benefit we can't do without. (I discuss this issue in greater depth later.)

WHY INVEST IN PE?

Most families who have accumulated significant wealth did so by building a successful business of some kind and selling it for lots of money. Thus, the first reason families should consider investing in PE is that it is culturally the most familiar kind of investment a family can buy. The people who run PE-backed firms are the wealthy families of the future (assuming they are successful)—in other words, people like you.

Beyond that, PE is a tax-advantaged investment. PE returns are taxed at long-term capital gains rates, and those taxes are deferred long into the future, allowing the investment to compound tax-free for a decade or more.

Finally, the potential returns on PE are much higher than the returns available on public equities, thus qualifying PE for representation in the "aspirational" portion of a family investment portfolio.[3]

PERSISTENCE OF RETURNS

As we will see in Chapter 17, managers of public equities might produce top quartile returns for a time, but those returns rarely persist for very long. But it's quite different in the world of PE, where partnerships that develop excellent track records tend to persist in the top quartile for many years—generations, in some cases. One explanation for this persistence has to do with the quality of the deal flow that these successful partnerships see. Once a PE firm establishes itself as superior to most of its peers, entrepreneurs will seek it out, and they will often accept a slightly lower-priced deal from a top firm rather than taking top dollar from a lesser firm.

The reason an entrepreneur might be willing to accept a slightly lower price is that top PE firms bring much more than capital to the party: They offer advice based on their own vast experience with similar firms; they can source executive talent the firm will need as it grows; and the depth of talent in top firms ensures that the entrepreneur won't have to settle for the second team when, as it always will, the going gets tough.[4]

THE IMPORTANCE OF DIVERSIFICATION

Assuming that a family can gain access to top quartile private equity funds, either via funds of funds or directly, the next step is to diversify the PE exposure as broadly as possible. Note that there are many dimensions of diversification. We can diversify by:

- The type of investment (venture, buyouts, mezzanine, distressed).
- The stage of the investment (in venture, we can invest in early-stage, mid-stage, or late-stage investments).
- The industry (technology, healthcare, manufacturing, etc.)
- Geography (not just Silicon Valley or any other narrow geographical location that may be susceptible to simultaneous economic swoons, but nationally and even globally).
- Deal size (in buyouts, we can invest in large buyouts, small buyouts, middle-market buyouts, etc.)
- Vintage year. I mention this issue last, but in some ways it is the most important. PE returns are cyclical, and it is virtually impossible to anticipate those cycles. The only way an investor can ride out the bad vintage years is to be sure to be invested during the good vintage years. And the only way to do that is to invest consistently year after year.

PRACTICE TIP

The length of the time commitment to a PE fund can hardly be overstated. Consider that a PE fund of funds will typically invest over a four-year period of time. The underlying funds in which it invests will have lifetimes of 10 to 12 years, plus one or two one-year extensions. Adding it all up, we are already at a 15- or 16-year lifetime for the fund of funds, and 20 years is well in sight. Twenty years is pretty much the investment lifetime for a wealthy family investor!

My point is that PE funds, and especially PE funds of funds, must be chosen with extreme care. Our clients will be partners with these funds for many, many years.[5]

PRIVATE EQUITY RETURNS

Private equity returns run in cycles and are strongly influenced by such factors as market conditions, credit markets, company valuations, liquidity for exits, merger and acquisition activity, and other factors, including the amount of money looking for exposure to the asset class.

Looking merely at the 12-year period ending in 2010 enables us to observe the turmoil that can afflict the world of PE. In the late 1990s, investor enthusiasm for investing in emerging technologies led to the now famous Tech Bubble, which burst dramatically in 2000. Returns stagnated for years as the industry retrenched. The bear market for public equities that stretched through 2000 and 2001 further depressed the PE markets, placing pressures on exits and therefore on returns.

Still, as the markets languished and as investors fled PE, PE firms investing in smaller buyouts continued to operate below the radar, ultimately producing handsome returns later in the decade.

As liquidity built during the strong public equity markets of 2005–2007, the market for large buyouts became extremely active and for a short period returns were spectacular. But when the credit markets collapsed in 2007, this party came to a quick end, shocking many overextended PE investors (especially endowed institutions[6]). At the same time, the secondary and distressed PE sectors took off.

My point here is that no one could have foreseen this turmoil or timed their PE investments to take advantage of the ups and downs of the various sectors. Instead, PE investing requires great discipline and steady commitment. Investors who fail to build strong vintage year diversification into their portfolios can get badly burned.

THE RETURN CHARACTERISTICS OF PE INVESTMENTS

Returns can vary dramatically depending on the type and stage of a PE investment. Historically, early-stage venture capital returns are higher than later-stage returns, which in turn are higher than buyout returns. Within buyouts, returns on small and mid-market buyouts tend to be higher than returns on large buyouts. This hierarchy corresponds with the differences in risk undertaken. Early-stage companies are prerevenue and the few winners can provide huge payoffs, more than making up for the many losers. In the buyout arena, firms are more mature, cash flow is positive, and business models are well-established. Risk is therefore lower, but so are the returns.

Fund Stage	20-Year Returns
All venture capital	19.2%
All buyouts	8.9%
Small buyouts	12.1%
Mid-market buyouts	11.6%
Large buyouts	11.9%
Megabuyouts	7.2%
Mezzanine	7.0%
S&P 500	8.2%[7]

As the chart suggests, longer-term returns follow the expected patterns. However, over short and even intermediate periods of time, returns can be quite unpredictable. For example, over the 10-year period ending 9/30/2010, venture capital returns were actually negative, whereas buyouts eked out a 4 percent return. Being the average for all reporting funds, this chart understates the possibility for returns if the investor has access to the top-tier performers.

GAINING EXPOSURE TO PRIVATE EQUITY

Most sophisticated asset allocation strategies for wealthy families will include an exposure to private equity. As noted above, the challenge is to create a durable program, gain access to managers that have a history of outperformance, and structure a portfolio that is well diversified across vintage years, geography, and the various stages of company maturity. There is also a challenge associated with reaching the target allocation, given the nature of the investment pattern.

Suppose that your asset allocation calls for a PE exposure equal to 20 percent of the overall portfolio, and that your portfolio totals $100 million. What is the best way to build the PE portfolio, given that the best PE firms require minimum investments of $5 million or more?

Your $20 million allocation to PE will be drawn down over a period of four to seven years and in year three or four the funds will begin to repatriate capital to you. In order to achieve vintage year and style diversification, you will need to make annual commitments of no more than $5 million, spread around among various stages of venture and different styles of buyouts. At most, you can commit about $1 million to any one partnership. But the best firms require $5 million.

For most families, the solution will be to structure a program around one or more funds of funds, committing to investing with each fund over a period of years to achieve the targeted diversification.

PE FUNDS OF FUNDS

Private equity funds of funds are a relatively new phenomenon. Although funds of funds have been around since the 1970s, they proliferated in the 1990s as individuals and smaller institutions began to demand access to the asset class but were too small to invest directly with the best individual funds.

Funds of funds represent an efficient way to build a diversified, best-in-class private equity program. Among the characteristics investors should look for in a fund of funds is longevity, access to top-tier managers, proven relationships with these managers, fund size, the ability to identify tomorrow's top-tier performers, reputation, and reasonable fees and terms. The investment experience of the fund of funds management is critical. The managers should have years of market experience, a vested interest in the fund, interests aligned with the limited partners, demonstrated manager selection capabilities, and proven relationships with and access to the top-tier managers.

A GLOBAL ASSET CLASS

Another reason to consider funds of funds is the gradual extension of PE investing beyond the shores of the United States. In Europe, for example—the largest economy in the world—PE opportunities are growing rapidly. At this writing, the opportunities are mainly in buyouts, resulting from the high level of cross-border merger and acquisition activity. Unlike in the United States, where larger buyouts represent 80 percent of the market, in Europe large and smaller buyouts are about equal in number. Buyouts represent about half the percentage of GDP in Europe as they represent in the United States,[8] so there is plenty of room for the market to grow. As is the case in the United States, returns are the highest with small and mid-cap funds, but these are the most difficult funds to access.

Asia offers an increasingly wide range of opportunities in private equity. From 2000 until the end of 2010, Asian PE increased fourfold to levels competitive with the United States and Europe. Moreover, it weathered the 1997 meltdown, the 2000 tech bubble, and the 2007 credit crisis better than other parts of the world. However, Asian venture and buyout funds are very difficult for families to identify, vet, and monitor.

Israel has traditionally been a venture capital market, but there is an emerging later stage and buyout component. Key drivers of PE in Israel include outsized national expenditures on research and development and one of the most highly educated populations in the world. Again, however, access to funds is very difficult.

PRACTICE TIP

True as it is that PE has become an increasingly global asset class, it must also be said the returns outside the United States have not been strong over longer time horizons. European venture capital returns, for example, have actually been negative over the past 20 years. Also, given the current uncertain state of the European community, it's difficult to predict how well PE funds will do in the intermediate-term future. Europe's disarray will certainly create opportunities, but it will also create many unexpected speed bumps for PE-backed businesses.

If you are planning to encourage your clients to build non-U.S. diversification into their PE portfolios, you will need to have in mind a thesis for how they will make enough money to justify the long lockup.

ILLIQUIDITY AND THE J-CURVE EFFECT

Investors in private equity should have a long investment time horizon, as returns on commitments do not materialize for years and the penalty for abandoning a commitment is severe. Most fund partnerships have a 12-year life with the possibility of one or two one-year extensions thereafter.

On top of the illiquidity, PE investors must be willing to navigate the dreaded J-curve effect: Returns in the early years are almost always negative.

This phenomenon referred to as the J-curve can be illustrated graphically, as shown in Figure 16.1.

Investors who are new to PE are often horrified by the sudden drop in value of their investment, but the J-curve is almost inevitable. It occurs for a number of reasons, but the primary ones are these:

- Organizational expenses of private equity partnerships are deducted immediately, so no sooner does an investor meet the first capital call than the return immediately turns negative.[9]
- Smart general partners will identify bad investments quickly and write them down or off, whereas good investments will take time to pay off.

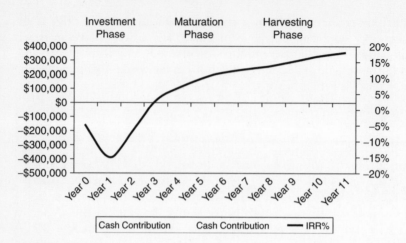

FIGURE 16.1   Fund Life Cycle and the J-Curve
Source: Greycourt.

- Most of the better PE firms follow very conservative policies when writing investments up or down: Bad developments cause immediate write-downs, but happy developments don't result in write-ups until some event occurs confirming the higher valuation.

RAMPING UP TO YOUR TARGET ALLOCATION

In private equity investing there is a considerable lag between commitments and actual investment of capital. Funds of funds commit to underlying private equity partnerships over a two- to four-year period. In turn, the underlying funds generally invest in operating companies over a three- to seven-year period. As a result, the investor in a fund of funds can expect that cash exposure to the asset class will rise rather slowly.

Compounding this, realizations will start as early as the third year and accelerate in years four through seven. As a result, in most cases less than 70 percent of an investor's PE commitment will ever be outstanding. For this reason, it is necessary to overcommit slightly to the asset class.

WATERFALL ANALYSIS

Waterfall analysis is a quantitative approach to thinking through the commitments required to reach an investor's target allocation and then sustaining

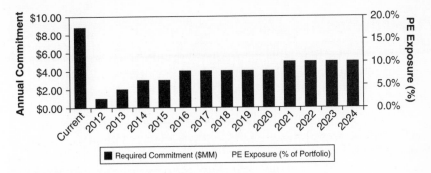

FIGURE 16.2 Private Equity Exposure Trajectory
Source: Greycourt.

the appropriate level of exposure. Diagramming the likely pattern of cash flows to and from various funds or funds of funds will help to determine how much and how frequently commitments should be made and how long it will take to get to the target exposure.

For example, Figure 16.2 shows the yearly required commitments for an investor with $160 million in assets to achieve a 15 percent allocation to private equity. The goal is to maintain a 15 percent exposure over time, despite unpredictable returns and varying capital call and distribution schedules. Another wild card is the anticipated performance of the underlying non-PE portfolio (the denominator in the allocation calculation).

Note that at the beginning of the period, the investor was *over*allocated to PE, so investments in the early years had to be lower than normal. This can raise havoc with vintage year diversification.

PRACTICE TIP

How can our clients know whether or not their PE portfolios are performing well enough to justify the risk and illiquidity associated with the asset class? It's a difficult question.

We can benchmark the client's returns against manager universes published by Venture Economics, Thomson Reuters, or Cambridge Associates, of course. But if overall PE results are poor during the period, our client might show well against the benchmark and still not be getting an appropriate return for the risk.

Most advisors will also want to benchmark PE returns against a long-equity index like the S&P 500. But because the S&P is highly

(Continued)

> **PRACTICE TIP** (Continued)
>
> liquid, our clients will want to achieve something more than long-equity returns on their PE portfolios. I typically use the S&P plus 500 basis points for venture capital and the S&P plus 350 basis points for buyouts.
>
> You may want to use higher or lower spreads, and you may want to use a small-cap or even microcap index for venture. But the principle of earning a spread over liquid equities is an important one.

SECONDARY PE INVESTING

Secondary investing is the business of buying limited partnership interests from investors in funds (or funds of funds) prior to their maturity. In other words, instead of investing as a limited partner in the original fund, you simply buy out a limited partner's interest in an existing fund. Typically, the limited partner will be a motivated seller who needs to raise capital and can no longer tolerate the illiquidity of his position.

Note that in most cases the general partner will control the sale. When an investor acquires a limited partnership interest in a PE fund, the limited partnership (LP) agreements typically provide that partners may not transfer their interests or commitments. To effect a transfer thus requires the approval of the general partner, who, as noted, will normally take control of the process. However, in the case of very large sales of LP interests, an auction may take place.

Although families can buy secondary interests directly, it's a far better practice to invest in a fund dedicated to buying secondary interests. This is a highly specialized sector of the PE market, and few families—or institutions, for that matter—will have the ability to gain access to interesting secondary opportunities, negotiate acceptable pricing, and deal with the general partners who control the game.

Among the advantages of secondary investing is that the money goes out faster because the fund interests are more mature, there is little or no J-curve effect, and returns occur earlier. Employed on an opportunistic basis, secondary investing can be significantly additive to a diversified PE program.

THE EVOLUTION OF SECONDARY INVESTING

Secondary investing got its start in the 1980s, but it gained serious traction in the institutional world in the early 1990s, when several large institutional investors in exited the PE business via secondary sales. In 2000, when the tech bubble burst, many PE investors, especially families, found themselves overcommitted to PE and very short of capital as the markets crashed.

Then, in 2008, the shoe was on the other foot, as large institutional investors, especially colleges and universities, faced serious liquidity crises as a result of their overcommitments to PE and the collapse of the equity markets—the so-called "denominator effect."[10] Although the institutions' PE exposures had risen well above target, and although the equity markets had dropped precipitously, PE partnerships were still issuing capital calls. Strangely, many institutions had not performed cash flow analyses that incorporated these conditions, and they found themselves in serious hot water.

Most family investors—other than those who got in trouble in 2000— probably learned about secondary investing as a result of the institutional problems I just described. Nimble secondary funds were able to pick up a large number of LP interests very cheaply during this period, although the window of opportunity closed fairly quickly.

SECONDARY INVESTING STRATEGIES

It's important to keep in mind that secondaries represent a very small part of the total PE market: For the last several years secondary funds have represented about 3 percent of the U.S. PE market and even less of the worldwide market.

Some secondary funds are stand-alone, narrowly focused funds that do nothing but acquire secondary interests. There are also primary funds or funds of funds that have the authority under their limited partnership agreements to make secondary purchases.

Stand-alone secondary funds fall into one of two broad categories: very large and "smaller." Very large, multibillion-dollar funds have a great deal of capital to put to work in a fixed period of time, and as a result they will generally pursue larger transactions. Investments of $50 million and greater most often involve an auction, and pricing can come under pressure. Smaller funds tend to pursue transactions where less competition exists and where the pricing is likely to hold up better.

The maturity of the PE interest being acquired via a secondary sale is a key determinant in establishing the price. The more mature the interest is (say, one that is in the sixth to eighth year of its life), the more will be known about the underlying investments. In the hypothetical case of a seven-year-old fund that has completed its investment period, all of the portfolio companies will be in place and can be analyzed. This, of course, cannot be done with a two-year-old fund, which will likely sell for a bigger discount from its net asset value.

IDENTIFYING HIGH-QUALITY SECONDARY FUNDS

A high-quality secondary fund will be independent and free from conflicts of interest (avoid bank-sponsored funds, where conflicts are virtually limitless), and will have an extensive database of funds and underlying investments that permit them to model out the potential value of each underlying investment. Deal sourcing is also an important consideration: Sometimes, strong relationships with general partners will provide access to transactions without a lot of competition. The reputation of the secondary fund manager for timely evaluation, discretion, and execution can be key to driving opportunities.

PRACTICE TIP

As advisors, we will naturally want to build out a diversified portfolio of PE investments for our clients. Thus, we will diversify by buying venture capital, buyouts, mezzanine, and opportunistic funds. We will diversify by industry sector (tech, etc.) and by PE manager. We will diversify by vintage year. And, of course, we will diversify by adding secondary investments on an opportunistic basis, when secondary pricing is attractive.

Note, however, that a secondary investment is only a secondary on the day it is bought. After that, it's simply a PE investment that can be categorized as venture, buyout, or whatever. Categorizing these funds as secondaries doesn't tell us anything useful about our clients' overall exposures to PE.[11] (On the other hand, of course, we will want to note which investments were acquired as secondaries so that we can calculate how successful our secondary program is.)

CONCLUSION: THE ULTIMATE ASPIRATIONAL ASSET

If a family that no longer owns an operating business is going to have any chance of maintaining its wealth across the generations, the family's portfolio must have a healthy allocation to private equity, and that private equity must be invested in top-quartile funds.

Almost everything about PE is a challenge, from finding and gaining access to the best managers, to building an appropriate exposure while cash is both going out and coming in, to navigating the J-curve, to tolerating the illiquidity associated with long lockups. All this hassle is worth it only because PE is the ultimate aspirational asset; a way for families to invest alongside entrepreneurs who are soulmates of the family members who built the wealth in the first place.

NOTES

1. This chapter relies heavily on two papers written by my partner at Greycourt, David Lovejoy, from which I have also borrowed several charts. See Greycourt White Paper No. 40: Private Equity Investing (April 2009), and Greycourt White Paper No. 45: Secondary PE Investing (2011), both available at www.Greycourt.com.
2. And this return disparity is understated as a result of survivorship bias; that is, the worst firms went out of business and their (lousy) returns are no longer included in the database.
3. In Chapter 19, I divide a family investment portfolio into assets that are designed to support current spending, assets that are designed to maintain family wealth over time in the face of inflation, and assets that hold out the possibility of increasing the family's wealth; that is, aspirational assets.
4. See Steven N. Kaplan and Antoinette Schoar, "Private Equity Performance: Returns, Persistence, and Capital Flows," *The Journal of Finance* 60, no. 4 (2005): 1791–1823.
5. Fortunately, most PE funds stop earning fees after about 15 years, giving the fund managers a serious incentive to bring the final investments to an end—if necessary, by selling them into the secondary market.
6. Remarkably, many otherwise smart institutions had failed to consider the possibility that distributions from PE funds could stop while capital calls could continue, and that this phenomenon could happen at a time when the public equity markets were down substantially (the so-called "denominator effect"). This created a major liquidity crisis that caused institutional investors to become forced sellers of their limited partnerships into the secondary market.
7. All data is sourced from Thomson Reuters and is as of September 30, 2010. These returns are for all reporting partnerships, so they understate the returns achieved by investors in top-tier funds.
8. However, in the UK, buyouts represent an even larger percentage of GDP than in the United States.

9. Another unhappy factor in the J-curve effect is that fees, including start-up fees, are applied against a smaller asset base (because only a small amount of the total commitment has been called down), making already-high PE fees look even more outrageous. This situation will, however, correct itself in time.

10. In other words, if an institution had a 20 percent target to PE and the value of its liquid portfolio had dropped significantly, the institution found that its exposure to PE was closer to 30 percent.

11. This issue was first brought to my attention by John Barker of Harvard Management Company.

CHAPTER **17**

Working with Money Managers

I'm more interested in the return of my money than in the return on my money.

—Mark Twain

Working with money managers[1] is the aspect of the investment process that is usually the most interesting for investors, but that all too often adds least to the growth of investor wealth. In fact, one of the principal methods of identifying investors who will encounter little success over time is to observe those who are most obsessed with money managers.

The reason that money managers typically subtract value from, rather than add value to, the investment process is not that money managers are incompetent, but that their services are, on the whole, overpriced relative to the value they bring to their customers. In the asset classes that matter most to investors—U.S. large- and mid-cap stocks and bonds—most managers will underperform over time by at least an amount equal to their fees and trading costs, to say nothing of taxes. In the more complex and obscure asset classes, where useful information is difficult to come by, talented and hardworking managers may modestly add value net of all costs.

The main reason investors spend so much time and emotional energy on working with managers, despite the modest-to-negative return we are likely to receive for our efforts, is that money managers are actual human beings, whereas almost all other aspects of the investment process are purely intellectual. It's a lot more fun and a lot more interesting to spend time talking with an intelligent money manager than it is to run mean variance optimization algorithms or participate in long conference calls with accountants about tax-managing our portfolios.

307

In this chapter I try to address a couple of the principal issues associated with money managers. Specifically:

- Why it is so difficult to identify best-in-class managers in time to profit by investing with them.
- Why it is that good past performance can be completely meaningless.
- I identify the (mainly qualitative) characteristics of best-in-class managers.
- I describe best practices in identifying best-in-class managers.
- I discuss, briefly, some approaches to optimizing the mix of managers in investment portfolios.

The issue of selecting money managers is very closely associated with the challenge of identifying optimal strategies for each asset class that will be included in our portfolios. Hence, this chapter should be read in conjunction with Chapters 11 through 16. Some information is duplicated in these chapters for the sake of clarity of the presentation.

THE BUSINESS OF MONEY MANAGEMENT

Before we look at working with traditional and alternative managers in depth, let's take an overall look at some of the challenges active managers face. We'll start by following a new U.S. large-cap management firm to see how it operates.

Hapless Asset Management

The principals of Hapless Asset Management, having worked extensively in the money management industry, understand all too well the dynamics of the business. They know, for example, that attracting new clients—especially private investors—is a difficult, time-consuming, and expensive activity. But they also know that once a client has signed on, the marginal cost of servicing that client's account will be negligible. After all, Hapless will buy and sell pretty much the same stocks for every client, so it can manage $10 billion almost as easily as it can manage $100 million. Sure, clients sometimes want to meet with Hapless too often (from Hapless's perspective), but most clients soon settle into a routine that is highly cost effective for Hapless. After all, clients are busy people, too.

Thus, the main challenge for Hapless is to keep the clients it gets. Those clients provide an annuity income for Hapless, and given the cost of obtaining new clients, Hapless wants to do everything it can to avoid losing accounts. The main way Hapless is likely to lose accounts is for the firm to generate truly dismal performance numbers. If the numbers are really awful, clients will defect after one year of bad performance. If the numbers are merely bad, clients may wait two years to dump Hapless. But dump they will. Hapless, therefore, wants to avoid really bad performance at any cost.

How does Hapless ensure that it will never experience terrible investment performance relative to the benchmark its clients are measuring it by (in this case, the S&P 500)? The answer is surprisingly simple: Hapless will manage its portfolios as closet index funds. Here's how this works. Let's suppose that General Electric represents 3 percent of the S&P 500 index and that Microsoft represents 2 percent (both about right). Let's suppose, further, that Hapless believes that GE's price will rise faster than Microsoft's. We might imagine that Hapless would load up on GE without any Microsoft at all—but that's because we don't understand how money management actually works.

What Hapless actually does is to modestly overweight GE in its portfolio and modestly underweight Microsoft. If we examine Hapless's portfolio, we might find that it consists of a 3.3 percent exposure to GE and a 1.7 percent exposure to Microsoft. Other stocks that appear in the S&P 500 might also be modestly over- or underweighted, and the rest will be held exactly at their index weighting. If Hapless is right about both its over- and underweightings, Hapless will generate a nice-but-modest outperformance versus the S&P 500. If Hapless is right about some weightings but wrong about others (the most likely case), Hapless will generate modest underperformance roughly equal to its fees and costs. If Hapless is more often wrong than right, it will generate negative-but-modest underperformance versus the S&P 500.

In other words, although Hapless may, in an occasional year, outperform its benchmark, in most years Hapless will experience underperformance, but only modest underperformance. Hapless knows that the same clients who would dump it in a second following really bad performance will stick around for years if Hapless can generate occasional outperformance but overall underperformance. In other words, just when the client's patience has nearly been exhausted by several years of underperformance, Hapless will have a good year, and the client will stick around. From the client's point of view, this behavior is perfectly rational. After all, it is expensive to terminate a manager, and there is no guarantee that a new manager will do any better than Hapless.

And consider what Hapless is actually charging in fees. Its stated fee is 1 percent. But remember that Hapless is actively managing only a tiny portion of the capital it's been entrusted with—the rest is indexed.[2] Let's say that Hapless's R-squared to the S&P is .96. In other words, 96 percent of

Hapless's investment results are determined by the results of the S&P 500. What Hapless is really doing is charging a 1 percent fee to manage 5 percent of our capital. But it's charging on *all* our capital. Thus, the sad reality is that Hapless is charging 20 percent per annum to manage our money. And people say hedge funds are expensive!

The net result of all this is that Hapless will build a growing and highly profitable money management business even though it is a fairly poor money manager, and even though it is imposing significant opportunity costs on its clients. In other words, if Hapless's clients had simply earned the return on the S&P 500 index, they would be wealthier. If those clients had been with a best-in-class manager, they would be a lot wealthier.

What is going on at Hapless, and what goes on at most long-only money management firms, is the creation of what is known as portfolio deadweight: Most of Hapless's portfolio looks suspiciously like the S&P 500 index. Hapless is making only modest bets on the stocks it likes and against the stocks it doesn't like. Hapless lacks the courage of its convictions because it can't afford, from a business point of view, to be wildly wrong in any year (and, God help it, in any two consecutive years). Therefore, no matter how confident Hapless may be that Microsoft is going up and GE is going down, Hapless will back that confidence with only modest over- and underweightings in those securities.

PRACTICE TIP

I've gone into some length on the subject of hapless Hapless Asset Management because many clients—and, let's face it, some advisors—aren't all that familiar with exactly how it is that money managers work and the various tricks they play.

In many firms, all the manager diligence is done by a special team of analysts who hardly ever interface with the client advisor team. But it's very important for advisors to understand in some detail how good—and, especially, bad—money managers go about their business.

If you work in a firm where client advisors don't work directly with managers, you'll need to spend some serious time on your own getting to know the asset management business. Otherwise, you'll be in the position of regurgitating whatever the manager diligence team passes on to you, rather than exercising the kind of skepticism that your client is expecting of you.

Survivorship Bias

Virtually every study of active management in the U.S. large-cap space shows that 70 percent to 75 percent of all managers will underperform the S&P 500 index over longer periods of time. But the truth is that the dismal performance of active management is actually far worse than it appears. If we were to conduct a study today of 1,000 randomly selected managers, we would, indeed, discover that roughly 75 percent of them have underperformed the S&P 500 over the past 20 years. But our study would have missed many managers, most of which had truly dismal records. We would miss them because they are no longer in business, having been liquidated or absorbed into other management firms that dropped their losing track records. But while those managers were in business they managed billions of dollars of client money, and managed it badly. They are part of the miserable track record of active management, whether their contribution can be measured or not. Thus, the challenge of finding managers who will outperform is even worse than it appears.

Survivorship bias shows up in another way as well. Investors often proudly show me that their portfolios are employing only, or mainly, managers who show long-term outperformance. Indeed, a snapshot of many family portfolios will show such a phenomenon. But if we viewed not the snapshot version of the portfolio, but the full-length movie version, we would see a very different story; namely, manager after manager who is hired after a few good years of performance but who then underperforms, is fired, and thus disappears from the current snapshot. But those managers held those investors' money, and the underperformance they generated has had a permanent negative effect on the investors' wealth.

Fees and Costs

Active managers, especially in the large- and mid-cap sector, but elsewhere as well, are working against a powerful headwind of fees and expenses. Managers charge fees that are stunningly high considering the little value they add to—and more often subtract from—investment portfolios. Most manager fee schedules start at 1 percent, then decline as the size of the account increases. But even very large family accounts are often charged 50 to 75 basis points. (There are 100 basis points in 1%.) According to Morningstar, the average U.S. large-cap mutual fund has an expense ratio (management fees plus 12b-1 fees) of about 150 basis points (1.5%).

But to these costs we must add on the round-trip costs of brokerage commissions (roughly 10–11 cents per share for large managers), the spread between bid and ask prices (slightly higher), the cost of market impact (roughly 25 cents) and opportunity costs (10–12 cents). Given that the average share price of a U.S. large-cap stock is about $27 (mid-2003), this means that, in addition to the manager's fee, we must add more than 2 percent for trading costs. In other words, merely to match the performance of the index, a manager must outperform it by roughly 3 percent per year—a truly Herculean achievement.

As noted, virtually all long-only managers charge asset-based fees. The idea behind this approach—which would be odd, indeed, in most other industries—is that the manager is adding more value in absolute terms to larger accounts than it is adding to smaller accounts. If Hapless Asset Management outperforms the S&P 500 index by 1 percent in any year, it has added $1 million to a $100 million account, but only $10,000 to a $1 million account.

But there are several problems with this justification. The first problem is that the asset-based fee has nothing to do with the actual cost of managing money. It doesn't cost Hapless Asset Management 100 times as much to service its big client as it does to service its small client, even though the big client is 100 times larger. Sure, sensible businesses don't typically price their services on a cost-plus basis, but competition in most industries eventually drives prices down quite close to cost, so that only the most efficient firms can survive. In the money management industry, however, we are such lousy consumers that this hasn't happened.

But it gets worse. Hapless Asset Management, along with most other money managers, is far more likely to subtract value than to add it. Let's say that Hapless underperforms the S&P 500 by 1 percent—a far more likely scenario. If Hapless charges our hypothetical $100 million client 50 basis points ($1/2$ of 1%) and charges our $1 million client 1 percent, Hapless has earned $500,000 on the big client and $10,000 on the small client. But the big client has lost $1 million and the small client has lost $10,000. What sort of alignment of interests is this? As noted above, Hapless Asset Management, along with most other asset management firms, has created a very successful and profitable business by subtracting gigantic amounts of money from client portfolios.

What's to be done? Unfortunately, most family investors are too small to wield the clout that would be required to change pricing practices in the money management business. Even investors that one would think of as being large enough to wield such clout—huge endowed institutions and pension plans—have had little success in forcing through radical changes in pricing. However, it is sometimes possible to negotiate incentive fees with managers who are very confident in their ability to add value to client portfolios. Even here, however, we need to proceed with caution, as poorly designed incentive fees can create counterproductive motivations.

Perhaps the most sensible form of incentive fee for a long-only manager takes the form of a fulcrum fee. In such a fee arrangement, we ask the manager how much outperformance he expects to deliver to our portfolio. Let's say that the manager claims to be able to deliver 80 basis points per annum above the benchmark on average. Let's say, further, that we expect the manager to deliver about 30 basis points above the benchmark. We will then create a fee structure that (a) will give the manager approximately his standard fee if he outperforms by 30 basis points, (b) will give him a much higher fee if he outperforms by 80 basis points, and (c) will give him a fee much lower than his standard fee if he delivers less than 30 basis points of outperformance.

Fulcrum fees should have both caps above them and floors under them. The purpose of the floor—which we set at about the manager's break-even operating cost—is to ensure that the manager pays attention to the account. Even during a period when the manager's style is out of favor and its performance is weak, we don't want the manager to ignore us or to terminate our account. (We want the account to be terminated only when we want it to be terminated.) The purpose of the cap is to eliminate any incentive on the part of the manager to take extravagant risks with our money in an attempt to earn a higher fee.

It's not enough just to be right. Suppose that back in the 1970s Hapless (or, more likely, a predecessor firm, because most money management firms don't survive that long) had had the foresight to anticipate the technology boom of the past 30 years and had loaded up on tech stocks. Hapless would have made a killing, right? Wrong. Hapless would have underperformed the broad market by roughly 130 basis points per year (1.3%). The reason is that lots and lots of investors anticipated a technology boom, and as a result much of the future appreciation in that sector had already been priced in. For Hapless to make a killing, it would have had to anticipate a development that very few others anticipated.

With all this background information in mind, let's look at why it is so difficult to identify managers who will outperform in the future—that is, while they have our capital under management—as opposed to in the past—when they didn't.

TRADITIONAL MANAGERS

> *Investing is easy. I just buy a stock and hold it 'til it goes up. If it don't go up, I don't buy it.*
>
> —Will Rogers

It's almost impossible to express how difficult it is to identify truly outstanding portfolio managers in time to profit by investing with them. By truly outstanding, I mean managers whose outperformance relative to the broad markets and to other managers will be so great as to result in significant wealth creation for their investors. Consider that since 1970 several thousand Americans have won large lotteries—lotteries large enough to result in significant wealth for their winners. But since 1970, how many Warren Buffetts have there been? More than one, to be sure. But not thousands. Not hundreds. Not even dozens. Statisticians will tell us that playing the lottery is a fool's game,[3] that in the aggregate lottery players lose far, far more money than they win, and that even the remote possibility of gaining great winnings doesn't begin to justify the cost of playing. What would statisticians tell us about the challenge of finding outstanding money managers?

And if identifying great managers weren't difficult enough, timing in the enterprise is everything. People who invested with the legendary hedge fund manager Julian Robertson early in the game had little idea how much money they were about to make. But people who invested with Robertson late in the game had little idea how much money they were about to lose. Same great manager, very different outcomes.

Finally, outperformance among managers tends to show little persistence over time, at least if we define outperformance to mean "consistently landing in the top quartile of all similar managers." Not long ago Greycourt looked at persistence even among managers in a sector of the market that is generally considered to be inefficient, and where talented managers should have room to run—namely, small-cap managers.

We prepared an analysis using a group of 57 small-cap growth managers and compared relative performance over time. Most investors believe that capable managers should be able to add value in inefficient sectors with reasonable consistency over time. Hence, the purpose of the exercise was to determine how often managers remained outstanding performers over time. Our analysis illustrates the difficulty managers face in maintaining their top performance rating over even relatively short periods of time. Of the top 15 managers at the beginning of the study, only two remained in the top 15 eight years later. On the other hand, the manager who finished dead last (57th) at the beginning was the 11th-rated manager by the end. In other words, investors hiring any of the top performers identified at the beginning of our study would have been sorely disappointed.

The Main Problem: Recent Good Performance Is Almost Irrelevant

The main mistake investors make in engaging managers is hiring a firm that has experienced good recent performance—say, a better-than-average five-year track record. The reason this is a mistake is that, more often than not, a good five-year track record says virtually nothing about how the manager is likely to perform over the next five years. That track record might indicate that the manager will continue its outperformance, but it is far more likely that the track record indicates one of the following:

The good track record is simply the result of "the law of small numbers." In his endlessly amusing book, *A Mathematician Plays the Stock Market*,[4] John Allen Paulos points out that we tend to misunderstand the role chance plays in the outcomes of apparently even games. Imagine that two people—I will call them George Soros and George Bozos—flip a fair coin 1,000 times each, competing to see who can come up with the most heads. We tend to imagine that, after that many flips, the outcome would almost always come out very even, with Soros and Bozos each getting about 500 heads and 500 tails. We infer from that conclusion that if one of the players actually ends up well ahead of the other, that outcome must be due either to an unfair coin or to the special skill of one of the players.

In fact, as Paulos points out, there is a far greater probability that after 1,000 fair coin flips, Soros or Bozos would be well ahead of the other, having flipped 525 heads to, say, 475 heads. We might call this the law of small numbers; that is, 1,000 flips may seem like a lot, but actually it's not enough observations to ensure that Soros and Bozos will come out even. Thus, if 10,000 people all flipped a fair coin 1,000 times, the aggregate results would tend to be that a goodly number would end up with pretty darn good records and an equal number would end up with pretty sorry records. A very few would have spectacular records and a very few would have abysmal records. Far fewer than we might expect would have even records.

This outcome looks alarmingly like the outcome of money manager five-year track records (which are based, after all, on only 60 monthly observations, or in some cases on only 20 quarterly observations): A tiny number have spectacular records, a tiny number have abysmal records, a goodly number have pretty darn good or pretty darn bad records, and only a few have average track records. None of this, however, means anything. Investors who engage managers purely on the basis of good five-year track records are likely to fall victim to the law of small numbers.

The good track record is simply the result of fortunate timing. Imagine a money manager who has been in business for 15 years and who, for 13 of those years, has reliably turned in undistinguished performance. But during the past two years, for reasons unknown to us or the manager, performance has been quite good. These two "lucky" years of performance pulled the manager's five-year track record up to the point where it is now quite creditable. As a result, many unfortunate investors, impressed with that record, will engage a manager who is clearly undistinguished and who can be relied on to continue in that vein.

The good track record is simply a result of style rotation. Let's consider two managers. We'll call them Value Capital Investors (VCI) and Capital Value Investors (CVI). Both are deep value managers who do well, naturally enough, when value stocks are in vogue and less well when growth stocks are in vogue. Both have been in business for many years and have built their businesses in the same way. Just after periods of value outperformance, when their track records are strong, VCI and CVI both aggressively market their records, building their asset bases. After periods of value underperformance, when their track records are weak, VCI and CVI both work hard to keep their clients from defecting. The result of all this is a repeating pattern of strong asset growth followed by weak asset growth or even asset contraction, followed by strong asset growth, and so on.

But there are two things wrong with this picture. The first is that investors are constantly making the wrong decisions about VCI and CVI: engaging them just when they are about to enter a period of weak performance and terminating them just when they are about to enter a period of strong performance. Investors are, in effect, buying high and selling low.

The second problem is that VCI turns out to be a very competent manager, whereas CVI is well below average: Investors should be engaging VCI and should be avoiding CVI. But investors don't do this because the differences in aggregate performance between the firms are overwhelmed by the sector rotation effect: Being a deep value manager had more impact on a manager's performance than did being a good manager.

The manager's performance has been "managed." Corporate executives have become adept at managing earnings, ensuring that investor expectations for quarterly per-share earnings are met, but in the process giving a misleading picture of the consistency of the company's operations. Money managers can also be quite adept at managing performance; that is, putting the best possible spin on a checkered track record. Recently, for example, a well-known—and well-regarded—aggressive growth manager touted its excellent one-year record (+60%) and its excellent 10-year record (+16.9%). What the manager failed to note was that in the years 1 through 3 it ranked in the 95th percentile among all mid-cap equity managers. In other words, for three years running the manager was among the worst 5 percent of all its competitors. So which picture was truer—the good long-term performance or the disastrous recent three-year performance? The answer is both. But the manager managed its performance claims to make it look far better—far more consistent—than it really was.

The good track record is genuine, but the manager is a changed firm. Finally, the manager's good five-year track record may be unimpeachable, but investors who engage the manager will find that they have hired a very different firm from the one that produced the good performance. The firm may have changed, for example, because the asset base of the firm has grown dramatically and the founding professionals can no longer both manage the business and pick good stocks. (There is no necessary correlation between people's ability to pick stocks and their ability to manage a business.) Or the firm may have changed because the investment professionals who produced the track record are no longer with the firm. Or the firm may have been sold, and the original owners are now rich and lazy or, worse, reporting to some bureaucrat in Duluth. In other words, in addition to the track record being real, it is always useful for investors to be sure that the firm that built the track record is the firm we are hiring.

Characteristics of Best-in-Class Managers

It is, alas, not possible to define the characteristics of best-in-class managers in a way that is detailed enough to enable investors to apply a simple template and see if the manager fits it or not. Too much judgment and experience are involved. Nonetheless, the main characteristics of best-in-class managers are simple enough to state. They are as follows:

- *Investment philosophy.* The quality of a portfolio manager's investment philosophy is perhaps the single most critical element in judging whether the manager is likely to be capable of sustained outperformance. Unfortunately, this issue is also likely to be of little help to individual investors in identifying best-in-class managers. The reason is that there is no such thing as a money manager who can't articulate an investment philosophy that sounds good. The only way to know whether or not what sounds good actually holds any water is to put the manager through a thorough, multilevel scrutiny, ending with an intensive on-site grilling of the manager and its senior team by an investment professional who has had vast experience interviewing and working with managers.

- *Discipline.* Even the most solid investment philosophy won't create wealth unless it is implemented in a disciplined manner. To determine whether the manager is a disciplined investor and is sticking to its philosophy in good times and bad, it is necessary to conduct a detailed review of the manager's performance during periods when the wind has been at its back and when the wind has been in its face. Attribution analysis and a close examination of investment decisions that turned out badly can shed important light on these questions. In particular, sell discipline—strict rules that determine when a security is to be sold—is important. As noted above, sell discipline tended to disappear during the bull market of the 1980s and 1990s. Under more normal market conditions, however, sell discipline is crucial. Otherwise, managers will tend to hold appreciated securities far too long and to believe that they are "smarter than the market," therefore holding on to underperforming securities that should be sold.

- *Experience.* Any manager can outperform over a short period of time, and investors who hire such managers after that period of outperformance will almost always—*almost always*—be disappointed. The five-year rule is intended to enable investors to observe a manager's performance over a full market cycle, that is, a period of time during which the manager's investment style and philosophy are in vogue as well as a period of time when they are out of fashion. Hence, five years might be too short a period of time or, in a few cases, it might be more time than we need.

- *Asset base.* Some investment philosophies and styles can be carried on at huge scale, but others will be successful only if they remain niche businesses. Bond managers can oversee tens of billions of dollars with relative ease. Indeed, scale matters in bond management because trading costs, especially the costs of trading municipal bonds, can eat up a large fraction of the potential returns. But small-cap managers face the opposite problem: The float of most small-cap stocks can be very thin, making the management of even a few hundreds of millions of dollars problematic. Many professionals believe that trading costs are so high with smaller stocks that any return advantage is completely negated. Thus, with small-cap stocks smaller really is better all around.

- *Alignment of interests.* Money management is a business, and like any business operator, money managers will attempt to maximize their profits. If those profits can only be maximized by acting in the interests of clients, the manager-client relationship is likely to be satisfactory to both parties. Unfortunately, there are many ways in which money managers can increase their profits at the expense of client investment returns. One obvious example is for the manager to emphasize asset gathering over alpha generation. It is far easier for a manager to increase its fee revenue by focusing on proven sales techniques than by focusing on the complex challenges associated with investment outperformance. As a result, most money management firms are really sales organizations, not money management organizations, and are to be avoided on that ground alone.[5] The general practice of charging asset-based fees is also problematic. If the manager's results are poor, the manager's fee declines but he still gets paid; the client, on the other hand, has lost real money.

- *Organizational stability.* A sound investment philosophy can only be implemented by an investment team that has worked together for years and that has experienced little, if any, turnover. Even among managers who have produced outstanding long-term track records, organizational instability is an excellent early warning sign that performance is likely to deteriorate. The same is true of asset management firms that have recently been purchased—this is almost always a sure sign of bad things to come.

- *Quality of the client base.* This may seem an odd characteristic to focus on, but in fact the quality of a manager's client base can make an important difference in the manager's ability to function with minimal interference and maximum stability. Typically, managers who have performed competently over the course of many years, but who are never (or rarely) the best-performing managers in any year, will wind up with a stable, sophisticated client base that understands what the manager is doing and that will be patient with periods of underperformance. Managers who have shot the lights out now and then, followed by periods of very poor performance, will tend to wind up with a client base consisting mainly of unsophisticated, "hot money" clients. It is virtually impossible for a manager to operate sensibly if clients are constantly pouring money into the firm and then pulling it out again.

- *Personal integrity.* This should go without saying. Although it may seem harsh, any blemishes on a manager's record should disqualify the firm from serious consideration. This includes regulatory problems at the firm level and also personal problems at the individual level.

- *Trust—but verify.* President Reagan, during the SALT negotiations, was fond of saying, "Trust—but verify." The same is true of managers. It is always interesting to hear a manager talk about its style, but a returns-based style attribution analysis rarely exaggerates. The professionals at a firm may appear to be the very soul of rectitude, but a background check will result in far fewer sleepless nights for investors. Broadly speaking, substantial families have no choice but to place their capital at risk. But narrowly speaking, substantial families never have to place their capital with any particular manager. Before we entrust our capital to a manager, we should always trust—but verify.

Objectionable Characteristics

In addition to the useful characteristics of managers just discussed, it's also important to look for the presence or absence of objectionable characteristics in asset management firms, such as a focus on asset gathering, a weak trading or back office operation, a predominance of inexperienced personnel, a bureaucratic organizational framework, a history of regulatory problems, an organization that is primarily engaged in activities other than money management, and so on. The presence of even one of these objectionable characteristics should raise an immediate alarm, requiring further investigation, and the presence of two or more should send investors running in the other direction.[6]

PRACTICE TIP

It's natural for inexperienced investors to say something like this to their advisors: "If you're so smart, how come so many of your managers underperform?"

The reality is that measuring manager performance is so fraught with difficulty that it's impossible to know whether out- or underperformance is based on skill or luck for many, many years. But your client doesn't want to hear that. And your client especially doesn't want to hear that the manager you engaged with such fanfare two years ago has just "had a run of bad luck."

Like it or not, as advisors we have to take responsibility for the managers we pick. But advisors who understand the perils of the manager-selection process will help educate their clients about it. And no matter how enthusiastic we may be about a new manager, it's crucial that we not overpromise and underdeliver. If we've done a good job picking managers, we need to help our clients do a good job being patient with their inevitable periods of underperformance.

Finding Best-in-Class Managers

There are many ways to go about the process of finding the best managers, but I like the three-stage process we use at my firm, Greycourt & Co., Inc. It works generally like this.

The early phases of this process rely largely on quantitative screening and evaluation criteria, whereas later stages are almost entirely qualitative in nature. Our ultimate goal is not to identify which managers have outperformed in the past—any fool with a computer can do that. Rather, our objective is to identify the reasons why selected managers have outperformed in the past and to judge whether those reasons are likely to persist into the future.

The first step (Level I) in our due-diligence process requires managers to be measured against a series of six objective criteria. These criteria vary somewhat from asset class to asset class but generally are as follows:

Criteria #1: Appropriate R-squared to the relevant benchmark.

Criteria #2: Product return rank was in the top third of the peer universe.

Criteria #3: Product return rank was not in the bottom quartile of the peer universe in any of the most recent five calendar years.

Criteria #4: Product risk-adjusted return rank was in the top third of the peer universe.

Criteria #5: Product upside capture was at least 100 percent.

Criteria #6: Product downside capture was better than the benchmark.

We use these screening criteria in two ways. First, the Level I screen allows us to quickly determine if we should spend our limited time meeting with salespeople seeking to introduce us to their products. Second, the Level I screen allows us to efficiently comb through publicly available manager databases such as Morningstar, PSN, and HFR to see if there are potentially interesting managers that we may not yet have knowledge of. It is important to note, however, that many of the managers we use or are interested in do not always pass all six of our Level I criteria. For example, we are often interested in concentrated equity managers who have low R-squared statistics but who otherwise are excellent. We have the discretion (which we use often) to pursue further research on any manager, whether or not they pass all six Level I criteria. Finally, though the Level I screening process works well for most long-only asset classes, it is somewhat less useful in evaluating alternative asset classes such as private equity, real estate, hedge funds, and so on.

The next step (Level II) in our manager process involves gathering as much information as possible about a potentially interesting manager. Initially, our information-gathering focuses on further screening out inappropriate managers. For example, we seek to determine if a manager is closed to new assets, whether they have reasonable minimum account sizes, whether their fees are competitive, what kinds of investment vehicles they offer (separate accounts, limited partnerships, mutual funds, etc.), or whether they have unusually high turnover which may cause them to be tax inefficient. These additional early Level II questions do not take much time to complete and often weed out another 25 percent to 50 percent of the managers who made it past the Level I process.

Once the list of qualified manager candidates has been narrowed, we seek to gather a broad array of information about each manager in order to formulate an opinion on how they were able to generate attractive results in the past. The type of information typically acquired includes:

- Manager pitch books
- A live manager presentation
- A completed Greycourt Manager Questionnaire
- The manager's Form ADV
- Relevant Web news and articles about the manager
- Comprehensive style-based return attribution analysis

All information gathered is immediately recorded in Greycourt's proprietary manager database so that it becomes instantly available to each of our investment professionals. We view our ability to access all manager information on a timely basis as critical to our ability to deliver high-quality and consistent advice to our clients.

Once we have evaluated all of a manager's information, a Greycourt investment analyst will prepare a brief two-page profile summarizing the manager's key attributes. At the same time, a Greycourt partner will begin to formulate an initial opinion (referred to internally as our Investment Thesis) seeking to articulate concisely why we believe the manager in question has succeeded in generating superior results in the past.

The third phase of our evaluation (Level III) is the most important and also the most qualitative. The objective of our Level III analysis is to attempt to validate the preliminary Investment Thesis established during the earlier Level II review. During this final phase, one or more of Greycourt's managing directors will meet with the senior members of the candidate manager's firm, usually in their offices. At these meetings we seek to better understand the manager's investment philosophy, risk controls, tax sensitivity, organizational structure, incentive compensation plans, operating infrastructure, compliance efforts, and interpersonal dynamics.

Our Level III efforts culminate in a peer review in which the sponsoring partner articulates, in writing, his or her view of the candidate manager's differential advantages; comments on the sustainability of those advantages; and identifies potential risk factors that might invalidate the perceived sustainable advantage. Partnerwide conference calls are held every week to discuss candidate managers who have completed all three levels of review. Very often the Level III peer review call results in additional questions being raised or further information being requested. Assuming that all additional questions are satisfactorily addressed, a formal vote is conducted in which all partners either approve or reject the candidate manager for inclusion on Greycourt's recommended list.

Monitoring Best-in-Class Managers

Once approved, we seek to monitor approved managers' continuing quality in several ways. First, we generate a report that measures the difference between each manager's monthly return and its relevant benchmark (this difference is referred to as tracking error). We then compare that month's tracking error to the manager's five–year historical tracking error. To the extent that a manager's tracking error in any given month is +/−1 standard deviation away from its historical tracking error, we initiate a call to the manager. During these calls we will ask them to describe what factor(s) caused them to perform unusually well or unusually poorly that month. Their responses are recorded in our database. Simply as a result of this monthly review process, we will, on average, speak to our managers three times per year. Our second form of review is to formally reevaluate each approved manager on an annual basis in order to reaffirm our belief in our stated Investment Thesis.

When one of our managers experiences a change of control, acquires another firm, or suffers the loss of a key portfolio manager, we immediately seek to understand how these changes may affect our stated Investment Thesis. The urgency with which we reexamine a manager undergoing a change depends on that manager's inherent volatility. For example, the departure of a key professional at a municipal bond manager is less alarming than the departure of a key professional in a small-cap growth firm. We seek to quantify our view of each manager's inherent risk by developing a numerical risk measure on each manager used. Developing this numerical assessment of manager risk is a regular part of our Level III analysis. Also, as noted earlier, part of our Level III review is to articulate specific risk factors that may invalidate our Investment Thesis. If one of those identified risks becomes a reality (such as a key professional's departure) we will fully reexamine the manager.

Managers are rarely terminated for poor performance alone. We terminate managers when it is deemed that they no longer maintain the differential advantages that caused us to hire them in the first place. Examples of reasons that have prompted us to terminate managers in the past include:

- Departure of a critical investment professional(s)
- Significant style drift
- Failure to limit asset growth to levels promised
- Failure to communicate or be responsive to requests for information

Obviously, this approach to identifying best-in-class managers will be far beyond the capabilities of most individual families. And there is nothing sacrosanct about the way Greycourt goes about the process. However, if your financial advisors aren't following something like the process as described above, perhaps you're working with the wrong advisors.

Active, Indexed, Fundamental, and Structured Products

When it comes to marketable securities, investors have a wide choice of strategies. Thus, wholly aside from the question of whether it is possible to identify outperforming managers in advance, investors have other arrows in their quiver as they attempt to achieve solid performance.

Active Management　　An active manager owns a basket of securities that is different from the index he is being measured against. If he is successful, his securities will outperform those of the index by a sufficient margin to overcome the drag of his fees, trading costs, and taxes. As noted above, there are "closet" index managers who charge active management fees, and these folks should in general be avoided, as they are bringing little to the party. By contrast, there are managers who own a basket of securities that is very different from the index, giving them a real chance to outperform and earn their keep—but also giving them a real chance of underperforming dramatically.

In fact, most good active managers will both outperform and underperform dramatically over the course of time. Consider Bob Rodriguez, the best-performing mutual fund manager of the last quarter century. Rodriguez runs the FPA Capital Fund, and typically owns no more than 30 stocks, despite the fact that he is being measured against the S&P 500 index. Despite the fact that he is the single best manager in the Morningstar universe, very few investors have benefitted from the extraordinary record of FPA.

In the late 1990s, for example, Rodriguez refused to play the tech game, and underperformed dramatically. His asset base was cut by more than half as investors left in droves. Again in 2005–2007, Rodriguez hated the market and underperformed again, resulting in more than $700 million of redemptions.[7]

Thus, in addition to the problem of trying to identify managers like Rodriguez in advance, there is the behavioral problem of sticking with the manager through thick and thin—something most investors don't have the stomach for.

Index Management　　A passive manager—think the Vanguard 500 Index Fund—simply tries to replicate the exact performance of the index it is measured against. This won't always be done by owning all the stock in the index, because mimicking the index performance can sometimes be managed in less expensive ways. Depending on how liquid the index is, tracking error can often be a problem, but with large indexes like the S&P 500, tracking error is minimal. By buying a well-managed index fund, you are guaranteeing that you will get the return of the index, less a small fee. You are also guaranteeing that you won't get any outperformance, of course.

Indexing tends to result in low turnover (and hence low trading costs) and also in lower taxes than active management, unless the active manager is extremely tax aware or trades very infrequently.

The problem with passive investing is that most indexes are capitalization weighted—in other words, if Google represents more of the index than, say, Johnson & Johnson, the index fund will own more Google. This is swell if you believe in momentum investing, but all too often it ends up causing you to buy high and sell low. Hence the interest in fundamental investing.

Fundamental Management   Fundamental investing is a version of passive investing, but it has characteristics of active investing as well. A fundamental index fund will not be capitalization weighted, but will select its securities with reference to other, more economically fundamental, factors; for example, sales, earnings, book value, cash flow, and dividends. Many of the products offered by firms like Dimensional Fund Advisors (DFA) are fundamentally weighted rather than capitalization weighted.

Because fundamental characteristics change slowly over time, fundamental investing tends to be less volatile than index investing. This can be good and bad, of course. If we are in the middle of a raging bull market and the S&P 500 is up 40 percent for the year, your friends in the cap-weighted index fund will also be up about 40 percent. But there you sit, wallowing in your fundamental index fund, up only 22 percent. What you are likely to do is to dump the fundamental index and plunge into the cap-weighted index, just as it's about to crash.

By their nature, fundamental indexes tend to have a smaller cap and value tilt versus cap-weighted indexes. This is good if you are a value investor and believe in the "small-cap effect," but it can hurt when value and small cap are out of vogue, as in the 1990s.

Finally, fees tend to be higher in fundamental index funds, so you will need to be confident that that's what you want.

Structured Products   Fundamental indexes are a kind of structured product, but there are other ways to create structured investments—for example, by equally weighting all the securities or by creating a rules-based portfolio. The rules might have to do with the liquidity and fairness of emerging markets exchanges, for example, or the quality of financial reports by companies.

A structured portfolio takes no position on the merits of individual securities, but instead seeks to outperform by adhering to certain rules, including rebalancing. Some studies have shown that an equal-weighted portfolio would have significantly outperformed a cap-weighted portfolio over the last 45 years,[8] primarily by avoiding the individual security concentrations that result over time in a cap-weighted portfolio. Rigorous rebalancing in these portfolios tends to result—over time—in the sale of appreciated securities (selling high) and the purchase of less highly appreciated securities (buying low).

The volatility of structured portfolios can vary widely, depending on cross correlations in the target market. For example, the volatility of a structured portfolio focused on U.S. equity markets will tend to be higher than the volatility of a U.S. equity cap-weighted index. On the other hand, the volatility of structured portfolios focused on emerging markets, currencies, or commodities tends to be lower than cap-weighted indexes.

ALTERNATIVE MANAGERS

Alternative managers are hedge funds and private equity funds. Because there are special issues associated with such managers, I've added a few paragraphs about working with each.

Working with Hedge Funds

Prophesy as much as you like, but always hedge.
—Oliver Wendell Holmes

As Gertrude Stein might say, a manager is a manager is a manager. But a hedge fund manager is a manager only more so—a manager on steroids, if you will. The earlier precautions about managers in general go for hedge fund managers, but they are all even more critical. Long-only managers can underperform, sometimes substantially, but they rarely blow up and lose all an investor's capital. Hedge funds do this quite regularly.

The fundamental concern about hedge funds is that the assets managed by hedge fund managers are not held in custody in the usual sense of the word. Custody issues are discussed in Chapter 22, but in brief, when an investor engages a long-only manager, the manager never actually gains control of the investor's cash or securities. Cash and securities remain in the hands of a bank or brokerage firm that is acting as the asset custodian for the investor. The portfolio manager has, in reality or in effect, a limited power of attorney to direct the investments in the account. The manager can cause the account to sell GE and buy Microsoft. But the GE stock doesn't leave the custodian's hands until the proceeds from its sale arrive, and the funds required to buy Microsoft don't leave the custodian's hands until the Microsoft stock arrives. (All this occurs electronically, of course, and is subject to the prevailing settlement rules.)

But when an investor engages a hedge fund manager, the cash and securities are held in accounts controlled by the hedge fund, not the investor. Typically, the cash and securities are held by a so-called "prime broker" for the hedge fund. But whereas in a traditional custody arrangement the investor is the custodian's client, in a prime brokerage arrangement the hedge fund is the broker's customer. The prime broker's loyalties—to say nothing of his lucrative business dealings—lie exclusively with the hedge fund. If the hedge fund manager wakes up some morning with a hankering to go to Brazil, he can simply wire all the funds in the hedge fund account to his private account in Sao Paulo and hop on the next plane. (He or she will have more trouble passing through security at Kennedy Airport than stealing our money.) The same is true if the manager wakes up in the morning with a hankering to buy his girlfriend a new Jaguar or to bet the house shorting an obscure tech stock whose price is about to go through the roof.

In short, when looking for a hedge fund manager to engage, we will want to keep in mind all the challenges discussed previously about long-only managers, then perhaps square them. And after we have finished all that diligence, we will want to add a whole new level of inquiry, namely thorough background checks (civil and criminal) on the principals in each hedge fund we are considering. Background checks won't necessarily identify hedge fund managers who will turn out to be incompetent or foolish, but they will identify managers who have checkered pasts and who are therefore exponentially more likely to keep checkering away—this time with our money.

PRACTICE TIP

When we pick a lousy traditional manager, the worst that usually happens is he underperforms and we replace him with someone better. But the downside with a hedge fund can be much worse. Hedge funds can simply underperform, of course, but hedge funds can also blow up as a result of poor risk controls or fraud. There are a few examples of advisory firms being destroyed by their association with hedge

(Continued)

PRACTICE TIP (Continued)

fund blowups, and many firms have been seriously crippled by client defection, litigation, and general reputational damage.

If you are going to work with individual hedge funds—and client pressure to do so is intense—you will simply have to devote some very serious research to the task. Especially on the ODD side—operational due diligence—many firms will find that it is more economical to outsource ODD to a specialist firm.

Even so, it's important to supervise the specialist and to understand what it is they are doing and why. After all, if you have a blowup or fraud in the clients' portfolios, blaming the specialist won't get you very far with your clients.

Working with Private Equity Funds

Private equity, broadly speaking, encompasses venture capital, management or leveraged buyouts, mezzanine financings,[9] and various kinds of illiquid distressed investing. These strategies can be executed directly, by investing in individual deals; indirectly, by investing in venture, buyout, or mezzanine limited partnerships (which then invest in direct deals); or very indirectly, by investing in funds of funds that invest in limited partnerships which then invest in direct deals.

The main consideration associated with PE managers is that investing with a PE fund is like getting married. Like it or not, you are largely stuck with the manager from the date you commit to the fund until the final underlying investment has been liquidated or sold. This can easily add up to a 15-year relationship, especially when investing in a fund of funds.

Because of the long lockup, the importance of up-front diligence can't be emphasized enough. Although it's not impossible to exit a PE fund, except in extraordinary circumstances the cost of getting out is likely to be higher than the cost of staying in.

PRACTICE TIP

When our clients commit to a PE fund or fund of funds, all the capital isn't called down immediately. Instead, the manager will call the funds as it finds opportunities to invest it. Our clients are therefore faced with a dilemma: They have committed their capital to a PE fund and are legally obligated to live up to that commitment. (The penalties

(Continued)

for failing to meet a capital call are draconian.) Yet, the PE manager takes no responsibility for the fact that our capital won't be called down for some time—usually, a period of three or four years. If we calculated PE returns on the full commitment amount from the date of the commitment to the date the fund terminates, our PE returns would look very much worse than the manager's reported results.

So the question arises: Where should committed-but-uncalled capital be invested? Many investors, not wanting to be caught short, keep that capital in a money market fund or some similar low-risk investment. But this creates a very serious opportunity cost for our clients. Money market fund returns are very low, typically equaling about the rate of inflation. PE returns (we hope) are very high. But when we blend the low returns the clients get on their money market funds with the high returns they get on their PE funds, the drag of the former on the latter will be substantial.

Instead, advisors should recommend that investors keep most of their committed-but-uncalled capital in equities—or at least spread across the entire portfolio—perhaps moving the funds to a short-term bond fund as the likely date of a capital call approaches. Over the long term, this strategy will reduce the overall return on our clients' committed PE capital, but not by nearly as much as if we kept their total commitment in cash.

CONCLUSION: AT LEAST MANAGERS ARE INTERESTING

Earlier in this chapter I wrote, "It's almost impossible to express how difficult it is to identify truly outstanding portfolio managers in time to profit by investing with them." I repeat it here because it's a truth that investors have a tough time internalizing. We remember vividly the few outstanding managers we've invested with, but the many disappointments tend to disappear into the mists of the past.

Even the best institutional investors make many, many manager mistakes, and at the end of the day they will be lucky if the mistakes don't outweigh the successes. An under-resourced family has little chance of succeeding.

On the other hand, working with managers is an interesting way to spend time—far more interesting than, say, poring over mean variance optimization models. So if you love working with managers, be my guest. But be honest with yourself and your family's money. If you find, as is likely, that on a net basis your managers are subtracting value from your portfolio, size active management down and passive management up.

NOTES

1. Parts of this chapter were originally published as Greycourt White Paper No. 32: The Challenge of Identifying Managers Who Will Outperform (2004), coauthored with my partner, Gregory R. Friedman. The paper is available at www.Greycourt.com.
2. A better way to work with a manager like Hapless would be to give Hapless only 5 percent of the money we want to invest in a U.S. large-cap portfolio and to index the other 95 percent.
3. Voltaire supposedly remarked that a lottery is simply a tax on stupidity.
4. New York: Basic Books, 2003. Paulos's other books are also well worth looking into, especially *Innumeracy: Mathematical Illiteracy and Its Consequences* (New York: Hill and Wang, 2001), and *A Mathematician Reads the Newspaper* (Norwell, MA: Anchor Press, 1997). On the subject of innumeracy, see Chapter 4.
5. Looking at the manager-client relationship as a problem of principal-agent theory, David Swensen (CIO at Yale) has acutely analyzed the problems investors face in trying to align manager interests with their own. See David Swensen, *Pioneering Portfolio Management: An Unconventional Approach to Institutional Investment* (New York: Free Press, 2000) 4–6, 197, 248–292.
6. One of the best summaries of desirable and undesirable manager characteristics was produced by The Investment Fund for Foundations. See TIFF's website at www.TIFF.org.
7. See Mina Kimes, "Bob Rodriguez: The Man Who Sees Another Crash," *Fortune* (June 6, 2011).
8. David Stein, Paul Bouchey, Timothy Atwill, and Vassilii Nemtchinov, "Structured Active Portfolio Management," Parametric White Paper (Summer 2011).
9. Most commonly, mezzanine financings are used in connection with a leveraged buyout to reduce the amount of equity capital the PE firm must invest. Mezzanine capital is subordinated to other debt of the borrower and is senior only to the common stock.

CHAPTER 18

Managing Investment-Related Taxes

I don't want to achieve immortality through my work. I want to achieve immortality through not dying.

—Woody Allen

Alas, like death, taxes are one of the few certainties investors face. Indeed, for most family investors, most of the time, taxes will prove to be the single largest drag on investment returns. Uncle Sam is our investment partner, and Governor Bill is also usually along for the ride, and sometimes even Mayor Benny. Thus, although tax avoidance should never be the sole motive for any investment decision, it is crucial that family investors take tax concerns into account.

But before we discuss effective tax management of our portfolios, let's pause a moment to emphasize the point about avoiding tax-motivated decision making. Much of the time, structuring an activity in a way that minimizes taxes will bring with it other costs. Sometimes these costs may be actual financial costs—as when we select an underperforming tax-aware manager over an outperforming gross-returns manager, or when we fail to diversify a concentrated stock position. Setting up strict trusts for our children or grandchildren can save money on taxes, but it can also ruin those people, turning them into trust fund babies even before they are born.

Another problem with managing investment-related taxes is that the tax issue is almost always conflated with risk in such a way that investors are typically faced with choosing between lower-taxes-and-higher-risk, or higher-taxes-and-lower-risk. Thus, to obtain capital gains tax treatment, we must typically hold our assets for at least one year (higher risk). We can lower our risk by buying assets that will (or can) be sold in a month, but that will subject us to higher ordinary income or short-term capital gains taxes.

DESIGNING PORTFOLIOS FROM AN AFTER-TAX PERSPECTIVE

Most financial advisors design client portfolios using expected *gross* returns for each asset class to be included in the portfolio. If we were pension plans, that would be fine. But as family investors, most of our assets are likely to be subject to the complicated regime of investment taxes—short-term gains, long-term gains, ordinary income taxes, the alternative minimum tax, plus whatever nightmares our state and city of residence have cooked up for us.[1]

If we think about this for a minute, we will quickly realize that each asset class will be affected somewhat differently by this crazy quilt of taxes. To take two very opposite examples, returns on private equity tend to be extremely tax advantaged: Our money comes back to us taxed at long-term capital gains rates and, in addition, the payment of the tax is delayed, representing an interest-free loan to us from the tax authorities. On the other hand, the return we receive on hedge funds is typically tax *dis*advantaged: These returns are taxed mainly at short-term capital gains rates and we pay the tax right away.

Given the differing impact of taxes on the different asset classes, it's clear that portfolios designed using expected gross returns will be highly inefficient for taxable investors. If a family investor wishes to obtain the same expected return as a tax-exempt investor, it will have to accept more risk. If a family investor wishes to maintain the same risk level as an institutional investor, it will have to accept lower returns.

We can't level the playing field completely for taxable investors, but we can go a long way toward ensuring that their portfolios will be as realistic and efficient as possible by designing them from an after-tax perspective. This is a more complex process than it might appear, and it is discussed at length in Chapter 9.

ASSET LOCATION

As discussed more fully in Chapter 19, families, unlike pension plans and endowment funds, typically have an enormously complex series of entities through which capital must be invested. These entities often exist as part of the family's tax and estate-planning strategies, but may exist for other reasons as well. The most obvious of these entities are private trusts, charitable trusts, partnerships, foundations, closely held businesses, and the individual portfolios of different family units and generations.

The tax consequences of investing in these different entities can be quite different, and hence it should be obvious that the location of an asset in a family's portfolio will have important implications for the growth of net wealth. A simple example is that sensible investors would not ordinarily put the same kinds of investments in a generation-skipping trust as they would put in a defective grantor trust. Similarly, managers appropriate for the patriarch's personal portfolio may be wholly inappropriate for the family foundation. Yet it is quite rare for a financial advisor to understand these implications and act accordingly.

ASSET CLASS STRATEGIES

The need to develop optimal asset class strategies is discussed at length in Chapters 11 through 16. For purposes of our present discussion, the important point is that the tax treatment of the various asset classes will significantly affect the selection of strategies that will be optimal for taxable investors. Over time, for example, we know that value strategies have outperformed growth strategies. But much of the return of value investing comes from the high dividend stream typically paid out by "value" companies, and, until recently, that dividend stream was taxed at very high rates. This doesn't mean that taxable investors should have avoided value stocks and value managers, but it does suggest that the relative exposure of a taxable investor to value strategies would have been different—lower—than the typical exposure a tax-exempt investor might seek.

Similarly, taxable investors should typically hold a lower exposure to most hedge fund strategies than will tax-exempt investors,[2] because the short-term gains produced by most hedge funds are taxed at a very high rate. Placing hedge strategies in an IRA or other tax-sheltered account can help, of course, but most substantial investors will not hold IRAs that are of any significant size relative to their entire asset base.

Similar analyses must be pursued in each asset class to ensure that tax considerations have been taken into account—not, I hasten to add, that tax considerations should always be decisive—in selecting optimal strategies in each category.

TAX-AWARE MANAGERS

The money management business, at least as a professional, thoughtful, disciplined activity, grew up in the institutional world. The overwhelming majority of competent money managers designed their investment strategies and disciplines for, and cut their teeth on, an institutional, nontaxable client base. Because those investors paid no taxes, tax considerations were never incorporated into the investment process. Meanwhile, most family investors were stuck in the trust company and private client backwaters, having their portfolios managed by individuals who were really salesmen or client relations people, not professional portfolio managers.

As families have become more sophisticated over time, they have naturally sought out more professional investment management for their portfolios. Unfortunately, this has taken too many families out of the frying pan and right into the fire. The reason is that the institutional money managers whose thoughtfulness and discipline appeal to sophisticated families are all too often money managers who don't pay the slightest attention to the tax consequences of their investment activities.

As the institutional business has stopped growing and, at the same time, become intensely competitive, many institutional managers have set their sights on wealthy families as a rapidly growing and hugely underserved market. Most, as noted, have simply sold their gross return performance, hoping that family investors will not take the trouble to convert the (often) attractive gross returns into the (usually) unattractive net-of-tax returns.

Some institutional money managers have actually modified their investment disciplines to incorporate tax considerations, but families should be wary of such managers for a whole host of reasons. Imagine, in general, a money management firm that has built up a respectable track record over the years by diligently pursuing a particular investment process. Then, simply because the manager wishes to gather assets more rapidly, the firm alters its investment process to incorporate strategies that are currently more popular with investors. Unsophisticated investors might be lured into engaging such a manager, but more experienced investors will look elsewhere. For one thing, the new process is unproven—engaging the manager would be almost like engaging a newly formed firm with no track record. But there is a more serious problem, namely, the cynicism of the change in the investment process. A firm that would engage in such an activity once is a firm that will engage in it again, and we should beware of doing business with such a firm.

Modifying a disciplined investment process to incorporate tax considerations may not seem like a cynical move, but all too often it is. Clearly, for example, the change in the investment process is being made solely to improve the firm's asset-gathering capabilities—namely, by appealing to a new market of affluent, taxable investors. More fundamentally, it will be a rare investment process that will work as well considering taxes as it does without considering taxes—simply layering a tax-aware element onto a process that never considered taxes is no different in principle from layering a value element onto a growth discipline.

To take a simple example, let's consider a momentum manager for whom rapid turnover is a fundamental aspect of its style. This firm buys stocks that have risen in price recently and sells them as soon as their price momentum slows down. As a result, some stocks may be held for only a few days or weeks. Virtually all of the gains generated by such a manager will be short term, taxed at high rates for a family investor. Adding to the process a tax overlay that requires stocks to be held for a full year (to receive long-term capital gains treatment) would be absurd. Such a modification of the process would, in fact, destroy it.

With many other investment styles and disciplines, the consequences of adding tax considerations may not be so obvious, but they are almost always serious. To ensure that tax considerations will make a meaningful and positive contribution to an investment process requires that tax considerations be an integral part of the process *as it is being designed*. Thus, for a money management firm to enter the market for taxable investors requires far more than simply reducing turnover or trying to harvest losses now and then. It requires the firm to design a new investment process from the ground up. This process will undoubtedly incorporate the disciplines of the firm's tax-exempt product and it will build on the firm's strengths. But the taxable investment product will be quite different from the tax-exempt product and the track record of the tax-exempt product will be largely irrelevant.

The point is that if a money management firm that has historically advised institutional investors wishes to advise taxable investors, the firm will have to make a very substantial investment in the project. This investment will include designing the product as a taxable product from the beginning, and will include building a significant track record with the product before it can be marketed widely or successfully to taxable investors.

Identifying Tax-Aware Managers

As noted earlier, for many years, managers—including, unfortunately, banks and brokerage firms whose primary clients were families—paid no attention at all to the tax consequences of their money management activities. More recently, managers have begun to pay lip service to the concept of tax efficiency, but managers who are truly tax-aware in their disciplines remain rare. As we look for tax-aware managers, some of the characteristics we should focus on include the following:

- *Managers whose styles include low turnover.* Notice, however, that low turnover is not, in and of itself, conclusive evidence of tax efficiency. For low turnover to translate into tax efficiency, without the employment of other techniques, the turnover must be *extremely* low, typically on the order of 10 percent. A manager whose turnover is 30 percent is likely to be no more tax efficient than a manager whose turnover is 100 percent. Nor is high turnover itself conclusive evidence of tax inefficiency. Consider a passive, tax-aware manager that is constantly harvesting small capital losses and using those losses to shelter gains elsewhere. Such a manager will exhibit very high turnover, but its activities will in fact be highly tax efficient. Thus, we will want to examine a manager's annual turnover, but we will need to examine it carefully and in context.

- *Managers who are conscious of holding periods and who avoid incurring short-term capital gains whenever possible.* Here the challenge is balancing investment gains against tax losses. Assume a manager buys a security with an anticipated holding period of 18 months and an anticipated price gain of 40 percent. If the company's performance falls apart early in the holding period, it will likely make sense for the manager to sell the stock, even if it results in a short-term gain. But if the performance falls apart in the 10th month of the holding period, it may pay the manager to hold on for another two months, because the lower tax may offset the price decline.

- *Managers who aggressively offset losses against gains in an attempt to zero-out the tax liabilities of their buying and selling activity.* Managers naturally tend to be very confident of their skill. But the fact is that few managers will generate enough alpha to offset the taxes they produce.[3] Thus, a manager who is truly tax aware will be willing to take a loss on a stock, rather than stubbornly hold on to it hoping its price will recover. Such behavior may well hurt the manager's gross-of-tax returns, but it will leave far more money in its clients' pockets.

- *Managers who manage tax lots.* Institutional managers simply accumulate stock positions and then deaccumulate them, in no particular order. But a portfolio manager who works with taxable investors must be aware of the tax lots it holds. For example, as the manager is accumulating a position in Ford Motor, the manager might buy some lots at $51, some at $53.50, some at $56, and so on. When it comes time to sell, the manager needs to identify which tax lot he is selling in order to minimize the tax consequence of the sale.

- *Managers who are willing to be flexible in reducing their clients' overall tax burdens.* Imagine a manager who is sitting on significant gains in securities whose prices the manager thinks will continue to rise. The manager has no losses in the portfolio, so it can't shelter the gains if they are realized. However, the manager's client calls and asks the manager to realize the gains on those stocks because the client has losses *elsewhere* in his portfolio that will cover the taxes on the gains. Will the manager sell the stocks? He won't *want* to sell, of course, because he expects the stocks to continue to rise. But if he is truly a tax-aware manager he will indulge the client's wishes, knowing that the client's gain is more important than his own gross returns for the period.[4] The same is true of a manager sitting on unrealized losses, who expects those securities to recover, and who has no offsetting gains in its portfolio. If the client has gains elsewhere in his portfolio, the client may ask the manager to realize the losses.

Of course, some desirable managers are engaged in strategies that are inherently tax inefficient—absolute-return-oriented hedge funds, for example. It would be counterproductive to insist that these managers somehow develop tax-efficient disciplines, because it is the very nature of their strategies to produce short-term gains and ordinary income. But the point is that when we have a choice between a manager who is tax aware and one who is not, we will almost always want the former, not the latter.

HARVESTING LOSSES

Although tax-aware managers can harvest losses that occur in their own portfolios, they will have no idea of the gain and loss positions held elsewhere in the client's accounts. As investors, however, we (or a financial advisor on our behalf) can carefully monitor activity across the portfolio and coordinate among managers to net out gains and losses, or at least minimize net gains. If Manager A has losses that can be realized and Manager B has gains he cannot offset, we can work with the two managers to net out the tax consequences across the two portfolios.

In this, as in so many other areas, the importance of engaging a qualified master custodian for our investment assets can hardly be overemphasized. Asset custody is discussed in Chapter 22, but for purposes of this discussion the importance of a master custodian lies in (a) the custodian's role as the keeper-of-record for tax cost basis information on all securities in the portfolio (including identification of tax lots), and (b) the custodian's ability to produce consolidated account statements. These services allow us to observe our tax position across the portfolio, regardless of who is managing our money or how many managers we have engaged. Often, we are able to do so online and in something approaching real time. Absent a central custodian, we are reduced to poring over paper statements that arrive at different times, or trying to download online information from many different, usually incompatible, sources.

Even among investors who use a custodian and practice tax loss harvesting, a common mistake is waiting until near the end of the year to cross gains and losses. Our managers are buying and selling securities throughout the year. If we wait until November or December to look at our unrealized gain-loss positions, we will have missed many, many opportunities to reduce taxes because most of the tax-realization events will already have occurred. Families will likely find that reviewing tax savings opportunities every quarter will prove optimal, most efficiently balancing investment and tax considerations.

PRACTICE TIP

Advisors have gotten better in recent years at building tax awareness into their work with wealthy families. But there is still a lot of work to do in terms of keeping tax issues at the forefront of everything we do for our clients. Taxes represent a *huge* drag on investment returns, and the more we can minimize that drag, the better off our clients will be.

That said, it's also important not to allow the tax tail to wag the investment dog. Getting this balance right isn't easy, especially when we are being pressed by clients to take action to reduce taxes even though it means making unwise investment moves. But, hey, that's why they pay us the big bucks!

CONCLUSION: YOU CAN'T EAT GROSS RETURNS

In a happier world, families would be like college and university endowments and not have to worry about the taxes generated by their managers. But because we're not likely to inhabit such a world any time soon, it's critically important to focus on high-quality managers who are tax aware in all their investing activities. Finding managers who can consistently produce alpha is an almost impossible challenge, but finding managers who can produce "tax alpha" is much easier, because the techniques required to minimize taxes are well known and effective.

NOTES

1. The best extended discussion of the tax issues associated with managing family investment portfolios can be found in Jean L.P. Brunel,

Integrated Wealth Management: The New Direction for Portfolio Managers (London: Institutional Investor Books, 2002), especially chapters 6 and 14–17.
2. In reality, other considerations militate against higher hedge exposure for tax-exempt institutions. The main constraint is the huge asset base managed by many institutions and the fact that hedge strategies are almost always capacity-constrained. Hence, it is quite difficult for a large institutional investor to obtain a significant exposure to hedge funds without seriously compromising the quality of the funds selected.
3. The classic journal article on this subject is Robert H. Jeffrey and Robert D. Arnott, "Is Your Alpha Big Enough to Cover Its Taxes?" *The Journal of Portfolio Management* (1992).
4. The manager could protect his position in any number of ways. For example, he could buy a security whose price behavior is closely correlated with the sold security. He could buy an ETF in the same industry. He could wait 31 days (to avoid the wash sale rule) and buy the security back.

CHAPTER 19

Asset Location and Implementation

In this chapter we will discuss two issues to which many investors and advisors give short shrift. The first is the asset location issue: how to decide which of the many family investment "pockets" to use for which investment assets. The second issue is the implementation issue: how to move from a mainly liquid portfolio to a fully invested position. (Or how to move from one strategy to a very different strategy, although one hopes this would be a rare event.) Properly negotiating these challenges can have an important impact on a family's wealth.

ASSET LOCATION ISSUES

Because that's where the money is.
        —Willy Sutton, when asked why he robbed banks

"Asset location," as its name implies, refers to the question of where to locate each of the investments expected to be employed in the overall portfolio. Unlike most institutional investors, private investors own their assets in many, many different forms. For example, it is not unusual to encounter, in one large family, assets held in the private accounts of different generations, in the private accounts of many different individuals, in the accounts of different collateral family units, in family investment partnerships and family limited partnerships, in charitable foundations, family trusts, IRAs, closely held corporations, LLCs, offshore vehicles, intentionally defective grantor trusts, dynasty trusts, and the alphabet soup of tax and charitable vehicles such as GRATs, GRUTs, CRATs, CLATs, CLUTs, CRUTs, NIMCRUTs, cascading GRATs, and so on. Each of these vehicles is typically created for a specific, largely noninvestment purpose, but each holds assets that must nonetheless be properly invested. The decision about which investments should go into which vehicles is mainly a tax-driven issue, but other issues will also be present and they will sometimes be decisive.

I could write an entire book just on the asset location issue, but in deference to my readers' patience I will only identify the issue as a crucial one and illustrate some of its complexities. Families will, in the main, have to rely on their legal, tax and investment advisors when to comes to asset location issues, but it is important at least to recognize the issue and understand its importance. The simple fact is that, all too often, the good work of our tax, trust, and estate planning advisors is undone by financial advisors who misunderstand the nature and taxability of complex vehicles.

PRACTICE TIP

One very common set of asset locations is the family's personal fortune and the capital held in a family foundation. As an advisor, you might be thinking that to the extent the family's liquidity needs relate to charitable commitments, those could in fact be discharged by the foundation. But this is true only in limited circumstances.

If the family makes a charitable pledge and that pledge is fulfilled by the foundation, the directors or trustees have engaged in a self-dealing transaction and can be subjected to large fines. On the other hand, the family is free to discharge individually any pledges made by their foundation.

Thus, although these may seem like minor differences, they are crucial ones, and as an advisor to wealthy families you need to be aware of how the IRS views the world.

Examples of Asset Locations and the Associated Investment Implications

In the following paragraphs I give brief examples of estate planning vehicles that are frequently employed by families, along with some of the more obvious investment implications associated with using those vehicles. I want to emphasize that the vehicles are discussed merely as examples of the issues that tend to arise; they are by no means exhaustive.

Asset protection trusts (APTs). These offshore (and sometimes onshore) vehicles are often used by clients in litigious professions or who fear large legal judgments. They are similar to spendthrift trusts—indeed, they are in effect self-settled spendthrift trusts—except that the trust is established in a jurisdiction with laws that make it difficult for creditors to enforce their rights (often via very short statutes of limitation and very limited discovery rules). A key provision is the presence of a "protector" who will not be subject to U.S. court orders. Unlike true spendthrift trusts, in an APT the presence of the donor as a discretionary beneficiary does not render the gift to the trust incomplete. Hence, APTs can effectively be used to remove assets from the estate of the donor. APTs must be created before a judgment is entered against the donor, and preferably before any claim has been asserted or even arisen.

Investment implications: All U.S. taxes must be paid on income and gains as they occur, exactly as though the trust were a domestic trust. Consequently, the investment considerations will be similar to those posed by a domestic portfolio. Assets placed in APTs may remain in trust longer, and hence have a longer investment time horizon associated with them, than the same assets may have had when held directly and domestically. On the other hand, many investors who establish APTs see them as an ultimate "anchor to windward" and will wish to see the assets in the trust invested very cautiously.

Charitable lead annuity trusts (CLATs). A CLAT pays a fixed amount to charity for a period of years, then passes (outright or in trust) to the children or other beneficiaries tax-free. A charitable deduction is available for the expected present value of the charitable payments. A significant amount of property can be removed from the donor's estate at no tax cost using properly structured CLATs.

Investment implications: Investment implications tend to depend on the charitable intent of the donors. Donors may wish to benefit charity, in which case high-income assets will be placed in the trust. If they wish to benefit the children, on the other hand, low-income, high-growth assets will be placed in the trust. Note that the investment advisor may be representing the donors or the ultimate family beneficiaries, or, in some case s, both.

Charitable lead unitrusts (CLUTs). A CLUT is simply a CLAT that pays to charity a percentage of the fluctuating value of the trust assets, rather than a fixed amount.

Investment implications: Generally, same as a CLAT. However, the fluctuating value of the payments to charity must be taken into account—the use of very low-yielding assets in CLUTs is usually unwise.

Charitable remainder annuity trusts (CRATs). A CRAT is the opposite of a CLAT: Assets in a CRAT pay a fixed amount of income to the donor for life or a period of years, then pass outright to charity—which can be a family foundation. Appreciated property is usually placed in a CRAT. The donor receives a charitable deduction for the value of the gift less the value of the income payments. CRAT payments must equal at least 5 percent of the value of the property.

Investment implications: Most donors will want to ensure the annuity payout to themselves, and may have little interest in how much ultimately passes to charity. However, this is not always the case. Remember that taxes paid by the beneficiary are determined by the nature of the income at the trust level. Highest taxable income must be distributed first.

Charitable remainder unitrusts (CRUTs). A CRUT is a CRAT that pays the donor a percentage (not less than 5 percent) of the fluctuating value of the trust. The donor can make additional contributions to a CRUT, unlike a CRAT. Surprisingly, a CRUT can pay out the lesser of 5 percent or the net income of the trust, making it ideal for appreciating assets that pay little or no income.

Investment implications: CRUTs are generally used when there is a serious charitable motive. Remember that taxes paid by the beneficiary are determined by the nature of the income at the trust level. Highest taxable income must be distributed first.

Dynasty trusts. This is a term typically applied to any trust that is designed to last for several generations. Dynasty trusts created in states that have abolished the rule against perpetuities (e.g., Alaska, Delaware, Idaho, South Dakota, Wisconsin) can theoretically last forever, although the Internal Revenue Service has proposed sunsetting provisions.

Investment implications: These vehicles have very long investment time horizons and few income demands. Most donors will want to see the assets in a dynasty trust invested aggressively, consistent with fiduciary principles.

Generation-skipping trusts. Gifts that skip a generation are subject to a high flat tax, plus the usual estate tax. There is a (fluctuating[1]) lifetime exemption available to each spouse. The parents create a trust and allocate their GST exemptions to it. GST trusts are limited in most states by the Rule Against Perpetuities, but by creating the trust in a state that has repealed the rule (see above), the trust can theoretically last forever. A GST dynasty trust can be leveraged considerably by combining it with a CLUT.

Investment implications: These vehicles have very long investment time horizons and few income demands. Most donors will want to see the assets in a dynasty trust invested aggressively, consistent with fiduciary principles.

Grantor retained annuity trusts (GRATs). Under a GRAT, the grantor retains the right to receive a fixed dollar amount for a specified number of years. Assuming that the grantor survives the annuity period and that the assets in the trust appreciate rapidly, a considerable amount will pass to the children free of estate and gift taxes. A gift is made upon the creation of the GRAT equal to the initial value of the assets reduced by the value of the annuity payments. Investors can also create zero-gift GRATs by setting the annuity amount so high that no gift is made. Gifts of closely held stock and limited partnerships are especially useful because they are already discounted for lack of marketability. The grantor is taxed on gains in the trust, and these tax payments represent additional tax-free gifts. So-called "cascading GRATs" are often used in situations where it is possible that an investment will appreciate extremely rapidly. If so, a substantial sum is passed tax-free to the children. If not, the GRAT simply expires harmlessly (assuming the grantor survives).

Investment implications: Investments in GRATs should be as aggressive as is consistent with the need to make the annuity payments (or more aggressively in the case of cascading GRATs).

Insurance wraps. Placing a tax-inefficient asset inside an insurance product (usually a modified endowment contract or a variable annuity contract) causes the tax consequences to pass to the insurance company while the gains remain in the policy as increasing cash value. The insured can access the cash value through low-cost policy loans or simple cash withdrawals. Many insurance wraps are structured through offshore insurance companies to avoid strict state rules on investment options. The ongoing costs of these programs is an important issue, and the IRS is cracking down on perceived abuses.

Investment implications: These vehicles are useful to shelter the income from growth assets that generate substantial ordinary income or short-term capital gains; for example, nondirectional hedge funds. Keep in mind that the insured cannot select the investments inside the policy.

Intentionally defective trusts. An intentionally defective trust is one that will not be includable in the grantor's estate but on which the grantor pays all taxes, even though the income or appreciation is going to the children. These taxes represent an additional untaxed gift. A trust can be "defective" by giving the grantor the right to "sprinkle" income or principal among a group of beneficiaries, by retaining the power to reacquire the trust assets by substituting property of equal value, or by providing that the trust income can be distributed to the grantor's spouse.

Investment implications: Because the donor pays all taxes, his or her tax picture must be kept in mind. It is usually preferable to invest in assets that generate long-term capital gains.

NIMCRUTs. A version of a CRUT containing an income makeup provision that allows more income to be paid out in later years, to the extent that income paid out in earlier years was less than the required percentage amount. Thus, rapidly appreciating property can be placed in a NIMCRUT while the donor is young; later, during retirement, the investments can be switched to high-yield assets paying the donor a very high income.

Investment implications: Invest in high-growth, low-income assets during the accumulation phase, and high-income assets (e.g., junk bonds) during the payout phase.

Offshore trusts. Offshore trusts offer investors no tax benefits if the donors or beneficiaries are U.S. citizens, but many wealthy clients will have non-U.S. citizens somewhere in their families. This presents the opportunity to site trusts in offshore jurisdictions and avoid all U.S. (and often foreign) taxes.

Investment implications: These depend entirely on the needs of the beneficiaries.

Private foundations. Foundations can be established as trusts or corporations. Corporate foundations tend to be simpler to administer and they avoid bizarre state limits on investments. Trusts, however, are better equipped to preserve family control across the generations. A private foundation is a grant-making organization which must make grants and other payments (or in IRS terms, qualifying distributions) equal to 5 percent or more of its average assets each year; pays a 1 percent or 2 percent excise tax, depending on the scale of the grant-making; must file a Form 990-PF with the IRS every year; and must make available to the public either its 990-PF or an annual report. Note that most foundations will likely find themselves the target of unsolicited funding proposals, and failure to respond to these funding requests can harm the family's reputation. Gifts to private foundations are limited to 20 percent of adjusted gross income, rather than the 50 percent deduction permitted for gifts to public charities. For this reason, many "smaller" foundations are set up as donor-advised funds at a community foundation.

Investment implications: Fearful of not generating enough income to meet the payout requirement, many foundations invest far too conservatively. During extended bear markets (as in the 1970s and early 2000s), the 5 percent payout requirement, plus the excise tax, can actually amount to a much higher percentage of the current asset base. Even during normal market conditions, overly cautious investment strategies can result in investment returns that are well below those needed to grow the foundation's assets in real terms (payout requirement + excise tax + inflation).

Revocable trusts. Also called revocable inter vivos trusts. These are best viewed as property management vehicles. Revocable trusts have no tax benefits and, in most states, few other benefits (despite the claims of a few unscrupulous lawyers and accountants). Assets placed in a revocable trust must be retitled in the name of the trust, and if the trustee is anyone other than the grantor, separate tax returns must be filed. In certain states revocable trusts can avoid some of the costs of probate, and such trusts can also, for wealthy families, be useful for complex asset management situations (where a durable power of attorney might be too simple), and to preserve privacy. In a few states a revocable trust can be used to prevent a spouse from receiving his or her statutory share of the grantor's property at death.

Investment implications: The only investment issue is the important point that well-drafted revocable inter vivos trusts can be effective asset and property management vehicles with less unwieldiness than a general power of attorney, and therefore assets such as real estate will typically be placed in them.

There are a thousand and one other issues associated with the proper location of investment assets in complex family portfolios, but the point is that these issues need to be addressed with care and sensitivity. The most brilliantly conceived investment portfolio and estate plan can be seriously undermined by the failure to locate assets in the right locations.

IMPLEMENTATION ISSUES

If the future were a repeat of the past, librarians would be rich.
—Warren Buffett

When a family experiences a major liquidity event, or when an invested portfolio is being substantially restructured, many questions arise about how to proceed. These questions have mainly to do with market timing considerations and risk tolerance issues, but other issues are involved as well, including good old-fashioned human emotions.

To examine these issues, let's imagine a family—we'll call them the Goldsmiths—who have just sold their family business for $100 million. The business was built up over four generations, and the current leaders of the family, Mark and Ellen Goldsmith, are acutely aware of their stewardship obligations. They recognize that sitting on $100 million of cash, though certainly reassuring in the short run, is simply a way for the family to become a little poorer every year. Yet they fear that if they quickly deploy assets into the capital markets, their hard-earned assets could disappear in an unexpected bear market. Because the family's liquidity event occurred in September of 2008, in the idle of a deep bear market, those fears are hardly unfounded. How should the Goldsmiths proceed?

Macro Considerations

We know, from history, that capital markets tend to rise roughly twice as often as they decline. This consideration suggests that the Goldsmiths should invest as quickly as possible, because the long-term odds of the markets going up are in their favor. And, indeed, most financial advisors will suggest that families invest proceeds from a major liquidity event quite quickly, typically over a few quarters or, at most, a year. Although this may be the right course for some families, I suggest that it is far too fast for most families.

For one thing, the long-term odds favoring rising markets disguise some very unhappy short-term possibilities: 1973–1974, for example, 1987, 2000–2002, and 2007–2009. Thus, the Goldsmiths must ask themselves the question whether getting even richer is as powerful a stimulus for them as getting a lot poorer would be. Because wealthy families are, by definition, already wealthy, and therefore capital preservation-oriented, getting richer is unlikely to provide as much pleasure as getting poorer will provide pain. If the odds of good markets versus bad markets were 10 to 1, perhaps the Goldsmiths would feel comfortable plunging into a fully invested position. But at roughly 2 to 1, the possibility of a bad outcome is simply too high.

Note that this is true not just for wealthy families but for everyone: Clever experiments by behavioral scientists have shown that we are more eager to avoid pain than we are eager to experience pleasure. Moreover, we know that for most of us the marginal value of each additional dollar we receive declines the more dollars we have.

Given the dire possibilities the Goldsmiths face, and the relatively little that is to be gained in the short run by getting even wealthier, an interesting default position for Mark and Ellen might be to invest their newly liquid fortune *over an entire market cycle.* In other words, absent a compelling reason to move more quickly or more slowly, they should plan to invest their liquidity over the course of something like 20 quarters.[2]

Note that in the case of the Goldsmiths, this would have meant that they would largely (though not entirely) have missed the market rebound that occurred in 2009, when the markets were up powerfully and broadly. But, of course, even if they had invested over the course of one full year, they would still have missed much of this appreciation. The point is that although having a few tens of millions of dollars more in paper wealth would have been nice, there was a nearly equal chance that the markets could have gone the other way, and that would have been very unfortunate, indeed.

Moreover, the Goldsmiths' money will likely be invested for generations; missing out on a bit of appreciation in the first few years of the portfolio's life will make virtually no long-term difference to the family. On the other hand, if the markets had collapsed with all the family's money fully invested, it could have required decades to make up the loss: A crucial aspect of successful investing is avoiding very bad results.

It is interesting to speculate about what might cause the Goldsmiths to invest their capital more quickly or more slowly. Let's take a look at some of the considerations that might cause the Goldsmiths to depart from the one-market-cycle default position.

Reasons for Investing More Quickly   Unfortunately, the most common reason for accelerating the investment period would be that stock prices were rising rapidly and the Goldsmiths feared that they were missing out on an opportunity. I say "unfortunately" because it will be a rare case, indeed, in which an investor could jump into a rapidly rising market and emerge unscathed at the very end of the cycle. Short-term bull markets—the only kind the Goldsmiths would miss by investing slowly—have an unhappy tendency to turn very suddenly into bear markets.

Consider the bull of the late 1990s and its sudden transformation into the bear of the early 2000s, or the bull of 2006–early 2007 that turned into the bear of late 2007–2008. These bull/bear periods were quite different from the period between 1982 and 1998, when stock prices rose consistently over a very long period. Remaining uninvested over that period would have been a true investment disaster, to be sure. But missing a brief and powerful bull ought to be of little concern to the Goldsmiths.

Another common-but-inadequate reason for moving more quickly is simple impatience. The Goldsmiths will naturally be aware that keeping their money in, say, a cash portfolio (see Chapters 9 and 14) will not only not grow their wealth, but may actually shrink it: Net of tax and costs, enhanced cash portfolios tend to produce less-than-inflation type returns. Inflation is truly a demon enemy of private capital, *but only over longer periods of time*. If the Goldsmiths invest over a five-year market cycle, their average uninvested period will be only two and a half years. The likelihood that an enhanced cash portfolio would result in any serious loss, even net of inflation, is pretty remote over such a brief period of time.

A better reason for investing more quickly than over an entire market cycle would be if the equity markets were significantly undervalued by historical standards at the time of the Goldsmiths' liquidity event. Market watchers can argue endlessly about what the "fair" value of stocks should be, but periods of *serious* over- or undervaluation are not difficult to identify, even prospectively. The problem for the Goldsmiths is not concluding that stocks are priced at or near historic low ranges. Their problem is having the courage to invest at such a time. Remember that when an entire equity market is selling cheaply, there is likely to be a reason for it.

In late 1974, for example, inflation had spiraled out of control, there were long gas lines everywhere, American preeminence seemed to have been lost to Germany and Japan, and the menace posed by the Soviet Union was very real. Many, many investors bailed out of the markets in 1974. These investors weren't just running from a periodic bear market—they had completely lost faith in the future of the American economy. And yet, late 1974 would turn out to be a terrific time to invest.

In short, *all* serious bear markets are associated with far more than low equity prices. In every case there will be far more to worry about, and it will be those worries that will keep the Goldsmiths from putting capital into the markets at the very time when that capital is likely to be most productive. The one-market-cycle rule can at least help build a little courage in the family.

Reasons for Investing More Slowly   Reasons to invest more slowly than one market cycle should be very rare. We have just discussed one unfortunate reason: The markets are in a serious bear phase and families will be fearful of putting *any* money to work, just when the return on that money is likely to be at its peak.

Another reason for moving cautiously has to do with the difficulty of making the transition from being a family that owns and operates a business to being a family that owns and operates an investment portfolio. Although in fact it is far more risky to own one business than to own pieces of many of them (that is, both the possible upside and the downside outcomes are far more extreme), it won't necessarily seem that way to the family.

In the Goldsmiths' case, the family had owned an operating business for four generations. By definition, it was a successful business, the family was in control, and the family was used to the risks the business posed. Investing in a traditional investment portfolio, though far less risky from an objective point of view, is a new experience for the Goldsmiths and they will naturally worry that they may not be very good at it. They will exaggerate the risks and underestimate the opportunities.

Thus, families new to investing will sometimes go through a very long period of remaining underinvested and of putting money directly into operating businesses, startups, and various and sundry other schemes, all because those activities seem more comfortable to them. Only after the family has suffered serious actual losses on its direct investments and serious opportunity costs by being out of the market will they throw in the towel and begin to put money to work in a sensible investment portfolio.

PRACTICE TIP

As advisors, we can sometimes have conflicts of interest with our clients even though we have gone to great lengths to eliminate all the usual conflicts.

For example, advisors shouldn't overlook the fact that many of us won't get paid, or won't get paid much, on the portion of the Goldsmiths' fortune that is invested in cash. All too often it is this consideration, more than anything else, that accounts for the advice to families get invested quickly.

It is possible to structure the advisory relationship, especially in the early years, in ways that eliminate or minimize this conflict. For example, by compensating their advisor equally on the total portfolio, whether the money is invested or uninvested, the Goldsmiths can at least dodge this particular advisory bullet.

Another possibility is for the advisor and the client to agree on a fixed fee for the first several years of the relationship, so that the advisor will have no incentive to move too quickly (or too slowly) in investing the client's capital.

Micro Considerations

Once Mark and Ellen Goldsmith begin to implement their investment portfolio, they will be investing in many different asset classes and, in all probability, in many different investment styles. One strategy the family might follow is simply to average-in to every asset class and style, and this is typically how it is done. Anything else is likely to smack of market timing.

A more astute tactic, however, might be to invest more quickly in areas that are believed to be undervalued and less quickly in areas that are believed to be overvalued.

This approach will have two salutary consequences. First, it will prevent the Goldsmiths from piling into sectors and styles that are currently "hot" and that are highly likely to collapse at some point. Murphy's Law being what it is ("If something can go wrong, it will"), that collapse will likely occur just after the Goldsmiths have bought in at the top of the market.

A second benefit for the Goldsmiths is that, by investing in out-of-favor categories more quickly, they are at least buying in cheaply. Although no one can know when an over- or undervaluation will correct itself,[3] we do know that it will happen and that we will not be nimble enough to get out of the way in time or to jump aboard in time. If we buy into overvalued situations, we can be pretty confident that we will pay handsomely for our folly at some point. If we buy into undervalued situations, we can't know when we will be compensated, but we know that, ultimately, we will be.

Thus, if it appears that value stocks are under-valued relative to growth stocks, the Goldsmiths will be wise to hire their value managers first and to invest more money with them more quickly. Of course, over the full investment period for the Goldsmiths, this valuation differential could easily reverse itself. In that case, the Goldsmith will want to slow down—or even reverse—the pace of investment with value managers and to pick up the pace with growth managers.

The same principles hold true of large-cap versus small-cap stocks, of domestic versus foreign stocks, of long versus short bonds, and so on. Over a full market cycle, most asset classes will enter a period of undervaluation, giving the Goldsmiths the opportunity to buy in at rational prices.

Yes, there is an element of market timing to this strategy, but it is market timing that is being done in a thoughtful way and with a conservative bias. In other words, the Goldsmiths aren't going to jump into a hot tech market with the thought that they will be able to time the markets well enough to get out before the collapse. The Goldsmiths are going to invest in *undervalued* assets a bit faster than they will in other assets. Sure, an undervalued asset can always become more undervalued, but the likelihood of a severe collapse in the prices of assets that are already undervalued is slim.

On the other hand, the likelihood of a collapse in the prices of assets that are already overvalued is very high. All value investing is, in effect, a form of market timing. We buy undervalued securities not because we believe that our downside risk is modest (though that is an important consideration), but because we believe that at some time in the future the true value of our securities will be recognized and their prices will rise.

Implementing in PE and Hedge

One area where valuation anomalies don't apply very well is private equity in general, and venture capital in particular. Although the "vintage year" of the investment will be extremely important to the investor's ultimate return, it is essentially impossible to know which vintage years will be good ones and which will be bad ones. Therefore, it will pay the Goldsmiths to invest their PE allocation regularly and systematically year after year.

Hedge fund investing falls somewhere between traditional investing and private equity. Hedge funds do correlate with the markets, though imperfectly, and hence jumping into hedge funds during periods of market overvaluation will likely prove unrewarding. On the other hand, a well-diversified portfolio of hedge funds will likely protect investors on the downside, while still achieving reasonable returns on the upside. As a result of this happy circumstance, investors may wish to move more quickly on the hedge fund side of their portfolio than on the traditional side, all things being equal.

Finally, real estate is an asset class that is subject to periodic booms and busts. Families who will be including real estate in their portfolios will want to take special care not to buy into overvalued real estate markets. Instead, they may wish to postpone gaining real estate exposure or target their initial exposure to sectors of the market that are reasonably priced.

CONCLUSION: IT'S NOT JUST A TECHNICAL ISSUE

Families are complicated beasts. I listed above a large number of possible "pockets" into which capital might be placed and need to be managed. And whenever we begin to manage capital, we face a series of implementation issues that will have long-term effects on our wealth for good or ill.

Asset location and implementation may seem like technical issues, but they matter a great deal. We overlook them at our peril.

NOTES

1. In other words, until the end of 2012 the exemption is $5 million. After 2012 it is scheduled to drop to $1 million.
2. This default position would not make sense for a family who had only temporarily moved to an uninvested position, perhaps as the result of terminating their investment advisor and moving temporarily to cash. (Note that terminating an advisor can often make sense; moving to cash—as opposed to keeping the invested positions intact—will rarely make sense.)

3. It is surprisingly easy to know intellectually when markets are reaching overvalued levels, because we know a great deal about corporate earnings and about what investors are willing, over longer periods of time, to pay for those earnings. What we can't know is when valuation anomalies will correct themselves. That is because extreme over- and undervaluations are caused by investor psychology, not by corporate earnings.

CHAPTER 20

Monitoring and Rebalancing Taxable Portfolios

All movements go too far.

—Bertrand Russell

The traditional techniques employed in the monitoring of investment performance and in the rebalancing of investment portfolios arose in the institutional world, where such matters are very clear cut. But institutions are quite different from families. In the first place, institutions are typically engaged in a *relative* performance game. If the S&P 500 is down 28 percent and the Widget Pension Plan's large-cap portfolio is down only 27 percent, Widget is happy and the managers of Widget's pension plan are happy. But under the same circumstances, few families would be happy to be down "only" 27 percent. Families tend to be *absolute* return investors, as eager to preserve their wealth as to grow it.

Another way in which family investors differ from institutions is in the emotional toll that portfolio changes take. Families are made up of human beings and managers are human beings. Firing a manager is, like firing an employee, a traumatic event for both parties. Institutions, on the other hand, are, well, institutions.

Finally, the nontaxability of institutional portfolios means that rebalancing activities, like manager terminations, are simpler and less costly for institutional investors. Long and careful research has shown the importance of rebalancing to achieving the best results from an asset allocation strategy, and hence many institutions automatically rebalance their portfolios when strategic ranges have been exceeded. Unfortunately for family investors, the research on the benefits of rebalancing was conducted on nontaxable portfolios. For families, the rebalancing issue is much more complex, requiring a careful and mainly intuitive weighing of the benefits of rebalancing against the negative tax consequences of doing so.

In short, institutional investors largely live in a world where performance monitoring and portfolio rebalancing is mainly a quantitative activity. Families live in a world where monitoring and rebalancing are far more qualitative than quantitative in nature, and hence they are aspects of the portfolio management process that are far more nuanced, more complex, and more judgment based.

PERFORMANCE MONITORING

Family investors may be receiving performance reports from a variety of sources. Money managers send reports to their clients, bank custodians send reports, and if the family has retained an overall advisor, such as an investment consultant, that advisor will also be sending reports. With so many sources of information about performance, we might imagine that most investors do a good job of monitoring investment performance. But nothing could be further from the truth. The source of the failure lies in the complexity of performance reports, in the differing kinds of reports we receive, and in the inability of many of us to interpret the reports appropriately.

Money Manager Reports

All money managers send account reports to their clients, but that's about all that can be said. Some managers send monthly reports, some send quarterly reports, some (especially alternative asset managers) send only annual reports. However frequently or infrequently they send out reports, some managers show only account balances, while others show performance for that period, and some show performance as well for prior periods. Among those managers who show performance, some compare that performance against appropriate benchmarks and some do not. Among those who show performance against benchmarks, some managers use consistent measuring periods and some do not.[1] Finally, managers report only on their own performance, not the performance of other managers, so families who rely only on manager reporting will find it difficult—indeed, well-nigh impossible—to produce consolidated reports for the entire portfolio.

As a result of these deficiencies, investors who rely solely on money manager reports to monitor their performance are likely to experience poor results. The only investors who might possibly get by with manager-only reporting are families with very large and sophisticated family offices that can compute—and recompute—manager performance results in ways that are consistent across the portfolio.

Bank Custody Reports

As discussed in Chapter 22, it will be a rare substantial family investor who should even think about managing a complex investment portfolio without engaging a bank to serve as custodian of the investment assets. The main reason for this is to safeguard the funds, but consolidated reporting is an almost equally important advantage. Unlike money managers, a custodian will send monthly account reports on every account in the portfolio,[2] as well as a total value for the portfolio as a whole. Typically, these reports show account values, along with cost basis information for each security, statements of income, principal appreciation, a gain/loss report, and so on. Bank custody reports typically do not show manager or account performance, but only the actual values in each account and in the overall portfolio. Some custodians will provide performance reporting for an extra fee. In that case, the bank is acting not simply as a custodian but as an overall advisor, and is producing reports similar to those produced by investment consulting firms, as discussed below.[3]

Investment Consultant Reports

The main shortcoming of performance reports, from whatever source, is that they tell us in quantitative terms how we have performed, but they don't tell us whether that performance is acceptable or unacceptable or what, if anything, we should do about it. What we need, in addition to the quantitative reports, is *qualitative* performance reporting.[4]

Families who have engaged investment consulting firms or other overall advisors should be looking to those advisors for a qualitative assessment of their performance. Consultants also provide quantitative reporting, of course—indeed, the better firms will reconcile manager-reported performance with the account values and cash flows shown on the custodian's statements (but see Conflicts between Reports, below). But the real value added by an overall advisor on the performance reporting side is to give us an informed, objective, *qualitative* report on how we are doing, preferably in simple English. Performance reports from managers generally start with a description of what happened in the markets during the reporting period. That's fine, of course, but unfortunately the reports stop there. While we might be mildly curious about our managers' takes on what happened in the markets, our attention is actually galvanized by what happened in our own portfolio, and most advisors don't provide that information.

While asking for a qualitative analysis of our own performance seems a simple enough request, in fact the business of supplying investors with qualitative assessments of their performance is extraordinarily difficult to pull off. In the first place, the advisory firm must have no conflicts of interest that might corrupt its assessment of performance. This eliminates 99 percent of all the financial advisory firms in the world. Next, the firm must actually employ senior investment professionals who are *able* to assess investment performance. Just to take a simple example, imagine a small-cap value manager that has underperformed its benchmark for two consecutive years. Should the manager be terminated, or should the firm be given more of our capital? Either decision could prove to be brilliant or disastrous, and the decision is rarely straightforward.

Finally, the firm must assign to its individual advisors a small-enough client load so that the advisors can actually take the time to prepare qualitative assessments. Brokerage firms typically assign hundreds of accounts to each rep, while bank relationship officers must manage scores of clients. Any advisor who handles more than about two dozen accounts will be in way over his or her head when it comes to providing qualitative, customized assessments of performance.

Typical consulting firm performance reports will consist of monthly reports on manager performance and quarterly reports on consolidated account performance. The monthly reports simply take the performance reported by the manager and compare it to an appropriate benchmark for the period and, typically, the year to date. The quarterly reports will reconcile manager account statements with the account statements produced by the custodian; will provide performance data on each manager and account, as well as for the consolidated portfolio; will comment specifically on the performance of each account; and will make any recommendations that the client should consider for that period.

Conflicts between Reports

Family investors who engage money managers and a custodian will find that the statements produced by the manager and the statements produced by the custodian frequently show different balances. While these differences are usually small, they are nonetheless alarming. (Imagine that, at the end of the month, we received a statement from our bank showing that our checking account balance was "somewhere around $52,000!")

The main culprit in discrepancies between managers and custodians has to do with the differing protocols used by each. When a security trade is made, the pricing of the trade is established by the *trade date*, but the actual proceeds change hands on the *settlement date*. For a money manager, it is the trade date that matters, because that date establishes the price the firm will receive from a sale or will pay on a buy, and it is that price that becomes a part of the firm's permanent track record. Hence, managers tend to prepare account statements using trade dates.

From the perspective of a custodian, however, what matters is whether the proceeds from a trade are successfully received into the account, and what the value of those proceeds is. Until the proceeds from a transaction are actually received into the account, the matter is purely hypothetical. Hence, banks tend to prepare accounts using settlement dates. Managers, in other words, are engaged in a performance game, while custodians are engaged in a money-counting game.

Inevitably, some securities transactions will straddle the closing date for the preparation of account reports. If the trade date for a transaction is September 30, the manager who made the trade will show the proceeds of the trade in its account statements. As far as the bank is concerned, however, no proceeds from the trade have been received into the account. Hence, the bank will not show those proceeds on its account statements for the period ending September 30.

Other discrepancies can arise as the result of decisions about accruing dividends and interest payments, the use of different securities pricing services, and so on. As noted earlier, many kinds of investment assets can't be held in a traditional custody account, and will be carried as a lone item entry by the bank. These line items are often not updated in a timely way.

Unfortunately, when we simply look at differing balances sent to us by managers and banks, it is impossible to know whether the discrepancies are related to harmless protocol-timing issues, or whether the errors may be more serious. Very large family offices will reconcile manager and bank statements, but most families will need to engage someone to handle this chore (and a chore it is!) on their behalf. The usual "someone" is an investment consulting firm that has built a sophisticated back office that downloads account data from the custodian on a daily basis.

Interpreting Performance Reports

As noted above, quantitative performance reports tell us very little. If our three U.S. large-cap managers all underperformed the S&P 500 for the month or quarter, should we be alarmed or not? It's impossible to know without knowing a great deal about the nature of the managers and the nature of the markets during that quarter. If our small-cap value manager suddenly begins to outperform its peers by substantial margins, should we be moving more capital to the firm or should we be deeply worried about style drift? What sort of benchmark should we be using to measure the performance of our overall portfolio, and should that benchmark be different over shorter and longer periods? If a blowup has occurred at a hedge fund included in our hedge fund of funds, should we be worried or is it inevitable that occasional blowups will occur?

As these questions suggest, interpreting quantitative performance reports is not a game to be played in short pants. The difficulties associated with interpreting performance reports have led family investors to make one of two opposite mistakes. Some families terminate managers or revise their portfolio strategies based on apparent-but-unreal performance deficits, resulting in excessive and expensive manager turnover and in sudden, amateurish changes in investment strategy. Other families, faced with the difficulties of interpreting performance, simply don't do it at all, living for years with underperforming managers and portfolios until some horrible event awakens them from their slumbers.

Unless a family is extremely experienced, or unless it can afford a very sophisticated family office, most private investors will need to engage an advisor to help interpret performance and make recommendations based on those interpretations.

PRACTICE TIP

A very big question is not so much whether the client can interpret complex investment performance reports, but whether the *advisor* can interpret them. Fortunately, the technology (especially regarding attribution analysis) is getting better.

Even so, for firms that have many clients and few senior advisors, the challenge of getting plain-English explanations of performance out to all clients is a huge one. Huge as it is, however, it's absolutely necessary if you want to be in the wealth advisory business. Assigning a senior advisor to draft explanations of performance, at least for issues that are common to most clients, will go a long way toward keeping clients happy.

Monitoring Manager Performance

We have touched on this topic before (see Chapter 17), but I would be remiss if I didn't emphasize the important point that most manager terminations are costly mistakes. Mistakes in the simple sense that the terminated manager outperforms the replacement manager over the next market cycle; costly in the sense that we not only give up the superior return produced by the terminated manager, but we must also pay the transaction costs, taxes, time, and emotional costs associated with moving from one manager to another.

Most manager terminations occur for what we imagine to be performance reasons. But in fact only a small minority of managers who are terminated really deserved to be terminated—and it is we investors who bear most of the costs associated with unnecessary terminations. Effective manager monitoring requires that we take each of the following steps:

- First, whenever a manager is engaged, we should prepare guidelines (see sample on the companion website for this book at www.wiley.com/go/stewardshipofwealth) for that manager and have those guidelines approved by the manager. The guidelines need not be extensive or elaborate, but they should cover such issues as:
  - The manager's acknowledgement that the account will be managed in accordance with the family's investment policy statement.
  - Performance expectations, including the benchmark, manager universe, and time horizon that will be used to measure the manager's performance.
  - The timing and nature of reports the manager will submit.
  - An agenda for meetings to be held with the manager, and the frequency of those meetings. Managers are superb at coopting the agenda of meetings, spending most of the time talking about the state of the markets, the view of the Federal Reserve Bank, the outlook for interest rates and the economy, and so on. Everything, that is, except the manager's performance.
- If the manager's performance is to be measured over an entire market cycle, it should be a very rare case that the manager would be terminated for performance reasons before that time has expired. Otherwise, we are probably overreacting to temporary market events or transient underperformance.
- We should take care to measure the manager against *appropriate* benchmarks and *appropriate* manager universes. A manager can produce lousy absolute performance and still be someone we want to keep in our portfolio: If the sector in which the manager works has produced dismal results, all managers working in that sector are likely to be doing the same. Trading one manager for another will accomplish nothing.
- On the other hand, substantial changes in the management firm itself should be cause for alarm even if performance has not deteriorated. Substantial changes mean that we are no longer dealing with the firm we engaged, but a somewhat different firm. The following changes should be of special concern:
  - Very substantial growth or shrinkage in the manager's asset base since the firm was engaged.

- Loss of key professional personnel.
- Sale of the firm or sale of a significant interest in the firm (significant enough to put lots of cash in the senior professionals' pockets).
- Significant personnel turnover or disarray even below the senior professional level.
- Failure of the senior professionals to provide for the continuation of the firm by bringing along younger professionals and sharing equity with them.
- Any (repeat *any*) ethical failure.

REBALANCING TAXABLE PORTFOLIOS

As noted above, most of the research on the benefits of rebalancing was performed on investment portfolios that were exempt from taxes. Because the tax costs associated with rebalancing taxable accounts can be very substantial, this research is suspect in the private client world. As a result, rebalancing of family portfolios needs to be more of a qualitative than a quantitative process, although of course it should be both.

As a review, we need to keep in mind the purpose of periodic rebalancing. Let's assume that we start with a portfolio strategy that is exactly aligned with our target asset allocation. As time goes by, our portfolio will drift away from the target allocation, as various sectors of the markets rise or fall faster than other sectors. Over time, our equity allocations will tend to grow much faster than our cash and fixed-income portfolios, but over the short term the opposite phenomenon could occur. In either event, the risk level of our portfolio will have changed, eventually substantially.

Suppose, for example, our target allocation has 55 percent in stocks, 35 percent in bonds, and 10 percent in hedge funds. In the absence of rebalancing, we may wake up some day to find that our portfolio is now invested 70 percent in stocks, 15 percent in hedge, and 15 percent in bonds. This is a vastly more risky portfolio than we set out to own, and in a bad market environment it will be hit hard—far harder than we are likely to tolerate without flinching badly.

Or assume that the markets have been in a bear phase. In the absence of rebalancing we may wake up to find that we are invested 40 percent in stocks, 15 percent in hedge, and 45 percent in bonds. This is far too cautious a portfolio for us. When the markets recover we will be largely left behind.

Instead of allowing our portfolio to drift with the whims of the market, we should be rebalancing periodically. But simply saying so raises a whole host of issues. Let's examine a few of the more important ones.

Setting Strategic Ranges

As with institutional investors, family investors will want to start with a target asset allocation strategy and then establish strategic ranges around these targets within which the portfolio will be allowed to move before rebalancing is considered. But a family's strategic ranges should generally be wider than an institution's. Allocation ranges that are too narrow will result in too-frequent rebalancing, and for taxable investors the cost of rebalancing will likely outweigh the benefits.

How wide should the "bands" be within which the portfolio can fluctuate? Too little attention has been given to this issue. As mentioned previously, most advisors use the same ranges for families that they have been using with institutions. But because the cost of rebalancing taxable portfolios is greater, the strategic bands should be wider. Even advisors who advocate wider bands for families tend simply to add and subtract 5 percent or 10 percent to or from the target allocation, resulting in silly outcomes. For example, an asset class with a target allocation of 40 percent might be allowed to fluctuate between 35 percent and 45 percent (12.5 percent either way), while an asset class with a 10 percent target allocation will be allowed to fluctuate between 5 percent and 15 percent (100 percent either way!)

A better approach would be to set the bands to describe a range of fluctuation that is consistent with the expected volatility of the asset class. For example, if an asset class has an after-tax standard deviation of 20 percent, why not start by setting the strategic ranges at plus or minus 20 percent? If an asset class has an after-tax S.D. of 8 percent, why not start with that as the strategic range? We can adjust these ranges upward or downward depending on how we feel about the tax issue, but the adjustments should be consistent with the expected volatility of the asset class, as well as its tax treatment.

Rebalance Back to What?

Let's assume that we have decided to rebalance our portfolio because our U.S. large-cap exposure, which has a target of 25 percent and a range of 20 percent to 30 percent, is sitting at 32 percent. Should we rebalance back to the target allocation (25 percent) or merely back to the top of the range (30 percent)? There is no purely quantitative answer to this question. If rebalancing can be done inexpensively, the better answer is to rebalance back to the target. But if rebalancing is going to be expensive, the better answer (assuming we are going to rebalance at all) is to rebalance only back to the top of the range. We need to keep in mind, however, that if we rebalance only back to the top of the range, a strongly rising market will require us to rebalance frequently.

A second issue to consider is whether valuations in the U.S. large-cap sector are high or low by historical standards. If we are at a 32 percent position in the sector but valuations remain low, we should be less eager to pay taxes and rebalance. But if valuations are high, rebalancing will be a more compelling idea.

How Often to Rebalance?

The issue here is highly qualitative, almost intuitive. My view is that taxable investors should set quantitative targets, not calendar targets. If an asset class has a 25 percent target exposure and a strategic range of 20 percent to 30 percent, we should *consider* rebalancing when the range is exceeded on either side. The default position should be to rebalance, but that default can be overcome if the cost of rebalancing is very high or if market valuations suggest that rebalancing won't prove rewarding. We should not rebalance automatically on a quarterly basis, as many institutional investors do.

The default position can also be overcome for valuation reasons, as noted above. If we are out of balance on the upside, and if valuations for the asset class remain low or reasonable,[5] we might postpone rebalancing, being reasonably confident that a price collapse is unlikely. If we are out of balance on the downside, there will be no tax consequence associated with buying into the asset class. The question will be where we get the cash to make the buys and what the tax consequences, and valuation conditions, are in the cash source market class.

We should also have in place an over- or underexposure level that *requires* rebalancing, regardless of the cost and regardless of what we think of market valuations. That level might be set at double the normal range, or at whatever seems reasonable (but probably not more than double). When we are out of balance by that amount we *must* rebalance. Otherwise, our enthusiasm or pessimism will seriously compromise our investment results.

Thus, the targets, strategic ranges, and maximum and minimum ranges for two hypothetical asset classes (the first with a 20 percent S.D. and the second with a 10 percent S.D.) might look something like this:

Target Exposure	Normal Range (rebalancing recommended)	Maximum Range (rebalancing required)
25%	20%–30%	15%–35%
15%	13.5%–16.5%	12%–18%

We would create the same targets, normal ranges, and maximum ranges for each asset class.

CONCLUSION: MONITORING AND REBALANCING ARE STEWARDSHIP ISSUES

Monitoring the performance of investment portfolios and rebalancing them in a disciplined fashion are not exactly the most exciting aspects of wealth management, but they are crucial to successful outcomes. We can do everything else right, fail here, and find that we have discharged our stewardship responsibilities poorly.

The phrase "in a disciplined fashion" was not an accident. There are two reasons why families fail to monitor portfolios appropriately and to rebalance them properly. The first is the boredom factor, and the answer to that is the same answer we would give to any boring-but-important job: discipline. It's simply part of the job we have to do, and we have to take the good with the bad. Otherwise, we are not intelligent investors carrying out serious stewardship responsibilities, we are simply dilettantes.

The second obstacle is overenthusiasm or overpessimism. If the markets are in a bull phase, we will be sorely tempted to let our gains run. Some of that is acceptable—markets do tend to be characterized by momentum. But there are limits. We originally set those limits (I hope) in calm moments, before we were faced with temptation. Then, no matter how strong the markets appear to be, and no matter how certain we are that they will continue to rise, once our maximum exposure has been reached we must—must—rebalance. Taking money off the table during strong markets is the way wealth is preserved.

Similarly, overpessimism can also be the enemy of wealth preservation. In a bear market our lower ranges will be frequently tested and often exceeded, and it can be very tempting to ignore the absolute minimum exposures we set for ourselves—or, worse, to abandon those market sectors altogether. All this will do is put us on the sidelines when the recovery occurs. We will have taken our lumps during the bear phase of the market, but we won't get the benefit of the bull phase. This is no way to run a portfolio.

PRACTICE TIP

Investors sometimes point out that disciplined rebalancing actually causes harm to a portfolio. For example, during much of the 1980s and 1990s, rebalancing in international and emerging markets equities generally took money out of better-performing domestic stocks and put it in underperforming foreign stocks, retarding the growth of the

(Continued)

PRACTICE TIP (Continued)

portfolio. True enough—but only true *in retrospect*, which is the case with every aspect of wealth management. If we had known that foreign stocks would underperform, we certainly would have avoided them, but that outcome was unknowable. People who claim they know in advance which assets will outperform—that is, market timers—have the worst of all investment track records.

Disciplined rebalancing will, on occasion, slightly hurt our clients' performance, rather than help it. But overall it will help far more than it will hurt, and we want those odds on our side. Most important of all—and it's crucial to communicate this to clients—rebalancing keeps the risk level of the portfolio within the bounds we and the client have already established.

NOTES

1. In other words, the measuring period might be selected to show off the manager's performance in the best possible light. See the discussion in Chapter 17.
2. Some investment accounts cannot be custodied in the normal meaning of the word. Private equity partnerships, hedge funds, real estate, and so on are examples of accounts that are not held in bank custody. The values of these accounts are typically shown by custodians as line item entries. In addition, mutual funds employ their own custodians, so that investors who want to see mutual fund accounts consolidated with their custodied accounts will have to ask their custodians to show them as line item entries as well.
3. There is also a growing list of firms that provide performance-only services.
4. Earlier in my career, when I was working in a large family office, we received extremely detailed, quantitative performance reports from our advisor every quarter. These reports were so extensive that they formed a pile 11 inches high on the corner of my desk. Somewhere in that pile was something I needed to worry about, but the likelihood that I would find it was extremely remote.
5. That is, if valuations are low or reasonable by *historical* standards. Convincing ourselves that, although P/E ratios of 40 are high by historical standards, they are reasonable because we are in a "new paradigm," is a recipe for investment disaster.

CHAPTER 21

Investment Policy Statements

*I think I did pretty well, considering I started out with nothing but
a bunch of blank paper.*

—Steve Martin

Everyone who participates importantly in the management of a large investment portfolio should think of themselves as fiduciaries, whether or not they are fiduciaries in the legal sense. Going into the process with this mind-set will result in getting a lot of things right the first time, without having to go back and redo everything after trouble arises. Thus, family members, members of an institutional or family investment committee, investment advisors, and so on should all have a fiduciary mind-set.

One extremely important fiduciary activity is to *document every significant policy that guides the management of the portfolio.* Some of these policies will be incorporated into an investment policy statement, some may be found in a separate spending policy statement, some may take the form of manager guidelines or guidelines for the management of cash. But it doesn't matter what the issue is—*if it's important, write it down!*

In this chapter I will discuss the major kinds of written investment policies most substantial investors will need, and will give examples of written policies that I consider to be well crafted.

THE INVESTMENT POLICY STATEMENT

The form of an investment policy statement (IPS) is to some extent a matter of individual preference. Some families prefer extensive, highly detailed policy statements covering every possible contingency, whereas others prefers brief, one- or two-page documents touching on only the most important points.

My personal feeling is that for a family, more is better, especially when the "more" focuses on the family itself: its antecedents, its culture, its hopes, its worries. A family IPS should be written with the thought that it will be read by a family member a generation or two down the road. It should therefore be interesting, easy to understand, nontechnical in its language, and should make the reader proud to be a member of a family that was concerned enough about the future to pen such a document.

Once a family has gone to all the trouble to design a sound investment portfolio and to think through how that portfolio will be managed and governed, the next important step is to write it all down. An investment policy statement is the written record of the work you have done, and it will serve as a guide to the management of the family's capital over the years. Though such policies can always be revisited and modified in light of experience, the development of and adherence to written policies will have several powerfully positive affects.

First, for fiduciary portfolios in the legal sense, in the rare but certain event of extremely adverse investment results, the existence of written policies will demonstrate the thoughtfulness and prudence with which you have approached the challenge of managing the capital. Modern concepts of prudence, as articulated, for example, in the Prudent Investor Rule, the Uniform Management of Institutional Funds Act, and similar laws, are not outcome oriented but *process oriented*. Virtually any security and any investment strategy can be prudent if it is adopted thoughtfully and with reference to the actual needs and objectives of the family, and with reference to the overall risk level of the portfolio. The fact that the security became worthless or the strategy failed is largely irrelevant, as many good ideas fail. On the other hand, even relatively uncontroversial investment strategies can be problematic if they were adopted with little thought, if they were inappropriate to the needs of the family, or if the trustees provided little ongoing oversight of their results.

Second, and more important, the existence of and adherence to thoughtfully developed investment policies and strategies that are appropriate to the needs and objectives of a particular family will go a long way toward preventing major investment disasters in the first place and ensuring that the long-term performance of the portfolio will be satisfactory.

Over time, the reasons behind even the best-designed portfolio can be forgotten or become confused. This is especially likely to be the case during periods of market turmoil, when the temptation to depart from long-term strategies can seem overwhelming. A specific memorialization of the reasons why long-term strategies were adopted can temper the desire to make ill-considered, short-term changes in the portfolio and can offer a measure of comfort during times of stress.

Moreover, many family portfolios are managed by individuals whose identities change periodically—family members and investment committee members, for example. In such cases disagreements can easily arise regarding the proper course to be taken, the role played by individual investments, or the reasons certain policies and strategies were adopted. The existence of a written investment policy statement serves as an objective method of resolving such disagreements, and, indeed, as a way of reducing the likelihood that such disagreements will arise.

Most financial advisors have forms of investment policy statements, but serious family investors will use those forms only as a general guide. If you simply adopt your advisor's form, it is unlikely that you will actually have thought seriously about the issues addressed in the statement. Instead, families should draft their own statements, putting the language in their own words. The important point is not the form or length of the statement, but that you prepared it yourself to meet your own needs, and that it remains a real, living document. I have placed a sample IPS for a family on the Web at www.wiley.com/go/stewardshipofwealth, password: curtis2012.

SPENDING POLICY STATEMENTS

Spending statements arose in the institutional context, because spending from the endowment is a critical part of the life of all but the smallest institutions. But spending statements can be extremely useful to family investors, too. Many family members will not be knowledgeable about the nexus between spending and preservation of the family's capital, and a spending policy statement can outline why it is crucial to keep spending under control. See www.wiley.com/go/stewardshipofwealth for a sample Spending Policy Statement.

CASH GUIDELINES

Some families maintain very substantial cash reserves for various reasons. (Note that one reason *not* to hold a large cash reserve is that it will act as significant drag on portfolio returns over time.) For families with substantial cash, cash management guidelines are an important aspect of investment policy. See www.wiley.com/go/stewardshipofwealth for a sample of guidelines for the management of cash.

MANAGER GUIDELINES

Every separate account manager should manage the family's portfolio according to written guidelines. For example, what are acceptable policies for holding cash in the portfolio? Are there minimum and maximum capitalization weightings that are acceptable to the family? How actively will taxes be managed? These and many other issues should be specifically addressed in the guidelines for each manager. The companion website (www.wiley.com/go/stewardshipofwealth) includes a sample manager guideline.

THE INVESTMENT COMMITTEE POLICY MANUAL

In recent years many families who have an investment committee have found it useful to adopt an operating manual for the committee. All too often, committee meetings wander here and there depending on what's happened recently in the markets. Often the meetings are dominated by the investment professionals (consultants, money managers, banks) who don't necessarily talk about the most important issues. I've placed an example of an operating manual at www.wiley.com/go/stewardshipofwealth.

LETTERS TO THE FAMILY

Although not formal fiduciary documents, a letter from the patriarch or matriarch to children, grandchildren, trustees, or more remote descendants can have even greater effect, because it is a very personal document. See the companion website (www.wiley.com/go/stewardshipofwealth) for samples of effective letters.

CONCLUSION: DON'T SKIMP ON DOCUMENTING YOUR DECISIONMAKING

Whether of not we are acting in a fiduciary manner as a legal matter, everything we do with our family's wealth is a fiduciary activity in the ethical sense: these activities matter to us, to our children, to our grandchildren, and even to more remote generations. The investment policy statement, for example, is the keystone document and it is almost impossible to spend too much time on it. But spending policies, manager guidelines and investment committee policy manuals are also very important and could be crucial for some families.

And let's not forget letters to the family. If you have spent an adult lifetime stewarding your family's wealth, writing down the key points you've learned will be a powerful influence on younger family members. In fact, I can envision a multigenerational series of such letters, each penned by the next steward in his or her turn over the years. What a wonderful legacy for any family!

CHAPTER 22

Miscellaneous Challenges for Private Investors

The purpose of this chapter is to touch on a variety of topics that, for one reason or another, don't seem to require a full chapter. Some if these issues are large and complex, but apply very rarely or only to a small group of private investors. Others are important but relatively straightforward. As an assist in navigating this long chapter, here is an outline of the topics covered:

Asset custody

Concentrated stock positions

Establishing a family office

Family investment partnerships

Philanthropy

ASSET CUSTODY

For almost all private investors, asset custody will form the base on which all else is built. A custodian—typically a very large bank—safeguards investment assets by holding them in a segregated account owned by the investor.[1] The fact that the account is segregated is important. By "segregated" I mean that the investor's assets are formally segregated from the assets of the bank that is serving as the custodian. In the unlikely event that the bank should go bankrupt,[2] the investor's assets will not be subject to the claims of the bank's creditors. Hence, although there might be some delay in retrieving the assets, and some cost and annoyance, the investor will in fact get his assets back.

This is not the case, it is important to note, with brokerage firms that are acting as a custodian. If the broker goes under, the investor's assets go with it. For this reason, all brokerage firms carry vast amounts of insurance, designed to protect investors against just this possibility. Unfortunately, one has to wonder whether the insurance firms themselves could survive the bankruptcy of a major brokerage house.

Surprising numbers of investors don't bother to have their assets held safely in a custody arrangement, but simply place the assets at the disposal of whoever is managing the money. In such a case they are placing themselves entirely at the mercy of the honesty of the money management firm and all its employees.

A few years ago a money manager named John Gardner Black set up his own "custodian," pointing out to investors that if they used his custody operation there would be no charge, whereas if they kept their money in custody with banks, the banks would charge several basis points (a basis point is 1/100 of 1 percent). A good many of Black's clients took him up on the offer, whereupon Black proceeded to spend their money on himself and his lifestyle. Black is now in jail, but his clients' money is gone.

In essence, a custodian holds and reports on all the client's investment assets, including cash and securities. Money managers engaged by a family will be given a limited power of attorney to direct the investment of the funds assigned to that manager (the custodian will set up separate accounts for each manager), but those managers will not have access to the cash or securities in the account. In other words, if a rogue manager attempts to misappropriate assets entrusted to him, he will not be able to gain access to the client's assets because no one, other than the client and those the client designates, can withdraw assets from the bank's custody or transfer them to other accounts.

Note that certain types of accounts are inherently not subject to actual custody, and are reported by the custodian only as line-item entries. Typical examples include mutual funds (each mutual fund has its own custodian), hedge funds (which are custodied, in a very limited sense, by a prime broker—see Chapter 15), private equity funds (which are not custodied at all), and so on.

What Services Does a Custodian Offer?

A master custodian will typically provide all the following services:

- Provide for safekeeping of the client's investment assets domestically and internationally
- Maintain accurate and timely records of the client's investments
- Consolidate assets as necessary for reporting purposes
- Clear and settle trades made at the direction of the client's money managers
- Transfer assets as directed only by the client

- Pay bills for various services (e.g., money manager fees)
- Provide multicurrency reporting for international assets
- Prepare reports on a cash or accrual basis
- Report transactions on a trade or settlement date basis
- Maintain records and processing trades on a tax-lot basis
- Maintain tax characteristics (interest, dividends, cost basis, etc.)
- Maintain compliance monitoring systems to ensure that managers adhere to whatever investment guidelines the client has put in place
- Provide unitized accounting and interim valuations
- Prepare tax returns[3]
- Maintain accounting for family investment partnerships (note that only a few very high-end custodians offer this service)

Finally, most institutions that offer custodial services also offer many other financial services, including banking, trust services, asset management, and so on. In rare cases it may make financial sense to allow a custodian bank also to manage certain assets for us. When a custodian has a best-in-class product in a particular asset class and is willing to discount its management fee because of the custody relationship (or to discount its custody fee because of the management relationship), the family may be better off allowing the custodian to manage those assets. But a custodian's asset management products must always be evaluated entirely separately from its custodial skills.

Evaluating Custodians

It's easy to identify the few financial institutions that aspire to excellence in the custody business. This is because asset custody is an extremely capital-intensive business, requiring massive and ongoing investments in technology and personnel merely to stay even with the competition. At the same time, custody is largely a commodity business with low profit margins. This unhappy combination of massive investment and low profits means that, globally, there are only a relative handful of institutions that have chosen to compete in this business.

However, once the small group of best-in-class custodians has been identified, it is more difficult to select the most appropriate custodian for our particular needs. At bottom, the decision comes down to extensive day-by-day experience with the performance of individual custodians handling different kinds of clients and assets. In making recommendations to clients about appropriate custodian candidates, the better advisors proceed as follows:

- Based on the advisor's knowledge of the client's needs and the skill set of the various best-in-class custodial institutions, the list of attractive candidates should be winnowed down to two or three.

- Each finalist institution should be sent an RFP (request for proposal) seeking answers to a large number of questions about the institution's custodial abilities, overall institutional strength, how they will meet the client's needs as investors, and so on. Responses to those RFPs can then be consolidated into a custodian comparison matrix for easy comparison by the client and its advisor.
- The client or its financial advisor should review each candidate's SSAE 16, an annual form global custody banks are required to file.[4]
- The primary contacts for each institution should be individually interviewed, focusing on areas of particular importance to our account.
- Fee bids should be sought from the institutions most likely to be appropriate to our needs.

Custody Pricing

Though asset custody is one of the true bargains in the investment business, it's easy to misprice custody services. Custodian pricing can be maddeningly complex, especially for taxable investors. Typically, a custodian will charge an overall fee that is asset based. This is simple enough and can easily be compared across vendors.

Unfortunately, the asset-based fee is only the beginning. Depending on the custodian, additional fees will apply for each managed account, for each line-item entry (e.g., mutual funds or hedge funds), for each transaction that is posted (dividends and income, for example) and so on. International separate accounts are typically more expensive because of the army of subcustodians that is required and the problem of dealing with multiple currencies. Because no two custodians will submit exactly comparable bids across the board, it's easy to select a custodian that appears to offer the best price, only to find out that we are being nickeled-and-dimed to death with other fees. Whenever possible, therefore, families should put in their RFP a reasonably exact picture of what the portfolio will look like. This won't make comparing custody bids easy, but it will help ensure that the family doesn't make a decision that turns out, inadvertently, to be penny-wise and pound-foolish.

Families will also want to be sure that they aren't paying for services they don't want or need. For example, most custodians will carry mutual funds as a line-item entry, updating the value of the fund and the number of shares held once a month. Another option is to have the custodian report the mutual fund in a way that allows the family to view the underlying shares. Finally, the family can hold the mutual fund completely outside the custody arrangement, receiving statements directly from the fund company and following pricing via the fund company's website.

The cost of the first option is typically something like $500/year—in many cases there is no cost at all. The cost of the last option is typically nothing (other than our time). The cost of the middle option is typically whatever basis point fee we negotiated. (For a ten million dollar account in the Vanguard Index 500 Fund, we might be paying 5 basis points for custody in addition to the 12 basis points we are paying for the Vanguard fund—a gigantic 42 percent increase in cost.) Few families will find a crucial need to drill down into the actual mutual fund holdings, and for those few who do, the best source is probably the Vanguard website.

PRACTICE TIP

You will likely notice that your clients have a recurring tendency to obsess about custody pricing, perhaps because it is so transparent.

It's not unusual to find a family agonizing over a one-basis-point (1/100 of 1 percent) reduction in their custody costs, spending months negotiating with the custodian. But even on a $100 million account, this will save only $10,000 per year.

Meanwhile, the same family will have engaged an active U.S. large-cap manager managing $10 million, to whom they are paying 85 basis points, and who has underperformed the Vanguard 500 Index Fund by 30 basis points per year over time. This arrangement is costing the family more than $100,000 per year, but nothing is done about it, perhaps because the manager isn't sending the family a bill for the cost every month.

Although no one should overpay for custody, it is obviously better to spend our advisory time on the $100,000 problems rather than the $10,000 problems.

Custody for Taxable Accounts

Until 10 or 15 years ago, custodians largely ignored the needs of taxable investors. Most large families tended to be captive clients of a local or national trust company anyway. But in recent years custodians have realized that taxable custody is by far the most rapidly growing part of the business, and they have made up for lost time by dramatically improving the quality of their services for taxable investors. Today, almost any bank that would be a serious candidate to custody a large institutional account will also be a serious candidate to custody a large taxable account.

Services provided to taxable investors will include those offered to nontaxable accounts, but will also include careful tending to tax issues, especially tracking the tax cost basis of securities across all the family's accounts. Without this familywide cost basis tracking, it will be extremely difficult to tax-manage the portfolio. For example, one manager may be sitting on nothing but unrealized gains, while another may be sitting on nothing but unrealized losses. If the first manager realizes its gains and the second doesn't realize its losses, the family will be stuck with a high—and completely unnecessary—tax bill.

In addition, most, though not all, custodians can provide accounting services for family investment partnerships (see the following discussion).

Securities Lending

In an effort to reduce or even eliminate the costs of custody, some families engage in securities lending transactions. A well-structured securities lending operation can not only offset the costs of custody, but can even be a small profit center. Unfortunately, securities lending is a dicey business, and only the largest and most sophisticated families should even consider engaging in it.

Securities lending exists to meet the needs of investors who wish to sell securities short—typically, hedge fund managers, but also including other investors. In a short-sale transaction, the manager borrows a security from another investor and sells it. Because the manager doesn't own the security it has sold, it will have to replace that security eventually, by buying it back in the open market. The manager hopes the price of the security will decline, in which case the security can be repurchased at a lower price, locking in a profit. But even if the price of the security rises, the manager will have to purchase it and return it to the investor who has lent it in the first place.

Because custodian banks hold millions of securities, they are obvious sources for brokers who want to locate securities their clients can sell short. Custodians will therefore establish securities lending businesses and may ask custody clients to make their securities available for lending. The technicalities of this business are too intricate to go into in depth, but in essence the borrower of a security pays for the privilege by paying an interest rate somewhat above the Treasury bill rate. Thus, for the lender of the securities, the transaction appears to be ideal: The lender is receiving interest for doing essentially nothing.[5] The realities, however, are more complex and troublesome.

In the first place, there are so many potential lenders of the most heavily traded securities (U.S. large-cap stocks)[6] that profit margins on the lending of such securities have disappeared. Most of the action therefore involves foreign securities and smaller securities, many of which are difficult to short. For most families, these sectors won't be large enough for the additional income to be meaningful.

A worse problem is counterparty risk—the risk that the security we have lent won't be returned, perhaps because the borrower or broker has gone bankrupt. Though such events are rare, they are not unheard-of, and one default can wipe out years and years of securities lending profits.

The reality is, therefore, that most families should avoid securities lending. It's a difficult business to understand, and the risks aren't, for the most part, worth the candle.

Brokers as Custodians

Unlike banks, brokers don't typically impose a separate charge for holding securities in custody. This is true both for traditional full-service brokers like Merrill Lynch and for discount houses like Charles Schwab. Instead, brokerage firms that hold our securities require that all or most trades take place through their own brokerage operations. As a result, it is important for us to compare the hidden cost of this directed trading against the fully transparent cost of bank custody. For smaller accounts and those invested mainly in mutual funds, broker custody may be less expensive. For larger accounts invested in separate account products, however, bank custody is likely to be more cost effective.

In addition, as noted above, brokerage firms don't hold our assets in accounts that are segregated from the brokers' own assets. In the event of a bankruptcy, creditors of the brokerage house can seize our assets right along with the broker's own funds.

PRACTICE TIP

The recent, spectacular failure of MF Global Holdings, Ltd., founded and headed by former New Jersey Governor (and, later, Senator), Jon S. Corzine, should serve as a cannon shot across the bow of investors—and their advisors—who have been asleep at the switch.

In its death throes, MF Global either intentionally or unintentionally (or, most likely, recklessly) used customer funds as its own. Those funds were seized by creditors and, at this writing, $1.6 billion of customer money is still missing. That's nearly a quarter of all the customer assets at the firm.

The principle needs to be kept firmly in our clients' minds and in our minds as advisors: Customer money in bank custody is safe, whereas no one knows what will happen to customer money in a broker's hands.

PRACTICE TIP

Largely for reasons of simplicity, many advisory firms use only one bank custodian or, worse, one broker as custodian. I understand the reasons for this practice, but if you want to advise wealthy families, you will simply have to drop it.

One reason for this is that many wealthy families will have long and close relationships—sometimes going back generations—with a bank, and they aren't going to want to have to move custody somewhere else.

But the fundamental reason is that families' needs are different and no one bank can best suit every family's purposes. Being in the wealth advisory business means, among other things, using best practices in everything you do for the client. Using only one custodian is not a best practice.

CONCENTRATED SECURITY POSITIONS

Put all your eggs in one basket—and watch that basket!
—Warren Buffett

Memo to investors: Follow this strategy only if the person watching the basket is Warren Buffett.

In point of fact, Mr. Buffett wouldn't think of putting all his eggs in one basket. Last I looked, Berkshire Hathaway owned more than 30 individual stocks, representing a well-diversified portfolio of companies ranging from huge multinationals to mid-sized firms to local retailers. If we (or even Warren Buffett) found ourselves sitting on the odd pile of cash—say, $100 million—what are the odds that we would invest it all in one stock? The odds aren't just low, they are zero. Only a lunatic would even think about it.

Yet, when we end up, one way or another, owning only one stock, how many of us immediately diversify the position away? Sure, the situations are different, but they are different mainly in that when we own one concentrated position, rather than cash, we are likely to have a tax issue (and an emotional issue).

But it's a mistake in the first place to think of ourselves as being worth $100 million if we have an imbedded $15 million tax liability. Our real net worth is $85 million. The tax authorities are making an interest-free loan to us, and there are many ways we can leverage that opportunity. But the tax is owed and will eventually have to be paid in one way or another.

Another, related, excuse goes something like this: If I sell my $100 million position in Tyco, where will I find another group of investments that will outperform Tyco net of the tax cost I'll have to pay? Merely to ask this question is solid evidence of the fact that we have missed the point. Diversifying a concentrated position isn't a matter of improving future returns, though that could easily happen. It's a matter of dodging the guided missile that is aimed precisely at our net worth.

Although a concentrated low-cost-basis position can arise in many ways, the most common circumstance occurs something like this. A family has built up a successful company over the years, and the time has come to consider selling out. The family is approached by a firm that is offering a stock-for-stock deal—in other words, the family would sell out not for cash, but for stock in the acquiring company. (There can be important tax reasons to structure the deal in this way.) The family looks at the recent performance of the acquiring company's stock and it looks quite good. The deal gets done. After the sale closes, the acquiring company's stock continues to rise, and all is well.

What's wrong with this picture? What's wrong with it is that the family is living in an unrealistic and temporary world in which their wealth seems to grow every day with no effort on their part. In fact, this is an incredibly rare (and, as noted, temporary) circumstance, and it has happened that way *because it had to happen that way*. If the acquiring company's stock had been a dog for years, the family would never have considered accepting a stock-for-stock deal. Companies are only able to make stock acquisitions during those temporary periods when their stock price is on a tear—during all other periods they have to pay cash or forgo making acquisitions. Thus, it isn't the case that the selling family has had the good fortune to sell to a company whose stock price seems extremely attractive—it always happens that way, and a family that reifies the phenomenon is making a serious mistake.

I don't mean to minimize the emotional complexity of a decision to sell all or a substantial part of a concentrated securities position. But the only way to avoid disaster is to decide in advance, in the calm before the storm, that you will not allow greed to overcome prudence. Sure, the terrific thing about holding a concentrated securities position is that it is a good way to build wealth. But the bad thing about holding a concentrated position is that it is a good way to go broke. Even if these were reciprocal outcomes for us—the pleasure of getting even richer being exactly equivalent to the pain of going broke—the trade-off would hardly be worth the candle. But notice that these are *not* perfectly equivalent outcomes: The downside is far worse than the upside is good.

Starting a business is a great way to build wealth (and also to destroy it—most businesses fail). But once the business has been built and is operating at scale, there is nothing but downside to holding on to all that stock. Big companies can't really grow much faster than the overall economy—competition is too fierce. Therefore, holding on to the stock isn't going to make you any richer than owning a diversified portfolio, even in the best case.

Ah, but the worst case—now that's a whole other enchilada. Think of those dot-com geniuses who started companies in 1998 and found themselves billionaires 20 months later. Their stock was selling for $300/share and (of course!) was going to $3,000! Why would they sell even one share? As it happened, those stocks took a big detour on the way to $3,000—namely to zero. Our dot-com geniuses went from being billionaires to being unemployed, almost overnight.

And what about the owners of Enron, Tyco, TWA, AIG, and the hundreds of failed brokerage firms and banks? Gone, all the wealth right down the drain.

But let's go back to our dot-com genius for a moment. Suppose, a few months before he started his dot-com, we had asked him what he would do if his interest in the company suddenly made him a billionaire. His answer would have been the sensible one: I would sell enough stock to ensure the security of my family and then take a flyer on the rest of the stock. So what happened once the entrepreneur actually found himself in that position? That's right—he suddenly became a genius, with infallible insight into where his stock price was headed.

Here's a factoid for you. In March of 2000, when every tech stock on the planet was preposterously overvalued and within days of crashing and burning, Duke University conducted a survey of tech chief financial officers. Eighty-two percent of those CFOs claimed their stocks were *under-valued*. Talk about mass hysteria.

It's easy for us to see the absurdity of the dot-com geniuses, and it's hard to feel sorry for them. So why can't we see it in ourselves?

Ah, I hear you saying, my company isn't a dot-com mirage, not by a long shot—my company is a Serious Global Business. Well, so were Enron and Tyco and AIG.

But your Serious Global Business doesn't have to fail for you to fail. Here's how it happens. Your Serious Global Business hits an air pocket. Maybe it's an accounting scandal, a failed strategy, a screwed-up merger. The stock price collapses from $40/share to $15/share. So what, you say. It will bounce back, this is temporary, I'm a long-term investor. Except that Competitor A comes along and buys your company, taking you out at $18/share.

At $40/share you were worth $100 million, but at $18 share, net of tax, you are worth about $38 million. If you were spending $5 million a year, that was 5 percent of $100 million. But it's 13 percent of $38 million. You'll be broke way inside of a decade.

Dealing with the Emotional Impact of a Concentrated Position

As I remarked above, I won't minimize the emotional complexity of a decision to sell out of a concentrated securities position. I've dealt with enough families in this circumstance to know better. The simple fact is that a family that owns a big single-stock position is fundamentally different from a family that owns a broadly diversified portfolio.

People who don't own very large blocks of stock find it hard to understand why people who do don't diversify. But that's because they are living in a totally different universe. A person who doesn't own a large block of stock begins by thinking, "If I had $100 million, would I invest it all in one stock? Of course not! I'm not an idiot! Ergo, people who own large blocks of stock are idiots!" (I just said this very thing, slightly more politely, in the paragraphs above.)

But a person who was born already owning a large block of stock, to say nothing of a person who built the company and therefore owns a large block of the stock, is thinking along very different lines:

- They are actually quite proud to be a large stockholder in the firm their great-grandfather founded and that means more to them than optimizing their investment returns.
- They are thinking that if they were to sell even one share of their legacy stock, Mom and Dad would disinherit them, and that would be a far worse catastrophe.
- They may be living below their means (see following) and don't care all that much if the stock price takes a (temporary) nosedive.
- They are actively involved in the company in some way and know a great deal more about it than all the people who are telling them to diversify.
- Big, successful companies do in fact go broke, but it doesn't happen very often. People who advise them to diversify are like people who say, "Houses sometimes burn down, therefore you shouldn't own a house."

- In important but hard-to-articulate ways, being a rich person who owns an important piece of an important company is a more interesting way to live than being a rich person who owns a passive portfolio.

So even if you won't diversify completely, I won't write you off as hopeless. But please consider the downsides of your concentrated position before deciding to hold on to it permanently.

PRACTICE TIP

Dealing with a client's concentrated equity position can be one of the most challenging aspects of our advisory work. For what it's worth, here's the advice I usually give my clients:

1. Best option: Sell the stock, pay the taxes, diversify the portfolio, and sleep soundly for the next three generations. Okay, they're probably not going to do this.
2. Next best option: Sell *half* the stock, pay the taxes, diversify the half they sold, *and live on that half*. For many owners of concentrated securities positions, this strategy—or something like it—may be the most appealing compromise.
3. Worst option: Keep the stock, blithely imagining that they are the luckiest investors ever born and therefore the stock price will always go up and never go very far down. But hope, I'm afraid, isn't a strategy. Your client's wealth is in grave danger.

Strategies for Diversifying Concentrated Positions

Strategies for diversifying concentrated stock positions come and go, as investors and the IRS play a never-ending game of catch-as-catch-can. Hence, it isn't worth going into extravagant detail about specific hedging and sales strategies, because any strategy could quickly become obsolete via action of the Service or a court. Nonetheless, the following are examples of strategies investors are using as this is being written:

- Outright sale of all or part of the position, especially while the 15 percent capital gains rate is still alive.
- Use of an exchange fund.

PRACTICE TIP

In some ways, the most important issue associated with using exchange funds is the behavioral one: Families tend to put lousy low-basis securities in exchange funds, not low basis-securities they expect to outperform dramatically.

As a result, unless the firm organizing the fund is very careful, our client will get diversification all right, but also a broad "dumbing down" of the investment position. Typically, investors in exchange funds will get a last look at the securities in the fund before having to make a final commitment. Take good advantage of this long last look!

- Puts, calls, and collars.

PRACTICE TIP

As with exchange funds, the main trouble with collars is probably behavioral. When Tycoon stock begins to plunge from its $50 price, our clients all too often begin to panic. "TRBL is clearly on its way to $25!" they think. "So why wait to get out until $38? Let's unwind the collar and get out while the getting's good!"

No sooner do we unwind the collar (at great expense) than TRBL, after dropping to $39, rises to $62. The same phenomenon occurs on the upside. No sooner do we establish our $38 to $63 collar than TRBL begins to skyrocket. "Obviously," the client thinks, "the stock is on its way to $100, and we're damned if we're going to get taken out at $63!" When the stock reaches $60 we unwind the collar—at great expense again—only to watch as the price touches $62, then begins a sickening plunge to $35.

A collar may or may not be a great idea—it's almost certainly a worse idea than selling all or part of the concentrated position—but once our client has entered into a collar, we and they should live with the results. Constantly unwinding collars, like constantly watching our puts expire worthless, is a good way to destroy our wealth even if the stock performs well.

- Variable prepaid forwards.
- Writing covered call options.

ESTABLISHING A FAMILY OFFICE

Many families who have experienced a significant liquidity event will consider setting up a family office.[7] However, the overwhelming majority of family offices are really convenience offices consisting of a very small number of individuals who typically have little influence over the family's important policy decisions. Instead, this staff handles routine chores such as bookkeeping, bill paying, and gatekeeping. The purpose of this section is to discuss more serious family offices: the reasons families consider establishing such an office, the typical duties of such offices, and a basic framework for designing and setting up a successful family office.

Why a Family Office?

There are thousands of family offices in the United States and many thousands more in Europe, Asia, and Latin America; powerful testimony to the attractiveness of the concept. The specific reasons families establish offices are as numerous as the families, but the most fundamental reason has to do with the challenge of stewardship: No one will take your issues as seriously as you will take them yourself.

For most of American history all but the wealthiest families[8] entrusted their assets to banks and trust companies, and the results tended to be dismal at best. Moreover, outside institutions were either indifferent to or completely ignorant of families' needs for advice on issues beyond asset management: philanthropy and intergenerational issues, for example. As a result, many families who began with substantial fortunes found that, three generations later, they were merely affluent at best. The point of a family office is to focus attention on the needs of the family, whatever those needs may be and however they may evolve over the generations.

What Is the Minimum Size for a Family Office?

The answer depends on the mission of the office. If the goal is simply to provide familywide accounting and bookkeeping, a family with as little as $50 million will find it economic to establish an office. On the other hand, a fully integrated[9] family office is probably accessible only to very large families, typically over $1 billion.

What Responsibilities Are Carried Out by a Family Office?

A full-scale family office will typically be responsible for the following activities, either by handling them directly or by outsourcing them:

> **Investment management.** For all wealthy families, Job #1 is to manage the wealth effectively, yet managing wealth on a large scale and

over the course of many decades is one of the most challenging issues most families will face.

Direct investing. Many families made their money through operating a business, real estate development, or venture investing. These skills can be applied to increase the family's wealth through direct investments in similar enterprises.

Accounting and reporting. If family members are to have any confidence in the management of the family's wealth, the family office will have to provide timely and accurate accounting, tax reporting, and performance reporting.

Coordinated estate, tax, trust, and insurance planning. Given the complex nature of the U.S. tax code, the confiscatory level of estate and gift taxation, the fiduciary responsibilities associated with complex trust planning, and the litigious nature of American society, families who neglect to coordinate their activities in these areas will find their wealth rapidly hemorrhaging.

Philanthropy. Philanthropy plays an important role in the lives of most members of wealthy families. But if charitable giving is to prove fulfilling and a method of binding the family together across generations, it will have to be pursued professionally, proactively, and with a focus on issues that resonate with family members.

Management of a closely-held business. Many families not only possess great liquid wealth, but also control an operating business. A family office can provide an ideal forum for discussing how such a business will be managed and governed, for dealing with issues posed by the fact that some family members work in the business and some don't, for thinking about capitalizing and recapitalizing the business, and so on.

Intergenerational conflict. It is a rare family, wealthy or otherwise, that doesn't experience intergenerational conflict at some point. For wealthy families, such conflicts can lead at best to unwanted publicity and at worst to deep emotional trauma and dissipation of the asset base.

Education of younger generations. A great challenge for wealthy families is raising children to be productive adults, fully capable of stewarding the family's wealth in their turn. A family office can play a highly positive role in helping educate younger generations about their future responsibilities and in offering opportunities to gain hands-on experience in dealing with those responsibilities.

Concierge services. This phrase refers to a variety of services typically needed by wealthy families, and may include bill paying, making travel arrangements, property management, oversight of aircraft operations, and so on.

Where to Begin?

The business of setting up a family office will differ from family to family, but the following steps will typically prove useful:

Where do you want to go? The first step is to think not about the family office, but about the family itself. What do you want to do with your wealth, with your talents, with your philanthropy, with your family business (if one still exists), with your children?

The mission statement. Once you know where you want to go as a family, the next step is to draft a mission statement for the family office. That mission statement will articulate the role of the family office in furthering the successful accomplishment of the family's goals.

The business plan. Now that you understand the mission of the family office, it's time to prepare a business plan detailing how that mission will be accomplished. The plan will discuss such issues as:
- The legal structure of the office (corporation, partnership, limited liability company, etc.)
- The specific activities the office will need to engage in
- Whether those activities will be carried out in-house or will be outsourced[10]
- Space needs
- The anticipated capital and operating costs of the office
- How those costs will be allocated among family members and entities[11]
- How the office will be governed and monitored
- The role of spouses (the problem is not usually the "spouse" problem, but the "ex-spouse" problem)
- How the office will report to the family.

Hiring family office personnel By far the most important consideration in hiring family office personnel is trust. For this reason, many families will launch their offices by hiring someone they have known and worked with for many years: the CFO of a family business, a trusted attorney or accountant, a seasoned family office manager, a long-time financial advisor. Beyond this, personnel decisions will shake out from the business plan. My advice, however, is *go slow*. It's a very bad outcome to hire a bunch of employees who now know all the family's secrets (and dirty laundry) and then have to terminate them.

Are There Alternatives to the Stand-Alone Family Office?

In recent years a great variety of alternatives to the stand-alone family office have been developed. Following are just a few of the options available:

Multifamily offices. A few families have gone into the business of offering family office services to families other than their own.

Law firms. Some larger law firms have organized special groups designed to provide an array of family office services to their wealthiest clients.

Accounting firms. The largest accounting firms offer services that enable families to outsource many family office activities.

PRACTICE TIP

It will be a very rare advisor who can truly advise a family from soup to nuts on whether and why and how to set up a family office. Instead, I highly recommend bringing in outside experts to advise the family.

Information about setting up a family office, as well as about alternatives to stand-alone family offices, can be obtained from the major affinity groups serving wealthy families, including the CCC Alliance,[12] the Family Office Exchange,[13] the Family Wealth Alliance,[14] and the Institute for Private Investors.[15]

FAMILY INVESTMENT PARTNERSHIPS

Most substantial families are probably familiar with family partnerships that are designed to reduce estate taxes.[16] But family partnerships can also serve investment purposes.

In a typical case, the senior living generation of a family will control most of the wealth. This generation is able to access the best managers (most of whom impose high minimum account sizes), can take advantage of fee break points, and they will also have available to themselves sophisticated investment strategies that require investors to be "accredited," that is, to have a certain minimum income and/or net worth. Younger generations may be stuck with inferior managers or mutual fund products. But by creating family investment partnerships (or limited liability companies—LLCs) to "pool" the family's investment assets, the senior generation can significantly expand the investment opportunities available to the younger generations while simultaneously reducing investment costs.

From the point of view of money managers, the client is not the individual family units but the partnership itself. Hence, the partnership is able to meet the high minimum account sizes demanded by many of the best managers. The middle and younger generations of the family might not otherwise have access to these managers. In addition, of course, the family partnership is able to take advantage of fee break points, giving all members of the family the advantage of lower investment costs. Finally, by investing through separate account managers, rather than mutual funds, younger family members can tax-manage their portfolios, significantly enhancing their net returns. The family can leverage these advantages by involving the middle and younger generations in meetings with money managers and other advisors, helping educate them about investment issues.

Family investment partnerships are sometimes established in a vertical fashion and sometimes in a horizontal fashion. In a horizontal partnership, the family creates an entire, diversified investment portfolio in which all members of the family participate (via the partnership). Horizontal partnerships provide maximum leverage, because all the family's assets are pooled into one partnership, but they can be clumsy investment vehicles. If there are three or four living generations, for example, what possible investment strategy would be appropriate for all the family members? When families organize horizontal partnerships, many of the more astute members of the family will put the core of their wealth in the partnership, but will keep other assets out in order to customize their own strategy.

Vertical partnerships are typically established for each asset class in which the family plans to invest. Thus, there might be separate partnerships for U.S. large-cap, U.S. small-cap, international, emerging markets, fixed income, hedge, private equity, and so on. Individual family members can put whatever percentage of their own assets they wish into each category, allowing for significant customization.

The main problem with vertical partnerships is complexity. Partnership accounting is always complex, and having to deal with ten partnerships, rather than one, can ratchet up the paperwork burden substantially. Fortunately, excellent software exists for managing these issues, and many of the better accounting firms and custodian banks can be engaged to handle the accounting, preparing Form 1065s, K-1s, and so on.

Finally, families can take the route of forming a single master partnership that has unitized funds corresponding to each asset class. The advantage is that only one Form 1065 and K-1 needs to be prepared. The disadvantage is that the 1065 cannot be completed until each asset class is finalized. Thus, a family member invested only in fixed income must wait until the 1065 is complete—which can't occur until the private equity K-1s have come in—in order to file his tax returns.

Note that there is no reason why a traditional family limited partnership designed for estate tax-discounting purposes cannot also serve as a family investment partnership. Indeed, there can be special advantages to doing so. When the IRS challenges family limited partnerships it will typically argue that there was no reason for the formation of the partnership other than avoiding taxes. If one reason for forming the partnership was to pool family investment assets, that can be a compelling business reason for a partnership that also claims discounted values for gift and estate tax purposes. On the other hand, the cohort of family units that is appropriate to participate in a family limited partnership formed for discounting purposes may be quite different from the cohort of family units that would be appropriate for a family investment partnership. Each family will have to work these issues out for themselves.

PRACTICE TIP

Many families wish include their foundations in the partnerships, but keep in mind that this can be controversial. If, for example, the foundation's assets are significant in relation to the family's assets, self-dealing issues might arise.

In addition, the IRS will scrutinize these partnerships carefully to ensure that cost basis is allocated properly among taxable and tax-exempt partners. My advice is to leave the foundation out.

PHILANTHROPY

This will be one of the shortest entries in the book for the simple reason that it's none of my business what you do with your money. And if there is a God in heaven I can guarantee you that He or She doesn't give a damn whether you give your money away or not. There are as many philanthropists in hell as in heaven. Henry Clay Frick said to Andrew Carnegie, perhaps the world's greatest philanthropist, when the latter asked to see the former: "I'll see you in hell."

Family foundations can be a wonderful way to give back to the community and they provide a useful training tool for younger generations in the arts of investing and philanthropy. Young people tend to be a lot more interested in giving money away than in investing it. But if they have to sit through the investment portion of the meeting in order to participate in the grant-making portion, they will gradually internalize the message that grant-making success depends on investment success.

But private foundations are highly regulated beasts and the regulations are getting more strict and becoming more rigorously enforced. In addition, foundations have (by law) heavy spending obligations, making the investment side of things very challenging.

Here are some things to be aware of:

- Keep your eye on the foundation's spending. By law, a private foundation must give away 5 percent of its asset base every year (as a rolling average), and the foundation must also pay a 2 percent excise tax (or pay a 1 percent tax and give the other 1 percent away, on top of the 5 percent). In addition, there are costs that don't count in the 5 percent calculation, and on top of that, many enthusiastic foundation directors end up giving away more than 5 percent on average: Because 5 percent is the minimum, you can only err, if you err, on the upside. In my experience, the average foundation is actually spending about 7 percent per year, and hence they are gradually liquidating themselves in real terms.[17]

- Avoid inadvertent self-dealing. The penalties for foundation trustees who self-deal are draconian. Most people avoid the obvious self-dealing issues (making a grant to your own child, for example). But here are two examples of self-dealing that trip people up:
  - Ethel attends a meeting of a nonprofit group and commits herself to make a $100,000 grant. Ethel has her family foundation make the grant. That's a no-no.
  - Frank hires a financial advisor to advise the family, its various trusts, and the family foundation. The foundation represents 20 percent of the overall asset base and pays 20 percent of the overall advisory fee. That's also a no-no. The IRS will take the position that by including the foundation's assets in the fee calculation, the family is paying a lower overall fee (lower in basis points) by taking advantage of the foundation. Result: self-dealing.

- Spend some serious time on your foundation's investment strategy. A high-spending investor, which a private foundation surely is, is caught in a kind of investment catch-22. Because of its high spending, the foundation needs to keep its portfolio highly liquid. But in order to avoid liquidating itself by spending more than it's making (including costs, excise taxes, and inflation), the foundation needs to trade liquidity for return. Balancing these issues isn't child's play.

■ Unless your family foundation is very large, consider a donor-advised fund. This will virtually eliminate the regulatory hassle and let you focus on the giving.

There are a lot of good things about the world of philanthropy—see Chapter 2—and I've been directly involved with organized philanthropy since I became president of the Laurel Foundation (one of the Mellon family charities) a quarter-century ago. But there is also a lot wrong with philanthropy, and most of it can be summarized in one word: arrogance. The cure can also be simply summarized: humility.

But humility is in short supply in the charitable world. There is a saying in the business that once you become a foundation president all your jokes become funnier and you will never again have an honest conversation. Arrogance, in other words, is baked into the ecosystem of organized philanthropy at the level of its DNA.

In recent years there has been a movement afoot to acknowledge foundation failures, the thought being that confession is good for the soul and that failure is a learning experience. Well, maybe so, but recall that when in his arrogance Icarus flew too near the sun, it was Icarus himself who paid the ultimate price. When a foundation initiative fails—and especially when a very large and powerful foundation's initiatives fail—the price isn't paid by the foundation but by the "target population," and that price can always be reckoned in turmoil and bitterness and sometimes in squandered lives. If you shot most nonprofit executives up with truth serum, what they would say about most charitable giving would fry your hair.

Still and all, giving your money away is good for you. More important, it's good for your kids to watch you do it. And even more important than either of those things, it's good for you, for your kids, and for the community in general to see you roll up your sleeves and get your hands dirty working on something you actually care deeply about.

I'm assuming, of course, that you are giving your money away sensibly, not just pouring it down some rat hole in the hope that it will get you in front of the right people or on the right boards.

By the way, "sensibly" means nothing more (nor less!) than funding something you feel passionate about. It might take you a while to find this topic—it might take you a lifetime—but once you find it, you'll know it. It's the only way most of us have to walk with the angels.

CONCLUSION: THERE ARE CHALLENGES EVERYWHERE WE LOOK

Just because I've styled a challenge as "miscellaneous" doesn't mean it isn't important. For some families, the question of what to do about a concentrated securities position dominates everything. And in addition to the challenges I've spent some time on in this chapter, there are others I could have talked about: overspending (see Chapter 21), asset protection planning (which can be important for highly visible families), and even obscure issues like the use of soft dollars by managers to compensate brokers, or by families to compensate their advisors.

But whatever the challenge, stewardship is stewardship. I hardly need to remind my readers that a great deal is at stake: for you, for your family, for your country, and for the broader world.

NOTES

1. Custodians are often referred to as "master custodians" because, in order for them to hold and report on the many types of financial assets investors own, a custodial institution will typically require the services of several (or many) subcustodians. For example, it is not practical—and is sometimes not possible, due to local laws and regulations—for a U.S. banking institution to have a custody operation in every country in the world. Instead, the master custodian will enter into agreements with local institutions to act as subcustodians for the master.
2. Unlikely, but hardly unheard-of. Most of the large banks in Houston, Texas collapsed in the 1980s, for example, as did Continental Illinois in Chicago and numerous other banks that proved not to be "too big to fail." Think Lehman Brothers, National City, Countrywide Financial, and so on.
3. Note that in the event of an IRS audit, the books of the custodian are considered to be the official "book of record" for tax data.
4. The SSAE16 is a thorough report on the internal controls at a custody bank and, effective in mid-2011, replaced the SAS70.
5. To make matters even more complex, there are firms that specialize in investing securities lending proceeds. In other words, these firms take the modest interest we receive for lending our securities and invest it to produce slightly more interest. A very large scandal involved one of these firms, First Capital Strategies, in the mid-1990s.
6. For example, the gigantic public and corporate pension funds.

7. This portion of the chapter is adapted from Greycourt White Paper No. 10: Establishing a Family Office (2006), available at www.Greycourt.com.
8. I believe that the first true family office in America was established by Judge Thomas Mellon in Pittsburgh in 1868. John D. Rockefeller set up an office for the Rockefeller family shortly thereafter.
9. That is, one handling, in-house, the full array of investment, accounting, legal, intergenerational, educational, and concierge services required by a complex family
10. Activities that are typically carried on in-house include direct investing, bookkeeping, accounting and reporting, philanthropy, education of younger generations, concierge services, and oversight of a family business. Activities typically outsourced include investment management (the chief investment officer function), asset custody, tax accounting, estate and trust planning, and such "soft" issues as intergenerational conflict, where an objective viewpoint is useful.
11. Note that if costs are to be allocated to a private foundation, a private letter ruling from the IRS should be obtained approving the allocation methods.
12. CCC Alliance LLC, 10 Liberty Square, 3rd Floor, Boston, MA 02109, 617-457-8368.
13. Family Office Exchange, Inc., 100 S. Wacker Drive, Suite 900, Chicago, IL 60606, 312-327-1200.
14. Family Wealth Alliance, 240 E. Willow Avenue, Suite 102, Wheaton, IL 60187, 630-260-1010.
15. Institute for Private Investors, 17 State Street, 5th Floor, New York, NY 10004, 212-693-1300.
16. The notion is that because the family members now own much of their wealth in an illiquid partnership, the IRS should accept a lower (discounted) value on those assets for estate tax purposes—in effect, a discount for lack of liquidity. This notion, by the way, drives the IRS crazy, and it tends to attack family partnerships on sight. The courts have, to date, issued decisions on family limited partnerships that are difficult to reconcile.
17. Internal Revenue Service statistics show that foundations routinely pay out far more than 5 percent of their assets. For the tax year ended 2008 (the most recent data available), smaller foundations on average had grant payout rates of 6.9 percent. See Cynthia Belmonte, "Domestic Private Foundations and Excise Taxes, Tax Year 2008," SOI Bulletin 31, no. 3, Available at http://http://www.irs.gov/pub/irs-soi/12pfwinbulexcise08.pdf.

Afterword

On Happiness

Happiness, madame, happiness.

—Charles de Gaulle[1]

Tolstoy was right: All happy families *are* alike, and that is true whether the families are rich, poor, or middle class. The characteristics that tend to lead to happiness are simply not wealth dependent. Indeed, science is telling us (we already knew this) that human beings have a genetic predisposition toward being happy or unhappy. We all know people who seem to have every reason to be happy, but who in fact are chronically morose and unpleasant to be around. On the other hand, we all know people who face a mountain of miseries but who are always cheerful and upbeat.

Thus, nothing in this book is intended to suggest that merely being wealthy will inevitably lead to happiness. It won't, any more than merely being poor or merely being middle class will inevitably lead to happiness. Happiness, to the extent that it goes beyond genetically wired predispositions, is almost always earned. We earn it by being productive, by overcoming obstacles that challenge us (but that aren't so daunting that they are impossible to conquer), by living in and helping to create a close and loving family environment, by making and keeping friends and acquaintances. None of this happens without effort, and hence the challenge of being happy is at its essence the same for all socioeconomic levels.

Of course, the specific form each of the challenges takes can be powerfully affected by our level of material well-being and by the social and cultural circumstances of our lives. A welfare mother, possibly barely more than a child herself, living in an urban ghetto or a bleak rural township with her three children, faces a certain set of challenges to her own happiness and that of her family, and those challenges are different from the challenges faced by a suburban soccer mom. The welfare mother's challenges can be so herculean that they will defeat her, leading to misery for herself and her fragile family. But they are not different in kind from those of the soccer mom. The path to happiness for both women is the path we articulated above—work, family, friends.

And the same is true for wealthy families. For this small but crucial group of Americans, the pathway to happiness is the same as it is for everyone else. And, unsurprisingly, the outcomes are about the same as well. The canard about the rich living lives of opulent emptiness is as bigoted—and hopelessly wrong—as the notion that all inner-city Americans are drugged-up gang members or that all suburban families are conformist boors. Happiness among the rich is about as evenly distributed as it is among just about any other group of Americans.

STEREOTYPES OF THE RICH

Many of the stereotypes about wealthy families are generated, or at least perpetuated, by silly Hollywood versions of the rich, where all the children are spoiled trust-fund babies, all the parents are emotionally stunted, all the lives are lived in dreary splendor. But, after all, we can't really blame Hollywood for this. Most of us are pretty boring, normal families, whereas dysfunctional families, like it or not, make for far more interesting viewing. If Tolstoy were alive today he might have written, "All happy families are bad sitcom material."

But even among the wealthy themselves, who should know better, there is a sense that their families face higher odds of being happy and productive. To be sure, the challenges facing wealthy families who aspire to happiness—that is, all wealthy families—are different from those of other families, in the same way that the challenges facing welfare families are different from those facing middle-class families. But the actual outcomes, as noted above, are about the same.

THE RICH AND THE "FAUX RICH"

Another issue that tends to cause confusion in this regard is the confounding of two kinds of prominent families: the truly rich, that is, those who control very significant amounts of private capital, and the "faux rich," those who merely enjoy extremely high incomes. The latter might eventually control significant capital, but the dynamic that drives their lives and their characteristic neuroses is the relatively sudden thrust from a middle-income (or worse) past to a very, very high-income present. Such people are more analogous to lottery winners than to the truly rich, and their typical patterns of behavior are similar to the dysfunctional practices of lottery winners.

There are very few ways in the United States or any other democratic society for anyone to legally earn a huge income, and in virtually every one of those sectors of the economy the jobs come with enormously high risk. Is the CEO of a Fortune 500 corporation really worth being paid hundreds of times as much as a factory worker? Maybe so, but many people will be skeptical, including many CEOs themselves. Worse, the job of any CEO can suddenly disappear, its occupant summarily fired, often for reasons wholly beyond the CEO's control. And along with the job, out the window go the high income and all the perks and the CEO's reputation. Private capital, on the other hand, if it is wisely managed (see Chapters 9 through 22, above), never goes away.

Let's compare two people we'll call Helen and Larry. In every sector of the economy, the incomes earned by the most successful people reflect not some extraordinary level of talent, but simply the *local value* of whatever talent exists. Let's begin by considering Helen, who is an exceptionally able administrative assistant to corporate executives (a person we would not long ago have called a secretary). Helen is organized, pleasant, diplomatic, reliable, and so on, and the executives to whom she reports during her career are very lucky to have her. Very few Americans are as good at their jobs as Helen is at hers. Unfortunately for Helen, there is only so much that her talents are worth—the local value of her talents as an executive assistant might allow her to lead a nice, comfortable lifestyle, but she will never become rich. In other words, Helen is a lot like most talented people—she will be successful and will enjoy her work, but her annual income will never make the front page of the *Wall Street Journal*.

Now we'll contrast Helen with another, roughly equally talented person. Larry is a television industry executive who has a specific talent, namely, the ability to anticipate what television shows Americans are going to like and watch. In the general scheme of things, this is a modest enough talent, roughly equivalent to Helen's. But Larry is lucky—the local value of his talent is enormous. The network pays Larry millions of dollars a year simply because the shows he has picked for the network tend to draw slightly more viewers than the shows other people have picked for other networks. This slight advantage means hundreds of millions of dollars in advertising revenue to Larry's network, so allocating a small percentage of that to keeping Larry happy seems like a bargain.

Meanwhile, Larry, a middle-class kid from Queens, has never seen so much money in his life. He spends it lavishly, so that everyone will know how important he is. Tiny slights—Larry was recently assigned a seat in the rear rows for a bonzo Hollywood opening, and not two weeks ago his regular table at Spago was occupied by a media mogul—wound Larry deeply, sending him into a rage. Larry routinely works 100-hour weeks, has been divorced twice, and is currently dating a gorgeous but brain-dead starlet. He would barely recognize his own children if they wandered into his office. What little spare time Larry has is spent with his personal trainer, trying desperately to remain buff in the face of advancing middle age.

But for all this, Larry is not the superficial twit he seems to be. He is simply a relatively ordinary guy who has suddenly been thrust into the position of earning a huge income and whose job, reputation, and salary are constantly in danger of suddenly going away. The grinding insecurity this engenders manifests itself in Larry's nauseating insistence on proving how important he is. But Larry is right to feel insecure. Sure enough, Larry's infatuation with modestly sexy sitcoms—his claim to fame in the industry—has overstayed its welcome. The public is tired of watching self-absorbed nincompoops exposing their neuroses at 9 P.M., and has turned its attention to reality shows. Caught completely off guard, his network's ratings plummet and Larry is summarily—and very publicly—fired. There went his high income, his power to green-light shows, his table at Spago—essentially everything that dominated Larry's life has disappeared in an instant. Helen, meanwhile, continues to climb the corporate ladder, getting herself assigned to ever-more-senior executives. And the truly rich, meanwhile, continue to be rich.[2]

THE REAL WAY THE RICH ARE DIFFERENT

The need to control the world around us is an instinct deeply embedded in the human soul. And a good thing it is, too; else we would all be naked and living in caves. If something is irritating us, we change it. Even if something is okay, but could be better, we change it. Wealthy families are no different from anyone else in this regard, with the singular distinction that it is far easier for the rich to buy control of their lives than it is for anyone else. And there lies the rub.

Most attempts to buy control of our world are harmless enough. A working-class family, rather than swelter through a hot, humid summer, will put a window air-conditioning unit in the parents' bedroom. A middle-class family will air condition most of the rooms that adults spend time in. An upper-middle-class family will install whole-house air-conditioning. But a wealthy family, having just purchased that charming old mansion put up in the nineteenth century, will install enough HVAC to keep all 22 rooms at a perfect 70 degrees all year round—and hang the (ridiculous) cost.

So what? The trouble comes when the habit of buying our way out of the normal irritations of life extends to buying our way out of irritations that are inextricably entwined with our happiness. Consider the three arenas of life that will largely determine whether or not we will be happy: raising children, preserving a happy marriage, and engaging in a productive work life. All three activities are fraught with a large variety of day-to-day irritations. Infants can be colicky, making our lives a living hell until they grow out of it. Toddlers learning the joys of independence make the phrase "the terrible twos" a colossal understatement. Preadolescents become involved in so many activities that we have to put our lives on hold just to drive them from place to place and attend their many (and often crushingly boring) events. Teenagers—well, no need to dwell on that subject. Then, suddenly, our children are grown and out of the house forever, and we spend the rest of our lives missing them.

As for marriage, never was a more bizarre arrangement invented. The idea that two adult human beings can share the same space, eat at the same table, supervise the same children, sleep in the same bed, *every day of their lives*, is preposterous. This is a good working definition of hell, if nothing else. And yet most of us not only get married, we often get married more than once (the triumph, as the saying goes, of hope over experience). The day-to-day irritations imposed on us by the institution of marriage are so numerous and so troublesome that long books are written about how to manage and minimize them. Nonetheless, like democracy, marriage is the worst of all possible outcomes—except for all the others.

Or consider work. No one who has ever held a job can possibly harbor any romantic illusions about the "joy of work." On a day-to-day basis, working is a pain in the neck. We have to get up earlier than we want to. We have to put on uncomfortable clothes. We have to commute through maddening traffic. We have to work with some colleagues we don't like and would never spend time with if we had any choice in the matter. Our bosses are invariably hopeless jerks. And, in the end, we are infuriatingly underappreciated and underpaid. When we meet some idiot who claims to "love his work," who "would do it for free if necessary," we know we have encountered a dangerous lunatic. Yet, virtually all of us do in fact work, including most of us who have no financial need to do so.

For most human beings, the irritations associated with raising children, staying happily married, and working productively are assumed to be nothing less than a part of the human condition. Unless we don't wish to pass our genes along, unless we wish to be alone and lonely, unless we're happy to starve to death in a gutter, we put up with these irritations and get on with our lives. And the ultimate result is happiness.

But suppose we didn't have to put up with them? Suppose we could, in fact, buy our way out of all or most of them? Wouldn't we be tempted to do it? Of course we would. And there lies the danger for the wealthy. In an attempt to control obvious irritations, we manage to buy our way out of happiness.

CHILDREN AND THE WEALTHY

If, for example, children are an irritation—as they certainly are—well, that is why God invented nurses, nannies, day care, tutors, boarding schools, and so on, and so on. If we are wealthy enough, we can move our children from birth through college without ever laying eyes on the little creeps. But this, of course, would be a serious mistake. As noted above, the irritations associated with raising children are inseparably bound up with the joys associated with raising children. We can't experience the latter without experiencing the former. Moreover, the way we deal with those irritations teaches our children volumes about what it means to be an adult, about maturity and patience, about what moms and dads are all about.

Yes, it's annoying in the extreme that little Freddie's soccer tournament is being held at a rural backwater three hours' drive away, and on a weekend when our office work is piled to the ceiling. And, yes, it's more than mildly provoking that little Susie's middle-school play happens to be scheduled on the same night as our favorite annual black-tie affair. But slipping Freddie 50 bucks as we head off to the office, or sending a dozen roses to Susie in lieu of our presence, are just more ways of buying our way out of happiness. No, we don't have to attend every single soccer tournament, and, no, we're not monsters if we sometimes favor black-tie affairs over middle-school plays. But we can't let those choices become habits.

The fact that we *can* buy our way out of these irritations, and thousands more like them, doesn't mean that we *should* buy our way out of them. The easier it is for parents to buy their way out of the irritating aspects of child rearing, the more likely we are to do it. It's extremely easy for the rich to do it, and hence not doing it—avoiding the temptation as often as possible—is one of the great challenges the wealthy face in pursuing happiness.

MARRIAGE AND THE WEALTHY

Sociologists tell us that more than half of all first marriages end in divorce, and that even higher percentages of subsequent marriages end in divorce.[3] But even these statistics understate the true rate of marriage failure, because many couples stay together for religious or financial reasons, or simply out of inertia. The simple truth is that long-term happy marriages are quite rare. And, given the challenges posed by living together with another human being, this should come as no surprise to us. The only way to eliminate divorce is to prohibit it, and the only way to eliminate unhappy marriages is to abolish marriage itself.[4]

The rich face all the same challenges to staying happily married as anyone else. But, in addition, we face the temptation to buy our way out of the irritations that inevitably accompany our marriages. The classic example of this is the spouse who routinely treats the other spouse badly, then "makes up for it" with an ISB (I'm Sorry Bauble), carefully sized to the scale of the offense. The message the offending spouse sends with the ISB is this one: "I can treat you any way I wish, as long as my offensive conduct is followed by an appropriate ISB." The message the offended spouse is sending is this one: "You can treat me any way you like, as long as you pay for it with an ISB."

There is nothing wrong with ISBs—even a poor spouse can afford a small bouquet of flowers or a fifth of Johnny Walker. The trouble comes about when the ISB is not a token of our remorse and our love, but a substitute for it. If we have done something that hurt our spouse, even inadvertently, the way to "make up for it" is to apologize sincerely, to let our spouse know that we are remorseful, to assure our spouse that we will do our best not to let it happen again. Skipping this extremely difficult step, and proceeding straight to the ISB, is simply a way of buying our way out of happiness, and it's a road that is especially easy for wealthy spouses to take.

Marriage is a difficult business, and most marriages will fail in one way or another. But being one half of a happy marriage is perhaps the most certain route to happiness for rich, middle-class, and poor alike. Simply being aware of the temptations that bedevil wealthy spouses can go a long way toward avoiding the pain that results from a failed marriage, or from being alone in life.

WORK AND THE WEALTHY

Among all the misconceptions about the wealthy that are harbored by people in general is the notion that the rich don't work. This odd idea seems to have gained currency in the same way as so many unsound notions about the rich—from Hollywood and from the rare, spectacular examples of international playboys and their ilk. What is, in fact, far more interesting and salient about the rich is how hard they tend to work despite not having any financial need to do so.

This issue of working hard, of being productive and of generating happiness out of that productivity, is perhaps best examined by looking at another example of the phenomenon, namely, the wives[5] of extremely successful men. Talented men, men who are destined for great success in life (and in this case we include financial success), tend to marry women who are a lot like themselves: talented women who can also look forward to great success in traditional terms. But what often happens is something else altogether. The couple wants to have children. Only the wife can have them, and she is probably (though not certainly) more maternally inclined. Society frowns on men who stay home while their wives work. All these and many other factors dictate that in most cases the wife will stay home with the kids.

Eventually, the last child toddles off to school and now the wife is faced with a question about what to do with her life. Her choices are so wide that it is difficult to know where to begin. And the world is a very different place for her than it was when she was first married. She could launch herself into a traditional career now, when she is probably in her late 30s, but she would be competing against and associating with colleagues who are far younger—not an attractive proposition.

Moreover, although the children are in school during the day, they come home at 3:00 p.m. What's to happen to them then? Who will pick them up, take them to their (increasingly numerous) activities and play dates? Someone could be hired to handle that chore, to be sure—money is no object for these successful families—but is that really the best way to handle it? Already the husband frequently arrives home after the kids are in bed—should the wife really emulate that work schedule?

And what about the wife's social life? That life has been built around a series of friends and activities that aren't constrained by the usual 10-hour professional workday. Should she give up these friends and these activities and start all over again?

Finally, there is the question of financial need. None of the above would matter a whit if the wife's income were crucial to the financial survival of the family. But we have already postulated that the husband can provide all the financial needs. Thus, these women have no financial need to work.

What becomes of this group of women, the talented wives of very successful men? Well, we know what becomes of them, because we all know so many of them. Some launch themselves into demanding careers, becoming every bit as successful, financially and otherwise, as their husbands.

But most of them, by far the great majority, carve out busy and productive lives that don't look like "traditional" successful careers, but that are crucially important to American society and richly rewarding to the women. These lives typically include elements of after-school child care, part-time work or work that pays far less than the women could ordinarily have commanded, and active volunteer or public service activities. The children of very successful men grow up to be well-adjusted and happy in considerable part because of the career "sacrifices" made by their talented wives. Nonprofit organizations and social service agencies are able to hire astonishingly talented women, despite the low salaries and benefits they offer. And at the core of most successful schools, churches, and organizations devoted to helping the less fortunate are talented and energetic women who, in another life, might have been at the very top of some profession or corporation.

No one looks down on such women. If anything, we wonder what motivates them to keep so busy, to accomplish so much, despite having no financial incentive to do so. And the same is true of wealthy families. Members of those families typically have no financial need to work, but the outcomes for them are exactly analogous to the outcomes of the wives of successful husbands. Some work 15-hour days, six-and-a-half days a week, as frantically driven as though the wolf were at their very door. A few do little or nothing. But the vast, overwhelming majority carve out busy and productive lives that may or may not look a great deal like "traditional" careers. But these lives are crucial to American society and richly rewarding to those who lead them. They are lives lived in devotion to family and society, and they enrich all our lives.

Given the enormous productivity of the wealthy, I am always puzzled by wealthy people—almost always the first generation, the ones who made the money—who say they plan to leave nothing, or very little, to their children, on the ground that inheriting a large pile of money will inevitably ruin them. For the most part, this is simple nonsense. Having money will ruin children if they lack character and otherwise it will not. If children lack character, they are already ruined, whether they have money or not. Therefore, the job of wealthy parents is not to disinherit their children, but to build character in those children and then to pass the stewardship of the family assets on to them in their turn. It is, in fact, remarkable how often the stewardship of wealth is better handled by second, third, and fourth generations than by the first.

FAILED STEWARDSHIP AND FAMILY UNHAPPINESS

From the point of view of the poor and of levelers everywhere, it might seem to be only simple justice for the rich to be wretchedly unhappy. Alas, this is not the case—the rich are as happy as anyone else, although the particular challenges to happiness that the wealthy face tend to be somewhat different.

But there *is* one certain route to unhappiness for the rich: If stewardship of the family's capital is so poor that it disappears, disappears to the point where the family is no longer wealthy and can no longer deploy its capital in creative ways, unhappiness will descend like a dark curtain on the family, perhaps for generations.

It is always a wrenching experience for any family to slip down the socioeconomic ladder, and it almost always leads to misery in one form or another. When a working-class family, clinging precariously to its hard-won respectability, slips back into poverty, an infinitely sad event has occurred. And in every high school, the most unhappy children are those whose parents are high achievers and whose expectations for their children are correspondingly—and all-too-often unreasonably—high. The fact that Daddy chairs the symphony board shouldn't have implications one way or the other for whether little Billy becomes a truck driver, but in fact the implications are huge. Even when the socioeconomic slippage occurs primarily as the result of broad economic dislocation—as in the Great Depression, when many families fell one or even two rungs down the ladder—the pain of the experience often persists for generations.

How much worse it is, then, for a family that is rich to cease to be rich solely because some generation of the family has failed in its stewardship of the capital. The sense of failure and the shame associated with that failure, the pressing weight of abused privilege, always results in unhappiness, and frequently it results in multigenerational neuroses that settle like a miasmal haze on subsequent generations. These are the families with dark secrets, the families with rigid and brittle personalities, the families with a perpetually negative outlook on life and its possibilities, the families pathologically concerned with appearances, with social slights, with the need to associate with the right people.

If we wanted to prioritize them, then, the challenges for the wealthy come down to these:

First, we need to stay rich. Failing this, the other priorities will rot and die.

Second, we need to do everything we can to ensure that younger family members will lead productive lives. This is a challenge for all families, of course.

Third, we need to improve the world we were born into, through the creative use of the capital we deploy.

Finally, if possible, we will want to grow our wealth in real terms. Important as this goal is, it is also important to note where it ranks among life's priorities.

WEALTH AND HAPPINESS

The first duty of a family in the possession of private capital, then, is to manage that capital competently. This is a serious and honorable business, it is hard and demanding work, and success in that enterprise is the only sure platform from which the family can pursue its own happiness. In addition, as I have noted at great length (see Part One of this book), its implications for the continued preeminence of America and for the continued economic and social progress of the rest of the world can hardly be overstated. The failure of stewardship is a momentous defeat for a family, and it is a momentous defeat for the society that depends so heavily on wealth as the engine of its competitiveness.

The goal of life is not wealth but happiness. But happiness cannot be pursued directly. It is the result of a process, and for wealthy families that process begins with the successful stewardship of their capital. Like everything else on which happiness ultimately depends, the stewardship of wealth is a process that is filled with day-to-day irritations and that requires effort and persistence. But it is neither impossible nor beyond the capability of any family that takes the issue of stewardship seriously. See Chapters 1 through 22.

NOTES

1. Late in their lives, Charles de Gaulle and his wife were being interviewed by an American television journalist. Although the interviewer had done his best to include Madame de Gaulle in the conversation, *Le Grand Charles* utterly dominated the proceedings. Finally, as the interview neared its end, the determined journalist turned directly to Madame de Gaulle and asked, "What is the most important thing in life?" Madame de Gaulle's command of the English language had never been robust, and her accent was usually impenetrable, but in this case she had understood the question perfectly. She settled back comfortably in her chair and replied, "A penis." A stunned silence followed. But General de Gaulle merely leaned toward his wife and said, "*Hap*piness, madame, *hap*piness."

2. For a compelling view of the volatility of the 1 percent—really, people like Larry, not the truly rich—see Robert Frank's recent book, *The High-Beta Rich: How the Manic Wealthy Will Take Us to the Next Boom, Bubble, and Bust* (New York: Crown Business, 2011).

3. Actually, as Charles Murray has recently pointed out, affluent families have significantly lower divorce rates than poor families: *Coming Apart:*

The State of White America, 1960–2010 (New York: Crown Forum, 2012).

4. Incidentally, by using the term "marriage" I am engaging in a bit of shorthand for any long-term, loving relationship. I realize that many people are offended by use of this term for couples who are simply "domestic partners." But these relationships are subject to the same challenges as more traditional marriages, and to the same satisfactions and joys.

5. Wives of successful men are a far better example than husbands of successful women partly because there are far more of them, and partly because the social pressure on men to work is so powerful that husbands of successful women tend overwhelmingly to engage in traditional work whether they really wish to or not.

About the Companion Website

If you ever start to feel too good about yourself, they have this thing called the Internet, and you can find a lot of people there who don't like you.
— Tina Fey, Golden Globes Acceptance Speech, 2009

Aside from correcting an overly developed sense of self-regard, the Internet offers other benefits to writers. Consider the chronic problem of "nice-to-have" material—material that might be very important to a few readers, but that is probably of little interest to most readers. Writers naturally want that material to remain in the book, while publishers—worried about trying to sell a book that weighs 10 pounds—want it out.

But then along came the Internet and all was sweetness and light again. "Need-to-have" material stays in the book, while the "nice-to-have" material gets posted on a website associated with the book and maintained by the publisher.

If you are among the smaller group of readers who want to see that material, you need only go to www.wiley.com/go/stewardshipofwealth and type in the password curtis2012. Specifically, you will find this material on the website:

- An additional chapter on conflicts of interest and the destruction of wealth.
- Guidelines for use with managers of municipal bonds, corporate bonds, cash, and small cap stocks (as an example of any active equity manager).
- A sample investment policy statement for a family, investment committee operating manual, and spending policy statement for a family.
- Examples of thoughtful letters written by senior generations to their children discussing financial management.

Enjoy.

About the Author

Gregory Curtis is the chairman and founder of Greycourt & Co., Inc., an open-architecture wealth advisory firm serving substantial families and select endowments on a global basis. Prior to founding Greycourt, Curtis served for many years as president of a Mellon family office and as president of the Laurel Foundation.

Curtis is the author of *Creative Capital: Managing Private Wealth in a Complex World*, and he is also the author of numerous white papers on a variety of investment topics. Curtis writes a blog for The Alliance Report.

Over the years Curtis has served on many investment committees for family and institutional investors. He currently serves on the investment committees for Carnegie Mellon University, The Pittsburgh Foundation, St. John's College, United Educators Insurance Co., and Winchester Thurston School, among others.

Curtis currently chairs the board of directors of The Pittsburgh Foundation (the community foundation for the Pittsburgh region); is a member of the board of directors of United Educators Insurance Co.; is a past chair of the board of St. John's College (Annapolis and Santa Fe) and past chair of the board of The Investment Fund for Foundations; and he has chaired or served on the boards of many other investment, educational, and cultural organizations. In addition to founding Greycourt and co-founding The Investment Fund for Foundations, Curtis is the founder and CEO of Moneybags LLC, the developer of the Moneybags financial app.

Curtis holds a BA degree from Dartmouth College, *cum laude* with high distinction in English, a JD degree from Harvard Law School, *cum laude*, and he is a graduate of The Endowment Institute at Harvard Business School. He also holds an honorary BA degree from St. John's College.

Curtis has six children and lives in Pittsburgh with his wife, Simin, the founder and CEO of the American Middle East Institute.

Index

The Moneybags© App

You've Read the Book

Now Get the App!

I developed the Moneybags© financial application to work hand-in-hand with my book, *The Stewardship of Wealth*. Why an app?

Because I recognize that the complex strategies discussed in the book can't be easily adapted for use by "smaller" investors. Suppose you are a middle-income investor, or perhaps a spouse or adult child in a wealthy family. Maybe you are an advisor to wealthy families but aren't wealthy yourself. Maybe you just want to learn about investing.

The point is that smaller investors need to observe best investment practices throughout the investment process just as much as wealthy investors do. Enter the Moneybags© app.

Once you download the app you walk through a series of screens that allow you to observe how a world-class (but smaller) portfolio is built, step-by-step. The app illustrates establishing a risk profile, designing a long-term (strategic) portfolio, adjusting the portfolio tactically, taking advantage of opportunistic investments, selecting managers, and monitoring and rebalancing the portfolio. Every step is explained, and if you want more information I refer you to the relevant chapter in *The Stewardship of Wealth*. From time to time I make changes in the portfolio, allowing you to observe how it evolves over time.

As a bonus, users of the app can order copies of *The Stewardship of Wealth* and receive access to my blogs, white papers, articles, and other investment writings.

The app is free to download. Simply look for it in the Apple AppStore or, if you use a different platform, log on to **www.MoneybagsApp.com**. Enjoy.